Domain-Specific Computer Architectures for Emerging Applications

With the end of Moore's Law, domain-specific architecture (DSA) has become a crucial mode of implementing future computing architectures. This book discusses the system-level design methodology of DSAs and their applications, providing a unified design process that guarantees functionality, performance, energy efficiency, and real-time responsiveness for the target application.

DSAs often start from domain-specific algorithms or applications, analyzing the characteristics of algorithmic applications, such as computation, memory access, and communication, and proposing the heterogeneous accelerator architecture suitable for that particular application. This book places particular focus on accelerator hardware platforms and distributed systems for various novel applications, such as machine learning, data mining, neural networks, and graph algorithms, and also covers RISC-V open-source instruction sets. It briefly describes the system design methodology based on DSAs and presents the latest research results in academia around domain-specific acceleration architectures.

Providing cutting-edge discussion of big data and artificial intelligence scenarios in contemporary industry and typical DSA applications, this book appeals to industry professionals as well as academicians researching the future of computing in these areas.

Dr. Chao Wang is a Professor with the University of Science and Technology of China, and also the Vice Dean of the School of Software Engineering. He serves as the Associate Editor of *ACM TODAES* and *IEEE/ACM TCBB*. Dr. Wang was the recipient of ACM China Rising Star Honorable Mention, and best IP nomination of DATE 2015, Best Paper Candidate of CODES+ISSS 2018. He is a senior member of ACM, senior member of IEEE, and distinguished member of CCF.

Domain-Specific Computer Architectures for Emerging Applications

Machine Learning and Neural Networks

Chao Wang

CRC Press
Taylor & Francis Group
Boca Raton London New York

CRC Press is an imprint of the
Taylor & Francis Group, an **informa** business

A CHAPMAN & HALL BOOK

First edition published 2024
by CRC Press
4 Park Square, Milton Park, Abingdon, Oxon, OX14 4RN

and by CRC Press
2385 NW Executive Center Drive, Suite 320, Boca Raton FL 33431

© 2024 Chao Wang

CRC Press is an imprint of Informa UK Limited

British Library Cataloguing-in-Publication Data
A catalogue record for this book is available from the British Library

ISBN: 978-0-367-37453-2 (hbk)
ISBN: 978-1-032-76895-3 (pbk)
ISBN: 978-0-429-35508-0 (ebk)

DOI: 10.1201/9780429355080

Typeset in Palatino
by codeMantra

Contents

Preface

Domain-specific computing is one of the most talked concepts in computer science and engineering in recent years, which refers to the customization and optimization of computing architectures with dedicated hardware and software for the needs of specific application domains to achieve higher performance and energy efficiency compared to general-purpose computing methods. Compared with general-purpose computing, domain-specific computing is more focused on solving domain-specific problems, and the design content of the system will be optimized for the characteristics and needs of the specific application domain to achieve higher performance or efficiency on specific tasks. The process of customization and optimization involves custom design on the hardware side, such as dedicated hardware accelerators for specific algorithms or operations, as well as custom development on the software side, such as optimized algorithms and codes written for specific domain requirements.

Currently, domain-specific computing has a wide range of applications in various fields, from scientific research to industrial production. Typically, in the field of artificial intelligence (AI) and machine learning, for complex algorithms such as neural networks, specialized hardware accelerators, such as graphics processing units and tensor processing units, can be designed to accelerate the training and inference process; in image and video processing, domain-specific computing also plays an important role, and specialized hardware can accelerate image processing, video coding and decoding, image recognition and other tasks, improving performance and energy efficiency; in emerging computing scenarios based on AI and image and video processing, such as autonomous driving and intelligent transportation, domain-specific computing can be used for perception, decision-making, and control to provide real-time, high-performance processing to ensure vehicle safety and smooth traffic.

Common training materials or textbooks at home and abroad often introduce more general customized methods and design ideas at the macro level, and there is a lack of relevant discussions on how to flexibly apply domain-specific computing methods in combination with the characteristics of different types of actual computing scenarios. Some of the classic textbooks related to the field of domain-specific computing, such as *Domain-Specific Processors: Systems, Architectures, Modeling, and Simulation* by Jörg Henkel et al., *Domain-Specific Languages* by Martin Fowler et al., *Designing Data-Intensive Applications: The Big Ideas Behind Reliable, Scalable, and Maintainable Systems* by Martin Kleppmann et al., usually only focus on hardware design or software design but lack the analysis and discussion of the co-optimization of the underlying hardware and the upper software layers within the same system. Due to the early years of the books, the coverage of the theories and methods in the books are somewhat different from that of the algorithms and applications that attract the most attention nowadays, and the hardware acceleration techniques based on new devices and semiconductor processes are not included. Domain-specific computing and its design theory and method are the core technology of manufacturing development and upgrading, especially in the current era of AI in which various types of compute-intensive and data-intensive algorithms continue to emerge, which is of key significance for reducing energy consumption and hardware costs, and a large number of high-level professionals are urgently needed to devote themselves to this field. But at present, the relevant education at domestic universities is relatively weak, and the ability to train practical talents is relatively insufficient.

Aiming at the lack of practical aspects of classic textbooks at home and abroad, combined with our years of teaching and research practice, and by sorting out the technical methods and development directions of the field, this book stands on the perspective of computer science and technology and takes the customized needs of different algorithmic application areas as a clue to discuss their respective domain-specific system design issues in different categories. The book covers mainstream algorithm types including neural networks, data mining, graph computing, etc., macro theory combined with specific cases, and takes the construction of domain-specific accelerator microstructures and acceleration systems based on field programmable gate arrays as clues. The system optimization analysis and specific hardware and software customization methods under different algorithmic scenarios are discussed in detail in different chapters. Due to space limitations, it is difficult to cover all the methods and ideas for different application fields under different hardware platforms. For a more detailed and comprehensive domain-specific system customization method for individual applications, interested readers can further refer to *AI Computing Systems* edited by Chen Yunji et al., and *Handbook of Signal Processing Systems* edited by Shuvra S. Bhattacharyya et al.

The publication of this book unites the efforts of many teachers and students in the Energy Efficient Intelligent Computing Lab, University of Science and Technology of China. Dr. Lei Gong, Prof. Xuehai Zhou, Prof. Xi Li, Haoran Li, Haoyu Cai, Yingxue Gao, Yang Yang, Songsong Li, Wenqi Lou, Xuan Wang, Jiali Wang, Yang Yang, Yangyang Zhao, Haijie Fang, Wenbin Teng, Zheyuan Zou, Yuxing He, Qiaochu Liang, Jize Pang, Hanyuan Gao, and many other researchers also took part in the preparation of the manuscript. The material of this book refers to a large number of relevant textbooks, courseware, and academic papers at home and abroad, and I would like to express my heartfelt thanks to the authors of the cited documents and apologize to the authors for the missing information sources. Due to the author's limited knowledge, there must be some improprieties in the book, please readers criticize and correct. For any comments and suggestions, please contact cswang@ustc.edu.cn.

The compilation of this book was supported by the National Natural Science Foundation, the Key Research and Development Program of the Ministry of Science and Technology, and the Youth Innovation Promotion Association. At the same time, Mrs. Randi Slack has done a lot of editorial work for the publication of this book, and I would like to express my sincere thanks.

Chao Wang
University of Science and Technology of China

1

Overview of Domain-Specific Computing

1.1 Background and Current Status of Domain-Specific Computing

With the increasing amount of massive data information and the widespread use of applications in the field of data mining, people have entered the era of big data. The advent of the era of big data brings not only opportunities but also challenges. Efficiently and stably accessing data information and accelerating the execution of data mining applications have become key problems that academia and industry urgently need to solve. In the emerging field of big data, machine learning, data mining, and artificial intelligence algorithms, as the core components of next-generation applications, have attracted more attention from researchers. Utilizing existing hardware and software means to carry out the design of a new algorithmic architecture has become a hot research topic nowadays.

Accelerating new algorithms in the era of big data is very different from the past. In the era of big data, there are many factors that make more and more users abandon the original CPU-based single-node processing platform and turn to other platforms and means to accelerate the execution of data mining/machine learning applications, some of which are as follows: (1) Massive data: The potential data scale of many application fields is extremely large, which makes it very impractical for a single machine to process data; (2) High data dimensionality: In some data mining applications, the number of features of instance data is large, and machine learning algorithms may need to segment the data features in order to process these data; (3) Complex models and algorithms: Some high-precision machine learning algorithms usually have a more complex model representation and often require a large amount of data calculation; (4) Inference time constraints: Some data mining applications such as speech recognition and visual object detection have real-time requirements, making single-computer processing unable to meet the needs; and (5) Multi-level prediction: Some machine learning algorithms can be represented in the form of multi-level pipelines, multi-level classifiers in the pipeline need to work in parallel, and single-node CPU processing platforms often cannot meet this demand.

DOI: 10.1201/9780429355080-1

To this end, Hennessy and Patterson's Turing Award Lecture in 2017 introduced the concept of domain-specific architectures, which argues that domain-specific computing will bring a new golden age of computer architecture. For a long time, computer architecture designers have focused on general-purpose computing. However, with the explosion of domain applications, there is a need to build a variety of specialized computing devices for a wide range of novel applications and algorithms to meet the needs of computing architecture performance, energy efficiency, scalability, and many other aspects.

There are many different acceleration platforms available on the market that we can utilize to implement machine learning algorithms that can handle massive amounts of data as well as achieve high efficiency. Generally, these acceleration platforms can be summarized into four categories, which are custom logic circuits (e.g. field programmable gate array (FPGA)/application specific integrated circuit (ASIC)), general-purpose graphics processing units (GPGPU), cloud computing platforms, and heterogeneous computing platforms. These acceleration platforms often exhibit different parallel granularity, are suitable for different application scenarios, and can also be combined to form heterogeneous systems to fully exploit the processing power of different acceleration devices.

It is not enough for the acceleration platform to rely on the hardware system alone, but it also needs a series of supporting software systems. There are still many different software systems that are suitable for different acceleration platforms, such as Hadoop, Spark, DryadLINQ, Pregel, and PowerGraph for cloud computing platforms, and compute unified device architecture (CUDA), OpenCL, and OpenACC for GPGPU platforms. These software systems take full advantage of the capabilities of the acceleration platform and are user-friendly. With these software systems, users only need to write software applications following the corresponding specifications and using the provided interfaces to obtain a lot of acceleration effect.

Cloud computing platforms and GPGPU are currently the most used general-purpose acceleration platforms. FPGA and ASIC are often used to implement specific accelerators for specific problems to achieve hardware acceleration. Heterogeneous computing platforms that use central processing unit (CPU), graphics processing unit (GPU), and FPGA together, such as Axel, OptiML, and Lime, should theoretically have good acceleration potential. However, they are still in the research stage due to the difficulty of implementation and many other problems, and so they have not been widely utilized. For cloud computing platforms, the current form of its composition is mainly a large number of CPU-based single-node computing clusters, which mainly use coarse-grained task-level parallelism to accelerate application execution. On the other hand, GPGPU mainly utilizes fine-grained data-level parallelism. FPGA/ASICs mainly utilize fine-grained data-level parallelism and pipelines to accelerate applications. The software systems of cloud computing platforms mainly include Hadoop and Spark based on the MapReduce programming model, and Pregel and PowerGraph based on the graph computing programming model. For GPGPU, its software systems are single program multiple data (SPMD)-based CUDA, OpenCL, and OpenACC. For FPGA and ASIC, there is currently no programming model and parallel platform suitable for it, and developers need to fully exploit the acceleration potential for different problems and different algorithms, using the hardware description language Verilog or VHDL to implement the corresponding hardware structure.

For cloud computing platforms and GPGPU, the current general-purpose CPUs are not ideal when dealing with machine learning algorithms because they are both data- and computation-intensive, and the data communication overhead of cloud computing platforms consisting of multiple CPUs has also become a stumbling block to efficiency improvement. GPUs also tend to be less efficient in processing data that is highly correlated and tends to have higher power consumption. Therefore, using FPGAs to design accelerator architectures for machine learning algorithms is a less involved but very promising research direction.

1.2 Current Domain-Specific Acceleration Means and Platforms

1.2.1 Current Acceleration Means

From the perspective of researchers, from a large aspect, the current means of accelerating machine learning algorithms can be roughly divided into three categories, namely, optimization at the software level, parallelization of machine learning algorithms, and improvement at the hardware level.

Optimization at the software level mainly includes optimization and improvement of the machine learning algorithm itself, and optimization and improvement of the algorithm runtime library environment. Improvement of the machine learning algorithm itself refers to the proposal of a new mathematical model for a particular algorithm to increase the execution speed of the algorithm, e.g. the proposal of the sequential minimal optimization (SMO) method for the support vector machine (SVM) algorithm. Optimization of the algorithm runtime library environment refers to the further optimization of the software environment in which the algorithm is running, such as the runtime library and operating system, to improve the efficiency of executing machine learning algorithms.

Parallelization of machine learning algorithms is currently the most common means of acceleration, which mainly parallelizes and distributes machine learning algorithms so that the algorithms themselves can achieve task-level parallelism and data-level parallelism on a specific hardware parallel platform. Many machine learning algorithms can be parallelized relatively easily and run well on multi-core, multi-node hardware platforms. Currently, the main hardware parallel platforms are cloud computing platforms and GPGPU platforms.

Improvement at the hardware level mainly refers to improving the existing processor architecture for the characteristics of machine learning algorithms, so that it can execute machine learning algorithms efficiently and quickly. The current architecture of general-purpose CPU is not suitable for dealing with machine learning problems because of the three characteristics of machine learning algorithms, namely, the combination of data- and computation-intensiveness, streaming data transfer and iterative computing, and low branch instructions. Machine learning algorithms are both data- and computation-intensive, leading to frequent memory access to obtain data and high-intensity, large-scale, and complex operations on data. For the CPU, its memory access efficiency and computational power are often unable to meet the requirements of large-scale machine learning applications. Machine learning algorithms generally read data and process them sequentially in a stream, and often have iterative calculations based on the entire data set, that is, a data processing often needs the entire data set to be processed before the next calculation can be performed, all of which results in a high ratio of CPU Cache Miss based on the least recently used (LRU) strategy, making the entire algorithm execution less efficient. Branch instructions tend to have a low proportion in machine learning algorithms, which makes the algorithm relatively straightforward, but it also illustrates the waste of branch prediction components that take up most of the CPU chip area.

1.2.2 Current Domain-Specific Acceleration Platforms

At present, the acceleration platforms for machine learning algorithms are mainly divided into four categories, which are cloud computing platforms, GPGPU platforms, FPGA/ASIC platforms, and heterogeneous computing platforms which integrate the characteristics of the above three platforms. These platforms tend to exhibit different parallelism granularity and are suitable for different machine learning problems.

The cloud computing platform is currently the most widely popularized, and the cloud computing platform can be used to distribute data processing and parallelize machine learning algorithms. Cloud computing platforms generally consist of a large number of isomorphic single-node CPU-based servers, with multiple nodes cooperating and working together, and often adopt task-level parallelism and data-level parallelism for problems. Cloud computing platform programming models can be roughly categorized into two types, namely, the MapReduce-based programming model and the graph computing-based programming model. Programs using the MapReduce programming model can be abstracted into two phases, namely, Map and Reduce. This model is more suitable for dealing with data with a relatively low level of dependency, while it is less suitable for data with a high level of dependency. Programs using the graph computing programming model can be abstracted into a computation based on a graph, where each node of the graph is computed based on the information of neighboring edges and nodes. This model is more suitable for situations with a high level of data interdependence.

GPGPUs are well suited for data-level parallel processing of data due to their specialized architecture. GPGPUs are often composed of multiple streaming multiprocessors (SMs) internally, and each SM consists of multiple streaming processors (SPs). Multiple SMs share a global memory, and SPs in each SM share multiple registers and shared memory. Essentially, GPGPU is equivalent to a multi-core architecture, and its different levels of memory devices are not automatically maintained like CPU but are specified by programmers, so GPGPU is well able to parallelize problems at the data level. The proposal and implementation of programming specifications such as CUDA, OpenCL, and OpenACC make GPU programming simple and fast, so GPU has become a widely used acceleration parallel platform.

FPGA and ASIC are currently mainly used to design specialized hardware accelerators for specific algorithms and problems themselves. FPGA is often an intermediate device used to verify and simulate the designed accelerator architecture, and when the verification is complete, the specialized ASIC accelerator can be customized. FPGA itself can also act as a specialized acceleration device due to its flexible programmability and reconfigurability characteristics, and the most suitable reconstruction for different problems makes FPGA to have great acceleration potential. However, FPGA and ASIC platforms are not very popular due to factors such as high design difficulty, and they mainly exist in embedded devices or applications in specific fields.

Heterogeneous computing platforms make use of a combination of CPU, GPU, and FPGA, and often adopt the scheme of clusters composed of heterogeneous computing nodes. However, heterogeneous computing platforms still have the problems of how to make good use of these computing resources and how to provide users with a concise programming model that is still immature and in the research stage. Some existing prototypes of heterogeneous computing platforms are Axel, OptiML, and Lime.

1.3 Metrics to Measure the Effectiveness of Domain-Specific Platforms

There are many different metrics to measure the acceleration effectiveness of domain-specific platforms, and these metrics tend to reflect different aspects of the acceleration platforms, some of which are speedup, efficiency, scalability, and resource utilization.

Speedup is the ratio of the time it takes for the serial version of a program to run to the time it takes for the parallel version of the program to run. It makes sense to parallelize the program only when the ratio is greater than 1, and often, the larger the ratio, the higher the acceleration effect on the parallelization of the program.

Efficiency refers to the ratio of the speedup of the program to the number of processing units, which often reflects the utilization rate of multiple processing units; the higher the efficiency, the higher the utilization rate of multiple processing units.

Scalability describes how the efficiency of a program fluctuates as the number of processing units increases. Scalability is generally related to efficiency; the higher the efficiency, the better the scalability of the program, and vice versa.

Resource utilization is primarily targeted at the use of FPGA platforms for acceleration. When using FPGA to design accelerator architectures, hardware resources are often very limited, so hardware resources cannot be blindly used in design, but we need to find a balance between resource and performance.

1.4 Content Structure of This Book

This book covers some of the major aspects of domain-specific computing, including domain-specific computing architectures and typical applications. Specifically, this book aims at the common big data and artificial intelligence scenarios in the existing industry, analyzes and summarizes some representative applications of related scenarios, analyzes the characteristics of applications, and proposes a series of domain-specific accelerator design methods and specific architectures. Specifically, the content of this book is structured as follows:

Chapter 2, Machine Learning Algorithms and Hardware Accelerator Customization, first analyzes some of the common existing machine learning algorithms and analyzes the acceleration of these algorithms. Based on the characteristics of existing machine learning algorithms, this chapter investigates common acceleration methods and hardware platforms, such as specialized chips, FPGA, GPU, and distributed systems. Each of the hardware acceleration architecture frameworks reflects the advantages of corresponding technical means.

Chapter 3, Hardware Accelerator Customization for Data Mining Recommendation Algorithms, focuses on the introduction of the common neighborhood-based collaborative filtering (CF) methods in recommendation algorithms and designs a specialized hardware architecture to implement the training accelerator and the prediction accelerator. The training accelerator supports five similarity measurements that can be used in the training phases of user-based CF and project-based CF in different phases of computing SlopeOne. The prediction accelerator supports the accumulation and weighted average operations of these three algorithms in the prediction phase. In addition, buses and interconnects between peripherals such as host CPUs, memory, hardware accelerators, and direct memory access (DMA) are designed. To facilitate user programmatic calls, this chapter also describes how to create and encapsulate the Linux operating system, as well as the user-layer function call interfaces for these hardware accelerators and DMA in the operating system environment.

Chapter 4, Customization and Optimization of Distributed Computing Systems for Recommendation Algorithms, focuses on the typical features of recommendation algorithms and how to adopt a Spark-based distributed system to realize the design of a domain-specific computing platform. This chapter includes a basic introduction to CF recommendation algorithms, content-based recommendation algorithms, and model-based recommendation algorithms, as well as a general deployment of distributed recommendation systems, including an introduction to key technologies such as weight blend and cross-blending.

Chapter 5, Hardware Customization for Clustering Algorithms, mainly focuses on the analysis of the features of the existing typical clustering algorithms, including K-Means, K-medoid, SLINK, and DBSCAN, to portray the basic algorithmic process and features, and to form the relevant groundwork for hardware deployments and accelerator customization, such as software and hardware function division, software and hardware collaborative design process, and code locality analysis. This is used as the basis for the hardware implementation of hardware acceleration systems, execution abstraction, and code mapping for clustering algorithms.

Chapter 6, Hardware Accelerator Customization Techniques for Graph Algorithms, mainly focuses on traditional graph computing algorithms and new graph neural network algorithms. This chapter analyzes the model implementation of graph computing systems and algorithms, examines the commonly used algorithms in graph computing such as PageRank, BFS, and WCC, and introduces the mechanisms of graph convolution and graph attention. On this basis, in terms of hardware deployment, distributed graph computer systems, stand-alone graph computing systems, graph computing accelerators, and graph neural network accelerators are introduced, and typical hardware acceleration systems, such as GPU, ASIC, and FPGA, are especially analyzed.

Chapter 7, Overview of Hardware Acceleration Methods for Neural Network Algorithms, focuses on different neural network acceleration methods, including ASIC, GPU, FPGA, modern memory, and parallel programming models and middleware for neural networks.

Chapter 8, Customization of FPGA-Based Hardware Accelerators for Deep Belief Networks, mainly summarizes the papers published on neural network accelerator in the field of EDA in recent years, and then classifies and analyzes the key techniques in each paper. For example, typical optimization goals include computation, storage, and performance power optimization. Typical techniques include pruning, weight compression, data sharing, data parallelism, and approximate computing. Finally, some new research hotspots and development trends of neural networks are given.

Chapter 9, FPGA-Based Hardware Accelerator Customization for Recurrent Neural Networks, begins with an introduction to deep belief networks, an analysis of the restricted Boltzmann machine, and common computational memory access pipeline techniques. On this basis, a hardware-customized acceleration platform for deep belief networks is introduced, and the basic implementation of the acceleration system framework, inner product computing, parallel processing, and pipeline mechanism are discussed. Based on this, various optimization methods are described, including storage optimization, structure reuse, and multi-platform parallel acceleration.

Chapter 10, Hardware Customization/Acceleration Techniques for Impulse Neural Networks, first introduces the basic principles of impulse neural networks; analyzes the impulse neuron model, the HH neuron model, the LIF neuron model, and the SRM neuron model; and describes the topology and algorithms of impulse neural network. On this basis, a hardware deployment/acceleration customization for impulse neural networks is introduced; digital–analog hybrid implementation and pure digital circuit implementation are described; and the existing new accelerators are reviewed and analyzed.

Chapter 11, Accelerators for Big Data Genome Sequencing, first analyzes Knuth–Morris–Pratt (KMP) and Burrows–Wheeler Alignment (BWA) algorithms and describes the typical operators of the algorithm process. On this basis, the principles of hardware acceleration are introduced, the specific design and implementation of the accelerators are described, and methods of building a software and hardware co-design framework and specific task mapping schemes are introduced.

Chapter 12, RISC-V Open Source Instruction Set and Architecture, begins with an introduction to the reduced instruction set computer-V (RISC-V) architecture, analyzing in detail the characteristics of the RISC-V architecture in comparison to traditional instruction set architectures. Then, the current research status of RISC-V in industry and academia is investigated and summarized, and the extended instruction sets and processors based on RSIC-V are introduced. On this basis, this chapter implements a convolutional neural network (CNN) extension based on the RISC-V instruction set and introduces the overall architecture, unit design, performance evaluation, and other aspects.

Chapter 13, Compilation Optimization Methods in the Customization of Reconfigurable Accelerators, first introduces the high-level comprehensive tools from source code to register transfer level code; then introduces the key techniques such as source code to source code optimization mechanism, domain-customized language, intermediate expression, and accelerator template mapping; and makes a more comprehensive summary and analysis of hardware accelerator customization optimization from the compilation perspective.

2

Machine Learning Algorithms and Hardware Accelerator Customization

2.1 Overview of Machine Learning

2.1.1 Introduction to Machine Learning

Machine learning is concerned with using data to construct appropriate predictive models to make predictions about unknown data. In general, the main task of machine learning is to select a function f from a certain class of function models and learn it based on a data set so that the function can accurately map the input domain X to the output domain Y, which is $f: X \rightarrow Y$. The input domain X often represents a collection of multiple sets of data, and the output domain Y represents the identity or result corresponding to each set of data.

Depending on the data used for learning, machine learning algorithms can be categorized into two types: supervised learning and unsupervised learning. In supervised learning algorithms, each set of training data in the data set used for training has a clear identification or outcome, and the algorithm uses the training data to construct a function f which will be used to make predictions on data with unknown identification or outcome. In unsupervised learning, the identity or outcome of an existing set of input data is often unknown, and most unsupervised learning algorithms assume that the data is subject to some kind of joint probability distribution, and the algorithms use this assumption to find the function f that best fits the input training data. Supervised learning is mainly of two types, namely, classification and regression. In classification, the output domain Y of the function f consists of a set of discrete values, and in regression, the output domain Y of the function f is a continuous real value, and the function f is a continuous real value. Unsupervised learning focuses on data clustering, which is the process of grouping data from an unclassified data set into classes according to attributes such as distance and similarity.

DOI: 10.1201/9780429355080-2

Both supervised and unsupervised learning share the distinction between learning and inference. Learning refers to the process of determining a prediction function f, while inference refers to the process of calculating $f(x)$ based on a certain instance x on X. Therefore, for machine learning algorithms, we can choose whether to accelerate the learning process or the inference process or both in parallel, depending on the specific application scenario.

In addition, according to the characteristics of the algorithm itself, machine learning algorithms can also be divided into two forms of batch learning and online learning. Batch learning is the traditional sense of learning, both first given a training set, training f, and then f used in the test data. Online learning is different from the traditional learning, and it is a kind of learning while predicting the process of the data, so the online learning often has real-time requirements. The online learning algorithms often appear more meaningful when accelerated than the batch learning algorithms.

2.1.2 Classification of Machine Learning Algorithms

According to the similarity of the presentation and implementation of machine learning algorithms, we can categorize the algorithms such as Bayesian-based algorithms and neural network-based algorithms. Of course, the scope of machine learning is so vast that some algorithms are difficult to categorize explicitly into a particular class, and for some classifications, algorithms of the same classification can target different types of problems. Some researchers [1] classified most of the machine learning algorithms into 12 types, where each type of algorithm tends to have similar models and solutions, and it is possible to design gas pedals by extracting common features in a particular class of machine learning algorithms to accelerate a particular class of machine learning algorithms. These 12 types of machine learning algorithms are listed in the following.

2.1.2.1 Regression Algorithms

Regression algorithms are a class of algorithms that attempt to explore relationships between variables using a measure of error. Regression algorithms are powerful tools for statistical machine learning. In the field of machine learning, people talk about regression, sometimes in reference to a class of problems and sometimes in reference to a class of algorithms, something that often confuses beginners (Figure 2.1).

Common regression algorithms include ordinary least square, logistic regression, stepwise regression, multi-variate adaptive regression splines, and locally estimated scatterplot smoothing.

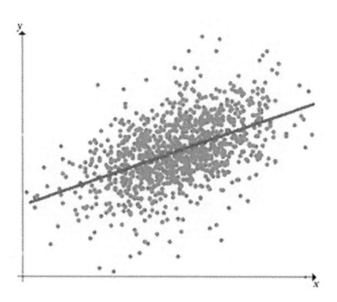

FIGURE 2.1
Using regression algorithms to make predictions about data.

2.1.2.2 Example-Based Algorithms

Instance-based algorithms are often used to model decision-making problems, such that a batch of sample data is often selected and then the new data is compared to the sample data based on certain approximations. In this way, the best match is found. For this reason, example-based algorithms are often referred to as "winner-take-all learning" or "memory-based learning" (Figure 2.2).

Common example-based algorithms include k-nearest neighbor, learning vector quantization (LVQ), and self-organizing map (SOM).

2.1.2.3 Regularization Methods

Regularization methods are extensions of other algorithms (usually regression algorithms) that adjust the algorithms based on their complexity. Regularization methods typically reward simple models and penalize complex algorithms (Figure 2.3).

Common regularization algorithms include ridge regression, least absolute shrinkage and selection operator, and elastic net.

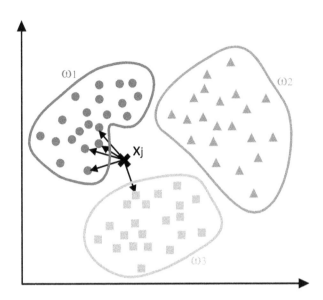

FIGURE 2.2
Matching an objective function using an instance-based algorithm.

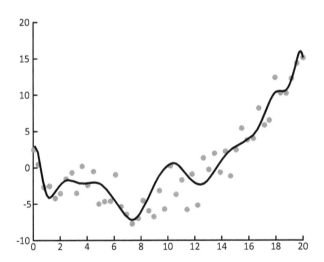

FIGURE 2.3
Reducing overfitting with regularization methods.

2.1.2.4 Decision Tree Algorithms

Decision tree algorithms use a tree structure to build a decision model based on the attributes of the data, and decision tree models are often used to solve classification and regression problems (Figure 2.4).

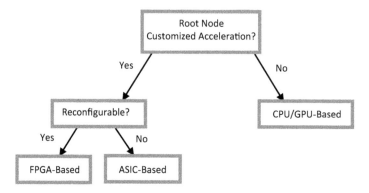

FIGURE 2.4
Solving classification and regression problems using decision tree algorithms.

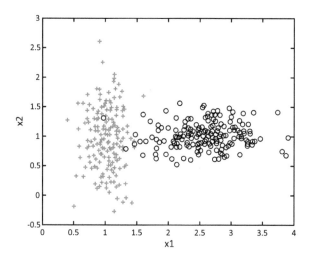

FIGURE 2.5
Solving classification and regression problems using Bayesian methods.

Common decision tree algorithms include classification and regression tree (CART), ID3 (Iterative Dichotomiser 3), C4.5, chi-squared automatic interaction detection, decision stump, random forest, MARS, and gradient boosting machine (GBM).

2.1.2.5 Bayesian Approach

Bayesian methods are a class of algorithms based on Bayes' theorem and are mainly used to solve classification and regression problems (Figure 2.5).

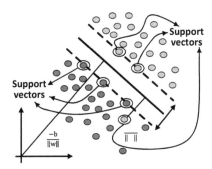

FIGURE 2.6
Solving classification and regression problems using kernel-based algorithms.

Common algorithms based on the Bayesian approach include the plain Bayesian algorithm, averaged one-dependence estimators, and Bayesian belief network.

2.1.2.6 Kernel-Based Algorithms

The most famous kernel-based algorithm is the support vector machine (SVM). Kernel-based algorithms map the input data into a higher-order vector space, in which some classification or regression problems can be solved more easily (Figure 2.6).

Common kernel-based algorithms include SVM, radial basis function, and linear discriminate analysis.

2.1.2.7 Clustering Algorithms

Clustering, like regression, is described sometimes as a class of problems and sometimes as a class of algorithms. Clustering algorithms usually group input data according to centroids or hierarchies. So clustering algorithms try to find the intrinsic structure of the data in order to group the data according to the greatest common denominator (Figure 2.7).

Common clustering algorithms include K-Means algorithm and expectation maximization.

2.1.2.8 Association Rule Learning

Association rule learning identifies useful association rules in large multi-variate data sets by finding the rules that best explain the relationships between data variables (Figure 2.8).

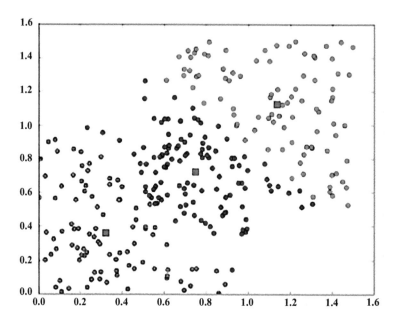

FIGURE 2.7
Data categorization using clustering algorithms.

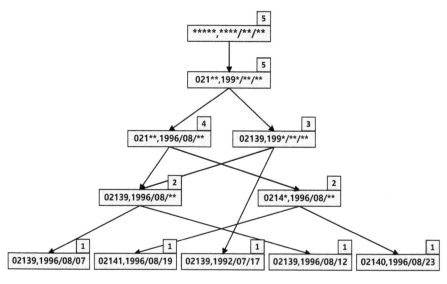

FIGURE 2.8
Using association rule learning to extract association rules in a multi-variate data set.

Common association rule learning algorithms include the Apriori algorithm and the Eclat algorithm.

2.1.2.9 Artificial Neural Networks

Artificial neural network algorithms mimic biological neural networks and are a class of pattern matching algorithms. They are usually used to solve classification and regression problems. Artificial neural networks are a huge branch of machine learning with hundreds of different algorithms (Figure 2.9).

Important artificial neural network algorithms include perceptron neural network, back propagation, Hopfield network, SOM, and LVQ.

2.1.2.10 Deep Learning

Deep learning algorithms are a development of artificial neural networks. It has won a lot of attention in the recent past, especially since Baidu has also started to focus on deep learning. With computing power becoming increasingly cheap, deep learning attempts to build much larger and more complex neural networks. Many deep learning algorithms are semi-supervised learning algorithms that are used to deal with large data sets where there is a small amount of unlabeled data (Figure 2.10).

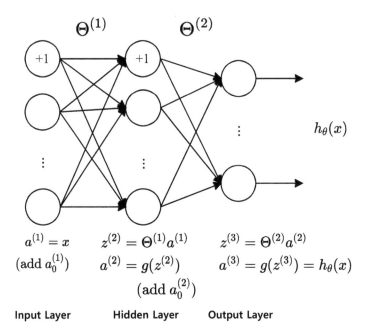

$$a^{(1)} = x \qquad z^{(2)} = \Theta^{(1)}a^{(1)} \qquad z^{(3)} = \Theta^{(2)}a^{(2)}$$
$$(\text{add } a_0^{(1)}) \qquad a^{(2)} = g(z^{(2)}) \qquad a^{(3)} = g(z^{(3)}) = h_\theta(x)$$
$$(\text{add } a_0^{(2)})$$

Input Layer   **Hidden Layer**   **Output Layer**

FIGURE 2.9
Artificial neural network structure.

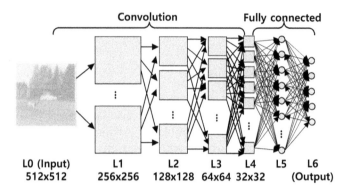

FIGURE 2.10
Neural network structure in deep learning.

Common deep learning algorithms include restricted Boltzmann machine, deep belief networks, convolutional networks, and auto-encoders.

2.1.2.11 Dimensionality Reduction Algorithms

Like clustering algorithms, dimensionality reduction algorithms attempt to analyze the intrinsic structure of the data, but dimensionality reduction algorithms attempt to generalize or explain the data using less information in an unsupervised learning manner. These types of algorithms can be used to visualize high-dimensional data or used to simplify the data for use in supervised learning (Figure 2.11).

Common dimensionality reduction algorithms include principal component analysis, partial least square regression, Sammon mapping, multi-dimensional scaling (MDS), projection tracking, and projection pursuit.

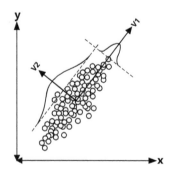

FIGURE 2.11
Using dimensionality reduction algorithms to analyze the intrinsic structure of data.

2.1.2.12 Integration Algorithms

Integration algorithms use relatively weak learning models that are trained independently on the same samples and then integrate the results to make an overall prediction. The main difficulty with integrative algorithms is which independent weak learning models to integrate and how to integrate the results. This is a very powerful and popular class of algorithms (Figure 2.12).

Common algorithms include boosting, bootstrapped aggregation (bagging), AdaBoost, stacked generalization (blending), GBM, and random forest, among others.

2.1.3 Machine Learning Algorithm Acceleration Focus

Accelerating the execution of machine learning algorithms is not simply a matter of accelerating certain parts of the algorithms, but rather, there are rules to follow. Since machine learning algorithms are compatible with data-intensive and computation-intensive characteristics, acceleration of

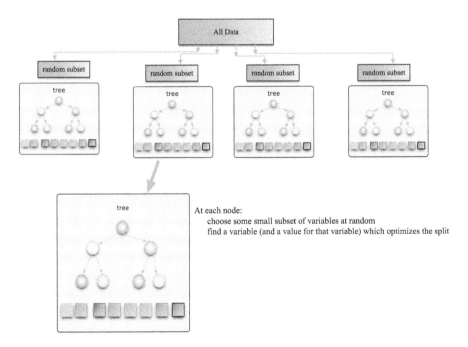

FIGURE 2.12
Integration of independent learning models for integrated prediction using integration algorithms.

machine learning algorithms can start from accelerating data communication and transmission and accelerating computation execution of algorithms.

According to more than 30 papers researched and my own understanding and summary, we can accelerate machine learning algorithms from four points, namely, accelerating the computational core of the algorithm, abstracting the common characteristics of the algorithm, parallelizing machine learning algorithms, and optimizing the data communication transmission of machine learning algorithms. Accelerating the computational core of the algorithm and parallelizing the machine learning algorithm belong to the aspect of accelerating the computational execution of the algorithm. Optimizing the data communication transmission of the algorithm belongs to the aspect of accelerating the data communication transmission, while the common features of the abstract algorithm and accelerating the features both include the two aspects.

These four points of view are not independent of each other, but are closely related to each other. For example, optimizing data communication transmission is a special case of abstracting and accelerating common features of machine learning algorithms; parallelizing machine learning algorithms can be done for the computational core of the algorithms; the common features of the abstracted algorithms may be the computational core of the algorithms or not; and it may not be meaningful to accelerate the execution of the common features that are not computationally central. Starting from these four points can help and guide us in accelerating machine learning algorithms.

2.1.3.1 Accelerating the Computational Core of an Algorithm

Regardless of the type of machine learning algorithm, different parts of the algorithm have different impacts on the execution time of the whole algorithm.

The computational core of the algorithm (kernel) is the most time-consuming part of the algorithm, and accelerating the kernel can significantly reduce the execution time of the whole algorithm. Therefore, for the kernel, we can either utilize multiple computing units such as general-purpose graphics processor (GPGPU) to perform parallel computation on different data, or use FPGA to solidify the kernel of the algorithm into multiple computing units to accelerate the execution.

Paper [2] lists the top three most time-consuming kernels for 15 machine learning algorithms, as shown in Table 1.1.

There are many more algorithms for machine learning than those listed above. Since we cannot enumerate them all, we will focus on summarizing the computational core of a particular class of algorithms in our future research work.

TABLE 1.1

Statistics of the Most Time-Consuming Computational Kernels for Various Machine
Learning Algorithms

Application	Top Three Kernels (%)			Sum (%)
	Kernel 1 (%)	**Kernel 2 (%)**	**Kernel 3 (%)**	
k-Means	Distance (68)	Clustering (21)	minDist (10)	99
Fuzzy K-Means	Clustering (58)	Distance (39)	fuzzySum (1)	98
BIRCH	Distance (54)	Variance (22)	Redistribution (10)	86
HOP	Density (39)	Search (30)	Gather (23)	92
Naive Bayesian	ProbCal (49)	Variance (38)	dataRead (10)	97
ScalParC	Classify (37)	giniCalc (36)	Compare (24)	97
Apriori	Subset (58)	dataRead (14)	Increment (8)	80
Eclat	Intersect (39)	addClass (23)	invertClass (10)	71
SNP	CompScore (68)	updateScore (20)	familyScore (2)	90
GeneNet	CondProb (55)	updateScore (31)	familyScore (9)	95
SEMPHY	bestBrnchLen (59)	Expectation (39)	IenOpt (1)	99
Rsearch	Covariance (90)	Histogram (6)	dbRead (3)	99
SVM-RFE	quotMatrx (57)	quadGrad (38)	quotUpdate (2)	97
PLSA	pathGridAssgn (51)	fillGridCache (34)	backPathFind (14)	99
Utility	dataRead (46)	Subsequence (29)	Main (23)	98

2.1.3.2 *Common Features of Abstract Algorithms*

Many machine learning algorithms show a lot of common features, and
accelerating for these common features can achieve better acceleration
results and show relatively general characteristics. The common features of
machine learning algorithms can be roughly summarized into five points,
including large-scale linear algebra operations, synchronous/asynchronous
iterative operations, algorithmic addition and multiplication, the use of commonly used excitation functions, and abstraction based on graphical models.

Large-scale linear algebra operations refer to the fact that most machine
learning algorithms often involve a large number of large-scale linear
algebra operations, and accelerating the execution of these operations can
improve the performance of the whole algorithm. Paper [3] designed a gas
pedal device to speed up matrix multiplication operations and achieved
good acceleration results on a variety of machine learning algorithms.

Synchronous/asynchronous iterative operations, on the other hand, means
that many machine learning algorithms need to repeatedly perform syn-
chronous/asynchronous iterations on data in the algorithm, and optimization of the iterative algorithm can significantly improve the performance of
the algorithm. Paper [4] designed an FPGA-based asynchronous iterative gas
pedal structure, which can be utilized to accelerate the execution of many
machine learning algorithms very well.

Algorithm multiplication proposed in paper [5] mainly refers to a part of machine learning algorithms in the learning or reasoning process that is often expressed in the form of multiplication-accumulation, and each multiplication corresponding to the degree of dependence on the data is often low, making it convenient for parallelization.

Commonly used excitation functions, on the other hand, indicate that many machine learning algorithms use many of the same auxiliary functions, such as the sigmoid function, in a certain step of their execution, and speeding up for these commonly used excitation functions can achieve a certain speed-up effect.

The abstraction based on the graph model proposed in paper [6] shows that the graph computation model can better and effectively deal with those data mining algorithms that have a high degree of data dependency, and therefore the process of abstracting data into a graph and then performing graph-based vertex computation can be accelerated.

It is important to note that, as mentioned earlier, common features abstracted from multiple algorithms may or may not belong to some part of the computational core of those algorithms. Therefore, if the abstracted feature is a computational core in many algorithms, it makes more sense to accelerate the execution of this feature; conversely, if the abstracted feature is just a very common computational step in most algorithms, it makes relatively little sense to design a gas pedal structure for this feature.

2.1.3.3 Parallelizing Machine Learning Algorithms

Parallelizing machine learning algorithms is currently the most used acceleration means, and task-level parallelism or data-level parallelism or a mixture of both can be used to parallelize most machine learning algorithms. Essentially, the essence of parallelizing machine learning algorithms is to parallelize the core computation of the algorithm in order to achieve better acceleration results.

As mentioned in Section 2.2, the three main platforms for parallelizing machine learning algorithms are cloud computing platforms, GPGPUs, and FPGA/Application Specific Integrated Circuit (ASIC) platforms. Cloud computing platform parallelism mainly utilizes task-level parallelism and data-level parallelism, and the parallel granularity is relatively coarse. For example, the Map and Reduce processes in the MapReduce model can be executed in parallel, and the vertices in the graph computation model with no dependencies can also be executed in parallel. GPGPU platform parallelism mainly utilizes data-level parallelism, and the parallel granularity is relatively fine. FPGA/ASIC platform parallelism mainly utilizes data-level parallelism, and the parallel granularity is relatively fine. FPGA/ASIC platform parallelization is a good choice to achieve the parallelization effect. The parallelism using FPGA/ASIC platforms mainly depends on the different architectures of the designed gas pedals, which can utilize both task-level parallelism and data-level parallelism. In addition, pipelining techniques are often used in gas pedals to increase throughput.

2.1.3.4 *Optimizing Data Communication Transmission*

Since machine learning algorithms are both computation- and data-intensive, accelerating the computation-intensive part of the algorithm alone is not enough, and the data communication such as access memory of the algorithm often becomes a bottleneck to improve performance. Optimizing data communication transmission and access models for machine learning algorithms is a starting point for accelerating the data-intensive part of machine learning algorithms.

The three existing acceleration platforms all face data communication problems to varying degrees.

For cloud computing platforms, parallel acceleration of certain machine learning algorithms may be less than ideal, which is often rooted in the huge overhead of data communication. Cloud computing platforms utilize a distributed file system to store data, with point nodes connected via Ethernet. If an algorithm requires data distributed across multiple nodes, or if the algorithm needs to access the data more frequently, the data transfer communication overhead can be significant.

For a GPGPU, utilizing it to accelerate machine learning algorithms also requires data transfer considerations. The data needed by the program is often stored on disk in the node and transferred to the global memory of the GPGPU via memory, a process that takes up a significant amount of time overhead. In addition, GPGPUs also have internal memory hierarchies of registers, shared memory, L1 Cache, etc., so the parallelization of algorithms using GPGPUs needs to focus on how to utilize these different storage components.

And for FPGAs and ASICs, when designing specialized gas pedals based on them, they are often faced with the process of transferring data from Host memory to Device memory. Moreover, FPGAs also have different frequencies of internal memory devices, so designers need to focus on how to design the storage part of the gas pedal, such as the intermediate values used in the iterative computation of the design of the corresponding cache and so on.

2.1.4 Commonly Used Public Data Sets for Machine Learning

Currently, there are many public data sets on the web, which often have high credibility and are used relatively frequently. Therefore, in the process of designing the gas pedal, we can consider utilizing these public data sets to test and compare the gas pedal prototype.

Commonly used public data sets include MNIST, Tsukuba, Maricopa, and Tweet.

2.2 Design of FPGA-Based Machine Learning Gas Pedals

This section is mainly a brief summary of nearly 30 papers previously researched on the design of gas pedal components for machine learning algorithms using FPGAs. Overall, these 30 papers address different starting points of the problem and design different gas pedal solutions, which can be categorized into four groups according to the kind of problem to be solved, namely, designing gas pedals for specific problems, designing gas pedals for specific algorithms, designing gas pedals for common features of algorithms, and designing general gas pedal frameworks using hardware templates. These four categories follow a process from specific to general, and the design difficulty tends to increase. For the first two categories, designing gas pedals is more common and less difficult, while for the last two categories, especially the last one, the design is more difficult and still in the research stage and not popularized.

From a research point of view, we should aim at designing a generalized gas pedal architecture for machine learning algorithms instead of limiting ourselves to specific application scenarios or machine learning algorithms, which would be very difficult but indeed very meaningful.

2.2.1 Designing Accelerators for Specific Problems

Designing gas pedals for specific problems using FPGAs is currently the most widely used area of FPGA-based gas pedals. Designing gas pedals specifically for a particular problem not only fits the needs of the problem well, but it is also relatively less difficult to design. Designing gas pedals for specific problems often accelerates the reasoning process of machine learning algorithms rather than the learning process.

A case study of designing a gas pedal structure for a specific problem is listed below. In paper [7], a dedicated gas pedal device is designed using FPGA to execute the C4.5 decision tree algorithm to accelerate the solution of the Online Traffic Classification problem. The Online Traffic Classification problem refers to the problem of determining the number of packets in the transport stream of a TCP connection/UDP establishment based on the number of packets of the TCP connection/UDP establishment. For example, analyzing eight packets transmitted by a TCP connection, it can be determined that the connection was established by QQ.

The gas pedal architecture designed in the paper is shown in the figure above. As shown in Figure 2.13, the overall gas pedal architecture is divided into two parts: the discretization module on the left and the classification module on the right. The discretization module is a process of preprocessing the input data, while the classification module actually makes classification decisions on the input data.

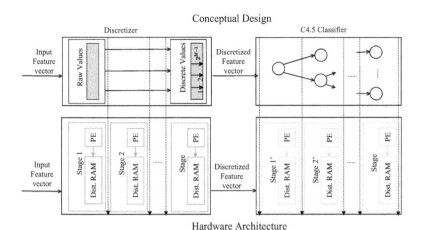

FIGURE 2.13
FPGA-based C4.5 algorithm gas pedal architecture designed in paper [7].

The attribute vectors of the data are fed from the left side to the discretization module, and after each level of the discretization processing unit, the data is discretized corresponding to a particular attribute value. The data is then fed to the classification module and after each level, the data goes one level down in the decision tree. A classification unit has all the intermediate/leaf nodes of this level in the corresponding decision tree stored in its local memory, and the next level of the classification unit receives the parameters (data attribute set, intermediate node address) and then finds the corresponding intermediate node to continue the classification.

The specific gas pedal structure designed in this thesis still has some shortcomings. For example, for the classification module, each layer of the decision tree is handled by a PE, which will inevitably lead to an imbalance in computational resources as the nodes of each layer are different, and thus the gas pedal component might have some performance bottlenecks when the input data size is relatively large.

2.2.2 Designing Accelerators for Specific Algorithms

Designing gas pedals for a particular machine learning algorithm using FPGAs is also a common application area for FPGAs. Gas pedals designed for specific machine learning algorithms can be applied to a specific problem, often only needing to configure specific parameters, or some small changes can be better adapted to the specific problem.

Currently, the research on this piece is not very sufficient, but only investigated the five machine learning algorithms of SVM, Apriori, Decision Tree, K-Means, and Bayesian graph based on DAG, which are listed in the following.

2.2.2.1 SVM Algorithm

The SVM algorithm is one of the most famous kernel-based machine learning algorithms. Most of the current papers mainly focus on the inference process of the SVM algorithm to design gas pedal devices. In the inference process of the SVM algorithm, for data that needs to be classified, it needs to be multiplied with all the support vectors to get the intermediate value, and then the intermediate value will be sent to the kernel function for processing to get the final result. Therefore, for the inference process of SVM, we can choose to accelerate the multiplication and summation part or the kernel function part, or both.

Paper [8] proposes a gas pedal architecture designed for the inference process of the SVM algorithm. The architecture mainly accelerates the part of the multiplication and accumulation of the vector to be classified and the support vector, while the computation of the kernel function is still executed in the CPU.

The overall gas pedal architecture is shown in Figure 2.14. There are multiple vector processor clusters on the FPGA; each vector processor cluster consists of multiple Vector Processing Elements (VPE) arrays; each VPE array consists of multiple VPEs; and each VPE is a vector processing unit that handles dot product operations between two vectors. During the execution of the gas pedal device, large-scale matrices are passed in as streams, small-scale matrices are stored on the on-chip memory, and all VPEs in each VPE array store a column of the small-scale matrix. In addition, the gas pedal device has a more fine-grained dot product operation, where each vector dot product operation is divided into multiple chunk dot products, and the size of this chunk is rationalized so that the data transfer between the FPGA and the Central Processing Unit (CPU) does not become a bottleneck.

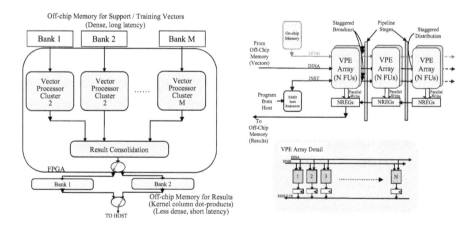

FIGURE 2.14
Accelerator architecture for FPGA-based SVM algorithm reasoning proposed in paper [8].

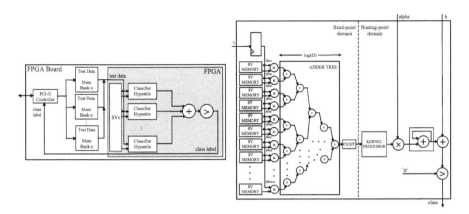

FIGURE 2.15
Improvements made in paper [9] for FPGA-based SVM inference gas pedals.

The gas pedal architecture designed in paper [8] does not accelerate the computation of kernel functions and does not support operations on heterogeneous data. In paper [9], these problems are improved and a novel architecture for cascaded SVM gas pedal is proposed.

Paper [9] proposes an improved structure for the shortcomings of paper [8], as shown in Figure 2.15. In this gas pedal structure, there are multiple Classifier Hypertiles acting as PEs of the gas pedal. For certain test data, each PE handles the operation between the test data and a portion of the support vectors separately. All the support vectors are stored in the on-chip memory of the FPGA, and all the test data are stored in the off-chip memory of the FPGA. For each test, data is streamed into multiple PEs. For each Classifier Hypertile (PE), in essence, it also goes for a multiply-accumulate operation. Unlike the previous MAC unit, Hypertile has a finer granularity, and it uses a multiplier for each attribute that corresponds to the accuracy of the attribute so that it can handle heterogeneous data better. In addition, the gas pedal architecture uses specialized computational units to accelerate the computation of kernel functions.

In addition to the improvement, paper [9] also proposes a novel structure of the SVM gas pedal, namely a cascaded SVM gas pedal, as shown in Figure 2.16. The so-called cascade is a pipelined concatenation of multiple SVM classifiers, each of which may have a different classification model and different classification capabilities. This is equivalent to using the idea of Boost algorithm, and both multiple weak classifiers are combined to form a strong classifier. For a certain level of SVM, if it cannot more accurately determine the type of the input value, then it will be given to the next level to deal with. It is logical that the latter classifier should be stronger than the former.

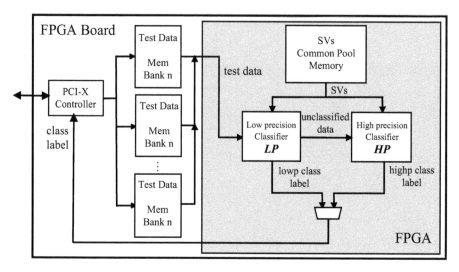

FIGURE 2.16
FPGA-based cascaded SVM gas pedal structure designed in paper [9].

The thesis designed a two-level classifier. The first level of the classifier can better classify the points farther from the hyperplane, using a simple kernel function, running faster, while the second level of the classifier can classify the points at the edge of the hyperplane (the first level of the classifier cannot judge the point), using a kernel function which may be more complex, running a little slower.

The widespread use of SVM algorithms makes accelerating SVM algorithms seem relatively relevant. More work has been done on the inference process of SVM algorithms and it is relatively well-developed, while relatively little work has been done on accelerating the learning process of SVM algorithms. In addition, for the inference process of the SVM algorithm, there are often preprocessing processes such as orthogonalization and regularization before data classification, which is often inefficient and occupies a high proportion of time on the CPU. Therefore, accelerating the execution of the preprocessing process is also a scientific research entry point.

2.2.2.2 Apriori Algorithm

The Apriori algorithm is an important algorithm for dealing with association analysis. The Apriori algorithm is mainly used to discover the association connection between things, and it obtains the degree of association by counting the number of times things appear to each other.

Paper [10] designed a gas pedal structure for the first half of the Apriori algorithm to accelerate the process of obtaining frequent item sets, as shown

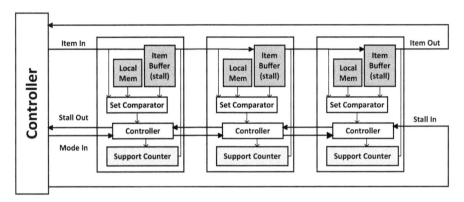

FIGURE 2.17
Structure of FPGA-based gas pedal for the Apriori algorithm designed in paper [10].

in Figure 2.17. The paper divided the first half of Apriori to calculate the support into three parts: Candidates Generate, Candidates Punnig, and Support Calculation. The gas pedal structure can be reused for all three phases and shows good acceleration results.

Candidates Generate is used to generate candidate frequent itemsets. If there are two K-frequent itemsets (already frequent itemsets) and their first k−1 items are the same, then a K+1 candidate frequent item can be generated from these two K-frequent itemsets. Candidates Punnig is used to do preprocessing on the K+1 candidate frequent itemset just generated, both for the K+1 candidate frequent itemset and for the K+1 candidate frequent itemset. Preprocessing, both for the K+1 attributes, removes any one attribute and test the remaining K itemsets in the set of K-frequent itemsets that have been generated. If one of the remaining K itemsets is not frequent, then the newly generated K+1 itemsets must not be frequent. Support Calculation is used to do the statistics for the K+1 candidate frequent itemsets that have been pre-checked, calculate the K+1 candidate frequent itemsets, and calculate the K+1 candidate frequent itemsets from these two K-frequent itemsets. The Support Calculation part is used to do statistics on the K+1 candidate frequent itemsets that have passed the pre-check, calculating the frequency of the K+1 candidate frequent itemsets in the whole data set, and only after a certain frequency, the K+1 candidate frequent itemsets can be considered as frequent, and then it is added to the set of K+1 frequent itemsets.

The Apriori algorithm is not well-researched; just read this one. However, since the Apriori algorithm essentially exhibits a techno-statistical process, the use of FPGAs to accelerate the Apriori algorithm should also have a better future. In addition, most Apriori algorithms require that the data should be pre-numbered in a dictionary order when processing the data, so the preprocessing process of sorting the data in a dictionary order should also be a potential acceleration point.

2.2.2.3 Decision Tree Algorithm

The decision tree algorithm is a more general machine learning algorithm that also has two processes: learning and reasoning. The computational core of the learning process of the decision tree algorithm is the calculation of the Gini coefficient (for the C4.5 algorithm) or the entropy gain factor (for the CART algorithm). There is a lot of research on both the learning and reasoning aspects of decision tree algorithms.

Paper [11] proposes a gas pedal structure for accelerating Gini coefficient computation for the learning process of the C4.5 decision tree algorithm. The structure is shown in Figure 2.18. Each successive attribute Gini coefficient computation can be done by defining its own Gini unit in the FPGA, and then all the Gini unit results are connected at the hierarchical level by comparing the components so that the minimum Gini coefficients can be selected.

This paper was published earlier. The advanced accelerator structure for decision trees should have been greatly improved, and it should be able to perform the entire decision tree learning process rather than a small part of it, which can reduce the communication delay between the data. In addition, most decision tree algorithms tend to require the input data to be discrete and thus can be accelerated for the preprocessing process of discretizing the input data.

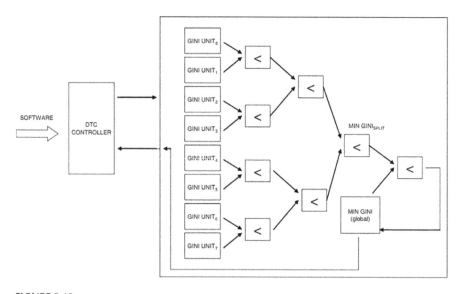

FIGURE 2.18
FPGA-based gas pedal structure for accelerated Gini coefficient computation proposed in paper [11].

2.2.2.4 K-Means Algorithm

The K-Means algorithm is one of the most common clustering algorithms, and its computational core lies in the process of finding the nearest center of mass at each point.

Papers [12,13] co-describe a gas pedal architecture that solidifies the entire K-Means algorithm, not just the computational core, into an FPGA implementation. The architecture is shown in Figure 2.19 and is overall divided into four modules, each of which corresponds to a particular implementation of the K-Means algorithm.

The Distance Kernel Block module accepts data from on-chip memory or off-chip memory, and calculates the distance from each point to all classes. If there are C classes, then the module has C DP units, and each DP unit calculates the distance from a point to a class, where the distance from a point to all classes is calculated at the same time, making full use of parallelism. The Minimum Distance Finder Kernel Block module accepts distance data from the Distance Kernel Block and finds the minimum distance from it. The Accumulation Kernel Block module accepts the distance data from the Distance Kernel Block and finds the class corresponding to the smallest distance from it. According to the class corresponding to the shortest distance from the previous module, the Accumulation Kernel Block module accumulates the features of the current data point into the accumulator of the corresponding class and increases the counter value of the corresponding class,

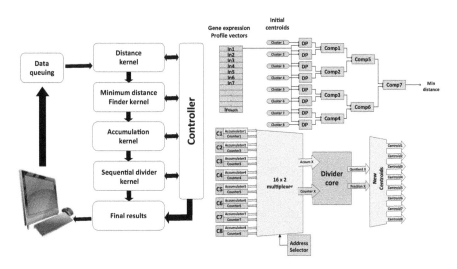

FIGURE 2.19
FPGA implementation of the overall K-Means algorithm gas pedal described in papers [12,13].

which corresponds to an accumulator and a counter for each class. When all the classes corresponding to the data points have been accumulated, the module sends the data to the next module. The Sequential Divider Kernel Block module is essentially a number of division units in a pipelined fashion, which will divide the accumulated values of each feature of each class of the data produced by the previous module with the value of the number of data counters in order to determine the next time the location of the new center of mass for each class.

The gas pedal structure designed for the K-Means algorithm is more researched and mature, so it is not of great scientific significance.

2.2.2.5 Bayesian Graph-Based Algorithms

Bayesian graph algorithms include graph models such as Bayesian belief nets and Markov random fields, which use graphs to describe an interconnected relationship between variables. Belief propagation algorithms that solve for Bayesian belief net models are a common computational core of Bayesian graph-based machine learning algorithms.

Paper [14] proposes a gas pedal structure that is only suitable for solving DAG-based Bayesian graph algorithms, as shown in Figure 2.20. Essentially, the structure is used to solve the topological ordering problem and not really for solving problems such as Bayesian belief nets. The paper devised multiple processing units, each of which uses a 20- to 30-stage ultra-deep pipeline to increase the throughput rate, and all of the processing units are connected to multiple memory modules via cross switches, with more memory modules than processing units. The architecture relies on static analysis of the problem to obtain an operational strategy, thus avoiding problems such as data correlation.

The structure devised in the paper has major drawbacks and shortcomings, and not many people have done the Bayesian graph-based machine learning algorithms. Hence, it is relatively difficult to implement them due to factors such as graph models.

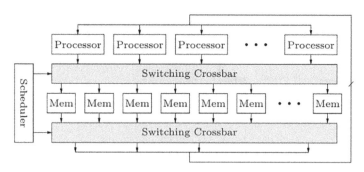

FIGURE 2.20
Structure of the gas pedal for DAG-based Bayesian graph algorithms proposed in paper [14].

2.2.3 Designing Accelerators for Algorithm Common Features

The previous two means of designing gas pedals are relatively specialized, and the designed gas pedals can only be applied to specific problems or specific algorithms. Designing gas pedals for common features of algorithms can accelerate the execution of a class of machine learning algorithms in a relatively general way.

We can design gas pedals using common features from two aspects: one is to find common features of a certain class of machine learning algorithms to design gas pedals according to the previous classification of machine learning algorithms, which has not been investigated in depth. The second is not limited to a certain class of machine learning algorithms, but to find common features in the whole machine learning algorithms, which is summarized according to the papers we read. The common three kinds of features extracted are linear algebra operations, iterative computation, and simplified algorithmic access.

2.2.3.1 Linear Algebra Operations

Most machine learning algorithms involve a large number of large-scale linear algebra operations in the process of learning or reasoning, which generally take up a large amount of computational resources, and therefore are often the core of the algorithm. Therefore, accelerating the linear algebra operations involved can effectively improve the overall performance of the algorithm.

Paper [3] pointed out that the intermediate step of many machine learning algorithms can be expressed in the form of matrix/vector product operation, and when the intermediate step operation is completed to produce intermediate data, the final step is often relatively simple to rank the intermediate data, find the maximum/minimum value, aggregate other approximation operations. For example, take the five algorithms depicted in Figure 2.21, which can all be represented in this form.

Therefore, paper [3] designed MAPLE, a gas pedal architecture, for matrix/vector product operations, and the overall architecture of MAPLE is shown in Figure 2.22.

MAPLE supports matrix/vector product operations. It is able to process intermediate data and perform normalization operations on them. For large and immutable matrices, it is often stored in off-chip memory and the data is streamed into MAPLE. For small and immutable matrices, it is partitioned and stored in multiple computation units of MAPLE. Each PE is a vector computation unit capable of performing multiply–add operations in a Cycle. Each PE has a Local Storage to store the columns of small-sized matrices. M PEs form a chain, and each Core has H chains. For each chain, the inputs are passed from left to right, and the outputs are passed from right to left. The outputs of each chain are connected to a Smart Memory Block, which is able

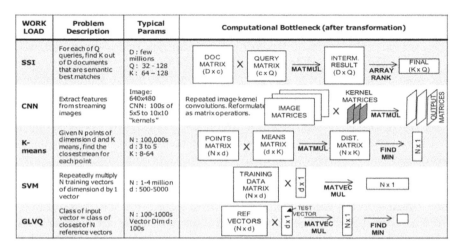

FIGURE 2.21
Representation of five algorithms using common features in paper [3].

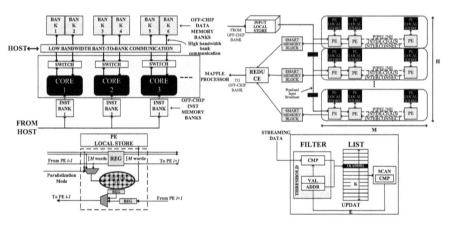

FIGURE 2.22
MAPLE, a gas pedal architecture for matrix/vector product operations proposed in paper [3].

to perform the approximation operations such as ranking, max/min, and aggregation on the outputs of each chain, and store the results that meet the approximation conditions.

2.2.3.2 Iterative Computation

In addition to linear algebra operations, another notable common feature of machine learning algorithms is repeated iterative computation. A large number of machine learning algorithms require repeated iterative computations until the final convergence result is obtained, so the number of iterations is often unknowable, and thus simply designing a gas pedal with a data flow model, as in paper [15], is far from sufficient. In addition, iterative computation is also divided into synchronous and asynchronous iterative computation. Synchronous iteration means that the next iteration of data needs to wait until the whole data has been iterated before it can be executed, while asynchronous iteration means that the next iteration of the data can be executed immediately without waiting for the whole data to be completed after an iteration.

The point at which iterative computation can be accelerated compared to linear algebra operations is not particularly clear, since different algorithms often utilize completely different iteration formulas. However, there are some common features of iterative computation, such as how to optimize the storage of intermediate values generated by iterative computation, or how to allocate and schedule the iterative data.

Paper [4] designed a gas pedal structure called Maestro, which is mainly used for accelerating asynchronous iterative machine learning algorithms, and the overall gas pedal structure is shown in Figure 2.23.

The paper divides all asynchronous iterative computations into two steps: Accumulate, in which a node collects a message m from another node with which it has an edge connection and stores the message in a local variable Δv, and Update in which the node uses Δv and the original weights v to derive new weights v. The node then applies a function to the node weights change amount Δv to get a value, and then sends that value to neighboring nodes and finally resets Δv to 0.

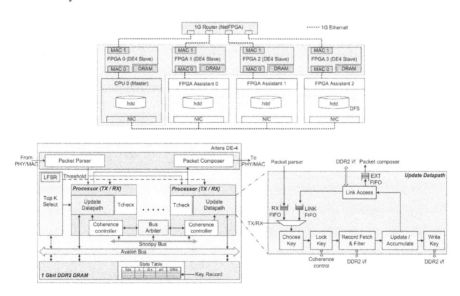

FIGURE 2.23
Maestro, the gas pedal architecture for asynchronous iterative machine learning algorithms designed in paper [4].

The system has one CPU acting as Master and four FPGAs acting as Slaves. The CPU-based Master is used for task distribution of Slaves and checking the stopping conditions. The FPGA-based multiple Slaves are used for the task distribution and checking the stopping conditions. Multiple FPGA-based Slaves run in parallel and are connected via Ethernet. Each Slave has a CPU/FPGA Assistant in addition to the FPGA, and the CPU/FPGA Assistant assists the FPGA to read and write information from the distributed file system.

The structure of the gas pedal designed in this paper actually adopts the idea of a graph computing model in cloud computing, so the incoming data of this gas pedal has graph-like association relationships, and the iterative operations performed are also vertex-based iterations, which are similar to the graph computing model in general.

2.2.3.3 Simplifying the Access Model of an Algorithm

The previous two common features mainly accelerate the computation-intensive part of machine learning algorithms, while optimizing the data-intensive part can also improve the execution efficiency of the algorithms as a whole. In fact, no matter whether in cloud computing platforms or GPGPUs, data communication transmission often becomes a bottleneck for further improvement of algorithm performance. Since a large number of machine learning algorithms have similar access models, gas pedals can be designed to accelerate a large class of machine learning algorithms by targeting these common features of data communication transmission and access.

Papers [16,17] propose a memory access structure called CoRAM, which can meet the needs of most machine learning algorithms and reduce the difficulty of developers in developing the memory access module a gas pedal, and the overall structure is shown in Figure 2.24.

When designing with CoRAM, the developer only needs to declare the CoRAM module in the verilog of the core function (equivalent to a black box), and the next data read and write operations are completed by CoRAM.

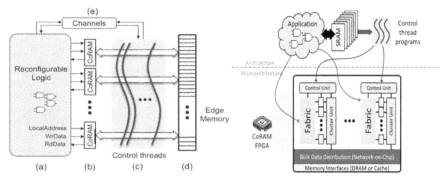

FIGURE 2.24
CoRAM, the access structure proposed in papers [16,17].

For completing the data access, CoRAM requires the developer to use the API provided by the CoRAM to define the behavior of the CoRAM using C, which greatly simplifies the design of the storage module. This greatly simplifies the design of the memory module.

Step (a) is the user-defined logic, and all the access operations of the user-defined logic are done through the CoRAM.

Step (b) is a number of CoRAMs, and the data read and written by the user will be stored in the CoRAMs. Each CoRAM has a Control thread to perform data read/write maintenance operations.

Step (c) is Control threads, and each Control thread is equivalent to an asynchronous finite state machine, which is used to maintain the migration of data between CoRAM and Edge Memory. The user-defined logic communicates with the Control threads through (e). Each Control thread consists of a number of Control actions, which can be interpreted as follows: a Control action is equivalent to an assembly instruction, and a combination of different assembly instructions forms a Control thread.

The essence of CoRAM is to simplify the design of the gas pedal access module, not specifically for machine learning algorithms to optimize the data communication and transmission part of the algorithm. It can only be said that CoRAM simplifies the algorithm's access to the memory model. Therefore, it is not known whether it can have an accelerating effect.

Optimizing the data-intensive part of machine learning algorithms has not been researched a lot, and only CoRAM is known. However, optimizing data communication transfer is indeed a potentially valuable research point, and it can accelerate a large number of machine learning algorithms in a relatively general way, so it can be a direction for future research.

2.2.4 Designing a Generic Accelerator Framework Using Hardware Templates

Compared to the previous three gas pedal design methods, designing gas pedals using hardware templates is a more generalized means. Generally speaking, these hardware templates are often the FPGA version of a certain programming model, which only requires the user to design a small part of the module for a specific problem and configure the parameters, and then the gas pedal framework can run automatically to accelerate the problem that the user is trying to solve when the parameters and modules are determined.

Thanks to the development of C to RTL tools, users can easily use C instead of s/VHDL for designing a specific module, which greatly simplifies the user's design and promotes the popularization of hardware template frameworks.

At present, three hardware template-based gas pedal frameworks have been investigated, namely, gas pedal frameworks based on the MapReduce model, gas pedal frameworks based on the Language Integrated Query (LINQ) model, and gas pedal frameworks based on the graph computation model. It can be seen that these acceleration frameworks tend to be implementations of the FPGA version of a particular programming model and are able to cover most of the machine learning algorithms.

2.2.4.1 Accelerator Frameworks Based on MapReduce Models

The MapReduce model is the most widely used model in cloud computing and is used in the implementation of many software systems such as Hadoop and Spark. Therefore, there are many research organizations trying to apply the MapReduce model in the hardware template framework for FPGAs.

The MapReduce model in cloud computing requires the user to customize the Map function and Reduce function, and then the work after that is left to the corresponding system to complete. For the FPGA-based MapReduce gas pedal framework, the user only needs to design the corresponding Map module and Reduce module, and configure the corresponding gas pedal parameters, and then the whole gas pedal no longer requires user intervention and can run automatically.

Paper [18] proposes FPMR, a hardware gas pedal framework based on the MapReduce model, and the overall framework is shown in Figure 2.25.

In FPMR, the Processor Scheduler is a very critical component that has two queues for the mapper and reducer, respectively. For Mapper, it has two queues, one for idle Mapper computation units, which holds the ID numbers of idle Mapper units, and the other is a Mapper task queue, which holds

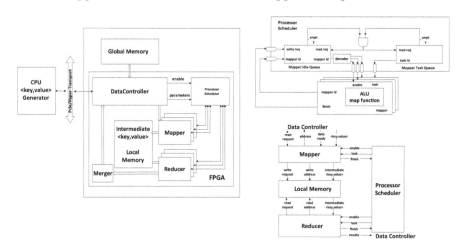

FIGURE 2.25
FPMR, a hardware gas pedal framework based on the MapReduce model proposed in paper [18].

Mapper tasks that have not yet been executed and is the same for Reducer, which use the FIFO strategy. In addition, the data transfer between the Mapper compute unit and the Reducer compute unit is done through Local Memory. In summary, the overall FPMR architecture is fixed, but only the Mapper and Reducer modules have changed. When using it, the user only needs to define the implemented Mapper and Reducer modules, and configure the corresponding gas pedal parameters.

Paper [19] again proposes Axel, a hardware gas pedal framework based on the MapReduce model. In fact, instead of being a gas pedal framework, Axel is a heterogeneous computing platform, and the overall architecture of Axel is shown in Figure 2.26. In Axel, a certain node acts as a Master for the general control of the cluster. For other slave nodes, the MapReduce computation model can be realized in two ways: in the one way, the CPU of the node carries out the general control, the GPU is responsible for the computation of the Map process, the FPGA is responsible for the execution of the Reduce process and exchanges between nodes through the bus of the FPGA. In the other way, the GPU and the FPGA are responsible for the computation of the Map process, and they work together to compute the Map. The CPU is responsible for the general control and Reduce, and exchanges information through the system I/Os. In addition, the most critical part of Axel is the Runtime Resource Manager, which runs on the top layer of each node in the system and is responsible for handling data distribution, task allocation of computation units, and inter-node communication.

For the research on gas pedal frameworks based on the MapReduce model, relatively more has been done so far. However, most of the research implementations have such and such problems, and relatively few have substantial breakthroughs.

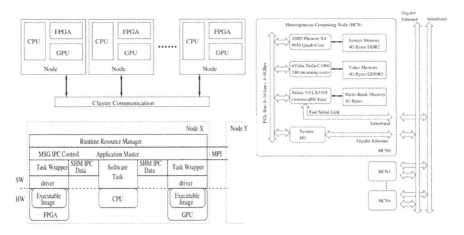

FIGURE 2.26
Axel, a hardware gas pedal framework based on the MapReduce model proposed in paper [19].

2.2.4.2 Accelerator Framework Based on Map Computing Model

Although the MapReduce model is the most common and widespread model in cloud computing, it has also exposed many shortcomings in use, such as its processing ability being very inefficient for algorithms with a high degree of data association. In recent years, a new graph-based model has been proposed, and the graph computing model can not only solve the deficiencies of the MapReduce model well, but it can also be very compatible with the MapReduce model, so it is very promising.

The graph computing model is not widely popularized in cloud computing and is temporarily in the trial stage. There are some systems that implement the graph computing model such as Pregel, GraphLab, and GraphX. There are even fewer gas pedal frameworks for graph computation models implemented on FPGA platforms, and the proposed gas pedal framework architectures have very large deficiencies. Therefore, the study of gas pedal frameworks for graph computation models has great research potential and value, and can be used as a research direction in the future.

Paper [20] proposes a gas pedal framework for graph computation models, but it is only a framework. For different graph computation problems, each member of the framework needs to be specially designed according to the problem. Therefore, the drawbacks are many, and the realization is not very valuable.

Paper [21,22] proposes a CoRAM-based graph computation gas pedal framework called GraphGen, which is shown in Figure 2.27. The framework needs to receive user-defined Graph Specifications and Design Parameters, and then generate the corresponding RTL-level code.

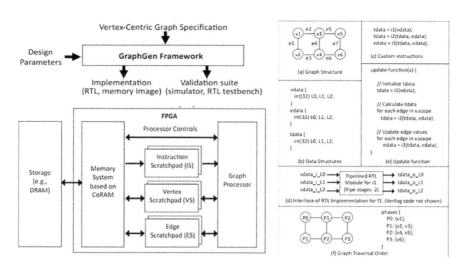

FIGURE 2.27
GraphGen, the CoRAM-based graph computation gas pedal framework proposed in papers [21,22].

The user-defined Graph Specification is the single most important input parameter. In the specification, the user not only needs to define the structure of the graph and the corresponding weight information, but also needs to provide the update function. Some of the function operations constituting the update function need to be provided by the user with the corresponding RTL-level implementations, and the user needs to specify the order of execution among the nodes. After the user provides the input parameters, GraphGen's compiler is responsible for generating the final RTL-level code, which will complete a series of subgraph partitioning, optimization, and other operations, and finally generate the RTL-described architecture.

Overall, the general gas pedal framework based on graph computation is relatively new and difficult to implement, so there are relatively few people doing it, and the implemented prototypes have a lot of shortcomings and deficiencies.

2.2.4.3 Accelerator Framework Based on LINQ Modeling

LINQ is a language similar to SQL invented by Microsoft. Unlike SQL, LINQ can embed user-defined functions in the basic operations of the language set, so we can easily rewrite a program in a LINQ way. In addition, the LINQ language has seven basic operations.

Paper [23] uses SOC to design LINQits, a hardware framework for accelerating the LINQ subset of the C# language, which allows the user to rewrite a program in LINQ form, and then use LINQits' tools to generate RTL-level code, which can be analyzed by the runtime library to decide whether to use the LINQ operations in LINQ. The runtime library analyzes the code to decide whether to use the reconfigurable logic units in the SOC to accelerate it.

The entire flow of LINQits mapping from software to hardware is shown in Figure 2.28.

The hardware artifacts (HAT) of LINQits need to be carefully designed to support the seven basic LINQ operations. The authors of this paper designed a HAT model that can support all but the Orderby statement. However, this model is not shown in the paper, but rather a HAT for partition, group, and hash, as shown in Figure 2.29.

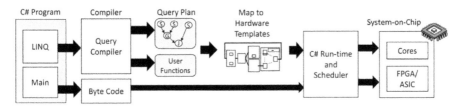

FIGURE 2.28
Flow of LINQits mapping from software to hardware.

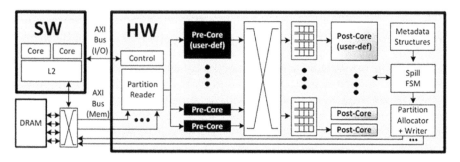

FIGURE 2.29
Hardware template for LINQits.

Overall, since the LINQ language is a Microsoft proprietary language, its degree of openness is not very high, and it is currently only popularized in Microsoft's product line. Therefore, this scientific research point for LINQ involving gas pedal frameworks should not be taken as a major research direction.

2.3 Conclusion and Outlook

2.3.1 Conclusion

Accelerating machine learning algorithms is a hot research topic nowadays. The mainstream general-purpose platforms are cloud computing platforms and GPGPU/GPGPU clusters. Although FPGAs/ASICs also have good acceleration capabilities, issues such as programming complexity have made them popular only in specialized areas.

Cloud computing platforms are mainly composed of CPU-based isomorphic compute nodes. Thanks to the large number of computing nodes, cloud computing platforms are able to process large amounts of data in a parallel and distributed manner. However, the CPU itself is not suitable for machine learning problems, and the bottleneck of cloud computing platforms is data communication transmission.

GPGPU platform is able to parallelize algorithms at the data level due to the special characteristics of the processor architecture. The use of GPGPUs to accelerate machine learning algorithms needs to focus on the utilization of different levels of memory of GPGPUs. Multiple GPGPUs can be clustered to handle larger-scale problems. However, GPGPUs are relatively energy-intensive and cannot efficiently process algorithms that cannot be data-parallelized.

FPGA and ASIC platforms are mainly used in specialized domains, and due to their low-level abstraction, they are highly difficult to program even with some general acceleration frameworks based on FPGA hardware frameworks. The main work and content of this chapter is a summary of the investigated FPGA-based implementations of machine learning gas pedals, and in doing so, it points out the shortcomings of some of the implementations.

2.3.2 Outlook

If FPGAs are to be utilized to accelerate machine learning algorithms, the following aspects can be started:

1. Acceleration of specific machine learning algorithms: This piece of research should be conducted on some popular and relatively complex machine learning algorithms. In addition, the study should focus on gas pedals for machine learning algorithms in the online learning category.

2. Acceleration of common features of algorithms: In this area, we should conduct extensive research on the computational characteristics of algorithms and abstractly summarize them, so as to find common features and design the corresponding gas pedal structure. In addition, we can focus on accelerating the preprocessing process of algorithms and optimizing the data communication and transmission process.

3. Research on the general gas pedal framework: This research should be based on a certain programming model, and the ultimate goal should be to design a more flexible gas pedal framework so that users can use it in specific application scenarios after simple modification or even without basic changes.

4. Research on heterogeneous computing platforms: Heterogeneous computing is a big concept that faces a lot of difficulties, so we can focus on how to make better use of GPUs, FPGAs, and other computing resources.

5. Research on processor architecture for machine learning algorithms: This should be the highest goal of research on machine learning gas pedals. Just like the introduction of DSP processors, with the widespread popularity of machine learning data mining applications, there should be processor architectures specialized in the execution of such applications.

References

1. S. Ray, "A Quick Review of Machine Learning Algorithms," 2019 International Conference on Machine Learning, Big Data, Cloud and Parallel Computing (COMITCon), Faridabad, India, 2019, pp. 35–39.
2. Choudhary A. N., Honbo D., Kumar P., et al. Accelerating data mining workloads: current approaches and future challenges in system architecture design. *Wiley Interdisciplinary Reviews: Data Mining and Knowledge Discovery*, 2011, 1(1): 41–54.
3. Cadambi S., Majumdar A., Becchi M., et al. A programmable parallel accelerator for learning and classification[C]. *Proceedings of the 19th International Conference on Parallel Architectures and Compilation Techniques*. 2010: 273–284.
4. Unnikrishnan D., Virupaksha S. G., Krishnan L., et al. Accelerating iterative algorithms with asynchronous accumulative updates on FPGAs. *2013 International Conference on Field-Programmable Technology (FPT)*. IEEE, 2013: 66–73.
5. Chu C. T., Kim S., Lin Y. A., et al. Map-reduce for machine learning on multicore. *Advances in Neural Information Processing Systems*, 2006, 19: 281–288.
6. Low Y., Gonzalez J. E., Kyrola A., et al. Graphlab: A new framework for parallel machine learning. arXiv preprint arXiv:1408.2041, 2014.
7. Tong D., Sun L., Matam K., et al. High throughput and programmable online trafficclassifier on FPGA. *Proceedings of the ACM/SIGDA International Symposium on Field Programmable Gate Arrays*. 2013: 255–264.
8. Cadambi S., Durdanovic I., Jakkula V., et al. A massively parallel FPGA-based coprocessor for support vector machines. *2009 17th IEEE Symposium on Field Programmable Custom Computing Machines*. IEEE, 2009: 115–122.
9. Papadonikolakis M., Bouganis C. S. Novel cascade FPGA accelerator for support vector machines classification. *IEEE Transactions on Neural Networks and Learning Systems*, 2012, 23(7): 1040–1052.
10. Baker Z. K., Prasanna V. K. Efficient hardware data mining with the Apriori algorithm on FPGAs. *13th Annual IEEE Symposium on Field-Programmable Custom Computing Machines (FCCM'05)*. IEEE, 2005: 3–12.
11. Narayanan R., Honbo D., Memik G., et al. An FPGA implementation of decision tree classification. *2007 Design, Automation & Test in Europe Conference & Exhibition*. IEEE, 2007: 1–6.
12. Hussain H. M., Benkrid K., Erdogan A. T., et al. Highly parameterized k-means clustering on FPGAs: Comparative results with GPPs and GPUs. *2011 International Conference on Reconfigurable Computing and FPGAs*. IEEE, 2011: 475–480.
13. Hussain H. M., Benkrid K., Ebrahim A., et al. Novel dynamic partial reconfiguration implementation of k-means clustering on FPGAs: Comparative results with GPPs and GPUs. *International Journal of Reconfigurable Computing*, 2012, 2012: 1.
14. Lin M., Lebedev I., Wawrzynek J. High-throughput Bayesian computing machine with reconfigurable hardware. *Proceedings of the 18th Annual ACM/SIGDA International Symposium on Field Programmable Gate Arrays*. Monterey, CA, 2010: 73–82.

15. Han L., Liew C. S., Van Hemert J., et al. A generic parallel processing model for facilitating data mining and integration. *Parallel Computing*, 2011, 37(3): 157–171.
16. Chung E. S., Hoe J. C., Mai K. CoRAM: An in-fabric memory architecture for FPGA-based computing. *Proceedings of the 19th ACM/SIGDA International Symposium on Field Programmable Gate Arrays*. Monterey, CA, 2011: 97–106.
17. Chung E. S., Papamichael M. K., Weisz G., et al. Prototype and evaluation of the coram memory architecture for FPGA-based computing. *Proceedings of the ACM/SIGDA International Symposium on Field Programmable Gate Arrays*. Monterey, CA, 2012: 139–142.
18. Shan Y., Wang B., Yan J., et al. FPMR: MapReduce framework on FPGA. *Proceedings of the 18th Annual ACM/SIGDA International Symposium on Field Programmable Gate Arrays*. Monterey, CA, 2010: 93–102.
19. Tsoi K. H., Luk W. Axel: A heterogeneous cluster with FPGAs and GPUs. *Proceedings of the 18th Annual ACM/SIGDA International Symposium on Field Programmable Gate Arrays*. Monterey, CA, 2010: 115–124.
20. Betkaoui B., Thomas D. B., Luk W., et al. A framework for FPGA acceleration of large graph problems: Graphlet counting case study. *2011 International Conference on Field-Programmable Technology*. New Delhi: IEEE, 2011: 1–8.
21. Nurvitadhi E., Weisz G., Wang Y., et al. GraphGen: An FPGA framework for vertex-centric graph computation. *2014 IEEE 22nd Annual International Symposium on Field-Programmable Custom Computing Machines*. Boston, MA: IEEE, 2014: 25–28.
22. Weisz G., Nurvitadhi E., Hoe J. Graphgen for CoRam: Graph computation on FPGAs. *Workshop on the Intersections of Computer Architecture and Reconfigurable Logic*. Nevada, 2013.
23. Chung E. S., Davis J. D., Lee J. Linqits: Big data on little clients. *ACM SIGARCH Computer Architecture News*, 2013, 41(3): 261–272.

3

Hardware Accelerator Customization for Data Mining Recommendation Algorithms

3.1 Background on Recommendation Algorithms and Their Hardware Acceleration

With the rapid increase in information technology and the vigorous development of the Internet industry, people move gradually from the era of lack of information into the era of information explosion. Massive overloading makes people blind and helpless in the face of numerous choices. How quickly and accurately to find the content of interest from a wide range of information has become a tremendous challenge to users. In response to this challenge, the recommended algorithm is born. The recommendation algorithm can exploit potential associations in the history of user behavior, which further helps to recommend the information that is more interesting to users or generate a predictive score for a non-contact item.

In the field of recommendation algorithms, the algorithm recommended based on collaborative filtering (CF) [1] is the most typical recommendation algorithm. This algorithm can be divided into two types: the algorithm based on the neighborhood model, and the algorithm based on the implicit semantic and matrix decomposition model. The algorithm based on the neighborhood model is the most basic mature algorithm, which mainly includes the user-based CF recommendation algorithm (user-based CF) [2], item-based CF recommendation algorithm (item-based CF) [3], and SlopeOne recommended algorithm [4]. These algorithms not only have detailed research but also have a very wide range of applications. The algorithm based on the implicit semantic and matrix decomposition model is a relatively new type of algorithm, which mainly includes Regularized Singular Value Decomposition (RSVD), Bias-RSVD, and Singular Value Decomposition++ (SVD++). This algorithm is the most famous research in the field of recommendation algorithms and originally originated in the Netflix Prize Contest [5].

The scale of data is in rapid growth with the advent of the Big Data age. The most noticeable feature of the Big Data era is the large size of the data.

DOI: 10.1201/9780429355080-3

For the recommendation system, it is directly reflected in the number of new users and new items that are constantly influx into the system and increasing user behavior or scoring of items. Whether it is collaborative filtering algorithms based on neighborhood models or those based on implicit semantics and matrix decomposition models, the ever-expanding data size makes the execution time of the algorithm longer and longer in the training stage and the forecasting stage. Besides, the recommendation system has to take a longer time to generate referral information for the user. Therefore, to reduce the response time of the recommendation system and generate the recommendation information for the user timely, it is necessary to accelerate the execution of the recommended algorithm.

At present, there are three commonly used acceleration platforms for algorithm acceleration: multi-core processor cluster, cloud computing platform, and general-purpose graphics processor (GPGPU). The multi-core processor cluster consists of multiple compute nodes, which are based on general-purpose CPU. It mainly uses MPI [6], OpenMP [7], or Pthread [8] to perform multi-process/multithreading on the task-level/data-level parallelism. The cloud computing platform is also composed of a vast number of computing nodes, which are also based on general-purpose CPU. It mainly uses Hadoop [9], Spark [10], or other computing frameworks to perform task-level/data-level parallelism in MapReduce. For GPGPU, it consists of a large number of hardware threads, adopts multi-threads to implement data-level parallelism, and mainly uses CUDA [11], OpenCL [12], and OpenACC [13].

For the CF recommendation algorithm, there is much related research work using the above three platforms to accelerate. Although this work is indeed productive, it also has some problems that cannot be ignored. For example, although multi-core processor cluster and cloud computing platform can be productive, the computing efficiency while dealing with the recommended algorithm task for a single computing node based on general-purpose CPU architecture is relatively low, and it is accompanied by high energy consumption. GPGPU has a high computational efficiency while dealing with recommended algorithm tasks due to its strengths on data-level parallelism, but it often results in higher energy consumption and runtime power overhead compared to general-purpose CPU.

In recent years, attempts have been made to exploit the use of specific-purpose integrated circuit chips (ASICs) and field programmable gate arrays (FPGAs) to study the design of hardware acceleration in order to increase the cost of energy while reducing performance. ASIC is a dedicated integrated circuit structure for specific areas of application, whose hardware structure cannot be changed after the chip produced. However, FPGA is a reconfigurable hardware structure that can customize different hardware structures for various applications. A front-end hardware design process is required whether using ASIC or FPGA, with the distinction lying in the final implementation. ASIC can obtain superior performance but with a high cost, while the implementation cost of FPGA is relatively low but often gets less performance than ASIC. At present, there are a lot of excellent hardware acceleration designs in the field of machine learning, especially in the field of deep learning. But for the CF recommendation algorithm, both the neighborhood model and the implicit semantic model, the related hardware acceleration research work is very few, and there are still some limitations and problems, so it is very important to study the hardware acceleration for the proposed algorithm.

In this chapter, we mainly study the hardware acceleration for the CF recommendation algorithm. This research work is mainly based on the CF recommendation algorithm of the neighborhood model. The primary consideration of the algorithm based on the neighborhood model rather than the implicit semantic and matrix decomposition model is that the latter has a wide range of applications and is the mainstream research direction in the field of future recommendation algorithms. But for the latter, the calculation model of each algorithm instance is different, and it is a learning method in essence, often needing to store the global data information for the iterative calculation to learn the optimal model parameters. These flexible computational models repeated iterative computations, and access to global data will significantly increase the difficulty of storing and computing resources with the extremely limited hardware-accelerated structural design. However, neighborhood-based algorithms are widely used in Amazon, Netflix, YouTube, Digg, Hulu, and other major internet systems, which are based on the statistical process in essence and have a more common computing model, without repeated iterative learning process. Also, it is very suitable to adopt hardware to implement for the reason that this algorithm requires a relatively small number of global information accesses. Therefore, this chapter chooses the CF recommendation algorithm based on the neighborhood model as the principal object of the hardware acceleration research.

3.2 Introduction to Collaborative Filtering Recommendation Algorithm

In this section, we first introduce the relevant concepts of the CF recommendation algorithm based on the neighborhood model. In addition to that, we will present two kinds of typical CF recommendation algorithms based on the neighborhood model, user-based CF algorithm, and item-based CF algorithm.

3.2.1 Collaborative Filtering Recommendation Algorithm Based on Neighborhood Model

With the rapid growth of data and information, people are interested in mining information more and more dependent on the help of the recommended system in the era of Big Data. According to the different requirements, the primary task of the recommended system can be divided into Top-N recommendation and score prediction. Top-N recommended tasks are mainly responsible for generating a recommendation list for the items that the user did not have a historical record, and the score prediction task is mainly responsible for generating specific interest rank for the items that the user did not evaluate.

The CF recommendation algorithm based on the neighborhood model [1] is a classical and mature algorithm. When generating a recommendation list or scoring prediction for a given user, this algorithm firstly searches for a specific neighborhood information set associated with users according to a certain condition, and then uses historical record of the user, combined with the content of the neighborhood information set, to generate the recommendation of the list of designated user items or the degree of preference of a certain item. According to the type of neighborhood information set, the CF algorithm based on the neighborhood model is mainly divided into user-based CF algorithm and item-based CF algorithm.

The user-based and item-based CF recommendation algorithms can be divided into two stages, namely, training and prediction. The training phase is often carried out in an offline style, and the prediction stage often needs to be carried out online. In general, the former takes much more time than the latter.

Both in the training and prediction phases, the user should use the history of the items, and this history of behavioral records can often be presented in a matrix, as shown in Figure 3.1. In this matrix, each row represents a user, and each column represents an item, and the intersection of rows and columns represents a user's specific behavior record or

	i_1	i_2	...	i_{j-1}	i_j	...	i_n
u_1	3	4		-	2.5		-
u_2	-	2		1	3		5
⋮							
u_{j-1}	2	5		-	-		2.5
u_j	3	-		2	4		3.5
⋮							
u_m	-	-		1.5	-		-

FIGURE 3.1
User-item score matrix.

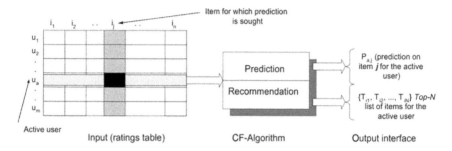

FIGURE 3.2
The execution process of the CF algorithm.

ranking value of an item. The value of the intersection is empty only if a user has not yet contacted or evaluated an item, which is indicated by "-" in the figure. It can be seen that the row vector represents the set of items that a user has had historical behavior or evaluation, and the column vector represents the set of users whose historical history or evaluation has been made for an item. For Top-N recommended tasks, which tend to use implicit user behavior records, the matrix is called the user-item behavior matrix and the value of each intersection is either empty or 1, which means that a user has access to a certain item. For a scoring task, it typically uses explicit evaluation information of users, so the matrix is also called the user-item scoring matrix, where the value at each intersecting position is an integer or real number that is within a certain range and represents the ranking value for an item.

Figure 3.2 briefly describes the process of the CF recommendation algorithm. For an item i_j that has no behavior or evaluation of the target user u_a, the algorithm will generate the interest or predictive score for i_j by using the data in the scoring table and the associated neighborhood information. For the score prediction task, the user u_a has obtained the score value of the item i_j. For the Top-N recommendation task, the prediction value of the other item is also required, and then the list consists of the first N items with the largest predicted value in all the items recommended to the user u_a.

3.2.2 User-Based Collaborative Filtering Recommendation Algorithm

User-based CF algorithm is one of the most classic algorithms in the field of algorithms. In a sense, the birth of this algorithm also marks the birth of the recommendation system. Goldberg et al. proposed user-based CF in 1992 and applied it to Tapestry [2]. Resnick et al. used this algorithm to build a news filtering system, GroupLens [14]. This algorithm has always been the most famous recommendation algorithm until the item-based CF appears. At present, user-based CF still exists in many recommended systems, such as Digg.

User-based CF recommendation algorithm is summarized in principle that is to find other users that have similar points of interest to the given user, and then recommend the items that these other users have contacted or shown interest to the given user.

User-based CF can perform either Top-N recommendations or scoring tasks. The algorithm needs to go through the following two phases regardless of the type of task:

- Training phase: To find and filter out the set that consists of K other users whose points of interest are most similar to the designated user, the specific K value can be set based on different requirements or reference experience.
- Prediction phase: To find the collection of items that the designated user has not had historical activities in the collection of the items that all K other users have historical records, generate the user's interest degree or score value (predicted value).

For the Top-N recommendation task, it is necessary to sort the items according to the prediction value in descending order after the completion of the prediction phase, and then recommend the first N items to the user.

In the actual use, the training phase of user-based CF is often carried out in an offline manner. The recommendation system will first compute the similarity among all users in the user set, and then sort the similarities between each user and other users in reverse order. We can directly get the specified user's K size of the neighborhood collection for the online mode of operation in prediction phase, without having to repeat the operation.

The most important work in the training phase of user-based CF is to find the neighborhood collection that is most similar to other users. For the similarity of this concept, there are many metrics and methods: the Jaccard similarity coefficient, Euclidean distance, Cosine similarity, and Pearson correlation coefficient, in which cosine similarity has two manifestations. It is necessary to perform the computation on the user's vector on the items evaluated by the two users regardless of which similarity is used. That is, i_1 and i_n of the user's vectors u_{j-1} and u_j, which are circled in Figure 3.1.

The specific score values are not required in the computation of the Jaccard similarity coefficient and cosine similarity, which means these two metrics are often used in Top-N recommended tasks. The computation of the similarity value of user vectors u and v in the Jaccard similarity coefficient as shown in Equation (3.1):

$$w_{uv} = \frac{|N(u) \cap N(v)|}{|N(u) \cup N(v)|} \quad w_{uv} = \frac{|N(u) \cap N(v)|}{|N(u) \cup N(v)|} \quad (3.1)$$

where the set of items evaluated by user u, v are denoted by $N(u)$, $N(v)$, respectively. The Jaccard similarity coefficient needs to compute the size of the intersection and union of two items.

The representation of the cosine similarity in the Top-N recommendation is shown in Equation (3.2):

$$w_{uv} = \frac{|N(u) \cap N(v)|}{\sqrt{|N(u)||N(v)|}} \qquad (3.2)$$

The specific scoring information is required in the computation of Euclidean distance, Cosine similarity, and Pearson correlation coefficient. So they are often used in scoring tasks. Euclidean distance is shown in Equation (3.3):

$$w_{uv} = \frac{1}{\sqrt{\sum_{i \in I} (r_{ui} - r_{vi})^2}} \qquad (3.3)$$

where the set I represents the set of items that the user u, v collectively evaluates and i represents an item in the set. r_{ui} and r_{vi}, respectively, represent the score of the user u, v on item i.

The representation of the cosine similarity in the scoring prediction is shown in Equation (3.4):

$$w_{uv} = \frac{\sum_{i \in I} r_{ui} * r_{vi}}{\sqrt{\sum_{i \in I} r_{ui}^2 \sum_{i \in I} r_{vi}^2}} \qquad (3.4)$$

The definition of the Pearson correlation coefficient is shown in Equation (3.5):

$$w_{uv} = \frac{\sum_{i \in I} (r_{ui} - \hat{r}_u) * (r_{vi} - \hat{r}_v)}{\sqrt{\sum_{i \in I} (r_{ui} - \hat{r}_u)^2 \sum_{i \in I} (r_{vi} - \hat{r}_i)^2}} \qquad (3.5)$$

where r_u and r_v, respectively, represent the user u, v in the item set I on their respective items' average score.

It is most important to use the similarity results of the training phase to generate the specified user's neighborhood set, then find the items collection that has not been contacted or evaluated, and generate prediction values for each item in the neighborhood set. This process can also be expressed by the formula, which often uses the summed sum or weighted average to compute the final result value.

When the user-based CF executes the Top-N recommendation, the prediction phase computes the user's interest in item i, as shown in Equation (3.6):

$$P_{ui} = \sum_{v \in S(u,K) \cap N(i)} w_{uv}, i \notin N(u) \tag{3.6}$$

where $S(u, K)$ represents the set of neighborhoods of K other users that are most similar to user u. $N(i)$ represents all user sets that have a behavioral record of item i. v represents a group that does not belong to set $N(u)$, which combines to a user in the intersection of the set $N(i)$ and the set $S(u, K)$. w_{uv} is the similarity between users u and v.

The prediction stage not only takes into account the scoring information but also requires the weighted average of the results, compared to Top-N's recommendation, as shown in Equation (3.7):

$$P_{ui} = \frac{\sum\limits_{v \in S(u,K) \cap N(i)} w_{uv} * r_{vi}}{\sum\limits_{v \in S(u,K) \cap N(i)} |w_{uv}|}, i \notin N(u) \tag{3.7}$$

3.2.3 Collaborative Filtering Recommendation Algorithm Based on Item

The item-based CF recommendation algorithm is one of the most widely used algorithms in the industry and is widely used in systems such as Amazon, Netflix, Hulu, and YouTube. Sarwar et al. proposed item-based CF [3]. Linden et al. applied the algorithm to the Amazon product system [15]. Compared with user-based CF, item-based CF can not only have more accurate recommendation results but can also overcome the shortcomings that make user-based CF inefficient at a larger user scale and unable to explain the results of the recommendation.

We can summarize that the goal of the item-based CF recommendation algorithm is that recommend those items to the specified user, and those items are most similar to the items that the user has previously contacted. Item-based CF algorithm does not adopt the contents of the property as a standard, but by analyzing the user's historical records of the items to compute the similarity of two items.

Training phase: Calculate the similarity values between all the items in the set and sort the similarity values between each item and other items in reverse order.

Item-based CF can perform Top-N recommended tasks and scoring tasks, and it also needs to go through the following two steps:

1. Training phase: compute the similarity values among all the items in the collection, sort the similarity values between each item and other items in reverse order.

2. Prediction phase: find the neighborhood set made up of K items that the specific user has not contacted or evaluated, then compute the predicted value for each item in the all-item neighborhood set.

The mentioned two phases can perform the scoring prediction tasks, while the process sorts the interest degree of item sets in descending order after the prediction phase for Top-N tasks, and then recommends the first N items to users. The item-based CF training phase is carried out in an offline style, and the prediction phase is often carried out online.

The main task of the item-based CF in the training phase is to compute the similarity between each item in the entire collection of items. For the similarity standard, the commonly used means of the same as described above are the five kinds of user-based CF. It is necessary to perform the computation on the users that commonly evaluate these two items when computing the items vectors regardless of which kind of similarity is used, which means that the circled out items i_{j-1}, i_j and the users u_2, u_j in Figure 3.1.

There are some differences in presentation for those five similarities described above between user-based CF and item-based CF. For the Jaccard similarity coefficient, when computing the similarity of two user vectors i and j, the method is shown in Equation (3.8):

$$w_{ij} = \frac{\left|N(i) \cap N(j)\right|}{\left|N(i) \cup N(j)\right|} \tag{3.8}$$

where $N(i)$ represents all the set of users who have had access or evaluation to the item i and $N(j)$ represents all the set of users who have conducted or evaluated the item.

Cosine similarity, when used in Top-N recommendation, is shown in Equation (3.9):

$$w_{ij} = \frac{\left|N(i) \cap N(j)\right|}{\sqrt{\left|N(i)\right|\left|N(j)\right|}} \tag{3.9}$$

The Euclidean distance is shown in item-based CF as shown in Equation (3.10):

$$w_{ij} = \frac{1}{\sqrt{\displaystyle\sum_{u \in U}\left(r_{ui} - r_{uj}\right)^2}} \tag{3.10}$$

where the set U represents the user's collection that collectively evaluates the item i, j, and u represents a user in the collection. r_{ui} and r_{uj}, respectively, represent the score of user u on items i, j.

The cosine similarity used for scoring prediction is shown in Equation (3.11):

$$w_{ij} = \frac{\sum\limits_{u \in U} r_{ui} * r_{uj}}{\sqrt{\sum\limits_{u \in U} r_{ui}^2 \sum\limits_{u \in U} r_{uj}^2}} \tag{3.11}$$

The definition of the Pearson correlation coefficient is shown in Equation (3.12):

$$w_{ij} = \frac{\sum\limits_{u \in U} \left(r_{ui} - \hat{r}_i\right) * \left(r_{uj} - \hat{r}_j\right)}{\sqrt{\sum\limits_{u \in U} \left(r_{ui} - \hat{r}_i\right)^2 \sum\limits_{u \in U} \left(r_{uj} - \hat{r}_j\right)^2}} \tag{3.12}$$

where r_i and r_j represent the average of the scores of all the users i and j in the user set U, respectively.

The main work of the prediction phase in item-based CF is that find the K item collection that is most similar to the specified item and has not been contacted or evaluated by using the similarity results obtained in the training phase, and then generate predictions for each item in the neighborhood of all items. Likewise, this process can be expressed by the formula, which tends to use the cumulative sum or weighted average to calculate the final predicted value.

Implementation of Top-N recommendation by using item-based CF, whose prediction phase will compute the degree of interest of user u in item j, is shown in Equation (3.13):

$$P_{uj} = \sum\limits_{i \in S(j,K) \cap N(u)} w_{ij}, \quad j \notin N(u) \tag{3.13}$$

where $S(j, K)$ represents the neighborhood of the K other items that are most similar to the item j. $N(u)$ represents the set of items in which user u has an activity record. Item i represents the item that belongs to the intersection of the set $N(u)$ and $S(u, K)$. w_{ij} is the similarity between items i and j.

Compared to Top-N's recommendation, the prediction phase of score prediction requires not only the score information but also the final weighting of the results, as shown in Equation (3.14):

$$P_{uj} = \frac{\sum\limits_{i \in S(j,K) \cap N(u)} w_{ij} * r_{ui}}{\sum\limits_{i \in S(j,K) \cap N(u)} |w_{ij}|}, \quad j \notin N(u) \tag{3.14}$$

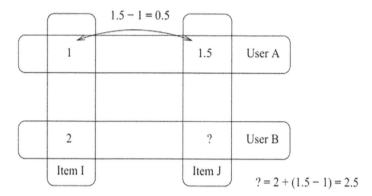

FIGURE 3.3
The example of SlopeOne recommendation algorithm.

3.2.4 SlopeOne Recommendation Algorithm

The SlopeOne recommendation algorithm is not a new class of algorithms in essence, but a variant of the type of CF recommendation algorithm based on items, which can be called a special item-based CF algorithm. Compared with the traditional item-based CF algorithm described earlier, the SlopeOne recommendation algorithm has the advantages of easy implementation and maintenance, fast response, and high accuracy.

The SlopeOne recommendation algorithm is mainly used for scoring prediction tasks and, of course, can also be used for Top-N recommendation. However, while implementing the Top-N recommendation, the SlopeOne algorithm often requires Boolean information that utilizes explicit user ratings rather than implicit user behavior. Figure 3.3 shows an example of the principle of the SlopeOne recommendation algorithm.

SlopeOne will first compute the average difference between all other items and items J. The specific method of computing the average difference degree is to subtract the score value on each of the two items at the same time, and then add the result and divide the number of components. In Figure 3.3, the other items are only item I and the common component is only user A, $(1.5-1)/1=0.5$. It is worth noting that the position of the two operands in the subtraction operation should be consistent. Then, for the predicted score of the user B to the item J, SlopeOne adds the score value of each item that the user has evaluated to the difference values between this item and item J, adds all the added results, and divides by the number of items which have evaluated by the user. In this example, it is $(2+0.5)/1=2.5$.

From the above example, we can see that the SlopeOne recommendation algorithm can be divided into two stages of training and prediction:

1. Training phase: To compute the average difference of all the items in the collection.

2. Prediction phase: For the item that has not been evaluated by the specified user, this phase computes the prediction values by using the scores of all evaluated items by the user and combining them with the average difference from the training phase.

The main work of the SlopeOne algorithm in the training phase is to calculate the average difference between each item in the item set. The computation of average difference between the items i and j is shown in Equation (3.15):

$$w_{ij} = \frac{\sum\limits_{u \in U} \left(r_{ui} - r_{uj} \right)}{|U|} \tag{3.15}$$

where the set U represents the set of users that collectively evaluates the item i, j. u represents a user in the set U. w_{ij} represents the average difference between the items i and j.

The SlopeOne algorithm uses the user-item score information and evaluates the difference value to generate a predicted score for an item in the prediction phase. For user u, the predictor for item j is shown in Equation (3.16):

$$P_{uj} = \frac{\sum\limits_{i \in R(u,j)} \left(w_{ij} + r_{ui} \right)}{|R(u,j)|}, \quad j \notin N(u) \tag{3.16}$$

$$R(u,j) = \left\{ i \in N(u), N(i) \cap N(j) \neq \varphi \right\}$$

where $N(u)$ represents the set of all the items that are evaluated by the user u, $N(j)$ represents the set of all the users who have evaluated the item j, $R(n)$ represents the set of all the items evaluated by the user u, and $R(u,j)$ represents a set of items satisfying a certain condition in which each item i in this set belongs to the set $N(u)$ and satisfies the condition that the intersection of the user set $N(i)$ which is corresponding to the item and the user set $N(j)$ of item j cannot be empty at the same time.

3.3 Hardware Acceleration Principle and Method

3.3.1 Hardware Acceleration Principle

The principle of hardware acceleration, in the general sense, is to assign those tasks that are not suitable to CPUs to the dedicated hardware accelerator. Thereby, it will reduce the workload of the CPU and in general enhance the system operating efficiency through the hardware to accelerate the efficient processing of the structure. At present, the most widely used hardware acceleration is the use of graphics processor GPU to speed up graphics and image processing tasks.

The general-purpose CPU is essentially a very large scale integrated circuit designed for general-purpose tasks. It has a lot of computing units, control units, and storage units, which can process data by executing the user-written instruction stream (program). The versatile hardware design architecture allows the CPU to behave very well in dealing with most tasks, but there are also some tasks that are not suitable to process on CPUs due to their unique characteristics, which further reduces the efficiency of CPUs.

A typical case that is not suitable for CPU processing is image processing. In an image processing task, each pixel in the image involves a large number of the same floating-point operations, and each picture has at least hundreds of pixels. For the general-purpose CPU, its internal often only has two to four cores; even taking into account the super thread technology, the real number of hardware threads is only about four to eight, and these hardware threads run in MIMD (multiple instruction stream multiple data stream). Therefore, the parallelism of CPU is relatively small, and it appears powerless to deal with the parallel tasks when there is a large amount of repeated work. However, GPU is dedicated to graphics and image processing and has specifically designed hardware processor architecture. The GPGPU has hundreds of thousands of stream processors, and each stream processor has a strong floating-point computing power, which is equivalent to having hundreds of thousands of hardware threads. These hardware threads run in SIMD (single instruction stream multiple data stream). Therefore, GPU has a strong parallel granularity and floating-point computing power, which makes it very suitable for dealing with the graphics image processing type of task.

The GPU has the ability to handle other non-graphical image tasks thanks to the promotion and development of CUDA [11], OpenCL [12], OpenACC [13], and other programming techniques and frameworks. In general, GPU has a large number of computing unit components, so its running power is often more than the same level of CPU. Due to the characteristics of its hardware architecture, GPU is suitable to process tasks that are easy to perform with data-level parallelism. For some tasks that are easy to perform data-level parallelism but do not require too many floating-point computations, the utilization of GPU can improve efficiency but at the same time have a lot of unnecessary energy consumption.

In recent years, for tasks or algorithms that are not suitable for CPU or GPU parallel processing, or tasks that can be parallelized on GPUs but come with significant energy costs, people have begun to design dedicated hardware acceleration structures based on ASIC and FPGA, to reduce the power and energy consumption as much as possible while achieving the purpose of accelerating the acceleration effect. For example, SODA [16] presents a software-defined FPGA-based accelerator for Big Data, which could reconstruct and reorganize the acceleration engines according to the requirement of the various data-intensive applications and is able to achieve up to 43.75× speedup at a 128-node application.

At present, hardware accelerator research for deep learning is the fiercest, and the representative is DianNao [17], which is proposed by Chen et al. DianNao is essentially a frequency of 1 GHz ASIC chip, which specifically customizes for the deep learning algorithm, and adopts parallel and pipeline and other acceleration methods. Compared to a 2 GHz SIMD CPU, DianNao achieves a 117.87× speed ratio while reducing the 21.08× energy consumption for the same task. In the same year, Chen and others also improved and expanded DianNao, forming a new acceleration chip DaDianNao [18]. A system with 64 DaDianNao accelerating chips achieves an acceleration ratio of 450.65× and a 150.31× power consumption compared to the high-end Nvidia Tesla K20M GPU. DLAU [19] presents a scalable deep learning accelerator unit on FPGA. DLAU accelerator employs three pipelined processing units to improve the throughput and utilizes tile techniques to explore locality for deep learning applications. Experimental results on the state-of-the-art Xilinx FPGA board demonstrate that the DLAU accelerator is able to achieve up to 36.1× speedup compared to the Intel Core2 processors, with a power consumption of 234 mW.

For the CF recommendation algorithm based on the neighborhood model, there is relatively little research on the related hardware acceleration. Although there are not many related works, many hardware acceleration techniques themselves are highly generalizable, and a method used in a particular algorithm can also be applied to other hardware acceleration implementations. Therefore, this design recommendation algorithm hardware acceleration structure will learn from other algorithms-related research work.

3.3.2 Commonly Used Hardware Acceleration Method

This section investigates and summarizes the research on hardware acceleration of machine learning algorithms. The research object mainly includes Support Vector Machine (SVM) [20,21], Apriori [22], K-means [23–25], DTC [26], deep learning [17,18,27], and similarity calculation [28,29] of the algorithm's dedicated hardware acceleration architecture, as well as general-purpose hardware acceleration architectures with the capability of accelerating a wide range of machine learning algorithms [30,31]

After research, we can find that most of the hardware acceleration research work will first look for the computation of hotspots and common features, then select the parts for hardware acceleration, and finally use a variety of methods and means for common features and calculation of hotspots to design hardware-accelerated structure.

This section summarizes the hardware acceleration methods that are frequently used in the above research work. These methods are mainly divided into two aspects: speeding up the computation process and reducing the communication cost. For accelerating the computation process, commonly used techniques include parallel computing, pipelining, approximation, and a variety of mixed techniques. For reducing communication overhead, data utilization techniques are often used.

3.3.2.1 Parallel Computing

Parallel computing is one of the most commonly used methods in hardware acceleration. For some tasks with high parallelisms, such as array addition and matrix multiplication, the execution time of the tasks can be greatly reduced by parallel computing.

In the related hardware acceleration research using parallelization technology, it is often seen that the hardware acceleration structure has multiple processing elements (PEs), each PE is responsible for a part of the whole task, and multiple PEs are in parallel to complete the entire task. In the case of two arrays of length L, for example, we assumed that there are N PEs. Each PE is responsible for adding two components of a certain dimension of the array. If the operation takes up to C cycles, $(L/N) * C$ clock cycles are needed to complete the whole task. Compared to non-parallel $L * N * C$ cycles, the parallelization of the way does reduce the time overhead.

3.3.2.2 Pipeline Technology

Pipeline technology is also one of the most commonly used methods in hardware acceleration. Suppose there is a task with three computational stages, each corresponding to a computation component, and each execution time of these three components is C cycles. If the pipelined approach does not apply, this will be able to perform a task until performing the next task. The period is 3*N*C, as Figure 3.4 shows.

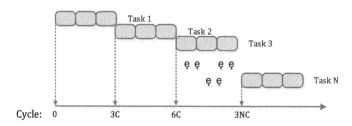

FIGURE 3.4
The time and space diagram of the non-pipeline mode execution case task.

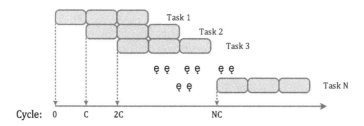

FIGURE 3.5
The time and space diagram of the pipeline mode execution case task.

If there is a completely pipelined design, when implementing multiple tasks, the new task does not have to wait for the completion of the former task. There are multiple tasks running on different stages at the same time. For the case task in Figure 3.4, there are up to three tasks executing at the same time, and for N tasks, it takes only $N*C + 2C$ clock cycles to complete the computation. Therefore, there is near 3x performance compared to the non-pipelined way, which is shown in Figure 3.5.

3.2.2.3 Approximate Computation

There is such a kind of tasks such as the recommended algorithm and deep learning. They are involved in a large number of real operations during the execution time. But at the same time, the real number of their processing is in a certain range, and the result of this task is an estimated value, or the accuracy requirements are not strict, which allows the existence of a certain range of errors.

For this type of task, we can replace floating-point operations with fixed-point operations in the design of hardware acceleration structure. The floating-point operation is more frequent than fixed-point operations, so the computation time is longer than that of fixed-point operations. If the floating-point operation is replaced by a fixed-point operation in a task that involves a large number of real numbers, a lot of time overhead will be reduced. As a result of the use of fixed-point computing, its accuracy is not as good as floating-point operations, so there will be some errors exist in the final computation of the task, compared to the floating point.

3.2.2.4 Mixing Technology

Most of the hardware acceleration work is often not a single use of the acceleration technology but will mix a variety of acceleration technologies to achieve the greatest performance improvement. Let's take a hypothetical specific task example, which is calculated as $(a + b) * c/(a - b)$.

The corresponding AT & T format assembly code with input variables 1, 2, and 3 is shown in Figure 3.6 for the X86_64 CPU.

```
1 movl     $0x1, %eax   ; eax = a = 1
2 movl     $0x2, %edx   ; edx = b = 2
3 addl     %edx, %eax   ; eax = a + b = 3
4 imul     $0x3, %eax   ; eax = (a + b) * c = 9
5 movl     $0x1, %ecx   ; ecx = a = 1
6 subl     %edx, %ecx   ; ecx = a - b = -1
7 movl     %ecx, %esi   ; esi = ecx = -1
8 idiv     %esi         ; eax = eax / esi = ((a + b) * c) / (a - b) = -9
```

FIGURE 3.6
Case task corresponds to the X86 CPU assembler.

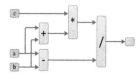

FIGURE 3.7
The task structure corresponds to the hardware implementation structure.

We can use the parallel and pipeline technology in the design of the hardware to accelerate the structure of the task. The designed hardware structure is shown in Figure 3.7. It can be seen that the hardware accelerator structure can calculate $a + b, a - b$ in parallel, and is a three-stage pipeline structure as a whole. If each level of hardware can be executed in full pipelining (one cycle produces one calculation result) for n tasks, and if the number of cycles spent by a divide operation is t, then the structure only needs to cost about $n + t$ clock cycles.

3.2.2.5 Reduce Communication Overhead

The above methods are mainly focused on the optimization and improvement of the computation process. However, data communication optimization is also another area of hardware acceleration.

In most of the research designs, hardware accelerators often play a complementary role, as a coprocessor with the host CPU to handle the task. Hardware accelerators need to obtain relevant data when processing tasks. These data are usually stored in the main memory. The cost of access to main memory based on AXI4, PCI-e, and other buses is often much higher than that of CPU direct access to main memory. Therefore, it is necessary to lower the data communication cost.

The main way to reduce the data overhead is to use data localization technology to tap the inherent nature of the task. The data that is frequently used should be resident in the hardware accelerator, thereby improving the data reuse rate and reducing the number of memory accesses. In addition, most accelerators have a storage hierarchy like CPU Cache, which can further reduce the cost of memory access.

3.4 Analysis of Collaborative Filtering Recommendation Algorithms Based on Neighborhood Models

3.4.1 Analysis of the Training Phase

This section will analyze the training phase of three algorithms: user-based CF, item-based CF, and SlopeOne, which will further mine the computational hotspots and common features.

As described in Section 3.2, user-based CF and item-based CF mainly include similarity computations and reverse order of similarity values in the training phase. SlopeOne contains only the average difference computation during the training phase. We used the ml-100k [32] data set to analyze the training stages of the three recommended algorithms. The results are shown in Table 3.1. It can be seen that the similarity/average difference computation takes more than 97% of the total time and is, therefore, a hotspot in the training phase.

User-based CF computes the similarity between two users when computing the similarity/average difference. Item-based CF computes the similarity between the two items. SlopeOne computes the average difference degree between the two items. It can be found that the computational behavior of user-based CF and item-based CF is very similar and can share the five similarity computation standards described above. The only difference is that the former is oriented to the user and the latter is oriented to the item, which is essentially because of the difference in input data. SlopeOne is oriented to the computation of the average difference for items and has a relatively fixed computation mode.

TABLE 3.1

Three-Recommendation Algorithm for the ml-100k Data Set Training Section Hotspot Analysis

Training	Metric	Similarity/Difference Calculation (%)	Similarity Sort (%)
User-based CF	Jaccard	98.99	1.01
	CosineIR	98.68	1.32
	Euclidean	98.82	1.18
	Cosine	98.73	1.27
	Pearson	98.79	1.21
Item-based CF	Jaccard	97.74	2.26
	CosineIR	97.43	2.57
	Euclidean	97.55	2.45
	Cosine	97.52	2.48
	Pearson	97.53	2.47
SlopeOne	SlopeOne	100.00	—

For the Jaccard similarity coefficient, Euclidean distance, two kinds of cosine similarity, and Pearson correlation coefficient, they can also be used to compute the two user vector or item vector. In this chapter, x, y represent two user and item vectors, respectively.

According to formulas (3.1) and (3.8), the computation of Jaccard similarity coefficient requires the knowledge of the number of non-empty scores N_x, N_y of the vector x, y and the number of common scores N_{xy} of the vectors x, y. Among them, N_x, N_y often can be obtained directly from the original data, thus only N_{xy} needs to be calculated, the formula as shown in Equation (3.17):

$$w_{xy} = \frac{|N(x) \cap N(y)|}{|N(x) \cup N(y)|} = \frac{N_{xy}}{N_x + N_y - N_{xy}} \tag{3.17}$$

N_x, N_y, and N_{xy} are also required to be known when computing cosine similarity calculations for Top-N recommended tasks according to formulas (3.2) and (3.9), as shown in Equation (3.18):

$$w_{xy} = \frac{|N(x) \cap N(y)|}{\sqrt{|N(x)||N(y)|}} = \frac{N_{xy}}{\sqrt{N_x * N_y}} \tag{3.18}$$

According to Equations (3.3) and (3.10), the computation of Euclidean distance needs to know the sum of the squares of squares $S_{x-y}{}^2$, where M is the collection of users or items that both these two vectors have historical behavior or evaluation records. And m is a member of the set M, as shown in Equation (3.19):

$$w_{xy} = \frac{1}{\sqrt{\sum_{m \in M} \left(r_{xm} - r_{ym} \right)^2}} = \frac{1}{\sqrt{S_{(x-y)^2}}} \tag{3.19}$$

According to Equations (3.4) and (3.11), it is necessary to know the squared sums $S_x{}^2$, $S_y{}^2$ of the self-score at the two vector-common offset positions and the multiplied sum S_{xy} when computing vectors x, y by using the cosine similarity in score predictions, as shown in Equation (3.20):

$$w_{xy} = \frac{\sum_{m \in M} r_{xm} * r_{ym}}{\sqrt{\sum_{m \in M} r_{xm}{}^2 \sum_{m \in M} r_{ym}{}^2}} = \frac{S_{xy}}{\sqrt{S_{x^2} * S_{y^2}}} \tag{3.20}$$

According to formulas (3.5) and (3.11), in addition to $S_x{}^2$, $S_y{}^2$, and S_{xy}, the computation of Pearson's correlation coefficient requires the common score number N_{xy} of the vectors x, y, and their respective relations to S_x, S_y at the common offset position. The simplified formula is shown in Figure (3.21):

$$
W_{xy} = \frac{\sum_{m \in M} r_{xm} * r_{ym} - \dfrac{\sum_{m \in M} r_{xm} * \sum_{m \in M} r_{ym}}{|M|}}{\sqrt{\left(\sum_{m \in M}(r_{xm})^2 - \dfrac{\left(\sum_{m \in M} r_{xm}\right)^2}{|M|}\right) * \left(\sum_{m \in M}(r_{ym})^2 - \dfrac{\left(\sum_{m \in M} r_{ym}\right)^2}{|M|}\right)}}
$$
(3.21)

$$
= \frac{S_{xy} - \dfrac{S_x * S_y}{N_{xy}}}{\sqrt{\left(S_{x^2} - \dfrac{(S_x)^2}{N_{xy}}\right) * \left(S_{y^2} - \dfrac{(S_y)^2}{N_{xy}}\right)}}
$$

The SlopeOne algorithm is used in the training phase of the formula as shown in Equation (3.14). It can be seen that SlopeOne needs to know S_{x-y}, the sum of difference at the common offset position, and N_{xy} when computing the two user vectors x, y, as shown in Equation (3.22):

$$
W_{xy} = \frac{\sum_{m \in M}(r_{xm} - r_{ym})}{|M|} = \frac{S_{(x-y)}}{N_{xy}}
$$
(3.22)

The computation of two input vectors x and y under those six similarity criteria is related to ten scalar values: N_x, N_y, N_{xy}, S_x, S_y, S_{x}^2, S_{y}^2, S_{xy}, S_{x-y}, $S_{(x-y)}^2$. After the computation of this scalar information, the only need is to perform addition, subtraction, multiplication, prescribing, and the last step of the division of the operation to obtain similarity or average difference.

For the original user-item behavior/score data, the application will often reorganize the structure of data after reading, and the organization is similar to the hash table structure [33]. Take the user-item score matrix in Figure 3.8 as an example. For user-based CF, the organization is shown in Figure 3.8a. The head node holds the number of items evaluated by a user. The linked node holds the item's number and the user's ranking value on the item. For item-based CF and SlopeOne, its organization is shown in Figure 3.8b: the

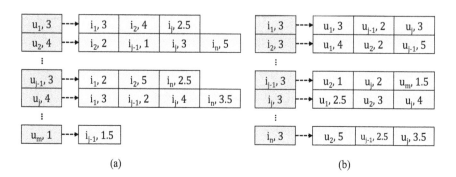

(a)   (b)

FIGURE 3.8
Two ways of reorganizing the user-item scoring matrix are shown in Figure 3.1. (a) user-based
CF. (b) item-based CF.

head node saves the number of an item evaluated by the user, while the
linked list node saves the user's number and the user rated the item.

According to the above data organization, the scalar N_x and N_y values can
be obtained directly from the head node information, and the remaining
scalar values need to be obtained after the vector x, y computation is com-
pleted. In the calculation of scalar N_{xy}, S_x, S_y, S_x^2, S_y^2, S_{xy}, S_{x-y}, and $S_{(x-y)^2}$, we
first need to perform the corresponding operations on the two components at
each common position of the vector, and then all of the partial results of the
operation should be summed.

3.4.2 Analysis of Prediction Phase

User-based CF, item-based CF, and SlopeOne algorithm in the prediction
phase according to the different types of tasks have different computing behaviors. For the scoring task, these three algorithms only need to
calculate the predicted value of the undetected or evaluated items of the
specified user in the prediction stage. For the Top-N recommendation task,
in addition to the need for computing the predictive values of the item,
selecting N items with the largest forecast for the designated user is also
needed. We also use the ml-100k data set to perform Top-N recommendations on the three algorithms in the prediction phase. The results are
shown in Table 3.2. It can be seen that the cost of the calculation of the item
is more than 90% of the total time spent, so it is the calculation hotspot of
the prediction phase.

There is the cumulative and weighted average of these two calculation
methods when user-based CF and item-based CF perform the calculation of
the expected value of the items. SlopeOne has a fixed calculation mode when
calculating the predicted value. The cumulative calculation is relatively simple and can be considered as a special case of weighted average calculations
and is therefore not discussed.

TABLE 3.2

Hotspot Analysis of Top-N Task in Three Predictors of ML-100K Dataset

Prediction	Metric	Prediction Value Calculation (%)	Top-N Item ($N=10$) (%)
User-based CF (neighbors: 80)	Jaccard	93.37	6.63
	CosineIR	95.14	4.86
	Euclidean	91.69	8.31
	Cosine	91.54	8.46
	Pearson	91.86	8.14
Item-based CF (neighbors: 80)	Jaccard	99.25	0.75
	CosineIR	98.83	1.17
	Euclidean	99.23	0.77
	Cosine	99.26	0.74
	Pearson	99.23	0.77
SlopeOne	SlopeOne	99.23	0.77

3.5 Hardware Acceleration System Hierarchy

The hierarchical structure of the hardware acceleration system for CF recommendation algorithm based on neighborhood is shown in Figure 3.9. We can see that the whole system runs in the Linux operating system environment, and it is divided into three levels, namely, the hardware layer, the operating system kernel layer, and the operating system user layer.

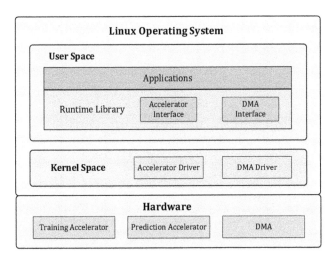

FIGURE 3.9
Hardware accelerator system hierarchy.

The hardware layer is the most important layer of the hardware accelera-tion system, mainly including training accelerator, predictive accelerator, Direct Memory Access(DMA), and other equipment. At runtime, the host CPU notifies the DMA to initiate a data transfer, and the hardware accelera-tor acquires the data by DMA.

The kernel layer of operating system mainly includes the driver of hard-ware accelerator, DMA, and other devices in the Linux operating system environment. The driver typically encapsulates the interface of the hard-ware device control register and creates the device file in the file system. Users can control the hardware device through the read and write device files directly.

The top layer is the user layer, which includes the runtime library and application layer. Although the user can read and write hardware regis-ters to control the hardware device to complete an operation directly, this approach is relatively cumbersome and requires the user to have enough understanding of the device. For the convenience of the user, the runtime library encapsulates the register read and write operations required by the accelerator and DMA functions and provides the upper interface for the user to invoke.

3.5.1 Training Accelerator Prototype Implementation

Figure 3.10 shows the implementation of the training accelerator prototype, which has four execution units and one control unit, where DMA adopts AXI-DMA IP cores provided by Xilinx. In each execution unit, the maximum supported vector length of the cache module is 8192. There are 32 PEs in the multifunction operation unit of the accumulation module, with five layers. AXI-DMA is connected with the memory controller in PS by the AXI4 data bus, while the host CPU controls the training accelerator control unit and AXI-DMA by AXI4-Lite bus.

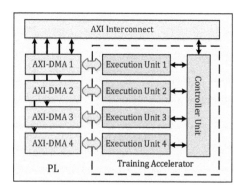

FIGURE 3.10
The overall structure of the training accelerator prototype.

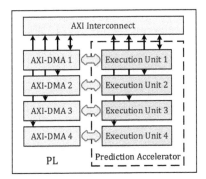

FIGURE 3.11
Predict the overall structure of the accelerator prototype.

3.5.2 Predicting Accelerator Prototype Implementation

Figure 3.11 shows the implementation of the prediction gas pedal prototype, which also has four execution units, and the DMA also uses AXI-DMA. In each execution unit, the cache module has a maximum support vector length of 8192. in the training gas pedal prototype, the host CPU, AXI-DMA, and the prediction gas pedal execution units are connected to the same bus.

3.5.3 Device Driver Implementation

Xilinx offers a Linux kernel that is optimized for the ZYNQ platform [34]. Digilent has further refined Xilinx's ZYNQ Linux kernel and added support for the ZedBoard development board. Hardware accelerator system selects Digilent-Linux 3.6 as a Linux kernel, based on ARM Ubuntu 14.10 Linaro 14.10 as the operating system root file system.

Training Accelerator Control Unit, Predictive Accelerator Execution Unit Controller, and AXI-DMA Device Drivers are implemented as mentioned above. Given the implementation of the details, due to the selection of the AXI4-Lite control bus and AXI-DMA, the number of accelerator control units and AXI-DMA register is more than previously designed, and the driver needs to support read/write operations for the extra registers.

The implementation of the AXI-DMA character device driver is based on memory map. DMA buffer adopts the reserve physical memory, that is, modifies the device tree file, and assigns the highest 64 MB memory on-board to four AXI-DMA before the start of ZedBoard. Therefore, each AXI-DMA has 16 MB for Reading/Writing operations. The drive module corresponding to the AXI-DMA will be mapped into the kernel space.

In order to verify the effect of this AXI-DMA driver module implementation, we implement the AXI-DMA driver in a traditional way and test the differences in performance between programs through two DMA drivers using the ArrayAdd IP core for adding two input arrays. The corresponding structure of the project is shown in Figure 3.12.

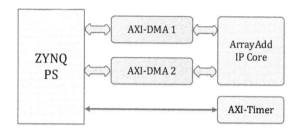

FIGURE 3.12
Test the hardware engineering structure used by the two driver implementations of AXI-DMA.

For two float arrays of length 1,024, the single-core ARM CPU itself takes 4,454 cycles. Taking the time for transferring the data between the main memory and IP core into account, for the AXI-DMA driver implemented in a traditional way, ArrayAdd IP core needs to spend 6,172 cycles to complete the task. However, it only needs to spend 2,840 cycles to achieve the AXI-DMA driver by memory map. It can be seen that the use of memory mapping technology to achieve the DMA driver can indeed reduce the data transmission costs.

3.6 Experimental Results and Analysis

3.6.1 Acceleration Ratio of Training Accelerator

We use the ml-100k, which contains 943 users, 1,682 items, and 100,000 data scores, to obtain the time spent on the operation of the five different platforms by calculating the similarity/average difference degree of the three algorithms in the training phase. We measure the speedup among the training accelerator, CPU, and GPU, where the time of the training accelerator includes the time of the accelerator calculation and the time of data transmission of the AXI-DMA. The CPU time contains only the calculation time. The time of the GPU includes the calculation time of the GPU and the data transfer copy time between the main memory and the GPU explicit memory.

The acceleration between the training accelerator and the same level of ARM CPU is shown in Figure 3.13. The leftmost column represents the speed ratio of the single-threaded CPU program running against itself, which is always 1 and serves mainly as a benchmark. The middle column represents the speed ratio of the double-threaded CPU program compared to the single-threaded CPU program. The rightmost column represents the acceleration ratio of the training accelerator compared to the single-threaded CPU program. CosineIR ignores the score of the cosine similarity.

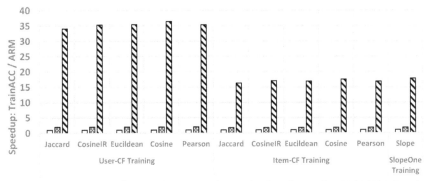

FIGURE 3.13
Acceleration ratio between the training accelerator and the ARM CPU under the ml-100k data set.

It can be seen that the acceleration ratio of the training accelerator and the single-threaded ARM CPU is around 35× for user-based CF. For item-based CF and SlopeOne, the acceleration ratio is around 16×. The speed of user-based CF is higher than that of item-based CF and SlopeOne because the former is the user vector, and the latter is the item vector. The length of the user vector is 1,682, and the length of the item vector is 943. When dealing with two vectors, the complexity of the CPU program is $O(n_x * \log n_y)$ when processing the two vectors, where n_x, n_y denote the actual number of the two vectors, respectively, and are usually positively correlated with the vector length n. It will be more efficient to implement the training gas pedal using a parallel pipeline, which has a complexity of $O(n/32)$. Therefore, the longer the vector length and the more scores in each vector, the better the acceleration of the training gas pedal.

The acceleration between the training accelerator and the Intel Core 2 CPU is shown in Figure 3.14. It can be seen that the speed ratio of the training accelerator compared to the single-threaded Intel Core 2 CPU is around 4.3× for user-based CF. For item-based CF and SlopeOne, the acceleration ratio is around 2.1×. As the frequency of 2.66 GHz Intel Core 2 CPU performance is higher than the frequency of 677 MHz ARM Cortex A9, training accelerator prototype about the CPU speed ratio has dropped significantly.

The acceleration between the training accelerator and the Intel Core i7 CPU is shown in Figure 3.15. It can be seen that the training accelerator is only about 2.3× acceleration ratio for the user-based CF. For the item-based CF, the training accelerator has no acceleration performance, the acceleration ratio is only about 1.1×, and the single-threaded CPU program performance is flat. Since the frequency of the Intel Core i7 CPU is 40 times faster than the training accelerator prototype, and the prototype has only four parallel execution units, there is not much advantage in the speedup.

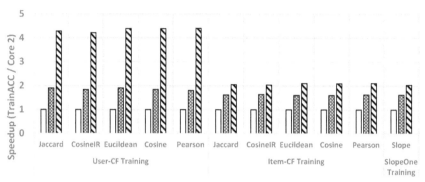

FIGURE 3.14
Acceleration ratio between the training accelerator and the Intel Core 2 CPU under the ml-100k data set.

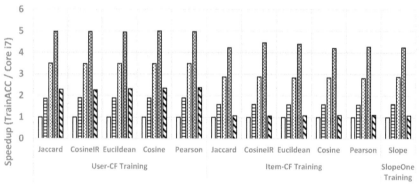

FIGURE 3.15
Acceleration ratio between the training accelerator and the Intel Core i7 CPU in the ml-100k data set.

The acceleration of the training accelerator and Nvidia Tesla K40C GPU is shown in Figure 3.16. GPU program adopts 128 thread blocks, and each thread block has 128 threads, a total of 16,384 threads. Each thread is responsible for pairs of similarity/average difference calculations. The Tesla K40C supports 2880 hardware threads. The peak running frequency of each hardware thread is 875 MHz, and both parallelism and frequency are much higher than those of the training accelerator. When the two vectors are processed, the time taken by the GPU's single thread is $O(n)$, while the training accelerator is of the order of $O(n/32)$, and this advantage is not helpful. In summary,

FIGURE 3.16
Acceleration ratio between the training accelerator and the Nvidia Tesla K40C GPU in the ml-100k data set.

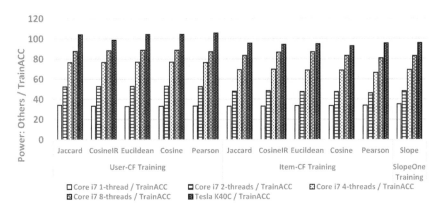

FIGURE 3.17
The power ratio between the contrast platform and the training accelerator in the ml-100k data set.

the training accelerator prototype compared to the Tesla K40C without any acceleration effect is also reasonable. Thus, if the main consideration of performance factors, GPU is indeed an excellent platform.

3.6.2 Power Efficiency

The power efficiency of the Intel Core i7 CPU, Nvidia Tesla K40C GPU, and the training accelerator is shown in Figure 3.17. It can be seen that the CPU running time power increases with the number of threads, about 33× to 88× of the training accelerator prototype, and the GPU's running power is about 100× of the prototype.

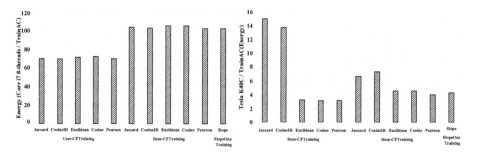

FIGURE 3.18
The energy efficiency comparison between the contrast platform and the training accelerator in the ml-100k data set.

3.6.3 Energy Efficiency

The energy consumption of the Intel Core i7 CPU compared to the training accelerator is shown in Figure 3.18a. For user-based CF, energy consumption is around 41×. For item-based CF and SlopeOne, energy consumption is around 21×. Thus, the training accelerator prototype compared to the CPU has great energy-saving advantages.

The energy consumption of the Nvidia Tesla K40C compared to the training accelerator is shown in Figure 3.18b. For user-based CF, energy consumption is around 5.5× for Jaccard and CosineIR and 1.1× for other standards. For item-based CF and SlopeOne, energy consumption is around 0.67×. The training accelerator prototype in energy consumption saving is not dominant, as the GPU advantage at runtime compensates for the power consumption disadvantage.

3.7 Conclusions

In this chapter, the training accelerator and predictive accelerator structure and instruction set are designed for the training phase and prediction stage of three neighborhood-based algorithms, namely, user-based CF, item-based CF, and SlopeOne. Both accelerators operate as a coprocessor under the control of the host CPU, and the training accelerator supports five different similarity calculation criteria required for user-based CF and item-based CF during the training phase. Besides, it also supports the difference calculation criterion, which is required in the training phase of SlopeOne. The prediction accelerator supports the summing and weighted averaging operations required by the three algorithms in the prediction phase. What's more, we design the interconnection among the host CPU, memory, accelerator, and DMA.

In this chapter, we design the device drivers for training accelerators, prediction accelerators, and DMA devices in the Linux operating system environment. We also design the device driver for the training accelerator control unit and the predictor accelerator execution unit controller by using the Linux character device driver framework model. For the DMA device driver, we also adopt the character device driver framework model and memory mapping technique.

For the convenience of users, we design and encapsulate the operating system user-layer interface for hardware accelerator and DMA. We mainly involve the training accelerator control unit, prediction accelerator execution unit controller, and the user-layer interface of DMA.

References

1. Chung E. S., Davis J. D., Lee J. Linqits: Big data on little clients. *ACM SIGARCH Computer Architecture News*, 2013, 41(3): 261–272.
2. Goldberg D., Nichols D., Oki B. M., et al. Using collaborative filtering to weave an information tapestry. *Communications of the ACM*, 1992, 35(12): 61–70.
3. Sarwar B., Karypis G., Konstan J., et al. Item-based collaborative filtering recommendation algorithms. *Proceedings of the 10th International Conference on World Wide Web*. New York, NY, 2001: 285–295.
4. Lemire D., Maclachlan A. Slope one predictors for online rating-based collaborative filtering. *Proceedings of the 2005 SIAM International Conference on Data Mining*. Society for Industrial and Applied Mathematics, Newport Beach, CA, 2005: 471–475.
5. Zhou Y., Wilkinson D., Schreiber R., et al. Large-scale parallel collaborative filtering for the netflix prize. *Algorithmic Aspects in Information and Management: 4th International Conference, AAIM 2008*, Shanghai, China, June 23–25, 2008. Proceedings 4. Springer, Berlin Heidelberg, 2008: 337–348.
6. Pacheco P. *Parallel Programming with MPI*. Burlington, MA: Morgan Kaufmann, 1997.
7. Dagum L., Menon R. OpenMP: An industry standard API for shared-memory programming. *IEEE Computational Science and Engineering*, 1998, 5(1): 46–55.
8. Stevens W. R., Rago S. A., Ritchie D. M. *Advanced Programming in the UNIX Environment*. New York: Addison-Wesley, 1992.
9. White T. *Hadoop: The Definitive Guide*. Sebastopol, CA, O'Reilly Media, Inc., 2012.
10. Zaharia M., Chowdhury M., Franklin M. J., et al. Spark: Cluster computing with working sets. *2nd USENIX Workshop on Hot Topics in Cloud Computing (HotCloud 10)*. Berkeley, CA, 2010.
11. Nvidia C. Compute unified device architecture programming guide. Nvidia Corporation, https://docs.nvidia.com/cuda/cuda-c-programming-guide/, 2007.

12. Stone J. E., Gohara D., Shi G. OpenCL: A parallel programming standard for heterogeneous computing systems. *Computing in Science & Engineering*, 2010, 12(3): 66.

13. Wienke S., Springer P., Terboven C., et al. OpenACC-first experiences with real-world applications. *Euro-Par 2012 Parallel Processing: 18th International Conference, Euro-Par 2012*, Rhodes Island, Greece, August 27–31, 2012. Proceedings 18. Springer, Berlin Heidelberg, 2012: 859–870.

14. Resnick P., Iacovou N., Suchak M., et al. Grouplens: An open architecture for collaborative filtering of netnews. *Proceedings of the 1994 ACM Conference on Computer Supported Cooperative Work*. New York, NY, 1994: 175–186.

15. Linden G., Smith B., York J. Amazon. com recommendations: Item-to-item collaborative filtering. *IEEE Internet Computing*, 2003, 7(1): 76–80.

16. Wang C., Li X., Zhou X. SODA: Software defined FPGA based accelerators for big data. *2015 Design, Automation & Test in Europe Conference & Exhibition (DATE)*. IEEE, San Jose, CA, 2015: 884–887.

17. Chen T., Du Z., Sun N., et al. Diannao: A small-footprint high-throughput accelerator for ubiquitous machine-learning. *ACM SIGARCH Computer Architecture News*, 2014, 42(1): 269–284.

18. Chen Y., Luo T., Liu S., et al. Dadiannao: A machine-learning supercomputer. *2014 47th Annual IEEE/ACM International Symposium on Microarchitecture*. IEEE, Washington, DC, 2014: 609–622.

19. Wang C., Gong L., Yu Q., et al. DLAU: A scalable deep learning accelerator unit on FPGA. *IEEE Transactions on Computer-Aided Design of Integrated Circuits and Systems*, 2016, 36(3): 513–517.

20. Cadambi S., Durdanovic I., Jakkula V., et al. A massively parallel FPGA-based coprocessor for support vector machines. *2009 17th IEEE Symposium on Field Programmable Custom Computing Machines*. IEEE, Washington, DC, 2009: 115–122.

21. Papadonikolakis M., Bouganis C. S. Novel cascade FPGA accelerator for support vector machines classification. *IEEE Transactions on Neural Networks and Learning Systems*, 2012, 23(7): 1040–1052.

22. Baker Z. K., Prasanna V. K. Efficient hardware data mining with the Apriori algorithm on FPGAs. *13th Annual IEEE Symposium on Field-Programmable Custom Computing Machines (FCCM'05)*. IEEE, Washington, DC, 2005: 3–12.

23. Hussain H. M., Benkrid K., Erdogan A. T., et al. Highly parameterized k-means clustering on FPGAs: Comparative results with GPPs and GPUs. *2011 International Conference on Reconfigurable Computing and FPGAs*. IEEE, Washington, DC, 2011: 475–480.

24. Hussain H. M., Benkrid K., Ebrahim A., et al. Novel dynamic partial reconfiguration implementation of k-means clustering on FPGAs: Comparative results with GPPs and GPUs. *International Journal of Reconfigurable Computing*, 2012, 2012: 1.

25. Jia F., Wang C., Li X., et al. SAKMA: specialized FPGA-based accelerator architecture for data-intensive k-means algorithms. *Algorithms and Architectures for Parallel Processing: 15th International Conference, ICA3PP 2015*, Zhangjiajie, China, November 18–20, 2015, Proceedings, Part II 15. Springer International Publishing, 2015: 106–119.

26. Narayanan R., Honbo D., Memik G., et al. An FPGA implementation of decision tree classification. *2007 Design, Automation & Test in Europe Conference & Exhibition*. IEEE, San Jose, CA, 2007: 1–6.

27. Yu Q., Wang C., Ma X., et al. A deep learning prediction process accelerator based FPGA. *2015 15th IEEE/ACM International Symposium on Cluster, Cloud and Grid Computing*. IEEE, Shenzhen, 2015: 1159–1162.
28. Perera D. G., Li K. F. Parallel computation of similarity measures using an FPGA-based processor array. *22nd International Conference on Advanced Information Networking and Applications (aina 2008)*. IEEE, Washington, DC, 2008: 955–962.
29. Sudha N. A pipelined array architecture for Euclidean distance transformation and its FPGA implementation. *Microprocessors and Microsystems*, 2005, 29(8–9): 405–410.
30. Cadambi S., Majumdar A., Becchi M., et al. A programmable parallel accelerator for learning and classification. *Proceedings of the 19th International Conference on Parallel Architectures and Compilation Techniques*. New York, NY, 2010: 273–284.
31. Liu D., Chen T., Liu S., et al. Pudiannao: A polyvalent machine learning accelerator. *ACM SIGARCH Computer Architecture News*, 2015, 43(1): 369–381.
32. Grouplens. MovieLens Datasets. Grouplens, https://grouplens.org/datasets/movielens/, 2023.
33. Segaran T. *Programming Collective Intelligence: Building Smart Web 2.0 Applications*. Sebastopol, CA: O'Reilly Media, Inc., 2007.
34. Xilinx. The official Linux kernel from Xilinx. Github, https://github.com/Xilinx/linux-xlnx, 2023.

4

Customization and Optimization of Distributed Computing Systems for Recommendation Algorithms

4.1 Application Context of Recommendation Algorithms in Distributed Systems

4.1.1 Recommendation Systems

In the wake of technological advancements, we find ourselves entrenched in the era of the Internet, a transformative journey spanning from Web 2.0 to the mobile Internet, and from cloud computing to mobile computing. The rapid evolution of the Internet has silently reshaped the contours of human life [1]. This evolution has brought about a dramatic surge in both user population and data volume. As of the end of 2016, the total count of accessible domain names had reached a staggering 42.28 million, with a corresponding 236 billion [2] web pages in existence. Presently, the principal conundrums between Internet users and data manifest as follows: (1) in the face of a colossal data reservoir, how can users swiftly pinpoint the information they seek, and (2) confronted with personalized user preferences, how can Internet applications cater to the diverse interests of users?

In order to solve the above contradiction between users and data, classified directories and search engines came into being. Classified directories, represented by Yahoo and hao123, categorize Internet data so that users can find information in different categories [3]. However, due to the escalating data volume and a surfeit of chaotic classifications, users encountered challenges in expeditiously locating information within the corresponding directories.

Therefore, search engine technology represented by Google and Baidu is rapidly emerging. The search engine automatically completes the collection and organization of information, receives the user's query, returns the query results to the user, and supports the relevance of sorting and giving summary information, which can effectively help the user to find the content of interest [4]. However, search engines rely on user-provided keywords for queries, and when user demands are vague, query results may not align with

DOI: 10.1201/9780429355080-4

user expectations. It is within this context that the concept of recommenda-tion systems was introduced.

A recommendation system is a filtering system that proactively provides information to the user and predicts the user's preferences for items based on information about the user or the item [5]. Currently, recommendation systems are widely used in e-commerce, advertising recommendations, and online news systems.

Recommendation systems have been in development for more than 20 years. The GroupLens system introduced by the University of Minnesota kicked off the research on recommendation systems by introducing the idea of collabora-tive filtering (CF) for the first time and constructing a formal model for the rec-ommendation problem [6]. Since then, Carnegie Mellon University introduced the WebWatcher system, designed to aid information retrieval [7]. Stanford University presented the personalized recommendation system known as Learning Information Retrieval Agents (LIRA), and the Massachusetts Institute of Technology developed the personalized navigation system, Litizia. In the application field, Amazon's product recommendation system, Netflix's recommendation system competition, and Google's advertisement alliance have effectively increased the number of users and turnover of the website.

However, a large number of practices have shown that the existing recom-mendation algorithms have limitations, and there is still no recommendation algorithm that can fully satisfy the needs of users. In order to make up for the shortcomings of a single recommendation algorithm and alleviate the problem of sparsity of preference data, the hybrid recommendation system combining multiple recommendation techniques has emerged.

Hybrid recommendation systems combine two or more recommendation algorithms to make up for the shortcomings of a single recommendation algorithm in order to obtain better recommendation results [8]. Hybrid rec-ommendation systems can be categorized into various frameworks, including multi-stage hybrid frameworks, weighted hybrid models, cross-harmonization systems, model blending systems, and holistic hybrid systems [1]. In order to further meet the needs of different application scenarios, researchers continue to optimize hybrid recommendation systems. The Netflix recommendation system competition serves as a notable example, where the ultimate victors harnessed a combination of multiple algorithms to significantly enhance accu-racy. Samsung Electronics, on the other hand, has ventured into the develop-ment of hybrid recommendation systems tailored for smart devices.

In 2006, Netflix hosted the recommendation system competition, with the aim of enhancing the precision of their recommendation system. After continuous improvement, the BPC (BellKor's Pragmatic Chaos) team came out on top with a 10.06% improvement in accuracy [9]. The Netflix system comprises offline, near-online, and online modules. The offline module is based on batch processing mode, using hybrid recommendation algorithms to train historical data and characterize users and items. The near-online module is based on the offline model and realizes fast updates. The online module responds to users' needs, using less complex algorithms to realize fast computation and display results in real time. Currently, the architecture of most recommendation systems is based on the improvement of Netflix's three-stage hybrid architecture.

In 2014, Samsung Electronics unveiled a patent for a hybrid recommendation system designed for smart devices. This system, founded on a distributed architecture, encompasses modules for log parsing, user profiling, recommenders, and result presentation modules [10]. The log parsing module reads log files from a database to extract relevant information. The log parsing module retrieves log files from the database, extracting pertinent information. The user profiling module employs MapReduce to construct user profiles. The recommender generates three categories of recommendations: the first category is based on CF algorithms, the second category is derived from Top-N recommendations, and the third category is grounded in content-based recommendations. The result presentation module computes a blended result utilizing these three recommendation categories.

In the past two years, hybrid recommender systems based on content feature relationships [11] and hybrid CF systems with autoencoders have gradually emerged to expand the scope of hybridization and effectively alleviate the cold-start problem [12].

The function of a hybrid recommendation system is to mine the user's interested content from massive data. Therefore, whether the recommendation result meets the user's needs is an important index to measure the system's performance. Based on user demands, hybrid recommendation systems typically grapple with two key problems:

1. Faced with copious data, hybrid recommendation systems must determine the most effective approach to combine recommendation algorithms, ensuring precise prediction of user preferences and delivering diverse recommendation results.

2. Hybrid recommendation systems combine multiple recommendation algorithms, which increases the complexity of the system. Therefore, when dealing with large-scale datasets, it becomes essential to ensure the efficiency of a hybrid recommendation system.

To address the first problem, hybrid recommendation systems usually combine each algorithm using a weighted hybrid approach. That is, according to the prediction results of each algorithm, calculate its corresponding weight. Currently, the commonly used method is the coarse-grained weight calculation method, where each algorithm is assigned a weight value. The weighted combination results are then determined based on the algorithm's prediction value and its respective weight. For the second problem, hybrid recommendation systems employ both batch processing and stream processing modes to ensure system responsiveness. Currently, the offline processing module uses batch processing to accelerate the training process, such as training large-scale historical data based on the MapReduce computational model and Mahout machine learning library.

Although the hybrid recommendation system has been more widely used, the following problems still exist: (1) hybrid recommendation systems, particularly those addressing rating prediction, often employ a coarse-grained weight calculation method. In this approach, developers iteratively experiment to ascertain the appropriate weights for recommendation algorithms. Regrettably, this method falls short in guaranteeing recommendation precision, demanding a high level of expertise from developers. (2) Hybrid recommendation results rely on the results of a single recommendation algorithm, which is greatly affected by the sparsity of preference data. Due to the rapid growth of Internet users, the sparsity of preference data increases, exacerbating the cold-start problem of hybrid recommendation systems. (3) Hybrid recommendation systems perform multiple recommendation algorithms and hybrid computation methods, leading to an increase in the system's computational volume, and there are a large number of iterative computations in the single recommendation algorithm, which will also increase the system's computational volume. As a result, the hybrid recommendation system model training time increases, failing to meet user expectations for system efficiency.

4.1.2 Distributed Systems

As the scale of Internet data expands, stand-alone servers are unable to meet the demand for high-speed growth of data processing. To enhance computational capabilities while optimizing cost efficiency, Internet companies represented by Google deploy distributed systems into practical applications. Distributed data processing platform integrates the resources of independent computers to provide computing services, featuring high performance, high throughput, fault tolerance, and scalability. In response to the needs of large-scale data processing, Apache and AMP Lab, respectively, realized their respective distributed data processing platforms and provided open-source code.

Hadoop is a data processing platform based on the MapReduce computing model developed by the Apache organization, which utilizes the idea of data redundancy to ensure the reliability of the system and the scalability of the system through the Master–Slave structure. The Hadoop ecosystem includes Mahout, HBase [13], and Hadoop Distributed File System (HDFS). Based on the Hadoop platform, developers can quickly develop distributed programs without having to understand the underlying structure, improving development efficiency. Currently, Hadoop is mainly used for offline processing of data.

Spark is a generalized large-scale data processing framework proposed by U.C. Berkeley AMP Lab in 2009. The framework is based on resilient distributed data sets (RDDs), which keep intermediate results in memory to increase computation speeds [14]. Capitalizing on in-memory computing and RDDs, Spark boasts computation speeds up to 100 times faster than Hadoop. Currently, Spark has evolved into a complete ecosystem, including distributed databases (Spark SQL), stream processing systems (Spark Streaming) [15], machine learning libraries (MLlib) [16], and graph computing frameworks (GraphX) [17]. Currently, Spark has a wide range of applications in machine learning, data querying, and stream processing.

Ray is a Python-based distributed computing framework being developed in the AMP Lab to simplify the writing of distributed machine learning programs and is currently in an experimental phase [18]. With the advent of the era of big data and artificial intelligence, machine learning algorithms have found an increasingly expansive range of applications. Ray emerges as a user-friendly platform that empowers developers to craft machine learning algorithms with ease. It automates parallel execution, thereby reducing the entry barriers to the field of machine learning. This platform permits the development of machine learning algorithms on a single machine while seamlessly enabling parallelization. In doing so, Ray contributes to simplifying the process of building and deploying machine learning solutions, ushering in greater accessibility for developers in this domain.

In addition to the above basic platforms, each Internet enterprise realizes personalized data processing platforms suitable for their business scenarios, such as AliCloud's E-MapReduce [19] and Huawei's FusionInsight enterprise-level big data platform [20].

In this chapter, we choose Apache Spark as the development platform, which is an efficient and generalized large-scale data processing engine based on the Scala language, and can automatically complete the work related to data partitioning and parallel computation. Spark provides programming interfaces for the developers, which enables the developers to develop parallel applications easily and efficiently.

Spark is based on in-memory computing and integrates machine learning, stream processing, graph computation, and data analytics to provide a one-stop solution for large-scale data processing. The Spark ecosystem, shown in Figure 4.1, encompasses modules like resource managers, distributed file

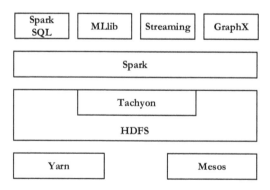

FIGURE 4.1
The Spark ecosystem.

systems, distributed computing engines, data querying tools, machine learning libraries, stream processing frameworks, and graph computing frameworks [21]:

Spark can use resource managers to realize the allocation, management, and recovery of global computing resources. Currently, the commonly used resource managers are Yam, developed by the Apache open-source community, and Mesos, developed by U.C. Berkeley.

Spark utilizes distributed file systems to facilitate the storage of large-scale data, ensuring efficient read/write operations and data reliability. Tachyon, for instance, is an in-memory distributed file system known for its high-throughput characteristics, eliminating the need for disk access during read and write operations [22]. HDFS is an open-source distributed file system based on Google File System architecture, with high efficiency, fault tolerance, and other characteristics [23]. Commonly used data files are usually stored in Tachyon, while a large number of data files are stored in HDFS.

The core of the Spark ecosystem is a distributed computing framework, which is based on the MapReduce idea and implements a memory-based distributed computing framework. Compared to Hadoop, Spark is more suitable for dealing with iterative computation, with the advantages of high performance, fault tolerance, and scalability.

Spark SQL is an interactive data query component based on the Catalyst engine that supports data formats such as Hive, CSV, JSON, and Parquet, and can fetch data through standard SQL statements [24].

Mllib implements commonly used machine learning algorithms and optimizes some of them, so developers can efficiently develop machine learning applications [16].

Spark Streaming fetches data from message queues, breaking down computation tasks into a set of short jobs and processing them in batch mode. Spark Streaming is a high-throughput, fault-tolerant, and scalable stream processing component [15].

GraphX is a graph computation framework based on the BSP model, supporting the Google graph computation engine Pregel API [17]. Currently, GraphX implements triangle counting, the maximum connected graph community detection algorithm, the pivot node discovery algorithm, etc., which are widely used in the fields of social networks, maps, and so on.

In order to realize a fault-tolerant data processing framework based on in-memory computation, Spark introduces a groundbreaking concept known as resilient distributed dataset (RDD). RDD represents a distributed, read-only, and partitioned collection of data. It comprises a list of partitions, a computation function, and a list of dependencies [14]. Spark can create RDDs from both in-memory data collections and external data files, and provides rich operations for RDDs. RDD operations are mainly categorized into transformation and action operations. Transformation creates a new RDD based on an existing RDD. The operation is lazy, meaning it will not be executed immediately after the submission, but will be executed only when the Action operation is submitted. The representative transformation operations are map, filter, reduceByKey, etc. The Action operation triggers a series of transformation operations to run and return the results of the calculations. The typical action operation is count, reduce, collect, and so on. The Spark computing framework based on RDD data structure has such features as high performance, fault tolerance, and versatility:

High performance: Since RDD is a distributed data collection containing multiple partitions, RDD operations can be executed in parallel to improve computational efficiency. Meanwhile, developers can specify the RDD storage level, and the intermediate result data does not need to be written to disk, realizing memory-based computation and improving performance. Currently, the memory-based computation of Spark is more than 100 times faster than Hadoop's MapReduce computation model.

Fault tolerance: Spark proposes the concept of lineage to ensure the fault tolerance of Spark based on the read-only characteristics of RDDs. When performing an operation, Spark performs a series of calculations to generate a new RDD based on the current RDD, and the lineage describes the transformation relationship between the RDDs. If the data in the RDD is wrong, Spark re-executes the computation process of the RDD based on the lineage information and then obtains the correct result.

Universality: Spark framework reads the data and then converts it to RDD format uniformly, and all kinds of operations of Spark are based on the RDD structure, which makes the various modules of Spark realize seamless connection, and builds a multi-functional and integrated data processing platform.

Spark uses a Master–Slave architecture to build a distributed computing framework, and its system architecture is shown in Figure 4.2 [21]. The Spark cluster consists of two types of nodes: the Master node and the Slave node.

Master is the core node of the cluster, which does not participate in the cluster computation, but is responsible for the cluster management and scheduling. All Worker nodes within the cluster send registration information to the Master node, effectively relinquishing control of their computational resources, including CPU, memory, and disk space, to the Master node for centralized management. The Master node monitors the operation status of each Worker node to ensure the rationality of resource allocation.

The Slave nodes are responsible for executing the jobs within the cluster. Depending on their functions, Slave nodes can be categorized into two types: (1) Driver node: These nodes run the main application process and serve as the logical starting point for the application. The Driver node divides the program into multiple task tasks, assigns these tasks to different Worker

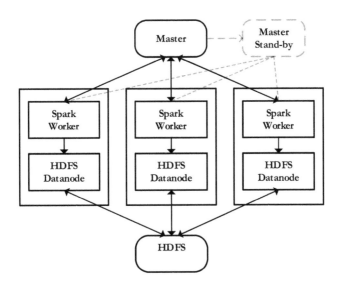

FIGURE 4.2
Spark system architecture.

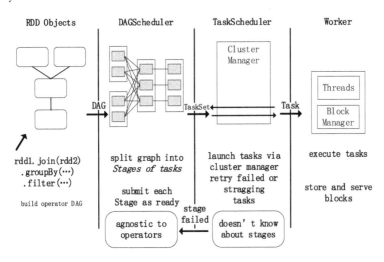

FIGURE 4.3
Flowchart of Spark execution process.

nodes, and coordinates the execution of tasks across various Worker nodes. (2) Worker node: Worker nodes are the actual nodes responsible for task execution. Within each Worker node, multiple Executor processes run, executing tasks and returning results to the Driver node. Additionally, Worker nodes provide in-memory storage for RDDs, enhancing data processing efficiency.

The operational mechanism of Spark is depicted in Figure 4.3 [25], illustrating the complete process of a Spark application from submission to execution conclusion. When a user submits a Spark application to the cluster, the Master node initiates a Driver node for it. The Driver node analyzes operations related to RDD creation, storage, and transformations within the main function, constructing a directed acyclic graph (DAG). Subsequently, it requests the necessary computational resources from the Master node. Upon receiving the resource request, the Master node dispatches commands to the registered Worker nodes to launch Executor processes. After the Worker nodes initiate the respective processes, they inform the Driver node, which then proceeds to allocate tasks. The Driver node distributes task assignments to various Executors, each independently performing task computations and subsequently returning results to the Driver node. Upon the completion of all tasks, the Driver node signals the termination of the application to the client program, concluding the execution of a Spark application.

With the advancement of information technology, the scale of Internet data has far exceeded the storage capacity of individual servers. Expanding memory and disk capacity would entail substantial cost increases. To address this challenge and achieve cost-effective storage for large-scale data, researchers have introduced the concept of distributed file systems.

HDFS is an open-source distributed file system developed by the Apache community, based on the design principles of Google File System, featuring high throughput, high fault tolerance, high reliability, scalability, etc. HDFS is deployed on extensive clusters of low-cost hardware and seamlessly integrates with the MapReduce computing model. It serves as a file system for upper-level applications, offering storage services for massive data sets, and constitutes a crucial component of the Hadoop ecosystem.

HDFS divides large data sets into equally sized blocks and stores them across different nodes, with a default block size of 64 MB. When applications read data, HDFS retrieves data from various nodes based on the metadata information associated with the block storage. This design embodies the concept of "write once, read multiple times." To realize this approach, HDFS adopts a Master–Slave architecture, where the Master corresponds to the NameNode and the Slaves are numerous DataNode nodes [26]. The NameNode serves as the core of the HDFS system, responsible for managing the file system's namespace, block allocation information, and metadata about block storage locations. It also monitors the addition, removal, and operational status of DataNode nodes. The NameNode is associated with a Secondary NameNode, responsible for backing up snapshots of the NameNode's files to aid in fault recovery. On the other hand, DataNode nodes receive read and write commands from the NameNode, facilitating data read and write operations.

When a user requests to read a file, HDFS initially sends the client's request to the NameNode node. The NameNode, using the file's block allocation information and metadata about block storage locations, determines the DataNode node closest to the client and returns its address to the user. Armed with this location information, the user can access the DataNode

node to read the data. When a user requests to write data, HDFS sends a write request to the NameNode node. The NameNode, within the namespace, creates a new file. The client writes data to the DataNode, and upon completion of the write operation, HDFS automatically backs up the new data file.

With the development of Hadoop and Spark, distributed computing frameworks have found extensive applications in fields such as data analysis and processing. To offer a rapid development tool for developers familiar with relational database management systems but less acquainted with distributed computing, Spark has integrated Shark, a distributed database. However, because Shark heavily relies on Hive's related technologies, this integration posed constraints on the integration and coherence of Spark's various modules. Consequently, Spark has developed its own distributed database, Spark SQL.

The official release of Spark 1.0 introduced the Spark SQL component. Spark SQL is an interactive SQL processing framework that adheres to SQL standards. It offers compatibility with various data formats, including Hive, Parquet, JSON, CSV, and JDBC, and provides programming language interfaces in Scala, Java, Python, and others. Furthermore, it enables interactive data querying through standard SQL statements [24]. Spark SQL leverages in-memory columnar storage technology and bytecode techniques to achieve significant performance improvements. As a result, Spark SQL has become a crucial means for accessing data within the Spark platform.

The overall architecture of Spark SQL is a combination of a query optimizer and an executor, with the Catalyst serving as the query optimizer and Spark as the executor. Catalyst, developed in Scala, is a flexible and extensible query optimizer. It translates SQL statements into executable plans and performs query optimization during the translation process. The result of Catalyst's translation is a query tree, which is then converted into a DAG for execution by the Spark executor.

4.2 Algorithmic Details

4.2.1 Concept of Recommendation Systems

In everyday life, users typically acquire information through two distinct approaches: active and passive methods. Active methods require users to have explicit needs, with representative examples being classification directories and search engines. In contrast, passive methods involve the system automatically selecting information for users, with recommendation systems serving as a representative pattern.

Recommendation systems operate based on user and item feature models to calculate information that users might find interesting [27]. For instance, when a user opens a video streaming website during their leisure time, the website recommends videos that match the user's interests based on their viewing, favoriting, and downloading history. Recommendation systems primarily consist of three modules: (1) the Data Module serves as the foundation of recommendation systems, storing user information, item information, and preference data used for model training. (2) The Algorithm Module represents the specific implementation of recommendation algorithms. Utilizing these algorithms, the system can predict unknown preference data. (3) The Recommendation Module, relying on the predictions generated by the Algorithm Module, provides users with item recommendations.

To meet the diverse requirements of different application scenarios and enhance the accuracy of recommender systems, researchers have introduced the concept of hybrid recommendation. The framework of a hybrid recommender system, as illustrated in Figure 4.4, allows for categorization based on various aspects such as data sources, architecture, algorithms, and blending techniques in practical applications.

(1) Multi-stage composite hybrid recommendation framework, exemplified by the Netflix recommendation architecture, comprises three modules: offline, near-online, and online. Each module computes recommendation results independently, and based on user requirements for response time, selects the corresponding results from the appropriate module. (2) Weighted hybrid recommendation systems employ the basic idea of calculating the weight of a single recommendation algorithm based on its predicted ratings, and the blended result is the weighted sum of the predicted ratings of each algorithm. Weighted blending techniques are widely used due to their simplicity and higher accuracy. This chapter enhances the weight calculation method to improve recommendation accuracy. (3) Hierarchical hybrid recommendation systems classify recommendation algorithms based on their precision. When dealing with different application scenarios, the system prioritizes algorithms with higher precision. Hierarchical blending techniques

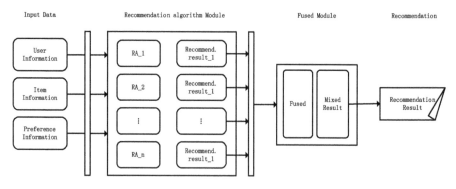

FIGURE 4.4
Framework of hybrid recommendation systems.

can consider multiple evaluation criteria, making it a more comprehensive blending technique. (4) Cross-harmonization recommendation systems use cross-harmonization techniques to blend the recommendation results of different algorithms in specific proportions, generating a mixed result. Cross-harmonization methods ensure diversity in recommendation results, providing better interpretability to the recommendations.

4.2.2 Collaborative Filtering Recommendation Algorithms

CF algorithms first appeared in email systems for message filtering [28]. It is the most mature recommendation algorithm at present and widely used in e-commerce systems and movie rating systems.

The fundamental idea behind CF algorithms is to group people and items by similarity. If two users, u and v, have similar ratings for a set of items, the algorithm considers them as similar users. Therefore, if user u likes a particular item, it is highly likely that user v will also like it. The execution process of CF algorithms, as illustrated in Figure 4.5, consists of three main components: the data module, similarity methods, and recommendation module:

Data module: CF algorithms analyze user behavior to construct a rating matrix [29]. The data item r_{ij} in the matrix represents the rating given by user i to item i. In Figure 4.5, the gray area represents known ratings, while the blank area represents unknown ratings that need to be predicted.

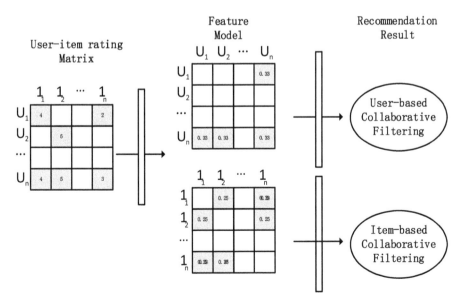

FIGURE 4.5
Workflow of collaborative filtering recommendation algorithm.

Similarity method: In CF algorithms, the feature model for users and items corresponds to the similarity matrix between users and items. Therefore, measuring the similarity between users or items is a crucial part of the algorithm. Common similarity calculation methods include Euclidean Distance, Cosine Similarity, Jaccard Similarity Coefficient, and Pearson Correlation Coefficient [27].

Recommendation module: If the target user u did not rate item i, the CF algorithm calculates u's rating of i using the rating of item i by u's similar user v and the similarity of (u, v). Based on the predicted ratings, the algorithm generates the final recommendation list.

CF algorithms, considering the relevance of the objects in question, are classified into two categories: user-based CF (user-CF) and item-based CF (item-CF) [27]: (1) User-CF Algorithm: The fundamental idea behind this algorithm is to group people by similarity, utilizing preference information to place similar users in the same set. It recommends items to the target user based on this grouping. (2) This algorithm operates on the principle of grouping items based on their similarity. If a user u has provided similar ratings for items i and j, the algorithm considers i and j as similar items. Therefore, if a user likes item i, they are highly likely to also like item j.

4.2.3 Content-Based Recommendation Algorithms

The content-based recommendation algorithm (CB) is a commonly used approach in the design of recommendation systems. Its fundamental concept involves creating and learning user profiles and leveraging the similarity between these profiles to recommend items that align with a user's preferences [30]. For example, in this algorithm, feature vectors are established based on information such as the title, genre, director, screenwriter, and lead actors of movies. If a user has shown an interest in <Harry Potter, Magic, J.K. Rowling, Daniel Radcliffe>, the CB algorithm would suggest that the user might also like <Where Fantastic Animals Are, Magic, J.K. Rowling, Eddie Redmayne>. Notably, the CB algorithm no longer relies on a rating matrix, making it an extension of CF recommendation algorithms and particularly well suited for handling textual, image, and video data.

The content-based recommendation algorithm framework, as depicted in Figure 4.6, consists of three main steps: profile creation, profile learning, and recommendation generation:

Profile creation: The profile serves as the foundation for content-based recommendation algorithms and typically refers to item profiles. Item profiles extract multiple features from items to create representative feature vectors.

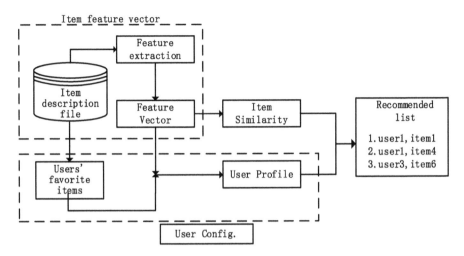

FIGURE 4.6
Architecture diagram of content-based recommendation algorithm.

Profile learning: Content-based recommendations utilize machine learning algorithms such as KNN, decision trees, and plain Bayesian algorithms to mine feature data, and construct and update user profiles.

Recommendation list generation: For a user's profile, denoted as *profile_u*, the CB algorithm calculates the association between *profile_u* and item feature vectors to generate a recommendation list.

4.2.4 Model-Based Recommendation Algorithms

CF and CB algorithms, which involve reading all data into memory to measure similarities, often lead to increased memory requirements for recommendation systems. Model-based recommendation algorithms can effectively address such issues.

The core concept of model-based recommendation algorithms is to uncover hidden associations between users and items. For example, users who like the same book likely share certain implicit features and books liked by the same user are bound to have some common characteristics. Model-based recommendation algorithms use rating matrices to train implicit user feature models and implicit item feature models. Based on these two models, the algorithms predict unknown rating data. The algorithm's workflow is illustrated in Figure 4.7. The key aspect of model-based recommendation lies in training implicit feature matrices. Currently, representative algorithms include matrix factorization and latent factor model (LFM) algorithms, among others.

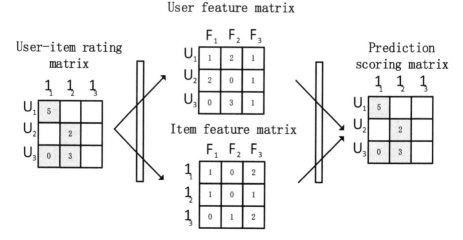

FIGURE 4.7
Framework of latent factor model recommendation algorithm.

4.2.5 Evaluation Metrics

Score prediction accuracy is an important metric of recommendation system accuracy, and it is a focal point for optimization in most research efforts. This includes two primary metrics: (1) root mean square error (RMSE) and (2) mean absolute error (MAE).

$$\text{RMSE} = \sqrt{\frac{\sum_{u,i \in T} \left(r_{ui} - \hat{r}_w \right)^2}{|T|}} \qquad (4.1)$$

$$\text{MAE} = \frac{\sum_{u,i \in T} \left| r_{ui} - \hat{r}_w \right|^2}{|T|} \qquad (4.2)$$

Top-N recommendation provides users with a recommended list, commonly used in website applications. The performance of a Top-N recommendation system is typically measured using two common metrics: Precision and Recall.

$$\text{Precision} = \frac{\sum_{u \in U} |R(u) \cap T(u)|}{\sum_{u \in U} |R(u)|} \qquad (4.3)$$

$$\text{Recall} = \frac{\sum_{u \in U} |R(u) \cap T(u)|}{\sum_{u \in U} |T(u)|} \qquad (4.4)$$

Coverage is an evaluation metric used to measure a recommendation system's ability to discover long-tail items. It is typically defined as the ratio of the number of recommended items to the total number of items.

$$\text{Coverage} = \frac{|U_{u \in U} R(u)|}{|I|} \tag{4.5}$$

4.3 Deployment of Recommendation Systems

4.3.1 Overall Framework of Recommendation Systems

The hybrid recommendation system designed in this study comprises two categories of recommendation algorithms: rating prediction-based recommendations and content-based recommendations. The rating prediction-based recommendations consist of three algorithms: user-based CF recommendation algorithm (user-CF), item-based CF recommendation algorithm (item-CF), and LFM algorithm. These algorithms, through a fine-grained weight calculation method, constitute the weighted hybrid subsystem.

Content-based recommendation consists of two algorithms: user content-based recommendation algorithm (user-CB) and item content-based recommendation algorithm (item-CB). Utilizing cross-blending techniques, these two algorithms are combined with the weight blending subsystem to form the final recommendation system.

4.3.2 Weighted Hybrid Subsystems

4.3.2.1 Distributed Recommendation Algorithm Library

In the Spark computing framework, data is stored in RDD structures, and fine-grained operations like map, reduce, and groupByKey are used for data transformations. Therefore, implementing user-based CF recommendation algorithms in Spark involves three main steps: constructing an RDD-based rating matrix, training user feature models, and rating prediction. Algorithm 4.1 outlines the logical structure of the distributed user-CF algorithm:

RDD-based rating matrix: The user's historical behavioral preferences are the basis of the recommendation algorithm. User-CF algorithm usually extracts user preference scoring data from user behavioral logs as the input to the algorithm. User-CF algorithm's input data is in the format of $((uid_1 :: item_1 :: rank_{11}),..., (uid_m :: item_n :: rank_{mn}))$, where *uid* represents the user number, *item* represents the item number, and *rank* represents the user's rating of the item. user-CF constructs an RDD-based rating matrix based on such rating data.

The user-CF algorithm first uses Spark's textFile interface to read the user's rating data of the items from the HDFS file system and divides each rating data into the key-value format of ((*uid, item*), *rank*) by matching the "::" delimiter, where *uid, item* is Int type, *rank* is Double type, and the RDD-based rating matrix is constructed by specifying the parameter of persist interface as *DISK_ONLY* and storing the data in disk.

Similarity matrix: Based on the rating matrix RDD, the user-CF algorithm calculates the user-user similarity matrix. Currently, user-CF algorithms commonly employ cosine similarity or the Jaccard formula to calculate user similarity. Both of these similarity metrics are reliant on the number of items for which users have provided common ratings, thereby analyzing user relatedness but overlooking preference information encapsulated within the ratings. Consequently, this section introduces an enhanced method for calculating similarity, namely, rating-based cosine similarity. Rating-based cosine similarity not only considers the number of items for which two users have common ratings but also thoroughly incorporates their rating data for the same items. The formula for its computation is as follows:

$$\text{similar}(u, v) = \frac{\sum_{i=1}^{n} r_{ui} * r_{vi}}{\sqrt{\sum_{i=1}^{n} (r_{ui})^2} * \sqrt{\sum_{i=1}^{n} (r_{vi})^2}} \tag{4.6}$$

The user-CF algorithm uses map and groupByKey operations to build user-item and item-user tables. Within the *user_item* table, each entry represents the set of items that a user has rated, while in the *item_user* table, each entry represents the set of users who have rated that item. The user-CF algorithm generates pairs of users who have rated the same item based on the *item_user* table, and the reduceByKey operation merges the same pairs of users. The Map operation indexes the pairs of users extracts the set of items that have been rated by each of the two users in the *user_item* table, and builds the user similarity matrix, which stores the data in the format of (*uid*, (*vid, sim*)).

After the above two steps, the user-CF algorithm builds the user similarity matrix *similaru*. The user-CF algorithm generates the recommendation list for the target user *t* as follows:

(1) Similar Users: The user-CF algorithm first finds users similar to the target user *t* based on the user similarity matrix, i.e., it reads the key-value pairs *similaru*[*t*] corresponding to the target user in the similarity matrix. Spark utilizes the filter operation to match the target user's identifier,

resulting in a collection of similar users. (2) Rating Prediction: Assuming that the set of similar users for user u is denoted as $V=(v_1, v_2,..., v_k)$, the algorithm proceeds to search the User-Item table for the collection of items rated by each user in V. Leveraging the similarity between user u and the users in V, the algorithm calculates the predicted ratings for the items in this collection for user u. (3) Recommendation Results: The predicted ratings of the target user for various items are stored in RDD format. To generate recommendations, the user-CF algorithm queries this RDD for data in the form of (*uid*, (*item*, *predict*)). It then utilizes a filter operation to exclude items already rated by the target user. The remaining items are sorted by predicted rating in descending order, and the top N items are selected to create a recommendation list.

Algorithm 4.1 Logical Structure of the Distributed User-CF Algorithm

The user-CF algorithm's pseudocode based on the distributed implementation in Spark.

01: **Input**: the rank matrix of user-item

02: **Output**: the predict rank matrix in RDD

03:

04: ***user_item*** = *rank*.map{case (*user*,(*item*,*rank*)) => (*user*,*item*)}

05: ***item_user*** = *rank*.map{case (*user*,(*item*,*rank*)) => (*item*,*user*)}

06: for (*item*,*user*) in ***item_user***:

07:    map {case(*item*,(*u*,*v*)) => ((*u*,*v*), I)}

08: end for

09: reduceByKey{case ((*u*,*v*), I) => (*u*,*v*)}

10:

11: for each (*u*,*v*):

12:    for *item* in ***user_item***[*u*]:

13:      if *item* in ***user_item***[*v*]:

14:        calculate based on equation 4.6

15:      end if

16:    end for

17: end for

The basic idea of the item-CF algorithm is similar to that of user-CF. It utilizes the rating matrix RDD and calculates the item-item similarity matrix to recommend similar items for it. The logical structure of the Spark-based item-CF recommendation algorithm is shown in Algorithm 4.2, which mainly consists of three steps: constructing the rating matrix, training the item feature model, and rating prediction:

   Rating matrix RDD: Item-CF algorithm is similar to the user-CF algorithm in that the initial user preference data is read using the textFile interface and mapped to the key-value pair format by the map operation. Similarly, it employs the persist interface with the DISK_ONLY parameter to store data on disk, thereby constructing a user-item rating matrix based on RDD.

   Training the item feature model: The core component of the item-CF algorithm is to compute the item-item similarity matrix. Similar to the user similarity matrix, item-CF first uses the map operation to build the user-item table (user-item) and the item-user table (item-user). Then the items rated by the same user are grouped into pairs based on the *user_item* table to generate item pairs, and the reduceByKey operation merges the same item pairs. Finally, the item number in the item pair is used as the index to find the list of user ratings in the *item_user* table and compute the item-item similarity matrix, denoted as **similarity**.

   Rating prediction: For the target user t, the item-CF algorithm utilizes the filter operation to match user t in the *user_item* table and obtains the set of items that t has rated. For each item in the collection, the rating prediction is realized by using the user t's rating of the item and item relevance. A recommendation list is generated by filtering, sorting, and selecting the top N items.

Algorithm 4.2 Logical Structure of the Distributed Item-CF Algorithm

Pseudocode for the item-CF algorithm based on Spark distributed implementation

01: **Input**: the rank matrix of user-item

02: **Output**: the predict rank matrix in RDD

03:

04: *rank* = readMatrix.Split("::")

05: ***user_item*** = *rank*.map{case (*user*,(*item*,*rank*)) => (*user*,*item*)}

06: ***item_user*** = *rank*.map{case (*user*,(*item*,*rank*)) => (*item*,*user*)}

07: for (*user*,*item*) in ***user_item***:

08:   if(*user,(i,j)*):

09:      map {case(*item,(i,j)*) => ((*i,j*), I)}

10:   end if

11: end for

12: reduceByKey{case ((*i,j*), I) => (*i,j*)}

13:

14: for each (*i,j*):

15:    for *user* in ***item_user[i]***:

16:      if *user* in ***item_user[j]***:

17:        calculate based on equation 4.6

18:      end if

19:    end for

20: end for

Hidden factor model recommendation (LFM) is a recommendation algorithm that exploits the implicit features of users and items. LFM fully exploits the implicit information in the user behavioral preference information, decomposes the sparse rating matrix into two low-rank matrices: user feature matrix and item feature matrix, establishes implicit correlation between the user and the item, and computes the unknown preference rating data. The logical structure of the LFM algorithm is shown in Algorithm 4.3, which consists of three main steps:

Rating matrix: LFM reads user behavior preference data through Spark's file interface textFile and uses the map operation to map the preference data into the format of ((*uid, item), rank*) to construct the user-item rating matrix R_{mn}.

Feature matrix: The core of LFM is to construct user feature matrix U_{mq} and item feature matrix V_{nq} based on the user-item rating matrix to establish the association between users and items. The algorithm first randomly initializes the two feature matrices U and V and calculates the error between UV^T and R_{mn}. Then, according to the fastest descent recursive formula, iteratively update the matrices U and V until the error between UV^T and R_{mn} is minimized. Currently, LFM commonly employs the stochastic gradient descent algorithm to iteratively calculate U and V.

Rating prediction: Based on the user feature matrix U and item feature matrix V, LFM calculates the prediction rating matrix UV^T.

Algorithm 4.3 Logical Structure of the Distributed LFM Algorithm

Pseudocode of LFM algorithm based on Spark distributed implementation

01: **Input**: the rank matrix of user-item

02: **Output**: the factor model of users

03:        the factor model of items

04:

05: *rank* = readMatrix.Split("::")

06: U = random(m,q)

07: V = random(n,q)

08:

09: for $UV^T\text{-}R_{mn}> \epsilon$ and iterations:

10:    calculate U based on random gradient decreases algorithm and V

11:    calculate V based on random gradient decreases algorithm and U

12:    iterations += 1

13: end for

4.3.2.2 Fine-Grained Weighting Methods

As described in Section 4.3.1, the coarse-grained weight calculation method assumes that each recommendation algorithm has the same bias and the same degree of bias; however, the experimental results prove that the predicted values of the recommendation algorithms may be higher or lower than the true values, and the range of prediction errors is large. Therefore, the assumptions of the coarse-grained weight calculation method are not valid. In this chapter, we propose a fine-grained weight calculation method (FWCM), which first uses the clustering algorithm to classify the prediction error of recommendation algorithms, then establishes a weight calculation model according to the optimization theory, and finally calculates weight vectors for the recommendation algorithms based on the weight calculation model. By classifying the prediction error, the FWCM algorithm assigns different weights to the prediction scores of the recommendation algorithms, which further improves the accuracy of the hybrid recommendation. This section introduces the design and implementation of the FWCM method and explains the establishment process of the weight calculation model in detail.

   The basic idea of the FWCM method is to subdivide the prediction error of the recommendation algorithm and assign different weights to different prediction scores in order to improve the accuracy of the hybrid recommendation results. The objective function of the FWCM method is the basis for weight calculation and optimization, which is formally represented as:

1. Suppose the recommendation system implements n recommendation algorithms and j denotes the jth recommendation algorithm;

2. u represents the user, i represents the item, and (u, i) represents the data item consisting of u and i;

3. R_{ui} is the score of u for i; r_{ui}^j is the predicted score of u for i in the jth recommendation algorithm;

4. For the jth recommendation algorithm, the prediction error of user u for item i is $D_{ui}^j = R_{ui} - r_{ui}^j$;

5. All scored items (u, i) are categorized into k classes based on the prediction error. $C_{ui} = (c_1, c_2, \ldots, c_k)$ represents the class assignment vector of a data item (u, i);

6. $\alpha_j = (\alpha_{j1}, \alpha_{j2}, \ldots, \alpha_{jk})$ represents the weight vector corresponding to recommendation algorithm j, including k weights;

7. $\alpha_j C_{ui}^T$. finalizes the weights corresponding to the predicted scores of (u, i) in the recommendation algorithm j.

The optimization objective of the FWCM method is to obtain the minimized sum of squares of the errors, so the objective function of FWCM is shown in Equation (4.7):

$$F(\alpha) = \sum_{u,i} \left(R_{ui} - \alpha_1 C_{ui}^T r_{ui}^1 - \alpha_2 C_{ui}^T r_{ui}^2 - \cdots - \alpha_n C_{ui}^T r_{ui}^n \right)^2 \tag{4.7}$$

$$s.t. \sum_{j=1}^{n} \alpha_j C_{ui}^T = 1 \tag{4.8}$$

The FWCM method first classifies all scoring items (u, i) into k classes based on the prediction error D_{ui}^j. For each rating, data item (u, i) corresponds to a class assignment vector $C_{ui} = (c_1, c_2, \ldots, c_k)$. The steps for computing the class assignment vector are as follows:

1. Initialization: The FWCM method initializes the class allocation vector to an ***all-0*** vector, i.e., $C_{ui} = (0, 0, \ldots, 0)$.

2. Class assignment: The FWCM method uses the K-means algorithm to realize the clustering process of scoring data. The K-means algorithm randomly selects the rating data items (u_0, i_0) as the initial clustering cluster centers, calculates the distances of each (u, i) to the center of the clusters, and assigns them to the cluster with the closest

distance. Then, it calculates the mean value of all the data items in the clusters as the new center. The above calculation process is repeated until the K-means algorithm obtains a local optimal solution.

3. After the above clustering process, each rating item (u, i) is assigned to a certain cluster. The FWCM method sets the value of the cluster corresponding to the class assignment vector of (u, i) to 1, i.e., the class assignment matrix of (u, i) is obtained. In other words, if (u, i) belongs to the second class, the class assignment vector corresponding to (u, i) is $C_{ui} = (0, 1, \ldots, 0)$.

The class assignment vector identifies the clusters to which the predictive scoring data belongs and can map the weights in the weight vector to the corresponding predictive scoring data, which helps in the computation of the mixture results.

The core essence of the FWCM method is to construct a weight calculation model to calculate the weight vector for the recommendation algorithm. Based on the objective function formula, optimization theory, and the Lagrange formula, we construct the Lagrange function with the following formulas:

$$L(\alpha) = F(\alpha) + \lambda \sum_{u,i} \phi(\alpha) \tag{4.9}$$

$$\phi(\alpha) = \sum_{j=1}^{n} \alpha_j C_{ui}^T - 1 \tag{4.10}$$

Following the principles of minimization theory for recommendation algorithm j, by taking the partial derivative of $\alpha\, C_{jui}^T$ such that $\dfrac{\partial L}{\partial \left(\alpha_j C_{ui}^T \right)} = 0$, we can derive the weight calculation formula as follows:

$$2 * \sum_{u,i} \left(\alpha_1 C_{ui}^T r_{ui}^1 C_{ui}^j + \alpha_2 C_{ui}^T r_{ui}^2 C_{ui}^j + \cdots + \alpha_n C_{ui}^T r_{ui}^n C_{ui}^j \right) + \lambda = 2 * \sum_{u,i} R_{ui} r_{ui}^j \tag{4.11}$$

The weight calculation formula (4.11) can be represented using matrices as follows:

$$XY = 2*\left(\alpha_1,\alpha_2,\ldots,\alpha_n,\lambda\right)$$

$$* \begin{bmatrix} \sum_{u,i} C_{ui}^T r_{ui}^1 r_{ui}^1 & \sum_{u,i} C_{ui}^T r_{ui}^1 r_{ui}^2 & \cdots & \sum_{u,i} C_{ui}^T r_{ui}^1 r_{ui}^n & \sum_{u,i} C_{ui}^T \\ \sum_{u,i} C_{ui}^T r_{ui}^2 r_{ui}^1 & \sum_{u,i} C_{ui}^T r_{ui}^2 r_{ui}^2 & \cdots & \sum_{u,i} C_{ui}^T r_{ui}^2 r_{ui}^n & \sum_{u,i} C_{ui}^T \\ \vdots & \vdots & \ddots & \vdots & \vdots \\ \sum_{u,i} C_{ui}^T r_{ui}^n r_{ui}^1 & \sum_{u,i} C_{ui}^T r_{ui}^n r_{ui}^2 & \cdots & \sum_{u,i} C_{ui}^T r_{ui}^n r_{ui}^n & \sum_{u,i} C_{ui}^T \\ 1 & 1 & \cdots & 1 & 0 \end{bmatrix}$$

$$= 2* \begin{bmatrix} \sum_{u,i} R_{ui} r_{ui}^1 \\ \sum_{u,i} R_{ui} r_{ui}^2 \\ \vdots \\ \sum_{u,i} R_{ui} r_{ui}^n \\ \sum_{u,i} 1 \end{bmatrix} = R$$

$$(4.12)$$

Based on formula (4.12), we can derive the calculation formula for the weight matrix X as follows:

$$X = R * Y^{-1} \qquad (4.13)$$

The results obtained by the FWCM method include class allocation vectors and weight vectors. These results serve as input data for the model fusion module and are used to calculate mixed rating data for users and items. The calculation is shown in formula (4.14):

$$\hat{r}_{ui} = \frac{\sum_{v} \operatorname{sim}_{u,v} * \left(\alpha_1 C_{ui}^T r_{ui}^1 + \alpha_2 C_{ui}^T r_{ui}^2 + \cdots + \alpha_n C_{ui}^T r_{ui}^n\right)}{\sum_{v} \operatorname{sim}_{u,v}} \qquad (4.14)$$

4.3.2.3 Module Design of the Weighted Hybrid Subsystem

In this chapter, the fine-grained weight hybrid subsystem is designed and implemented, and its architecture is shown in Figure 4.8. The system primarily comprises five modules:

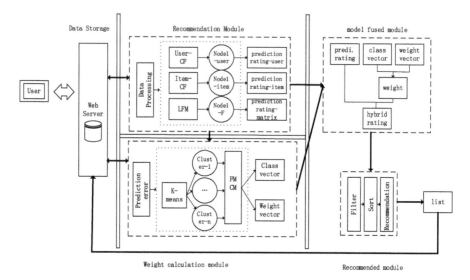

FIGURE 4.8
The architecture of fine-grained weighted hybrid subsystem.

Data storage module: The main function of this module is to collect
log data, clean and format it, and implement distributed storage for
large-scale data. The data storage module collects log files of user
behavior information and item feature description files, cleans the
missing values and outliers in the data files, and converts the data
into a unified data structure, which is stored in the distributed file
system. The data from this module can be used as input to the recommendation algorithm module, hybrid module, and recommendation module.

Recommendation algorithm module: The main function of this module is to establish a recommendation algorithm library, implement
distributed recommendation algorithms, and predict the user's
preference information. The recommendation algorithm module
reads the preprocessed data files, extracts feature information using
the recommendation algorithm, builds the feature model of users
and items, and calculates the user preference data based on the feature model.

Weight calculation module: The main function of this module is to
calculate the weight vector corresponding to each recommendation
algorithm using the FWCM method. This module first reads the prediction rating data of the recommendation algorithm module and
calculates the prediction error. Then, it calculates the weight vector
of the algorithm using the FWCM method. The module outputs the
class assignment vector and the weight vector.

Model hybrid module: This module is responsible for calculating the hybrid results. The model fusion module calculates the weighted sum of the recommendation algorithm's predicted scores and the corresponding weights based on the input predicted score data, class assignment vector, and weight vector.

Recommendation module: The main function of this module is to provide users with recommendation results. The recommendation module filters and sorts the mixed results according to the results of the model fusion module and generates a personalized recommendation list for the user.

4.3.3 Cross-Harmonization System

4.3.3.1 Distributed Recommendation Algorithm Library

A user-content-based recommendation algorithm (user-CB) trains item preference profiles based on user feature vectors. By comparing other user feature vectors with the preference profile of an item, it recommends the item to the most relevant users. Therefore, the user-CB based on Spark, as shown in Algorithm 4.4, mainly consists of the following three steps:

Constructing feature vectors: Similar to building user-item rating matrices in rating prediction recommendation algorithms, user-CB recommendation algorithms construct user feature vectors based on description files as the foundational data for system training. Content-based recommendation algorithms usually extract several keywords from a series of description files to form a feature vector for the user. Therefore, the format of the feature vector is (*userFactor_1, userFactor_2,..., userFactor_n*), where *userFactor* represents a feature keyword. User-CB algorithm utilizes the textFile interface to read user feature vector files from the distributed file system, storing each user feature vector in Vector format. By specifying the parameter of the persist interface as *MEMORY_ AND_DISK*, the user feature vectors are stored in memory and disk, completing the construction of feature vectors.

Training preference model: User-CB trains item preference profiles based on user feature vectors for liked items. First, it uses the filter operation to match users who like a particular item, obtaining a set of users. Then, it maps user feature vectors to item preference vectors using the map operation. Finally, through the reduceByKey operation, it merges identical features to obtain item preference profiles.

Recommendation list: User-CB compares the correlation between user feature vectors and item preference configurations to recommend items to relevant users. The algorithm utilizes the look operation to find matching features. The more the number of matches, the more relevant the two are.

Algorithm 4.4 Logical Structure of the Distributed User-CB Algorithm

Pseudocode for the user-CB algorithm based on Spark distributed implementation

01: **Input**: the description file of user and item

02: **Output**: the similarity between user and item profile

03:

04: *user_factor* = readMatrix.Split(' ')

05: for *user* in *user_factor*:

06:     for *item* in *description file*:

07:         if *user* like *item*:

08:             map{case($f1,f2, ...,fn$) =>*item_profile*}

09:         end if

10:     end for

11: end for

12:

13: calculate *similarity* between *user_factor* and *item_profile*

14:

15: for *user* in *similarity*:

16:     for *item* in *similarity[user]*:

17:         recommend *item* to other users

18:     end for

19: end for

The item content-based recommendation algorithm (item-CB) is similar to the idea of user-CB. It trains the user's preference profile based on the item feature vector, compares the correlation between the user's profile and the item feature vector, and recommends relevant items for the user. Therefore, the item-CB algorithm implemented based on Spark is shown in Algorithm 4.5, which mainly includes the following three steps:

Constructing feature vectors: The item-CB algorithm extracts keywords from the description file and composes item feature vectors as input data for system training. The format of the item feature vector is (*itemFactor_1, itemFactor_2,..., itemFactor_n*), where *itemFactor* represents the feature keyword. The process of constructing item vectors is similar to that of user vectors in user-CB.

Training preference models: The item-CB algorithm trains the user preference profile based on the feature vectors of the items that the user prefers. The filter operation initially matches all items liked by users, followed by using the map operation to map item feature vectors to user preference vectors. Finally, the reduceByKey operation combines identical features to generate user preference profiles.

Recommendation lists: The item-CB algorithm compares the degree of match between a user preference profile and the item's feature vector, and recommends the highest-relevance items to the user.

Algorithm 4.5 Logical Structure of the Distributed Item-CB Algorithm

Pseudocode for the item-CB algorithm based on Spark distributed implementation

01: **Input**: the description file of user and item

02: **Output**: the similarity between user profile and item

03:

04: *item_factor* = readMatrix.Split(' ').Map

05: for *item* in *item_factor*:

06:    for *user* in **description file**:

07:      if *user* like *item*:

08:        map{case(*f1,f2, ...,fn*) =>*user_profile*}

09:      end if

10:    end for

11: end for

12:

13: calculate *similarity* between *user_factor* and *item_profile*

4.3.3.2 Module Design for Cross-Harmonization Recommendation Systems

The overall architecture of the Spark-based cross-harmonization and recommendation system designed and implemented in this chapter is shown in Figure 4.9. The system primarily comprises four modules:

Data storage module: The primary function of this module is to collect, clean, and transform log data and implement distributed storage for large-scale log data. The data storage module collects data such

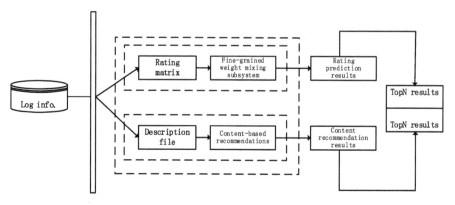

FIGURE 4.9
Architecture of Spark-based cross-harmonization recommendation system.

as user information logs, item information logs, and user behavior logs. It cleanses the data by handling anomalies, missing values, and empty values, and then transforms it into a uniform data structure for storage. This module utilizes distributed file systems to store large-scale data, such as HDFS and Tachyon.

Fine-grained weight hybrid subsystem: This subsystem utilizes the user-item rating matrix to compute unknown rating preference data to achieve rating prediction recommendations.

Recommendation algorithm module: The main function of this module is to implement a distributed CB algorithm for building feature profile files of users and items, and then predicting unknown user preferences. The recommendation algorithm module reads the formatted data file, uses the recommendation algorithm in the module to train the feature model, and realizes the preference prediction based on the feature model.

Recommendation module: This module is the interaction module between the system and the user, and its primary function is to provide the user with recommendation list information. The recommendation module reads the recommendation results of each recommendation algorithm and uses cross-harmonization technology to generate a personalized recommendation list for the user.

4.4 Conclusions

In this chapter, we have introduced the customization of recommendation systems in a distributed environment. We analyzed their application background and implementation details. Based on the distributed data processing platform Spark, we provided a specific solution for implementing a high-precision, efficient, diverse, and scalable hybrid recommendation system. This solution improves the accuracy and diversity of recommendation results while reducing the training time for models. Regarding the customization solution presented in Section 4.3, there is still room for further optimization and improvement, including:

Improve the recommendation algorithm module: Currently, the Spark-based hybrid recommendation system primarily implements three common types of recommendation algorithms: CF recommendation algorithms, model-based recommendation algorithms, and content-based recommendation algorithms. While these three types of algorithms cover most everyday use cases, they may not fully meet the recommendation needs in scenarios involving demographic information, geographical location, and other factors. Therefore, there is room for further enhancement of the algorithm library in the Spark-based hybrid recommendation system.

Optimizing recommendation results: The Spark-based hybrid recommendation results are generated using cross-harmonization, which involves taking the Top-N results from various recommendation algorithms to form a hybrid recommendation list. While cross-harmonization is a simple and practical approach, it may lack interpretability in the resulting recommendations. Therefore, further optimization of hybrid recommendation results is needed.

Introducing a real-time recommendation module: Despite the efficiency improvement brought about by Spark's in-memory computing, the Spark-based hybrid recommendation system may still not meet the requirements of applications that demand real-time recommendations, such as ride-sharing apps and restaurant review platforms. Therefore, the next step should involve building a real-time recommendation module to cater to a wider range of scenarios.

References

1. Lisa W. *Personalized Information Recommendation Based on Stochastic Wandering Model*. Dalian: Dalian University of Technology, 2011.
2. China Internet Network Information Center. The 39th Statistical Report on China's Internet Development [R/OL]. (2017-01-22)[2023-08-14]. https://cnnic.cn/n4/2022/0401/c88-1121.html.
3. Chen X., Fan X. Exploring the structure and principle of Yahoo's classification system. *Library and Intelligence Work*, 1999 (9): 33–36.
4. Hua, B. Google search engine technology realization. *Modern Library Information Technology*, 2004, S1: 40–43.

5. Adomavicius G., Tuzhilin A. Toward the next generation of recommendation systems: A survey of the state-of-the-art and possible extensions. *IEEE Transactions on Knowledge and Data Engineering*, 2005, 17(6): 734–749.

6. Resnick P. An open architecture for collaborative filtering of netnews. *Proceedings of CSCW'94*. New York, NY, 1994.

7. Joachims T., Freitag D., Mitchell T. Webwatcher: A tour guide for the world wide web. *Proceedings of International Joint Conference on Artificial Intelligence*. Nagoya, 1997: 770–777.

8. Zhang Y.F. Recommendation System Research Report and Overview. (2013-04-02) [2023-08-14]. https://www.yongfeng.me/attach/rs-survey-zhang.pdf.

9. Koren Y. The Bellkor solution to the Netflix grand prize. *Netflix Prize Documentation*, 2009, 81(2009): 1–10.

10. Zhou J., Xiong Z., Li X., Liu X., Zhang Y., Lv G. Hybrid recommendation system for smart devices and its method: 201210253651.2 [P]. 2014-02-12.

11. Aslanian E., Radmanesh M., Jalili M. Hybrid recommendation systems based on content feature relationship. *IEEE Transactions on Industrial Informatics*, 2016. doi: 10.1109/TII.2016.2631138.

12. Strub F., Mary J., Gaudel R. Hybrid collaborative filtering with autoencoders. arXiv preprint arXiv:1603.00806, 2016.

13. Yang Z. Research and Implementation of Distributed Column Storage Technology for Data Warehouse. Kunming: Kunming University of Science and Technology, 2012.

14. Zaharia M., Chowdhury M., Das T., et al. Resilient distributed datasets: a Fault-Tolerant abstraction for In-Memory cluster computing. *9th USENIX Symposium on Networked Systems Design and Implementation (NSDI 12)*. Berkeley, CA, 2012: 15–28.

15. Zaharia M., Das T., Li H., et al. Discretized streams: an efficient and Fault-Tolerant model for stream processing on large clusters. *4th USENIX Workshop on Hot Topics in Cloud Computing (HotCloud 12)*. Berkeley, CA, 2012.

16. Meng X., Bradley J., Yavuz B., et al. Mllib: Machine learning in apache spark. *The Journal of Machine Learning Research*, 2016, 17(1): 1235–1241.

17. Xin R. S., Gonzalez J. E., Franklin M. J., et al. Graphx: A resilient distributed graph system on spark. *First International Workshop on Graph Data Management Experiences and Systems*. New York, NY, 2013: 1–6.

18. Ray Core [EB/OL]. (2016-08-07)[2023-08-14]. https://github.com/amplab/ray-core.

19. E- MapReduce [EB/OL]. (2023-02-16)[2023-08-14]. https://help.aliyun.com/product/28066.html.

20. FusionInsight [EB/OL] (2018-01-01) [2023-08-14]. https://www.huaweicloud.com/product/FusionInsight.html.

21. Zaharia M., Chowdhury M., Franklin M. J., et al. Spark: Cluster computing with working sets. *2nd USENIX Workshop on Hot Topics in Cloud Computing (HotCloud 10)*. Berkeley, CA, 2010.

22. Li H., Ghodsi A., Zaharia M., et al. Tachyon: Reliable, memory speed storage for cluster computing frameworks. *Proceedings of the ACM Symposium on Cloud Computing*. New York, NY, 2014: 1–15.

23. Shvachko K., Kuang H., Radia S., et al. The Hadoop distributed file system. *2010 IEEE 26th Symposium on Mass Storage Systems and Technologies (MSST)*. IEEE, Washington, DC, 2010: 1–10.

24. Armbrust M., Xin R. S., Lian C., et al. Spark sql: Relational data processing in spark. *Proceedings of the 2015 ACM SIGMOD International Conference on Management of Data*. New York, NY, 2015: 1383–1394.
25. Wang, J. L. *Big Data Spark Enterprise Level Practice*. Beijing: Electronic Industry Press, 2015.
26. Song G. Research and Implementation of Recommendation System Based on Mahout, Hadoop. Changjiang University, 2016.
27. Xiang L. *Recommendation system practice*. Beijing: People's Posts and Telecommunications Press, 2012.
28. Goldberg D., Nichols D., Oki B. M., et al. Using collaborative filtering to weave an information tapestry. *Communications of the ACM*, 1992, 35(12): 61–70.
29. Ye J. Research on Personalized Recommendation Technology Introducing Policy Preferences. Southeast University, 2016.
30. Nie S. Design & Implementation of Intelligent Dating Website Based on Content Recommendation/Collaborative Filtering Recommendation Algorithm. Central China Normal University, 2015.

5

Hardware Customization for Clustering Algorithms

5.1 Hardware Customization of Clustering Algorithms

Clustering algorithms, as a category of unsupervised machine learning algorithms [1], are widely applied in various domains, such as market research, pattern recognition, data mining, image processing, customer segmentation, and web document classification [2]. According to the different division methods, the commonly used clustering algorithms can be divided into the following categories: division methods, hierarchical methods, density-based methods, grid-based methods, and model-based methods [3–5]. It is necessary to use different clustering algorithms for analysis to achieve optimal clustering results in different application domains and dealing with different types of data. For instance, the K-means algorithm [6], known for its simplicity and fast runtime, can handle data with spherical distribution well. However, when dealing with irregularly distributed data, especially data sets with significant noise, the K-means algorithm often fails to meet people's needs. In such cases, the DBSCAN algorithm [7] can achieve better clustering results. Overall, a variety of clustering algorithms are widely utilized in different application domains.

With the rapid development of the internet and e-commerce, there has been an exponential growth in the volume of data collected, accumulated, and urgently needing processing across various industries [8]. As a result, the scale and dimensions of data have been continuously expanding. The massive and high-dimensional data greatly reduces the efficiency of clustering analysis and seriously restricts the development of various industries. Especially in this high-speed development of the information age, the speed of information extraction has become a key factor affecting success. Given the widespread application of clustering algorithms and the significance of information extraction speed, the acceleration of clustering algorithms holds great significance and has become an urgent need in today's society.

DOI: 10.1201/9780429355080-5

Currently, there are two main platforms for accelerating clustering algorithms: cloud computing platforms and hardware acceleration platforms. Cloud computing platforms often employ frameworks and tools such as Hadoop or Spark to partition functions and data sets for the application. The partitioned tasks or data are then distributed to each PC node, where they are processed, and the results are returned to the host machine. Hardware acceleration platforms primarily consist of graphics processing units (GPUs), field-programmable gate arrays (FPGAs), and application-specific integrated circuits (ASICs). These platforms take advantage of the hardware's fast speed and use hardware instead of software or central processing units (CPUs) to implement specific functional logic. Additionally, a large number of built-in hardware logic components allow hardware acceleration to better accelerate algorithm execution in a parallel and streaming manner. Within hardware acceleration platforms, GPUs, FPGAs, and ASICs each have their own characteristics and application domains. GPUs are mainly used in the field of graphics processing, which have a large number of parallel processing units and utilize the mode of data-level parallelism to accelerate the execution of a variety of applications, such as matrix multiplication and image processing. However, due to the presence of a large number of parallel devices and their support for general-purpose and flexible computing, GPUs have higher power consumption compared to FPGAs. ASICs are specialized integrated circuits suitable for customized circuit acceleration, offering high speed but lacking flexibility and reconfigurability. FPGAs are favored for their stability, relatively low cost, high degree of parallelism, and reconfigurability. They have gained popularity for accelerating various applications. Its hardware characteristics also make it an ideal platform for customizing clustering algorithms.

5.2 Clustering Algorithm Details

The clustering algorithm [9] is an unsupervised type of algorithm commonly used in machine learning and data mining. It is a division of the original data set. The similar data objects are divided into a cluster so that the data objects in one cluster have a high degree of similarity and the data objects in different clusters have significant differences [10].

5.2.1 K-Means Algorithm

The K-Means algorithm is the simplest and most widely used of all clustering algorithms [11]. Algorithm Input: The data set to be divided $D = (d_1, d_2, d_3 ..., d_n)$; cluster of labels $C = (c_1, c_2, c_3 ..., c_k)$; $d_i (1 \leq i \leq n)$ represents a data object; and

$c_t (1 \le t \le k)$ represents a cluster label. Algorithm Output: The set of cluster labels corresponding to the data object $ID = (id_1, id_2, id_3 ..., id_n)$, id_t $(1 \le t \le n)$ represents the cluster number of the cluster which contains data object dt, the range of idt is $C = \{c_1, c_2, c_3 ..., c_k\}$. The basic principle of the algorithm is as follows:

1. Arbitrarily select the K data objects in the original data set in the original data set as the center of the original cluster, and give it a different label c_t to represent different clusters.
2. For each data object d_i in the original data set, do the following:
   a. Calculate the distance between d_i and all clusters.
   b. Find the minimum value of the distance value from operation a), find the cluster number of the center of the cluster to which the distance value corresponds, and then divide the data object d_i into the specified cluster.
3. Do the following for each cluster:
   a. Summarize the sum of each data object in the cluster.
   b. Divide the summarized sum value in (a) by the number of data objects in the cluster and the resulting data is the new center of the cluster.
4. Repeat steps 2 and 3 until the number of iterations reaches the convergence threshold or the data object in the cluster no longer changes.

From the principles of the K-means algorithm outlined above, it is evident that the algorithm is simple and efficient, and minimizes the sum of squared errors for the K clusters. However, the algorithm also has several shortcomings: (1) The algorithm requires prior knowledge of the number of clusters into which the data objects should be divided. In real life, many applications are not aware of the number of clusters. (2) The algorithm relies on setting initial cluster centers. If the selection of cluster centers is inappropriate, the overall results of the algorithm may be suboptimal. (3) The algorithm uses the arithmetic mean when updating the clusters, which is not very sensitive to the effect of noise and isolated points and will lead to less-than-ideal clustering. (4) While the algorithm performs well with data distributed in a spherical manner, it yields poor results for data sets with irregular distributions.

5.2.2 K-Mediod Algorithm

Another clustering algorithm, the K-Medoid algorithm [12], also known as the Partitioning Around Medoid (PAM) algorithm, is proposed based on the K-means algorithm. The PAM algorithm and the K-means algorithm have similar ideas; the only difference is the operation of updating the center of the cluster. Algorithm Input: The data set to be divided $D = (d_1, d_2, d_3 ..., d_n)$; the set of labeled clusters $C = (c_1, c_2, c_3 ..., c_k)$: $d_i (1 \le i \le n)$ represents a data object; and $c_t (1 \le t \le k)$ represents a cluster label. Algorithm Output: The set of cluster labels corresponding to data objects $ID = (id_1, id_2, id_3 ..., id_n)$; $id_t (1 \le t \le n)$ represents the cluster number of the cluster which contains data object dt; and the range of id_t is $C = \{c_1, c_2, c_3 ..., c_k\}$. The basic principle of the algorithm is as follows:

1. Arbitrarily select K data objects in the original data set as the center of the original cluster and give it a different label c_t to represent different clusters.
2. For each data object d_i in the original data set, do the following:
   a. Calculate the distance between di and all clusters.
   b. Find the minimum value of the K distance values from operation (a), find the cluster number of the center of the cluster to which the distance value corresponds, and then divide the data object di into the specified cluster.
3. Do the following for each cluster c_t :
   a. Do the following for each data object d_t:
      i. Calculate the distance between d_t and c_{t_i}, where c_{t_i} represents the $i-$ th element in cluster c_t
      ii. Accumulate the distance obtained in i.), and get the sum of the distances.
   b. Find the minimum value of the sum of the distances in operation a), and the data object corresponding to this minimum value is the center of the cluster needed for the next iteration.
4. Repeat steps 2 and 3 until the number of iterations reaches the convergence threshold or the data object in the cluster no longer changes.

The PAM algorithm can solve the impact of noise or isolated points, but the algorithm still has the following shortcomings:

1. Since the operation of the center of the cluster is time-consuming, it is not suitable for large data sets.
2. The algorithm requires prior knowledge of the number of clusters into which the data objects should be divided. In real life, many applications are not aware of the number of clusters.
3. Need to set the initial cluster center, but the choice of the center point will affect the final data set clustering results. The clustering analysis of the data of the spherical distribution is more effective, but the clustering effect is very poor for the randomly distributed data set.

5.2.3 SLINK Algorithm

K-means and PAM algorithms are both clustering algorithms based on partitioning strategies, requiring prior knowledge of the number of clusters before conducting cluster analysis. However, in many real-life applications, the number of clusters is unknown. To overcome this limitation, the SLINK algorithm emerged as a viable solution. SLINK algorithm belongs to the hierarchical clustering family, specifically the single-linkage agglomerative hierarchical clustering algorithm [13]. The basic principles of the SLINK algorithm are as follows: Each data object in the data set $D = \{d_1, d_2, d_3 \ldots, d_n\}$ is assigned a cluster label, denoted as set $ID=(id_1, id_2, id_3, \ldots, id_n)$, with a distance threshold R.

1. Compute the distance matrix DM for the data set D. The matrix element, $DM_{s,j}$, represents the distance between data objects d_i and d_j in D, that is, the distance between id_i and id_j. DM is also referred to as the inter-cluster distance matrix.

2. For each row L_i ($0 \le i \le n$, where i is an integer) of the distance matrix DM, find the minimum value in that row and the corresponding column. Store the minimum value in the LineMin[i] array and the index of the corresponding column in the MinNB[i] array. The search for the minimum value in each row starts from the diagonal position and continues to the end of each row.

3. Find the minimum for the LineMin array, assuming it is LineMin[s], the label of the corresponding column of this minimum value is MinNB[s], which means the minimum is the distance between d_s and $d_{\mathrm{MinNB[s]}}$.

4. Modify the LineMin array and the MinNB array: The minimum value in the LineMin is changed to the maximum value of the floating-point type to ensure that it will not be selected at the next minimum value seeking; change values of the elements in MinNB whose value is MinNB[s] to s.

5. Update the distance matrix DM, change the minimum value in the matrix to the maximum value of the floating-point type to prevent the data from being used for the second time, and then update the distance matrix between clusters using the following formula:

$$DM_{s,j} = Min\{DM_{s,j}, DM_{MinNB_s,j}\}, \quad MinNB_s \le j \le n$$

Merge clusters s and MinNB[s] to form a new cluster and update the ID set.

6. Find the minimum value and its corresponding column index for the row s, and store the values in LineMin[s] and MinNB[s]. Repeat steps 3 - 6 until the minimum distance between any two clusters is greater than R.

From the principle of the algorithm, it can be observed that the SLINK algorithm does not require prior knowledge of the number of clusters and there is no requirement for the distribution of the clustered data set. However, compared to the previous two algorithms, the operation of the SLINK algorithm is more time-consuming and the singular values also have an impact on the clustering results.

5.2.4 DBSCAN Algorithm

The DBSCAN algorithm is density based; the basic principle is to find out the region of high-density distribution from the set of data with different density distributions, that is, the region where the distribution of data points is denser, and for the region with sparse density, we call it as segmentation region [14]. The original data objects are classified into three types:

1. Core point data: Points which contain more than min_{num} neighbors within a radius R.
2. Boundary point data: The number of neighbors included in radius R is less than min_{num}, but its distance from one or more core points is less than R.
3. Noise point data: Data objects in the data set that do not belong to the core or boundary point categories. These points have few neighbors, and none of their neighbors are core points.

R and min_{num} are two thresholds that are used to define the high-density region, that is, the area where the radius R contains more than min_{num} data objects centered on a particular point. Algorithm Input: The data set to be clustered $D = (d_1, d_2, d_3 ..., d_n)$, the radius R, the threshold value min_{num} and the label of the cluster corresponding to the data object $C = (-1, -1, -1, ..., -1)$, where $d_i (1 \leq i \leq n)$ represents the data object and -1 means that the data object was not assigned to any cluster before clustering. Algorithm Output: $C = \{c_1, c_2, c_3, ..., c_k\}$, where the elements in C will have many identical values other than -1, representing that these data objects belong to the same cluster. The exact steps of the algorithm are as follows:

1. Calculate the distance matrix DM for the data set D, where $DM_{i,j}$ represents the distance between data objects d_i and d_j.
2. For each row in the DM, count the number of distance values smaller than R. If the count is greater than min_{num}, mark the point as a core point and record its neighbors.
3. Read an unrecognized data in D in sequence, determine whether the data is the core data: if it is the core point, create a cluster label, and add the cluster label to the core point and its neighbor node, and set the processed tag for the data object that has been divided, and then

carry out the operation of step 4; conversely, carry out the operation of step 3, until all the data objects have been processed.

4. Check if the neighboring nodes of a core point are also core points in order:

   a. If a neighboring node is a core point and has not been marked as processed, assign the cluster label to all its neighbors, mark them as processed, and recursively call step 4.

   b. If a neighboring node is not a core point, sequentially check the next neighboring node. If the next neighboring node satisfies condition a), execute operation a). Otherwise, execute operation b) until all neighboring nodes have been evaluated, and then return to the previous recursive call.

5. Repeat operations in steps 3 and 4 until all the data objects in *D* are judged, which means the entire data set has completed density-based clustering.

The algorithm exhibits excellent tolerance to noise and achieves effective clustering results for data sets with arbitrary distributions. However, it has the drawback of being operationally complex, involving recursion, and having a relatively high time complexity.

5.3 Hardware Deployment/Acceleration Customization-Related Work

5.3.1 Introduction to FPGA Acceleration Technology

FPGA, born to solve customized circuits, is the product of the development of programmable devices. It mainly consists of the look-up table, configurable logic block, clock resources and clock management unit, block memory RAM, interconnect resources, dedicated DSP module, input and output blocks, gigabit transceiver, PCI-E module, and XADC module [15]. The main principle of FPGA operation is to set the state of the on-chip RAM, that is, to program the RAM to set different functional logic (Figure 5.1).

FPGA acceleration methods include parallel computing, pipeline design, data locality, and so on. Parallel computing is mainly based on the characteristics of the algorithm and the part of the algorithm that can be parallelized is allocated to different hardware logic units to execute. Parallel computing is categorized into data parallelism and computational parallelism. Data parallelism means that some data in the algorithm are unrelated to each other, and these independent data are assigned to multiple hardware execution units (PEs) with the same logic function for simultaneous computation; computational parallelism means that the data is not divided but directly input into

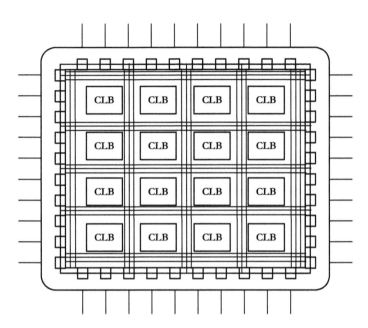

FIGURE 5.1
FPGA basic structure diagram.

a hardware execution unit PE, which itself has the function of parallel computation, such as hardware logic unit addition tree, vector subtraction, and vector multiplication. Pipelining is another commonly used parallel optimization method for FPGAs, where a segment of a functional logic block is partitioned to form multiple logic chunks, and then the time delay of the entire functional logic block is reduced by setting multiple register groups. Ideally, the pipeline will complete the functional logic computation once in each cycle, which enables the FPGA to have a great throughput rate, and the whole acceleration effect will be very considerable. Data locality refers to the characteristics of the algorithm. If there is a locality between the data in the algorithm, the FPGA can internally cache the data to improve data utilization by reducing the number of off-chip accesses to the data and to achieve the purpose of acceleration.

5.3.2 Functional Division of Hardware and Software for Accelerated Systems

This work of this part primarily involves two aspects: (1) divide the acceleration system into hardware and software, and implement the key codes of the algorithms in hardware accelerators; and (2) analyze the functional logic and locality of the key codes of the algorithms, and extract common functional code (common operators). The reason for performing software–hardware partitioning of the acceleration system is that the accelerator must effectively support four clustering algorithms. However, FPGA hardware resources are limited, and it is not feasible to fully implement all four algorithms on the FPGA. Therefore, the focus is on accelerating the key code of the algorithms. The main method is to analyze the more time-consuming key codes in the algorithms through some profiling tools and then implement these key codes on the FPGA side to improve the running efficiency of the whole algorithms. The primary method is analyzing the time-consuming key code in each algorithm through some analysis tools and then achieving these key codes on the FPGA side to improve the efficiency of the entire algorithm. The second aspect of the work is to balance the contradiction between the generality and performance of the accelerator. As the generality of the accelerator increases, its performance is inevitably affected. Due to the limited hardware resources of FPGA, designing specific hardware logic for the hotspots of each algorithm would result in repetitive and wasteful hardware logic for the same code functionality. By extracting common functional code and implementing the hardware logic for this common functionality in the accelerator, the shared hardware logic can be utilized among different algorithms. This approach significantly reduces the utilization of FPGA's hardware resources. The saved hardware resources can then be allocated to accelerate other parts of the algorithms, leading to an overall performance improvement of the accelerator. The specific approach involves progressively refining the hotspots of the four algorithms until common functionalities are identified. These refined functionalities are then extracted and serve as the fundamental functional logic units in the accelerator design. At the end of the chapter, the local analysis of the algorithm is given, which reveals the existence of the data in the algorithm and the use of the algorithm for the local use of the data.

5.3.2.1 *Process of Software–Hardware Co-Design*

This chapter mainly uses the combination of hardware and software to achieve a general-purpose acceleration platform for four clustering algorithms. The design of this platform involves two main components: the software subsystem and the hardware accelerator. When the acceleration platform handles the specific application, it will call the particular clustering algorithm through the CPU interface. The algorithm, through the corresponding driver, calls the hardware accelerator to deal with the time-consuming key code. The accelerator accelerates the hot code and returns the calculation result to the CPU. Then the processor continues to run the calculation results until the entire algorithm is completed. The whole acceleration framework is shown in Figure 5.2. The software subsystem design work includes the preparation of accelerator hardware drivers and user-oriented acceleration platform interface design. The design of the hardware accelerator includes the design of the accelerator frame, the choice of the accelerator scheme, the design of the accelerator instruction set, and the implementation of the slicing technology. From Figure 5.2, it is evident that the runtime library contains three important interfaces: the acceleration system interface, the intellectual property (IP) core interface, and the direct memory access (DMA) interface. First, the acceleration system interface calls the IP core interface to start the hardware accelerator, then the acceleration system interface calls the DMA interface to transfer data into the accelerator, and finally, the accelerator executes the hardware logic to complete the computation.

The implementation of the entire acceleration system is achieved through collaborative software and hardware processing. Figure 5.3 illustrates the complete flow of the accelerator's software and hardware design, with detailed steps outlined in Ref. [16].

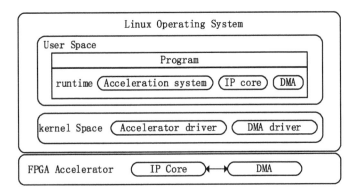

FIGURE 5.2
The overall framework of the acceleration platform.

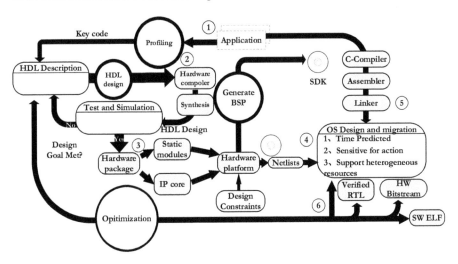

FIGURE 5.3
The process of accelerator software and hardware co-design.

Based on the above collaborative hardware and software design process, the concrete steps of the whole process of the accelerator hardware and software design are as follows:

1. Find out the key code of the clustering algorithm through the technique of hotspot analysis.
2. Refine the functional logic of the algorithm and identify the same functional logic units (common operators).
3. Design the IP Core of the hardware accelerator. This part of the work includes the selection of the acceleration scheme, the design of the instructions, and the implementation of each hardware logic unit.
4. Design and develop the driver program for the accelerator core.
5. Design software subsystems to achieve the cooperative work of hardware and software.
6. Evaluate the performance of the accelerator, acceleration ratio, and energy efficiency ratio.

5.3.2.2 *Hotspot Code Analysis and Hardware and Software Partitioning Results*

This chapter chooses the profile tool to count the running time of each function of the algorithm in Linux. GNU profiler is often used to analyze and test the time of various functions or operations in the Linux program, to find more time-consuming code or function. Figure 5.4 provides the instructions for using the profiler tool, with the source code file being K-means.c. The specific process for hotspot analysis can be found in Ref. [16]. In that article, the time proportions occupied by each function in the algorithm are provided, along with a brief outline of the software and hardware partitioning results for the acceleration system.

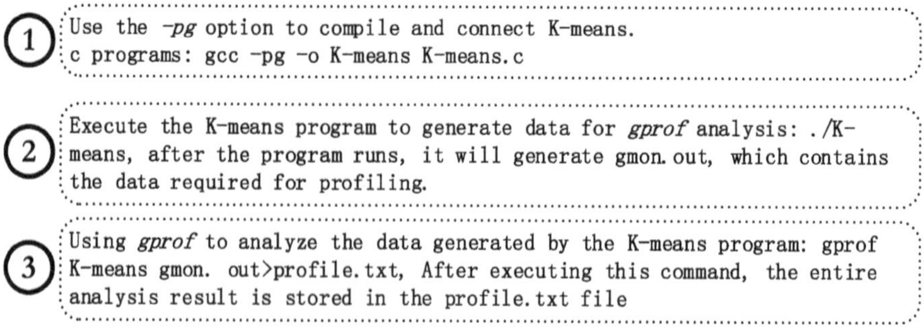

① Use the *-pg* option to compile and connect K-means.
c programs: gcc -pg -o K-means K-means.c

② Execute the K-means program to generate data for *gprof* analysis: ./K-means, after the program runs, it will generate gmon.out, which contains the data required for profiling.

③ Using *gprof* to analyze the data generated by the K-means program: gprof K-means gmon.out>profile.txt, After executing this command, the entire analysis result is stored in the profile.txt file

FIGURE 5.4
Usage of the profiler.

The K-means algorithm is implemented entirely on the FPGA. The PAM algorithm is divided into two parts: the division of clusters and the update operation of clusters. Both are implemented on the FPGA, but they need the cooperative operation of the CPU between each other. This is because the FPGA cannot store large-scale data sets, and the data required for cluster update operations must be transferred from the CPU. In the SLINK algorithm, the operations of updating the distance matrix and finding the minimum value in each row are performed on the CPU. The rest of the algorithms are implemented on the FPGA side. For the DBSCAN algorithm, the calculation of the distance matrix is implemented on the FPGA, while other parts of the algorithm are implemented on the CPU.

The flowchart depicted in Figure 5.5a illustrates the collaborative process between the operating system and the accelerator to achieve accelerated performance of the K-means algorithm. The entire process can be outlined as follows:

1. The CPU reads data from the DDR and transfers the data to the Block RAM (BRAM) of the FPGA.

2. The FPGA receives the data and operates distance calculation.

3. Within the FPGA, the operation of finding the minimum value of distances is executed, and the data is partitioned into different clusters.

4. Determine whether the number of iterations to meet the threshold inside the FPGA: If the threshold is met, the Send_Centroid function is executed, transmitting the cluster labels of the data objects to the DDR of the operating system, and the algorithm completes the computation. Conversely, the data objects and the data within the clusters are added, and steps 5 and 6 are performed.

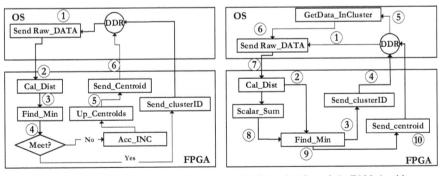

(a) Execution flow of the K-means algorithm   (b) Execution flow of the PAM algorithm

FIGURE 5.5
Collaboration of hardware and software for accelerating the system under (a) K-means and (b) PAM algorithms.

5. Use the average method to update the center of the cluster inside the FPGA.

6. FPGA transfers the new center point to Double Data Rate (DDR) under the operating system. This is an iteration of the algorithm. Then repeat steps 1 – 6.

Figure 5.5b gives a flowchart of the collaboration between the operating system and accelerator to accelerate the PAM algorithm. The whole steps are as follows:

1. The CPU reads data from the DDR and transfers the data to the BRAM of the FPGA.

2. The FPGA receives the data and operates distance calculation.

3. Within the FPGA, the operation of finding the minimum value of distances is executed, and the data is partitioned into different clusters.

4. The FPGA transfers the results of the computation to the DDR of the operating system.

5. The CPU under the operating system reads data from the DDR and counts the data objects in each cluster.

6. The CPU transfers the data objects in each cluster to the inside of the FPGA.

7. The FPGA receives the data and operates distance calculation.

8. The distance accumulation operation is performed inside the FPGA.

9. FPGA finds the smallest element from the array of cumulative sums that is the new centroid of that cluster.

10. Transferring information about the centroid of each cluster into the DDR to complete one iteration of the algorithm's operation and then the operations in steps 1 – 10 are iterated until the number of iterations reaches the convergent threshold.

The flowchart presented in Figure 5.6a illustrates the collaborative process between the operating system and the accelerator to achieve the accelerated performance of the DBSCAN algorithm. The entire process can be outlined as follows:

1. The CPU reads data from the DDR and transfers the data to the BRAM of the FPGA.

2. FPGA receives the data and operates distance calculation.

3. Transfer the calculated distance matrix to the DDR.

4. The CPU gets the distance matrix from the DDR and counts the core point data.

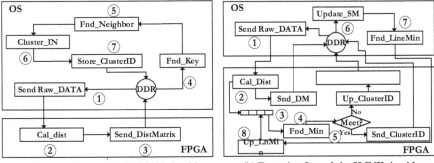

(a) Execution flow of the DBSCAM algorithm   (b) Execution flow of the SLINK algorithm

FIGURE 5.6
Collaboration of hardware and software for accelerating the system under (a) DBSCAN and (b) SLINK algorithms.

5. Count the neighboring nodes of the core point.

6. Operate clustering to complete the division of data objects.

7. Store the result of clustering in DDR.

The processing flowchart depicted in Figure 5.6b outlines the collaborative process between the CPU and FPGA in the SLINK algorithm. The overall processing flow can be summarized as follows:

1. The CPU reads data from the DDR and transfers the data to the BRAM of the FPGA.

2. FPGA receives the data and operates distance calculation.

3. Transfer the calculated distance matrix to the DDR.

4. FPGA internally looks up the minimum value within the row minimum array.

5. Determine whether this minimum value satisfies the stop condition, if so, execute the Send_ClusterlD function to transfer the label of the cluster of the data object to the DDR; otherwise, execute the Up_ClusterlD and Send Clustered_Info functions, and then execute steps 6 – 8.

6. The CPU gets the information about the clusters from the DDR and updates the distance matrix of the clusters.

7. Calculate the minimum value of the row to be updated and transfer the data inside the FPGA.

8. The FPGA internally performs the update operation of the minimum value of the row and repeats the operations in steps 4 – 8.

5.3.2.3 Extraction of the Same Code and Locality Analysis

1. Extraction of the same code

    The results of the hardware and software partition of the acceleration system are given in Figures 5.5 and 5.6. To utilize the hardware resources more effectively to improve the performance of the accelerator, the key codes of the four algorithms need to be analyzed and refined to extract the same functional logic units (common operators). Table 5.1 presents the refined functional logic units extracted from the key codes of the four algorithms: Vector_Sub, Vector_Fab, Vector_Mul, Scalar_Sum, Find_Min, Vector_Add, Vector_Div, SQRT, and Up_Vector. The corresponding operations are as follows: vector subtraction operation, vector absolute value operation, vector multiplication operation, scalar summation operation, minimum value search operation, vector addition operation, vector division operation, square root operation, and vector update operation.

    From Figures 5.5 and 5.6, we can see that the same functional logic of each algorithm is distance calculation and finding of the minimum value. Due to the adoption of both Manhattan and Euclidean distance calculations, which share common functionality in their similarity metric computations, a more granular refinement was conducted when extracting common operators. This finer-grained refinement specifically addresses the distance calculation aspect, as depicted in Table 5.1. The Manhattan formula contains vector subtraction, vector absolute value, and scalar summation. The Euclid formula contains vector subtraction, vector multiplication, scalar summation, and the square operation. Indeed, this finer-grained partitioning facilitates the sharing of hardware logic not only among different algorithms but also between the two similarity metrics within each algorithm. As a result, the utilization of hardware resources is significantly enhanced. Distance calculation is a common and critical component shared among the four algorithms, making it a priority for acceleration. Given its significance, for the unique functional logic units present in each algorithm, the accelerator must devise dedicated hardware logic units specific to each algorithm's requirements.

TABLE 5.1

Functional Logic Units after Key Code Refinement for the Four Algorithms

Arithmetic	Functional Logic Unit
K-means	Vector_Sub, Vector_Fab, Vector_Mul, Scalar_Sum, Find_Min, Vector_add, Vector_Div, SQRT
PAM	Vector_Sub, Vector_Fab, Vector_Mul, Scalar_Sum, Find_Min, SQRT
SLINK	Vector_Sub, Vector_Fab, Vector_Mul, Scalar_Sum, Find_Min, Up_Vector, SQRT
DBSCAN	Vector_Sub, Vector_Fab, Vector_Mul, Scalar_Sum, SQRT

2. Locality analysis

By analyzing we know that calculating the distance is the functional logic common to all algorithms and is a very time-consuming key code. In this regard, we give a local analysis of the distance calculation and will discuss optimization techniques in Chapter 4. The distance calculation operation in the K-means and PAM algorithms refers to the distance calculation between n data objects and the centroids of m clusters, while the distance calculation in the DBSCAN and SLINK algorithms is the calculation of the distance between pairs of data objects. While there may be differences in the data objects used in these four algorithms, they share the same data type. Hence, it is feasible to store the data for all four algorithms in a single array, eliminating the need for separate data storage for each algorithm. On the FPGA side, two vector arrays can be utilized for storage, minimizing the usage of hardware resources for data storage and providing a foundation for optimizing the functional logic.

Algorithm 5.1 Pseudocode for the Cluster Division Operation in the K-Means Algorithm

Algorithm 5.1 Original Distance Calculation Algorithm

Input: N is the Data Size

Input: M is the Number of Clusters

Output: Dist[X,Y] denotes the Distance Array

1: **for** i<-0 to N **do**

2: **for** j<-0 to M **do**

3: Read_Obj(I;&Objects[i])

4: Read_Means(j;&Centroid[j])

5: Dist[i;j] = Dist_Cal(Objects[i]; Means[j])

6: **end for**

7: **end for**

As evident from Algorithm 5.1, the data corresponding to each cluster centroid is repeatedly utilized N times. However, FPGA's hardware resources are limited, and at times, the number of clusters (m) can be quite large. It is not feasible to store all the data in BRAM due to resource constraints, resulting in the majority of the data being stored off-chip. Since each data object in the code is associated with m clusters, multiple off-chip memory accesses are required when processing each data object. This leads to the bandwidth of data transfer becoming a bottleneck in accelerating the performance of the accelerator. The original code structure fails to effectively utilize the principle of data locality, as the data are evicted without being cached, resulting in excessive off-chip memory accesses. In the subsequent sections of this chapter, we propose a solution using partitioning techniques to address the issue of frequent off-chip memory accesses, thus leveraging the benefits of caching data.

5.3.3 Introduction to the Framework Structure of the Accelerator

5.3.3.1 Basic Framework for the Accelerator

The simplest approach to implement four algorithms using FPGA is to directly hardware-harden them. However, this method significantly reduces the flexibility and scalability of the accelerator. If the key code of a certain algorithm is the same as the four algorithms or only has a small difference, it becomes necessary to redesign a new accelerator. In this chapter, we adopt the approach of designing an instruction set for the accelerator to achieve acceleration of four distinct algorithms. By executing extended instructions' semantics on the FPGA side, the corresponding hardware logic for each algorithm is implemented. The functionality of the algorithms is achieved through the process of instruction execution. This approach significantly enhances the flexibility of the accelerator. If a particular application can solve the problem by reorganizing the instruction set, then it only needs to input some corresponding instruction sets. The accelerator will then read the instructions, decode them, and execute the corresponding operations.

Figure 5.7 illustrates the fundamental structure of the entire acceleration platform, which primarily consists of a CPU, DDR, control unit, execution unit of the accelerator, DMA, and instruction cache, among others. The CPU

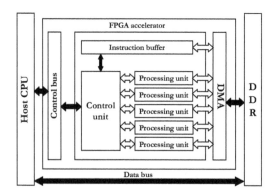

FIGURE 5.7
The overall framework of the accelerator.

is responsible for facilitating communication with the hardware accelerator, enabling collaborative acceleration of the entire algorithm. DDR acts as a bridge for data exchange between software and hardware. The accelerator utilizes DMA to transfer data from DDR to the FPGA internally. The FPGA then transfers the computed results back to DDR through DMA. The CPU reads data from DDR via the data bus and performs computations. The accelerator's controller primarily manages instruction retrieval and execution. The instruction cache stores the set of instructions transferred from DDR via DMA. The execution unit comprises hardware logic units corresponding to each instruction and their respective memory storage units. The entire accelerator operates in SIMD (Single Instruction, Multiple Data) mode, meaning that the same instruction operation is executed on different input data sets. Each execution unit consists of identical hardware logic, and the execution units work in complete parallelism. The number of execution units is limited by the hardware resources of the experimental platform. Once the accelerator is initiated, the CPU utilizes DMA to transfer the instruction set from DDR to the instruction cache in the FPGA. The controller then sequentially reads instructions from the instruction cache and executes the corresponding hardware logic functions, such as data loading, vector subtraction, vector summation, and data storage operations. The accelerator functions like a processor, completing the algorithm's functionality by fetching instructions, decoding them, and executing the specific instruction set.

5.3.3.2 The Internal Structure of the Execution Unit

The core of the accelerator is its execution unit, and this section provides an introduction to the internal structure of the accelerator's execution unit. As depicted in Figure 5.8, the execution unit comprises two main components: a memory storage module and a functional hardware logic module. The execution unit has three input arrays and two output arrays for memory storage: Objects is a two-dimensional array to store the data objects to be divided;

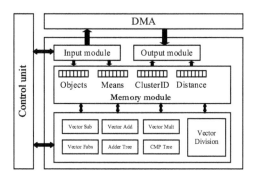

FIGURE 5.8
Internal structure of accelerator execution unit.

Means is a two-dimensional array to store the center points of the clusters; ClustedID is a one-dimensional array to store the labels of the clusters in which the data objects are located; and Distance is a one-dimensional array to store the distances between the points. There are some other memory units in the design, such as Para, a parameter array for storing data set information, and a temporary array for storing intermediate results.

The hardware logic corresponding to the instruction set is divided into two parts: the I/O instruction hardware logic unit and the computation hardware logic unit. The I/O instructions consist of an input module and an output module. The former encompasses various instructions for data loading, while the latter includes instructions for data storage. The computation instructions include vector subtraction, vector multiplication, vector absolute value, vector addition, scalar array summation, finding the minimum value of an array, vector division, and other operations.

The execution flow of the whole execution unit is as follows: (1) The controller reads the first instruction from the instruction cache: Load instruction. (2) The controller decodes and executes the hardware logic corresponding to the instruction, that is, it reads the data from the DDR to the specified on-chip array by calling DMA through the corresponding hardware logic unit in the input module. (3) The controller reads the instruction from the instruction cache. (4) The controller decodes and executes the hardware logic corresponding to the instruction. (5) The controller repeats the operations in (3) and (4) until it finally reads the last instruction from the instruction cache: the Store instruction; then it decodes and calls the corresponding hardware logic unit in the output module to output the computation result from the on-chip to the off-chip DDR via DMA.

5.3.3.3 Selection of Acceleration Schemes

From the analysis of the hotspots in the algorithms, it is evident that distance calculation constitutes a significant proportion of all four algorithms. Therefore, accelerating the computation of distances between n A-type data points and m B-type data points is particularly important. Currently, there are two main schemes for accelerating this part of the code. One acceleration scheme is to employ parallelism when calculating the distances between each A-type data object and all B-type data objects and the other scheme is to use a streaming approach. In this section, we will provide a brief overview of these two acceleration schemes, highlighting their respective advantages and disadvantages. Subsequently, we will present the chosen approach for this chapter.

1. *Parallel Acceleration Scheme*:
    Figure 5.9 illustrates the specific design of the parallel acceleration scheme, where multiple processing units (PEs) can execute in parallel with each other, and the functions of the PEs are all the same.

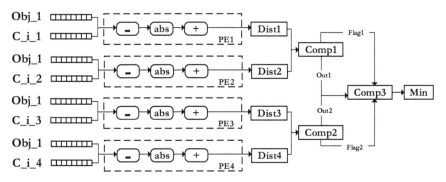

FIGURE 5.9
Schematic diagram of parallel scheme for distance calculation.

Each PE is divided into three stages: the first stage is a subtraction operation, the second stage is an absolute value operation, and the third stage is an addition operation. By sequentially executing the three stages, the distance calculation operations for a single dimension can be completed. Through pipelining, each PE can accumulate the calculations on each dimension, thereby accomplishing the point-to-point distance calculation. Additionally, the parallel operations of multiple PEs can handle the distance calculation between a data object and multiple cluster centroid points.

Due to the large size of the data being processed, it is not feasible to store the data in register format within the FPGA. Instead, the data need to be stored in BRAM. However, BRAM supports only two-port read/write operations per cycle. Therefore, to achieve parallel computation between a data object and multiple cluster centroid points, it is necessary to replicate multiple copies of the same data object. This additional overhead of parallel operations is the redundant storage of data. If data object Obj1 needs to perform parallel computation with eight cluster centroid points, it would require storing four copies of Obj1's data in different BRAMs. This approach trades space for time to accelerate the distance calculation between data and multiple cluster centroid points. Suppose the maximum supported parallelism of the accelerator is 32. When the number of clusters exceeds 32, the calculation needs to be performed in batches. Each batch would involve calculating the distances between Obj1 and 32 centroid points, followed by aggregating the results.

2. *Pipelining Acceleration Scheme*:

The principle of the pipelining scheme lies in the utilization of pipelining for distance calculation between a point and all cluster centroid points while employing parallel operations across dimensions for distance calculation between a point and a single cluster centroid. As shown in Figure 5.10, the whole distance calculation is

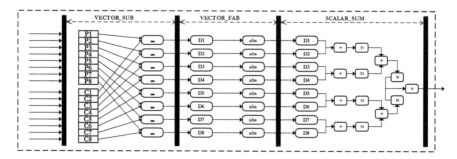

FIGURE 5.10
Schematic diagram of distance calculation for the pipeline scheme.

divided into three stages: the first stage is the subtraction operation of vectors, the second stage is the absolute value operation of vectors, and the third stage is the cumulative operation of scalars, which uses an addition tree to achieve the desired functionality. The three stages are executed sequentially to complete a single point-to-point distance calculation. By implementing a pipelined execution of these three stages, the distance calculation between a data object and all cluster centroid points can be accomplished. In FPGA, the data can be partitioned across different BRAMs based on dimensions, facilitating parallel operations across dimensions. By adding pipelining instructions to these three stages, the proposed design can be achieved. To ensure the desired result of processing one distance calculation per cycle, different arrays are introduced within the addition tree operation. This arrangement ensures that the data sources for each stage of the addition tree are distinct, effectively resolving data dependencies. As can be seen in Figure 5.10, the required hardware logic units include vector subtraction, vector absolute value calculation, and the addition tree operation. Assuming the accelerator supports parallelism of 8, it implies that calculations on eight distinct dimensions can be processed concurrently. Additionally, within each cycle, the data object can complete the calculation operation with one cluster centroid point.

According to Ref. [16], in the era of big data, the number of clusters is generally large. Therefore, considering this aspect, the pipelining approach offers superior acceleration benefits. As the data dimensionality increases, if the accelerator cannot parallelize computations across all dimensions, it becomes necessary to process dimension calculations in batches. However, when using the pipelining approach to compute distances between a point and multiple cluster centroids, the dimension calculations are no longer handled in batches but are parallelized across all dimensions. This can lead to insufficient hardware resources in the FPGA and prevent the accelerator from completing the design. If the pipelining approach is not utilized, the overall acceleration effect is significantly inferior to parallel processing. Based on this, we can conclude two points:

1. For data sets with lower dimensions, the pipelining acceleration approach may be more advantageous compared to parallel
   acceleration.
2. For large-scale data sets, the implementation of pipelining schemes
   becomes impractical, and the design of accelerators faces difficulties.
   In comparison, parallel acceleration schemes emerge as a favorable
   choice. Specifically, parallel schemes exhibit superior adaptability to
   the dimensions of the data when compared to pipelining schemes.

Taking into consideration the balance between the generality and perfor-mance of the accelerator, this chapter chooses the pipelining scheme, which offers superior acceleration effects, for the design. Each of the two schemes has its advantages and disadvantages and the main work of this chapter is to design the corresponding hardware for the pipelining scheme.

5.3.3.4 Implementation of Hardware Logic Units

The chosen acceleration scheme adopts an outer-level computation pipelin-ing approach combined with inner-level dimension parallelism. The acceler-ator design encompasses two primary types of instructions: I/O instructions and computational instructions. To enhance the execution efficiency of the accelerator, the instruction set is intentionally designed without data source and destination addresses. This means that any instruction operation involv-ing data retrieval or storage has fixed addresses and eliminates the need for decoding operations. Consequently, multiple read-and-write instruc-tions targeting different data sources or destination addresses are designed within the I/O instruction category. The computational instructions in the accelerator have pre-defined starting addresses for both the source and des-tination addresses within the FPGA. As the same instruction is repeatedly executed, the source and destination addresses of the computational instruc-tions undergo offsets accordingly. The complete instruction set is shown in Table 5.2.

From the table of the instruction set, we can see five coarse-grained instructions: K-means, PAM _CLU, PAM _UPD, SLINK, and DBSCAN. These instructions are designed to improve the acceleration performance of the acceleration, and each coarse-grained instruction executes a set of instructions in the above table in the process of executing. The function of the algorithm can be accomplished by reading, decoding, and executing the instruction in a single pass, which is much more efficient compared to reading, decod-ing, and executing multiple instructions. In addition, we can achieve accel-eration of algorithms with similar functionalities by transmitting multiple

TABLE 5.2

Instruction Set and Function of Each Instruction

Command Name	Introduction of Command Functions
LOAD_OBJ	Read data from the DMA and load it into the Objects array within the FPGA
LOAD_CLU	Read data from the DMA and load it into the Means array within the FPGA
LOAD_TMP	Read data from the DMA and load it into the TMP array within the FPGA
LOAD_PARA	Read data from the DMA and load it into the PARA array within the FPGA
STORE_TMP	Transferring data from the TMP array to the DDR via DMA
STORE_ID	Transferring data from the ClusterID array to the DDR via DMA
STORE_DIST	Transferring data from the distance array to the DDR via DMA
STORE_LOCA	The subscripts of the two closest clusters are passed to the DDR via DMA
VECTOR_SUB	Vector subtraction operation
VECTOR_FAB	Absolute value operations on vectors
VECTOR_MULT	Multiplication operations on vectors
SCALAR_SUM	Summing scalar arrays
SQRT	Distance open operation
FIND_MIN	Finding the smallest value in an array
CLUSTER_IN	Label the data objects with clusters based on the minimum value of the distance
VECTOR_ADD	Addition operations on vectors
VECTOR_DIV	Division operations on vectors
VECTOR_UP	Update the cluster label, update the row minimum, update the number of positions of the row minimum
K-MEANS	Executing this instruction executes a collection of instructions
PAM_CLU	Executing this instruction executes a collection of instructions
PAM_UPD	Executing this instruction executes a collection of instructions
DBSCAN	Executing this instruction executes a collection of instructions
SLINK	Executing this instruction executes a collection of instructions

instructions. Therefore, this design not only guarantees performance but also enhances the flexibility of the accelerator to a certain extent.

Distance computation is a shared logical function among the four algorithms and constitutes a crucial and time-consuming component. Hence, it should be prioritized as the module for acceleration in our design. In our design, we have incorporated two different similarity measurement standards, namely Manhattan and Euclidean, for distance computation. Consequently, there are two distinct sets of instruction sets corresponding to the respective distance calculation methods.

$$\text{The Manhattan formula: Dists} = \sum_{i-1}^{n} |x_i - y_i|.$$

To implement this formula, only three instructions are required, in the following order: vector subtraction, vector absolute value, and scalar summation. Both vector subtraction and vector absolute value operations are performed in parallel across dimensions, while scalar array summation is achieved using an addition tree. The hardware logic for the entire distance computation is illustrated in Figure 5.11.

Figure 5.11 presents the specific hardware logic for the three instructions: VECTOR_SUB, VECTOR_FAB, and SCALAR_SUM. The data sources for the VECTOR_SUB instruction are the Objects array and the Means array, while the destination data is stored in the vector Dist; the source and destination addresses of the VECTOR_FAB instruction are both the vector Dist; the data source for the SCALAR_SUM instruction is the vector Dist, and the destination data is stored in the Distance array. The dimension of the vector given in the figure is 8. In our design, we have implemented vector subtraction, vector absolute value, and an addition tree at a level of 32. When the data dimensions are smaller than 32, the accelerator will pad some vector dimensions with zeros. Performing vector subtraction, absolute value, and scalar summation operations on zero-filled dimensions does not have any impact. This ensures the correctness of the data computation and serves as the foundation for the adopted pipelined acceleration design approach.

$$\text{Euclid formula: Dists} = \sqrt{\sum_{i=1}^{n}(x_i - y_i)^2}.$$

The implementation of this formula requires the sequential execution of four instructions, VECTOR_SUB, VECTOR_MULT, SCALAR_SUM, and SQRT. Figure 5.12 provides the specific hardware logic design for each instruction, which follows the same principles as Figure 5.11. The only difference is that the second instruction is replaced with VECTOR_MULT instead of VECTOR_FAB. The square root operation is relatively more time-consuming compared to subtraction and multiplication operations. When the vector dimension is low, using the Euclidean formula is more time-consuming compared to the Manhattan formula. When the vector dimension is very large, the square root operation accounts for a very small proportion of the overall computation time during point-to-point distance calculation. On the other hand, the Manhattan formula utilizes an absolute value function, which needs to be applied to each dimension of the vector. Consequently, the

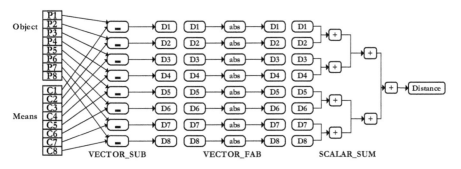

FIGURE 5.11
Hardware logic design with Manhattan computing.

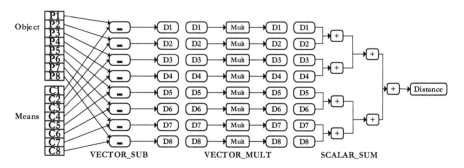

FIGURE 5.12
Hardware logic design with Euclid computing.

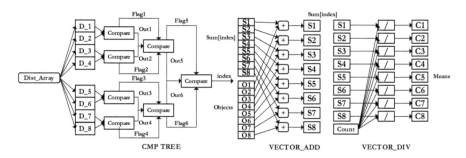

FIGURE 5.13
Hardware implementation of FIND_MIN, VECTOR_ADD, and VECTOR_DIV.

time spent on this operation becomes significant. Therefore, compared to the Euclidean formula, the Manhattan formula is more time-consuming.

Figure 5.13 presents the hardware logic design for the comparison tree, vector addition, and vector division operations. In the FIND_MIN instruction, the first step is to determine the number of data elements in the array to be sorted. Then, the CMP_TREE is used in batches to process the data, and the final comparison result is obtained. The data source for the FIND_MIN instruction is the Distance array, and the destination data is stored in the register index. The VECTOR_ADD instruction performs the accumulation operation on vectors. Once the data is divided into a cluster, the VECTOR_ADD instruction is used to execute the accumulation operation. The VECTOR_ADD instruction takes a two-dimensional array, Objects, and sum as input data, and stores the output data in the two-dimensional array, sum. Once all the data is partitioned, the sum array will contain the accumulated sum of the data vectors for each cluster. This sum array serves as one of the data sources for the VECTOR_DIV instruction. After executing the VECTOR_DIV instruction, the result is stored in the Means array, which represents the new cluster centroids required for the next iteration operation.

Table 5.3 provides the sets of fine-grained instructions used by each coarse-grained instruction. The coarse-grained instructions are a collection

TABLE 5.3

Instruction Sets Corresponding to Coarse-Grained Instructions

Coarse-Grained Instruction	Instruction Set Used
K-MEANS	vector_sub, vector_fab, vector_mult, scalar_sum, find_min, vector_add, vector_div, sqrt
PAM_CLU	vector_sub, vector_fab, vector_mult, scalar_sum, find_min, sqrt
PAM_UPD	vector_sub, vector_fab, vector_mult, scalar_sum, find_min, sqrt
SLINK	vector_sub, vector_fab, vector_mult, scalar_sum, find_min, vector_upd, sqrt
DBSCAN	vector_sub, vector_fab, vector_mult, scalar_sum, sqrt

of fine-grained instructions that correspond to the key code of the algorithm. This design eliminates the need to read and decode many fine-grained instructions, thereby improving the performance of the accelerator to some extent. In addition to the listed fine-grained instructions, the execution of the five coarse instructions may also involve simple Arithmetic Logic Unit (ALU) operations such as addition, subtraction, and comparison operations.

5.3.3.5 Solution for Frequent Off-Chip Access to Storage

From the analysis of algorithm locality, it is evident that when calculating the distance matrix, the limited hardware resources prevent storing all the data on-chip. Consequently, frequent off-chip memory accesses are inevitable. Moreover, the speed of transferring data from off-chip to on-chip is slow, which makes the bandwidth a limiting factor in the acceleration performance of the accelerator. To solve the problem, we propose a technique, tile, to minimize the occurrence of off-chip accesses. The original distance calculation is shown in Code 5.1, where each data object needs to calculate the distance with all the centroids in sequence, that is, each data object is associated with all the centroids. Assuming there are $N=60,000$ data points and $m=600$ clusters and the FPGA can only store 100 center points internally, the original code structure would lead to 6 off-chip memory accesses for each data partition operation. Therefore, the N data points would require a total of $60,000 \times 6 = 360,000$ off-chip memory accesses, with each access involving reading the center point data for 100 clusters. Indeed, such frequent off-chip memory accesses inevitably impact the acceleration performance of the accelerator and become a bottleneck for performance improvement. The original code structure leads to the centroid data stored inside the FPGA being swapped out without being reused. This means that the locality of the data is not utilized effectively. If the data stored internally in the FPGA is reused before being overwritten, the number of off-chip memory accesses can be reduced. This is because the algorithm itself determines the number of times each cluster center point is used, and if the on-chip data is effectively reused before being replaced, the frequency of data retrieval from off-chip memory decreases. To fully exploit the data locality of the algorithm, we use the technique of tiling.

From Algorithm 5.2, it can be observed that the tiling technique involves partitioning the N data objects and m center points into blocks of a certain size. Each computation is performed on a block-by-block basis, where the center point data within a block is repeatedly used by the data objects within another block. This approach ensures that the entire block of cluster center point data stored in the FPGA is effectively utilized before being overwritten. As a result, the utilization efficiency of on-chip data is significantly improved, reducing the number of data transfers from off-chip to on-chip.

Assuming that the number of cluster centroids that can be stored within the FPGA chip is S and the number of data to be divided is T due to the limitation of hardware resources, the number of off-chip memory accesses generated before and after adopting the Tiled partitioning technique can be expressed as follows: $\text{Num}_1 = \dfrac{N \times m}{S}$ and $\text{Num}_2 = \dfrac{N}{T} \times \dfrac{m}{S}$. From the equation, it can be seen that the number of off-chip visits before tiling is r times higher than that after tiling, and each off-chip visit has to read S data. This shows that the slicing technique does reduce the number of off-chip accesses.

Algorithm 5.2 Pseudocode for Distance Computation after Refactoring Using Tiling Technique

Algorithm 2 Tiled Distance Calculation Algorithm

Input: S is the Block Size of Means Array; T is the Block Size of Objects Array

Output: Dist[X,Y] denotes the Distance Array

1: for i<-0 to N/T do

2: Read_Obj(T, &Objects[i_T])

3: for j<-0 to M/S do

4: Read_Means(j;&Centroid[j])

5: for ii<-i*T to (i+1)*T do

6: for jj<-j*S to (j+1)*S do4.

7: Dist[ii;jj] = Dist_Cal(Objects[ii]; Means[jj])

8: end for

9: end for

10: end for

11: end for

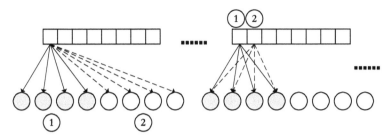

FIGURE 5.14
Execution of the algorithm before and after utilizing the tiling technique.

Figure 5.14 provides a clearer illustration of the principles behind the Tiled partitioning technique. In the diagram, different shapes represent different types of data, while colors represent the data storage methods. The square shapes represent the data to be partitioned, and the circular shapes represent the centroids of the clusters. The gray color represents data stored in the FPGA on-chip memory, while the white color represents data stored off-chip. The original computation method involves calculating the distance between each data point to the centroids of all clusters in a sequential manner. The steps are as follows:

1. Calculate the distance between the data point to be partitioned and the centroid data points stored on-chip.
2. Load the centroid data points of clusters that are not stored on-chip from off-chip memory into on-chip memory through off-chip memory accesses.
3. Repeat steps 1 and 2 until distances are calculated for all centroid data points of the clusters.
4. Repeat the above three steps for each data point to be partitioned.

Since the above steps are performed for each data to be divided, the computation for each data point requires numerous off-chip memory accesses. This frequent off-chip memory access becomes a bottleneck. However, the Tiled partitioning technique effectively addresses this issue. In Tiled partitioning, the center of computation shifts from individual data points to multiple data points, referred to as block-based computation. The overall computation steps are as follows:

1. Calculate the distances between each data point within a block and the centroid data points stored on-chip. Store the distance results temporarily.
2. Load the centroid data points of clusters that are not stored on-chip from off-chip memory into on-chip memory.

3. Repeat steps 1 and 2 until distances are calculated for all centroid data points of the clusters.

4. Load the data to be partitioned, stored off-chip, into on-chip memory in block units. Then, repeat the above three steps for each block until all data points have been partitioned.

5. Due to the block-based nature of Tile technology, the central data within an intra-cluster is fully utilized before it is swapped out which greatly enhances the locality of data usage. In algorithmic implementations, the number of times the central data of all clusters is reused remains constant. However, the utilization of the Tile technique enhances the frequency of reusing cluster center data during off-chip memory access, thereby reducing the number of transfers from off-chip to on-chip for data transmission.

5.4 Chapter Summary

As previously discussed, a wide range of real-world applications require the use of various clustering algorithms, making the acceleration of these algorithms highly necessary. In this chapter, we present a customized hardware acceleration platform solution that supports four types of clustering algorithms: K-means, PAM, SLINK, and DBSCAN. Additionally, the accelerator can employ two different similarity metrics for each algorithm, thereby greatly enhancing the flexibility and versatility of the accelerator. Based on this platform solution, there are still opportunities for further optimization and improvement that readers can explore.

First of all, in terms of data dimension, due to the limited hardware resources of FPGA, the design of the pipelining scheme is used so that the maximum data dimension supported by the accelerator is 32. Applications with data sets exceeding 32 dimensions are no longer supported. In this chapter, an alternative acceleration design approach is proposed, namely the parallel scheme. Although the parallel scheme may not achieve the same level of acceleration as the pipelining approach for data sets with the same dimensionality, it offers a significant extension in terms of supported data dimensionality. Hence, employing the parallel scheme is a favorable choice for applications involving high-dimensional data sets.

Second, the design presented in this chapter is tailored for a single FPGA, which inherently possesses limited hardware resources. This limitation significantly constrains the performance of the accelerator. If the data and functions can be divided and allocated to different FPGAs and the algorithm synchronization and data consistency can be achieved through data transfer between FPGAs, the acceleration performance of the whole accelerator can be greatly improved.

References

1. Lang W., Chen K., Zhang G., Lang W., Chen K., Zhang G.. Research on the application of unsupervised learning in cognitive networks. *Telecommunications Express: Networks and Communications*, 2014 (2): 3–6.
2. Han J., Fan M., Meng X. *Data Mining: Concepts and Techniques*. Beijing: Machinery Industry Press, 2012.
3. Hong Y., Kwong S. Learning assignment order of instances for the constrained k-means clustering algorithm. *IEEE Transactions on Systems, Man, and Cybernetics, Part B (Cybernetics)*, 2008, 39(2): 568–574.
4. He L., Wu L., Cai Y. A review of clustering algorithms in data mining. *Computer Application Research*, 2007, 24(1): 10–13.
5. Sun J., Liu J., Zhao L. Research on clustering algorithm. *Journal of Software*, 2008, 19(1): 48–61.
6. George A. Efficient high-dimension data clustering using constraint-partitioning k-means algorithm. *International Arab Journal of Information Technology*, 2013, 10(5): 467–476.
7. Hwang S., Hanke T., Evans C. Automated extraction of community mobility measures from GPS stream data using temporal DBSCAN. *Computational Science and Its Applications-ICCSA 2013: 13th International Conference*, Ho Chi Minh City, Vietnam, June 24–27, 2013, Proceedings, Part II 13. Springer, Berlin, Heidelberg, 2013: 86–98.
8. Ma C., Zhang H. H., Wang X. Machine learning for big data analytics in plants. *Trends in Plant Science*, 2014, 19(12): 798–808.
9. Zhou T., Lu H. Research progress of clustering algorithm in data mining. *Computer Engineering and Applications*, 2012, 48(12): 100–111.
10. Bai D. Research on the application of data mining in coal comprehensive statistical system. Hebei University of Engineering, 2010.
11. Xiong S., Ji D. Exploiting capacity-constrained k-means clustering for aspect-phrase grouping. *Knowledge Science, Engineering and Management. 8th International Conference, KSEM 2015*, Chongqing, China, October 28–30, 2015, Proceedings 8. Springer International Publishing, 2015: 370–381.
12. Zhang Q., Couloigner I. A new and efficient k-medoid algorithm for spatial clustering. *International Conference on Computational Science and Its Application*. Springer, Berlin, Heidelberg, 2005: 181–189.
13. Zhao Y., Karypis G., Fayyad U. Hierarchical clustering algorithms for document datasets. *Data Mining and Knowledge Discovery*, 2005, 10: 141–168.
14. Arlia D., Coppola M. Experiments in parallel clustering with DBSCAN. *Euro-Par 2001 Parallel Processing: 7th International Euro-Par Conference*, Manchester, UK, August 28–31, 2001 Proceedings 7. Springer, Berlin Heidelberg, 2001: 326–331.
15. He B., *The Definitive Guide to Xilinx FPGA Design*. Beijing: Tsinghua University Press, 2012.
16. Jia F. Research and design of FPGA-based acceleration platform for clustering algorithm. University of Science and Technology of China, 2016.

6

Hardware Accelerator Customization Techniques for Graph Algorithms

6.1 Graph Algorithms Background

6.1.1 Traditional Graph Computation Algorithms

With the gradual maturity and development of big data, cloud computation technology, and the Internet industry, human life has entered the era of data explosion [1]. Big data possesses the distinctive characteristics known as the "4Vs," namely, Volume, Variety, Velocity, and Value [2]. As one of the most classical and commonly used data structures, much of real life's data is often abstracted into multiple graph structures [3]. The vertices in a graph can represent different entities and the edges in a graph can represent the relationships between different entities [4]. Examples of common graph structure data types include social networks, web graphs, transport networks, and genome analysis graphs [5]. Additionally, the scale of graph data has been growing rapidly, for example, in 2011, Twitter Inc. posted more than 2×108 tweets per day [6], while in 2013, that number increased to 5×10^9 tweets per day [7]. As machine learning and data mining applications become more widespread, the scale of graph data has continued to expand. On the other hand, since large-scale graph data exhibits extreme irregularity [8,9], the computation process on traditional MapReduce [10] and Hadoop [11] systems generates a large amount of data communication, which in turn results in computational inefficiency [12]. How to efficiently process and analyze large-scale graph data is currently a major research hotspot in academia and industry. To tackle the aforementioned challenges effectively, many graph computation systems have been proposed for efficient graph data processing, which mainly include distributed graph computation systems, stand-alone graph computation systems, and graph computation accelerators.

For designing graph computation systems based on distributed platforms, there are many representative works in the industry, such as Pregel [13], PowerGraph [14], GraphLab [15], GraphX [16], Giraph [17], Chaos [18], and Gemini [19]. Notably, GraphX has been integrated into Spark [20], offering efficient graph data processing capabilities to users of the Spark platform.

DOI: 10.1201/9780429355080-6

Additionally, Giraph has been adopted by Facebook as a dedicated computational system for handling large-scale social network graph data. During the design process of distributed graph computation systems, researchers often focus on issues such as graph data partitioning, load balancing, data communication, system fault tolerance, and optimization of distributed algorithms. Even though distributed graph computation systems are capable of handling ultra-large-scale graph data, these aforementioned challenges pose significant hurdles for the designers of distributed systems, and for programmers, how to write, debug, and optimize distributed graph algorithms is a considerable difficulty as well. With the continuous improvement of computation and storage resources in single machines, it has become possible to implement large-scale graph data processing on single machines. In recent years, both academia and industry have also turned their attention to the design of single-computer graph computation systems, such as GraphChi [21], X-Stream [22], GridGraph [23], Ligra [24], VENUS [25], AsyncStripe [26], and MOSAIC [27]. Significant progress and breakthroughs have been achieved in the research on stand-alone graph computation systems which utilize traditional general-purpose processors as their computational cores. These systems make it possible for users to complete the processing of larger-scale graph data on their computers.

However, with the continuous advancement in graph computation technology and the rise of heterogeneous technology, researchers find that the traditional general-purpose processors appear to be weak in the face of large-scale, computation-intensive and memory-intensive tasks. As a result, there is a growing interest in accelerating computational tasks through heterogeneous computation. For graph computation, according to the different acceleration platforms, they can be divided into graphics processing unit(GPU)-based graph computation accelerators (e.g., CuSha [28], Medusa [29], Gurirock [30]), application specific integrated circuit(ASIC)-based graph computation accelerators (e.g., Graphicionado [31], Ozdal et al. [32], Tesseract [33], TuNao [34]), and field programmable gate array(FPGA)-based graph computation accelerators (e.g., GraphGen [35], FPGP [36], ForeGraph [37], Zhou et al. [38], GraphOps [39]).

In the design of GPU-based graph computation accelerators, designers often focus on increasing computational parallelism, reducing synchronization overhead among numerous cores, and so on. However, the inherent irregularity of graph-structured data poses new challenges for graph computation on GPUs. Moreover, the large number of computation cores in GPUs leads to relatively high power and energy consumption in the computational platform. For instance, the Nvidia GeForce GTX780 GPU used in CuSha has 2304 computation cores, 3 GB of video memory, and a thermal design power of 250W [40]. The Nvidia Tesla C2050 GPU used in Medusa has 448 CUDA cores, 3 GB of video memory, and a maximum power consumption of 238W. The Nvidia Tesla K40c GPU used in Gunrock features 2880 CUDA cores, 12 GB of video memory, and a power consumption of 235W.

Due to the high computational power consumption of GPU platforms and the low computational efficiency of traditional general-purpose CPUs, researchers have explored the utilization of customized hardware for accelerating graph data processing to improve the computational and access efficiency of graph data processing. Two prominent approaches in this domain involve the use of ASIC-based graph computation accelerators and FPGA-based graph computation accelerators, both of which have lower power consumption. ASIC hardware accelerators are often able to achieve higher efficiency than hardware accelerators on FPGAs because custom ASIC hardware accelerators have a higher computational frequency compared to hardware accelerators on FPGAs. However, ASIC hardware accelerators lack the flexibility that FPGAs offer. Consequently, they exhibit limited adaptability when faced with a wide range of graph processing algorithms. The reconfigurable and programmable nature of FPGAs compensates for this drawback of ASICs. The comprehensive comparison among traditional general-purpose processors, CPUs, GPUs, ASICs, and FPGAs is shown in Figure 6.1.

With the deepening research on novel storage materials, these materials have gradually found applications in graph computation systems. For example, Malicevic et al. [41] argue that traditional dynamic random-access memory (DRAM) cannot keep up with the continuously growing scale of graph data, so they introduced a new type of byte-addressable non-volatile memory (NVM) into graph computation systems and employed a hybrid storage system combining DRAM and NVM to store graph data. The experimental

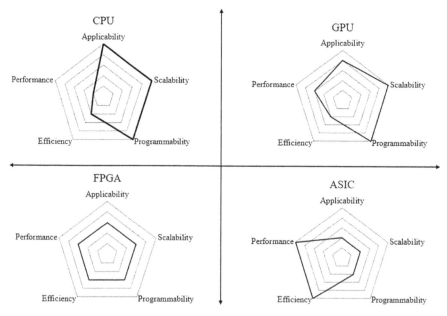

FIGURE 6.1
Comprehensive comparison of CPUs, GPUs, ASICs, and FPGAs.

results have demonstrated significant acceleration compared to the graph computation system using only DRAM or only NVM.

6.1.2 Graph Neural Network Algorithm

In recent years, with the rapid development of artificial intelligence technology, deep neural networks have attracted widespread attention due to their powerful modeling capabilities and have been successfully applied in the fields of natural language processing, image recognition, and so on, such as convolutional neural networks (CNN), long short-term memory (LSTM), and attention mechanism networks (Transformer). The aforementioned networks can only process structured Euclidean spatial data, such as images, text, and speech. However, data in many real-life scenarios are in the form of graph structures, which are considered non-Euclidean spatial data. Unlike image and text data, the local structure of each node in graph data varies. The complexity of graph data poses significant challenges to existing machine learning algorithms due to its irregular nature. Graph data exhibits variations in graph size and node order, and each node in a graph may have a different number of neighboring nodes, making some important operations that are easy to compute in images (e.g., convolution) no longer directly applicable to graphs. Researchers began to focus on constructing neural network models on graphs, which led to the definition and design of a neural network structure, graph neural network (GNN), specifically for graph-structured data processing. By leveraging the modeling capabilities of CNNs for local structures and the inherent node dependencies prevalent in graphs, GNNs ingeniously introduce a method for extracting features from graph-structured data and use the feature information extracted from graph-structured data for classification and prediction. As an emerging deep learning technique for graph data, GNNs have received extensive attention from both industry and academia [42–44]. At the end of 2018, the field of GNNs published three review-type papers at the same time, which is a "coincidence" reflecting the academic recognition of the technique. Subsequently, papers related to GNNs also accounted for a sizable share of the top academic conferences in 2019. According to the latest NeurIPS (CCF-A conference) 2021 paper acceptance keyword statistics, research papers related to GNNs have entered the top three and received widespread attention. As a basic data structure, graphs have been widely studied and applied in the era of big data when combined with deep learning networks [45–47].

The continuous development of GNN algorithms has also driven research in the field of architecture for designing efficient graph application frameworks, and it has become urgent to adapt efficient architectures for upper-layer algorithms. To efficiently execute GNNs, a series of software system frameworks have emerged on general-purpose proces-sors, such as Deep Graph Library (DGL) [48], Pytorch Geometric (PyG) [49], and Neugraph [50]. However, due to the inherent complexity of graph data structures, coupled with the fact that general-purpose processors are carried by fine-grained instructions, generality comes with a performance loss. The actual execution of GNNs on general-purpose processors encoun-ters challenges in terms of computational inefficiency and memory access inefficiency, which are manifested in the form of low cache hit rates and large stop-and-wait overheads in the pipeline. The inherent characteristics of graph data contribute to the inefficiency of GNN program execution on general-purpose processors.

To address the aforementioned issues, some researchers are also exploring the use of heterogeneous computing to accelerate graph deep learning tasks. Designing efficient hardware architectures for these tasks on dedicated pro-cessors presents three main challenges:

Challenge 1: Graph deep learning needs to handle unstructured graph data, which brings unique challenges. The process of graph pro-cessing faces the following three difficulties: (1) Large-scale data: Real-world graph data sets are massive, far exceeding the capacity of on-chip caches, so it is necessary to choose an appropriate slicing strategy; (2) Poor memory locality: Graph structure data is unstruc-tured, and its corresponding adjacency matrix exhibits extreme spar-sity, sometimes reaching as high as 99.9%. This results in random and frequent data accesses, leading to memory access bottlenecks. (3) Load imbalance: Graph data follows a power-law distribution, resulting in highly uneven data distribution. Consequently, load imbalance issues arise during the computation process.

Challenge 2: GNNs contain two main imbalanced workloads, the graph computation phase (aggregation phase) and the neural net-work phase (combination phase). The graph computation phase can be abstracted as a sparse–dense matrix multiplication pattern, while the neural network phase can be abstracted as a general matrix mul-tiplication (GEMM) pattern. Most existing dedicated processors are designed for single workload tasks. For instance [51,52], research has proposed a dedicated processor paradigm for dense applications [53] and has implemented a dedicated accelerator for sparse applica-tions. To realize a dedicated processor for GNNs, it is necessary to support both sparse and dense computation patterns within a single processor. However, the graph computation phase is a visit-intensive application and the neural network phase is a memory-intensive application. Moreover, these two phases also face stop-and-wait overheads during pipelined execution. The two execution processes will face a large amount of stop-and-wait overhead if they are not reasonably scheduled. How to design an efficient dedicated hardware architecture for GNN applications has become a research challenge and deserves further study.

Challenge 3: GNNs have received a lot of attention in various application areas. At the same time, there has been a proliferation of emerging GNN models, ranging from the initial graph convolutional neural network (GCN) to GraphSage networks, and further to graph attention networks (GAT), along with an ongoing development of various other types of networks. Designing an efficient solution that caters to GNN models of different sizes and types, while also ensuring user-friendliness and scalability, poses a significant challenge. Currently, numerous related researches on the design of dedicated accelerators for GNNs have been carried out. These studies can be broadly categorized into two types: two-stage processors and unified processors. In the case of two-stage processors, hardware architectures are separately designed for graph computation and neural network architecture. On the other hand, unified processors employ a unified hardware architecture for both graph computation and neural network tasks.

6.2 Graphical Algorithm Model

In this section, we take traditional graph computation algorithms and graph deep learning algorithms as examples to introduce the model implementation of their algorithms.

6.2.1 Graph Computation Models

Graphs possess strong abstraction and flexibility. Compared with traditional data organizations such as linear tables and hierarchical trees, graphs have stronger representation capabilities in terms of structure and semantics and are one of the most commonly used and important data structures. In reality, a multitude of data exists in the form of graphs. In recent years, with the continuous growth of graph data size, along with the increasing requirements for graph computation capability, a large number of computational systems oriented to graph data processing have been proposed. Large-scale graph data primarily consists of vertices, edges, and weights. During graph data processing, the most common graph computation models are the vertex-centric computation model (vertex-centric) and edge-centric computation model (edge-centric). The following sections will provide separate introductions to each of these models.

6.2.1.1 Vertex-Centric Computation Model

In the field of graph computation, the vertex-centric computation model is widely used in the design and implementation of graph computation systems, such as GraphChi [21], VENUS [25], and Gemini [19], due to its easier implementation and its applicability to various graph algorithms. The computational model is shown in Algorithm 6.1. The vertex-centric computational model divides the processing of graph data into three phases: Gather–Apply–Scatter. The vertex-centric computational model sequentially traverses the vertex set of the graph data, visiting each vertex in the vertex set. For a given vertex, during the Gather phase, this computation model traverses the "in-edges" set of the vertex v and collects the state values of all source vertices pointing to the edges of vertex v. The state values of these adjacent vertices are combined using a certain rule to generate an update value. In the Apply phase, the computation model updates the vertex with the computed update value. In the Scatter phase, the computation model traverses the "out-edges" set of the vertex v and propagates the newly generated update value along its out-edges to all the target vertices. With these steps, the vertex-centric computation model completes the computation for the specific vertex v. A schematic of the vertex-centric computational model is shown in Figure 6.2, which performs sequential access to the vertex set while randomly accessing the vertex's set of edges in a non-sequential manner. From the diagram, the random edge access pattern of this model can also be observed.

Algorithm 6.1 Vertex-Centric Computational Model

1	**for** *each vertex v in* **V do**
2	*Gather:*
3	**for** *each edge e in v.inEdges()* **do**
4	gather **updates** from incoming edges of **v**;
5	**end**
6	*Apply:*
7	Apply **updates** to vertex **v**;
8	*Scatter:*
9	**for** *each edge e in v.outEdges()* **do**
10	scatter the property of vertex v through the outgoing edges of v;
11	**end**
12	**end**

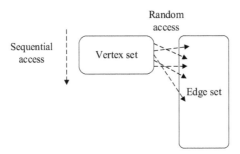

FIGURE 6.2
Schematic of the vertex-centric computational model.

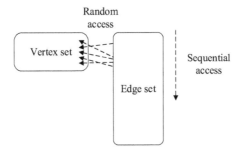

FIGURE 6.3
Schematic of the edge-centric computational model.

6.2.1.2 Edge-Centric Computation Model

The edge-centric computational model is another commonly used computational model in the field of graph computation. This model is well-suited for various types of graph algorithms and has therefore been widely employed in the design and implementation of graph computation systems, such as X-Stream [22], GridGraph [23], and Chaos [18], among others. The edge-centric computational model also divides the processing of the graph data into three phases: EdgeScatter–UpdateGather–Apply. This computational model is shown in Algorithm 6.2. In the EdgeScatter phase, the edge-centric computational model sequentially accesses each edge in the graph data, reads the state values of the source vertices of the edge, generates the update value update, and propagates the update value update to the target vertices of the edge. In the UpdateGather phase, the edge-centric computational model accesses the list of update values and collects those belonging to the same target vertex, denoted as "u.destination." In the Apply phase, the computational model updates the collected update values to the target vertex u.destination. The schematic diagram of the edge-centric computational model is shown in Figure 6.3, which performs sequential access to the set of edges and random access to the set of vertices.

Algorithm 6.2 Edge-Centric Computational Model

  1 **while** *not done* **do**
  2   *EdgeScatter*:
  3   **for** *each edge e in* **E do**
  4   generate and send **updates** over e;
  5   **end**
  6   *UpdateGather*:
  7   **for** *each update **u** in* **updates do**
  8   gather the updates of **u.destination**;
  9   **end**
10   *Apply*:
11   Apply **updates** to **u.destination**;
12 **end**

6.2.1.3 *Other Computation Models*

Some other computational models in the field of graph computation are used in the design and implementation of graph computation systems, such as block-centric computational models and path-centric computational models. The block-centric computational model, as introduced in Refs [54,55], is utilized for graph computation system design. Unlike the vertex-centric model, which uses vertices as the granularity of computation and is considered a fine-grained computational model, the block-centric model offers a coarser granularity. This characteristic enables the reduction of iteration time for graph algorithms, particularly those of the iterative type, requiring multiple rounds of iteration or SuperSteps to achieve convergence for vertex-centric computational models. Literature [56,57] proposed the path-centric graph computation model, to ensure the locality of the graph data and improve the storage efficiency of the graph data. The path-centric computation model divides the graph data based on the tree structure, which ensures the "order" of the data within the subgraphs, and thus improves the data locality. Furthermore, literature [56,57] accessed the graph data sequentially as much as possible to reduce the performance loss caused by random access.

6.2.2 Synchronous and Asynchronous Computation Methods

In the field of graph computation, the computation of graph algorithms can be divided into two categories: synchronous and asynchronous computation methods. Consider a graph $G = (V, E)$, where the set of vertices of the entire graph data is denoted as V, the set of edges as E, the vertices to be computed as u, the set of incoming edges of vertex u as E' ($E' = u.inEdges()$), $E' \in E$. The source vertices of each edge in E' are denoted as $v_1, v_2, ..., v_m$ and the subset of vertices formed by these vertices is denoted V', $V' \in V$.

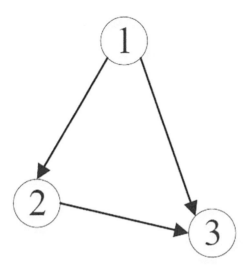

FIGURE 6.4
Example diagram.

In the iterative calculation, the state values of v_1, v_2, ..., v_m during the i-th iteration are denoted as $state^i_{v1}$, $state^i_{v2}$, ..., $state^i_{vm}$. Synchronous computation means that in an iterative type of graph algorithm, the execution of the algorithm is carried out in rounds (iterations), and the updated values generated by the current iteration cannot be used by the current iteration but can only be used during the next iteration, that is, $statei+1u = f(state^i_{v1}, state^i_{v2}, ..., state^i_{vm})$, and f is the update function during the computation. Algorithm 6.3 outlines the pseudocode of the PageRank algorithm in synchronous execution mode. In Figure 6.4, we illustrate the example graph that will be processed by the PageRank algorithm in the upcoming discussion. Subsequently, Figure 6.5 showcases the PageRank algorithm in synchronous execution mode as it operates on the graph depicted in Figure 6.4. From Algorithm 6.3, it can be observed that the PageRank algorithm under synchronous execution mode initializes the oldPageRank of all vertices as 1.0 and the newPageRank as 0.0 during the initial stage. After each round of iteration in the synchronous execution mode of the PageRank algorithm, the new state vector needs to be exchanged with the old state vector, enabling the new state vector to be used in the next iteration. As depicted in Figure 6.5, sumdiff and average_diff serve as indicators to determine the convergence of the algorithm. Their calculation is shown in formulas (6.1) and (6.2):

$$\text{sumdiff} = \sum_{i=1}^{|V|} \left| \text{newPageRank}[i] - \text{oldPageRank}[i] \right| \tag{6.1}$$

$$\text{average\_diff} = \frac{\text{sumdiff}}{|V|} \tag{6.2}$$

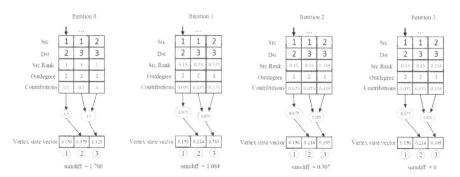

FIGURE 6.5
PageRank algorithm-synchronized execution mode.

In the synchronous execution mode, the PageRank algorithm converges after four iterations. In Figure 6.5, when the PageRank algorithm is executed synchronously, with Iterations set to 3, the value of sumdiff becomes 0. This indicates that the algorithm has reached a converged state.

Algorithm 6.3 PageRank Algorithm in Synchronous Execution Mode

```
 1  vertices ← |V|; edges ← |E|;
 2  inDegree[1,2,..., vertices] = {0,0,...,0};
 3  outDegree[1,2,..., vertices] = {0,0,...,0};
 4  oldPageRank[1,2,..., vertices] = {1.0,1.0,..., 1.0};
 5  newPageRank[1,2,..., vertices] = {0.0,0.0,...,0.0};
 6  temp = 0;
 7  for each edge e[i] in E do
 8      inDegree[e[i].destination]++;
 9      outDegree[e[i].source]++; i++;
10  end
11  while not convergent do
12      for each vertex v in V do
13          Gather:
14          for each edge e[k] in v.inEdges() do
15              temp = temp + oldPageRank[e[k].source] /
                      outDegree[e[k].source];
16          end
17          Apply:
18          newPageRank[v] = 0.15 +0.85 * temp;
19          temp = 0;
20          swap(oldPageRank,newPageRank);
21      end
22  end
```

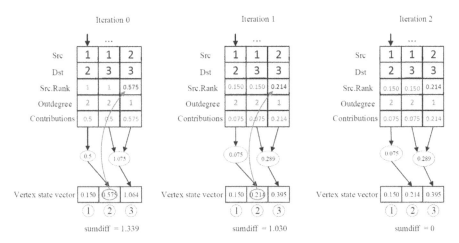

FIGURE 6.6
PageRank algorithm-asynchronous execution mode.

After each iteration, the latest state values obtained from the computations using v_1, v_2, ..., v_m are denoted as $state^{ik1}_{v1}$, $state^{ik2}_{v2}$, ..., $state^{ikm}_{vm}$. The previous explanation outlined the synchronous computation mode, whereas asynchronous computation refers to a scenario in iterative graph algorithms where the update function selects the most recent state values of v_1, v_2, ..., v_m as inputs for computation, that is, $state^{i+1}_u = f(state^{ik1}_{v1}, state^{ik2}_{v2}, ..., statekm^i_{vm})$, with f being the update function during the calculation. Algorithm 6.4 shows the pseudocode of the PageRank algorithm in asynchronous execution mode (DST in line 12 of the code denotes the set of target vertices comprising all edges of the graph data). Figure 6.6 shows the execution flow of the PageRank algorithm in asynchronous execution mode. As can be seen from Algorithm 6.4, the PageRank algorithm in the asynchronous computation mode pre-initializes the oldPageRank and newPageRank vectors to 1.0 and 0.0, respectively, and the state value of a vertex is passed to the oldPageRank region of the vertex after updating it for subsequent computation processes (e.g., code line 20), and lines 22–29 of the code set the state values of isolated vertices to 0.15, which only needs to be set at Iterations=0 since the state values of these isolated vertices do not change during subsequent calculations. As can be seen in Figure 6.6, the PageRank algorithm in asynchronous execution mode requires only three iterations to complete the processing of the example graph in Figure 6.4.

Algorithm 6.4 PageRank Algorithm in Asynchronous Execution Mode

```
 1  vertices ← |V| ; edges ← |E| ;
 2  inDegree[1,2,..., vertices] = {0,0,...,0};
 3  outDegree[1,2,..., vertices] = {0,0,...,0};
 4  oldPageRank[1,2,..., vertices] = {1.0,1.0,..., 1.0};
 5  newPageRank[1,2,..., vertices] = {0.0,0.0,...,0.0}
 6  temp = 0;
 7  for each edge e[i] in E do
 8        inDegree[e[i].destination]++;
 9        outDegree[e[i].source]++; i++;
10  end
11  while not convergent do
12        for each vertex v in DST do
13              Gather:
14              for each edge e[k] in v.inEdges() do
15                    temp = temp + oldPageRank[e[k].source] /
                              outDegree[e[k].source];
16              end
17              Apply:
18              newPageRank[v] = 0.15 +0.85 * temp;
19              temp = 0;
20              oldPageRank[v] = newPageRank[v];
21        end
22        if Iterations == 0 then
23              for j=1 to vertices do
24                    if inDegree[j] == 0 then
25                          newPageRank[j] ← 0.15;
26                          oldPageRank[j] = new PageRank[j];
27                    end
28              end
29        end
30  end
```

6.2.3 Introduction to Graph Computation Systems and Graph Algorithms

This section briefly introduces the classical stand-alone graph computation systems represented by GraphChi, X-Stream, and GridGraph, followed by the classical graph algorithms represented by PageRank, breadth-first search algorithm (BFS), and weakly connected components (WCC).

6.2.3.1 Graph Computation Systems

1. GraphChi

   As one of the most classical stand-alone graph computation systems, GraphChi adopts the vertex-centric computational model and is implemented in C/C++. During the design process of a stand-alone graph computation system, minimizing the frequency of random accesses to graph data caused by locality is crucial, so GraphChi is designed with a parallel sliding window mechanism to reduce the random accesses and increase the sequential accesses to the graph data. GraphChi's graph data processing workflow is shown in Figure 6.7. For a given graph $G = (V, E)$, GraphChi initially preprocesses the graph data into several subgraph data by partitioning the vertices into P disjoint intervals, where the vertices in each interval are consecutive. Each vertex interval corresponds to an edge set file, called Shard, which stores edges with vertices in the current vertex interval as target vertices, and is sorted based on the source vertex. Thus, for each vertex interval, the edge set file corresponding to that vertex interval stores all the "incoming edges" of the vertices in that

src	dst	value	src	dst	value	src	dst	value
1	2	0.3	1	3	0.4	2	5	0.6
3	2	0.2	2	3	0.3	3	5	0.9
4	1	1.4	3	4	0.8		6	1.2
5	1	0.5	5	3	0.2	4	5	0.3
	2	0.6	6	4	1.9	5	6	1.1
6	2	0.8						

Execution Interval: vertices 1-2   Execution Interval: vertices 1-2

src	dst	value	src	dst	value	src	dst	value
1	2	0.273	1	3	0.364	2	5	0.545
3	2	0.22	2	3	0.273	3	5	0.9
4	1	1.54	3	4	0.8		6	1.2
5	1	0.55	5	3	0.2	4	5	0.3
	2	0.66	6	4	1.9	5	6	1.1
6	2	0.88						

Execution Interval: vertices 3-4   Execution Interval: vertices 3-4

... ...

Execution Interval: vertices 5-6

FIGURE 6.7
GraphChi graph data processing flow [21].

interval, and the "outgoing edges" of that vertex interval need to access the remaining $P-1$ edge set files. Therefore, the parallel sliding window mechanism requires GraphChi to sequentially access the "incoming edge" file once and the "outgoing edge" file $P-1$ times from disk when processing a subgraph.

2. X-Stream

Unlike GraphChi, X-Stream adopts an edge-centric computational mode for the streaming processing of graph data. X-Stream divides the processing of graph data into three phases: Scatter, Shuffle, and Gather. During the Scatter phase, X-Stream computes the state value of each edge's source vertex and determines whether it needs to be sent to the target vertex of that edge. In the Gather phase, X-Stream applies the updated values generated by the source vertex to the target vertex. To enhance the effective bandwidth of the disk, X-Stream focuses on sequentially reading edges. However, this approach results in random access to vertices. To reduce the random accesses to the vertices, X-Stream partitions vertices into several disjoint intervals of equal size. Within the design of X-Stream, a stream partition consists of vertex intervals, edge tables, and update tables. The following describes the processing flow of *X-Stream* in detail. The graph $G = (V, E)$ is shown in Figure 6.8, which is a directed graph, consisting of four vertices and seven directed edges, and the flow of X-Stream processing the graph is shown in Figure 6.9. The whole process is divided into three phases: Scatter, Shuffle, and Gather.

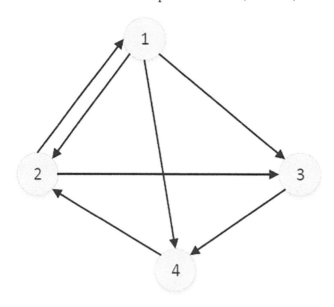

FIGURE 6.8
Example diagram $G = (V, E)$.

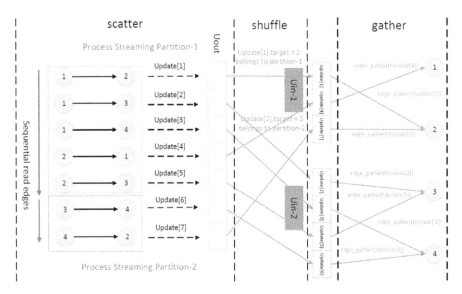

FIGURE 6.9
X-Stream plot data processing flow.

Before the graph data is processed, X-Stream divides the graph
G into two subgraphs: Partition-1 (containing vertices 1, 2) and
Partition-2 (containing vertices 3, 4). In the Scatter phase, X-Stream
traverses the edges of both partitions sequentially, generates the
corresponding *Updates*, respectively, and stores the *Updates*(1~7) in
the Uout. In the Shuffle phase, X-Stream classifies each *Update* to
the corresponding *Uin1* or *Uin2*, for example, *Update(1)* is generated
by *edge(1, 2)*, and the target vertex is 2, so *Update(1)* is stored to *Uin1*,
while *Update(2)* is generated by *edge(1, 3)*, and the target vertex is 3,
so *Update(2)* is stored to *Uin2*. Finally, in the Gather phase, *X-Stream*
traverses all the *Updates* in *Uin1* and *Uin2* sequentially and performs
the edge-gather operation, which collects the update values corresponding to the same target vertex and produces the final update
value to be updated over the vertex.

3. GridGraph

   GridGraph is also an edge-centric stand-alone graph computation system. Unlike *X-Stream*, which divides the graph data into one
dimension, GridGraph divides the graph data into two dimensions
based on the source vertices and target fixed points. In the preprocessing phase, GridGraph divides the vertices into P equal-sized
intervals, denoted as $C_1, C_2, ..., C_i, ... C_P$. Correspondingly, GridGraph
divides the edges of the graph into $P * P$ edge blocks, denoted as B_{11},
$B_{12}, ..., B_{PP}$. For example, given a graph $G = (V, E)$ where $V = \{1, 2, 3,
4\}$ and P is set to 2, we have $C1 = \{1, 2\}$ and $C2 = \{3, 4\}$. The edge (1, 2)

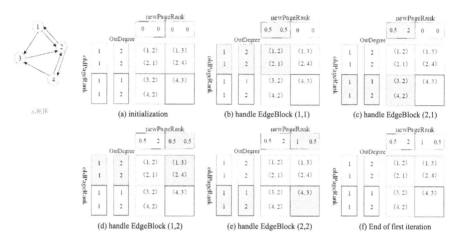

FIGURE 6.10
GridGraph graph data processing flow, including (a)–(f) [23].

belongs to *B11* (since the source vertex 1 ∈ *C1* and the target vertex 2 ∈ *C1*), while the edge (1, 3) belongs to *B12* (since the source vertex 1 ∈ *C1* and the target vertex 3 ∈ *C2*). Due to the irregular nature of the graph data, some of the "edge blocks" may be small in size, resulting in performance loss, so GridGraph merges multiple smaller "edge blocks" to improve the effective utilization of disk bandwidth. The process of processing graph data by GridGraph using the PageRank algorithm is shown in Figure 6.10. In the initial phase, GridGraph sets the newPageRank value of all vertices to 0.0 and their oldPageRank value to 1.0. In the computation process, GridGraph sequentially reads the PageRank value of each edge block, retrieves the PageRank value of the source vertex, and updates the PageRank value of the target vertex according to the PageRank computation formula. As shown in Figure 6.10b– e, the internal processing of each "edge block" uses a multi-threaded mechanism to compute the state value of the target vertex in parallel, and at the end of the graph algorithm, GridGraph writes the corresponding data (*metadata*, etc.) back to the external memory.

6.2.3.2 *Introduction to Graph Algorithms*

In the realm of graph computing research, the performance of many classical graph algorithms is often used as an important index for evaluating the graph computation system, such as the web page ranking algorithm PageRank, the BFS, the single-source shortest-path algorithm (SSSP), the strongly connected component, and the WCC. PrefEdge [12] classified the graph algorithms into three categories, which are graph traversal algorithms (such as BFSs,

SSSP algorithms, and depth-first traversal algorithms), fixed-point iteration algorithms (such as web page ranking algorithms and triangular counting algorithms), and feature description algorithms (such as sparse-matrix multiplication by vectors algorithms and graph spectral algorithms). During graph data processing, graph traversal algorithms may traverse vertices multiple times, but each traversal is focused on a subset of the graph data. In contrast, fixed-point iteration algorithms use the iteration convergence condition as termination criteria. For example, iterative ranking algorithms, such as the webpage ranking algorithm, often use the number of iterations and the average state difference of the vertices Δ as the algorithm's convergence condition. Throughout the execution of the algorithm, each iteration requires accessing the entire graph data, and all vertices are updated accordingly. On the other hand, feature description algorithms typically require a complete traversal of the entire graph data, making them more complex than the aforementioned two categories.

6.2.3.3 PageRank Algorithm

The PageRank algorithm, considered one of the top ten classical algorithms in the field of data mining, finds extensive application in search engines for web page ranking and recommendation purposes. In this algorithm, web pages are abstracted as vertices of the graph data, and the jump link relationships between web pages are abstracted as edges of the graph data. In the initial stage of the algorithm, the initial PageRank values of all vertices are set to 1. Subsequently, in each iteration, the state value of each vertex is calculated according to formula (6.3):

$$PR^{i+1}[t] = 1 - d + d * \sum_{s|(s,t)\in E} \frac{PR^i[s]}{\text{OutDegree}[s]} \qquad (6.3)$$

In Formula 6.3, d is a constant parameter, which is often set to 0.85, E is the set of edges of the graph data, and (s, t) is the edge to be processed, where s stands for the source vertex of the edge, t stands for the target vertex of the edge, and OutDegree[s] stands for the out-degree of the source vertex s.

6.2.3.4 Breadth-First Search Algorithm

The BFS algorithm is one of the most classical graph traversal algorithms in graph theory. It takes the vertices and edges of a graph as input and sets the vertex r as the root node. At the end of the algorithm, the BFS algorithm will construct a breadth-first search tree with vertex r as the root node. For the unweighted graph, in the initialization phase of the algorithm, the algorithm sets an initial distance value of *distance* (depth from the root node) for each vertex. The distance value of the root node is initialized to 0, while the rest of the vertices are initialized to 1. During the execution of the algorithm, the distance value of each vertex is updated to the minimum number of edges from the root node to that vertex. The algorithm's computational formula is shown in formula (6.4):

$$\text{distance}[t] = \min\left(\text{distance}[s] + 1\right) \quad s \,|\, (s,t) \in E \qquad (6.4)$$

In the given context, the variable s denotes the source vertex of an edge, while t represents the target vertex of the same edge. Additionally, *distance[t]* represents the distance between vertex t and its adjacent vertices.

6.2.3.5 Weakly Connected Components

For a given undirected graph $G = (V, E)$, a connected component C refers to a subset in which any vertex is reachable from any other vertex. The problem of WCC aims to identify $C_1, C_2, ..., C_k$ in graph G such that $\cup i Ci = V$, and the vertices in different components are not reachable from each other.

6.2.4 Graph Neural Network Algorithm

Figure 6.11 represents the execution process of the GNN algorithm. The GNN algorithm first performs aggregation of its neighbor vertices through the aggregation function Aggregate(), and then performs the feature transformation operation through the combination function Combine(). After k iterations, each vertex captures the feature vector of its k-hop neighbors and is represented by the transformed feature vector. In this discussion, we mainly focus on the inference process of the GNN algorithm. The inference process involves several phases, namely Sample, Aggregation, Combination, and Pooling. Let us now delve into the details of each stage.

> **Sample**: When a vertex has many neighboring nodes, to reduce the complexity of the computation phase, the sampling function, denoted as Sample, is usually applied before the aggregation

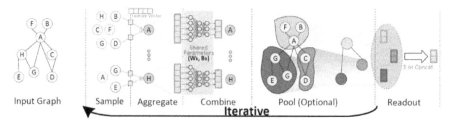

Input Graph   Sample   Aggregate   Combine   Pool (Optional)   Readout

Iterative

FIGURE 6.11
GNN algorithm process.

function, known as Aggregate. In this way, it can extract a subset of neighboring vertices from each vertex as new neighbors [58], which is used for subsequent computation. This process is represented mathematically as shown in Equation (6.5), where $N(v)$ represents all the neighbor nodes of vertex v, and $S(v)$ represents the filtered neighbor nodes.

$$S(v) = \text{Sample}(N(v)) \tag{6.5}$$

Aggregation: The aggregation process is responsible for aggregating for each graph vertex the feature information of its neighboring nodes, which are usually represented as vectors. This process operates on unstructured graph data and is also referred to as the graph computation phase. From an arithmetic point of view, this phase can be regarded as Sparse-matrix Multiplication Matrix (SpMM), characterized by its dynamic and irregular operations.

Combination: The aggregation process is responsible for mapping the aggregated vertex feature vectors to low-dimensional feature vectors. This phase is similar to the execution model of a multi-layer perceptron (MLP) in neural networks, where the *weights* and *biases* are shared among multiple vertices. From an arithmetic point of view, this phase can be abstracted as GEMM mode, characterized by its static and regular computation features.

The following Equations (6.6) and (6.7) are the formulas for the two phases of aggregation and combination during the k-th round of the inference process. In these equations, u is the filtered neighbor node, $S(v)$ denotes the filtered neighbor node, and h^{k-1}_u is the feature vector of vertex u after $k-1$ rounds of inference. a^k_v is the feature vector of vertex v after aggregation. And h^k_v is the feature vector after the operation of the combination phase.

$$a^k_v = \text{Aggregat}(h^{k-1}_u) : u \in S(v) \tag{6.6}$$

$$h^k_v = \text{combin}(a^k_u) \tag{6.7}$$

Pooling: Pool function is typically used after the combination of functions Combine to transform the original graph into a smaller graph, thereby reducing the computational load.

During the inference process of GNN algorithms, the aggregation and combination phases consume a significant amount of time in the execution of GNN models.

6.2.4.1 Graph Convolution Network

Graph convolutional networks (GCNs) extend the convolutional operation, commonly used in traditional data such as images and text, to graph data and have emerged as one of the most successful graph learning networks. The core idea behind GCNs is to learn a mapping function, denoted as f(.), which aggregates the feature vectors of each vertex v with its neighboring feature vectors to generate a new feature representation for the vertex v. GCNs serve as the foundation for many complex GNN models, including autoencoder-based models, generative models, and spatio-temporal networks, among others.

In summary, the core idea of GCN is to downscale a node's high-dimensional neighborhood information in a graph to a low-dimensional vector representation, which has the advantage of capturing the global information of the graph, and thus representing the vertex features effectively. The layer-to-layer propagation of the GCN is shown in formula (6.8). Here, A represents the sparse adjacency matrix after a simple transformation, H represents the vertex feature matrix of the l-th layer, W represents the weight transformation matrix of the l-th layer, and Act denotes the nonlinear activation function.

$$H^{(l+1)} = Act\left(AH^lW^l\right) \tag{6.8}$$

6.2.4.2 Graph Sample and Aggregate, GraphSAGE

Instead of learning the feature vectors of all nodes in a graph, the GraphSage network learns a mapping that generates feature vectors for each vertex. The GCN described above belongs to the class of transductive learning approaches, which cannot directly generalize to unknown nodes. The GCN described above belongs to the direct push learning process and cannot generalize directly to unknown nodes. In this process, the model learns feature vectors for each node directly on a fixed graph. However, in many cases, graphs evolve, with changes in network structure and the emergence of new nodes, and the direct push GCN needs to be re-trained. So it is difficult to land on machine learning systems that need to quickly generate unknown node feature vectors on machine learning systems. At this point, GraphSage graph networks were investigated, the basic idea of which is to learn how the information of a graph vertex is aggregated by the features of its neighboring nodes. Once this "aggregation function" is learned, along with the knowledge of each node's features and neighbor relationships, it becomes possible to incorporate additional vertices into the graph structure without necessitating retraining. The layer-to-layer propagation formula is shown in (6.9) and (6.10). Here, h_u^k denotes the feature of vertex u in the k-th layer, W^k denotes the weight vector of the k-th layer, $Aggregate$ denotes the aggregation function, *Concat* denotes the connection function of the feature vectors, and *Act* denotes the nonlinear activation function.

$$h_{N(v)}^k = \text{Aggregate}\left(\left\{h_u^{k-1}, u \in N(v)\right\}\right) \qquad (6.9)$$

$$h_v^k = \text{Act}\left(W^k.\text{Concat}\left(h_v^{k-1}, h_{N(u)}^k\right)\right) \qquad (6.10)$$

6.2.4.3 Graph Attention Network

The attention mechanism is nowadays widely used in sequence-based tasks, as it offers the advantage of amplifying the influence of the most important parts of the data. This property has proven useful for many tasks in applications such as machine translation and natural language understanding. Currently, there is a growing number of models that incorporate attention mechanisms, and one such model is the GAT, which introduces the attention mechanism into the design of GNNs. It uses the attention mechanism in the aggregation process to integrate the outputs of multiple models. In the GCN presented above, all neighboring nodes are treated equally. However, in real-world scenarios, different neighboring nodes may have varying degrees of importance to the central node. The GAT is a spatial-based GNN that incorporates an attention mechanism to assign weights to adjacent nodes during the feature aggregation process. It applies a self-attention mechanism, similar to the one used in Transformer networks, to calculate the attention of a node with respect to each neighboring node. The resulting attention features are then concatenated with the node's features, forming the final representation of the node, based on which it carries out practical tasks such as the classification of nodes.

6.2.4.4 Graph Isomorphism Network

Graph representation learning aims to generate a vector representation for a graph based on node attributes, edges, and edge attributes. With graph representations, we can perform various graph prediction tasks. Among the different approaches, the graph isomorphism network (GIN) is considered one of the most influential graph representation learning networks. The main challenge that GIN addresses is the ability to differentiate between different graphs, such as nodes, edges, and weights. The process of graph representation learning using GIN mainly contains the following two processes: first, computing node representations, and second, applying Graph Pooling (or Graph Readout) to obtain the graph representation. The effectiveness of GIN can be attributed to two factors. First, GIN has a larger number of network layers compared to other models, allowing it to capture more informative features. Second, GIN uses a summation function to aggregate the neighborhood information of its vertices, which allows GIN to learn more about the network structure compared to other aggregation functions such as maximum or minimum values.

6.3 Hardware Deployment/Acceleration Customization-Related Work

To cope with the various challenges posed by large-scale graph data processing, academia and industry have designed a variety of dedicated graph computation systems for efficient graph data processing and analysis, such as distributed graph computation systems, stand-alone graph computation systems, CPU-based graph computation accelerators, ASIC-based graph accelerators, and FPGA-based graph accelerators.

6.3.1 Distributed Graph Computer System

As mentioned earlier, a significant advantage of distributed graph computing systems is their capability to handle massive-scale graph data. In recent years, notable examples of such systems in the academic community include Chaos [18] and Gemini [19]. Chaos, a graph computing system developed by Intel Corporation and EPFL, is a distributed extension of the stand-alone graph computing system X-Stream [22], and leverages external storage devices such as mechanical or solid-state hard drives to store graph data. With the growth in the size of distributed clusters, Chaos can handle graph data scales of up to 1×1012 edges. The system adopts the edge-centric computation model for the processing of graph data, where vertices are stored in the node's memory and edges are stored in the node's external storage. This design allows for random vertex access within memory and sequential access to edges, thus optimizing disk bandwidth utilization. Since the bandwidth of the network environment in which Chaos operates far exceeds the disk bandwidth of the nodes, Chaos distributes the large-scale graph data randomly and uniformly to each node without considering the locality of subgraphs on each node. Additionally, Chaos implements dynamic load balancing through work stealing. The system consists of 32 16-core machines, each equipped with 32 GB of memory, a 480 GB SSD (with a bandwidth of 400 MB/s), two 6 TB disks (with a bandwidth of 200 MB/s), and a network environment of 40 GigE. Overall, compared to the single-machine version of Chaos, the 32-machine Chaos achieves a 20× speedup for the BFS algorithm and an 18.5× speedup for the PageRank algorithm. However, Chaos is limited by the network aggregation bandwidth of the cluster and the storage capacity of all the devices in the cluster. Gemini is a distributed graph computing system completed by Tsinghua University and Lai Yang Qatar

Research Institute. This system offers an alternative approach to optimizing the processing of large-scale graph data. It designs a Chunk-based graph data partitioning method to ensure the locality of graph data on each sub-node, and the computation is performed using a sparse–dense hybrid push–pull computational model. Gemini classifies active edge sets into two categories based on their size: dense active edge sets, with more than $|E|/20$ edges, and sparse active edge sets, with fewer edges than $|E|/20$ (where $|E|$ denotes the total number of edges). The sparse active edge sets are more efficiently processed through push operations, propagating the source vertex's state along outgoing edges to the target vertices. On the other hand, dense active edge sets are more efficiently processed through pull operations, collecting the source vertex's state along incoming edges to the target vertices. Therefore, Gemini's programming abstraction selects between push and pull models based on the sparse–dense pattern of the subgraph data on each node. Sparse subgraphs are stored using the compressed sparse row (CSR) structure, while dense subgraphs are stored using the compressed sparse column (CSC) structure. Furthermore, Gemini organizes the nodes in the distributed cluster in a ring topology. It also optimizes inter-node communication between nodes using high-performance computing communication libraries (e.g. AllGather in MPI) and implements fine-grained work stealing to achieve dynamic load balancing in the distributed system. By these methods, it is ensured that the scalability of the system is improved as much as possible without the loss of computational efficiency. In experiments conducted on an 8-node distributed cluster with Infiniband EDR Networks (supporting up to 100 Gbps bandwidth), each node consisting of 2 Intel E5–2670 v3 CPUs (12 cores each, with 30 MB L3 Cache) and 128 GB of memory, Gemini achieved an average speedup of 19.1× compared to other distributed systems such as PowerGraph [14], GraphX [16], and Powerlyra [59].

6.3.2 Stand-Alone Graphical Computation System

With the continuous enhancement of computational and storage resources in stand-alone systems, it has become possible to design and implement large-scale graph data analysis and processing on a single-machine platform. In recent years, both academia and industry have shown increasing interest in research on stand-alone graph computing systems. Based on the comparison between the scale of graph data and the memory capacity of stand-alone systems, stand-alone graph computation systems can be divided into two categories: memory-based in-memory systems and external memory-based out-of-core systems. In-memory stand-alone graph computation systems refer to those where the vertices, edges, and other temporary data structures of the graph data can all be stored in the memory of the stand-alone system during the data processing phase, as represented by the Ligra [24]. On the other hand, out-of-core stand-alone graph computing systems are those where only a portion of the vertices, edges, and other temporary data structures of the graph data can be stored in the memory of the stand-alone system during the data processing phase, and additional storage space is required from external storage. MOSAIC [27], the latest research achievement, can be taken as an example of such system. Ligra is a lightweight graph data processing framework based on shared memory, under which graph traversal algorithms such as breadth-first search, graph radius estimation, graph connectivity components, web page ranking, and SSSPs, can be easily implemented. It refers to the set of active vertices in each iteration as the vertex subset. During system initialization, Ligra sets a threshold ($|E|/20$), and when the total number of "out-edges" for all vertices in the vertex subset does not exceed this threshold, Ligra categorizes it as a sparse type of active vertex set. It then traverses the "out-edges" collection of this vertex set, reads the state values of the source vertices, performs calculations, and propagates the computed updated values to the target vertices (EDGEMAPSPARSE). On the other hand, when the total number of "out-edges" for all vertices in the vertex subset exceeds the threshold, Ligra categorizes it as a dense type of active vertex set. It then traverses the "in-edges" collection of this vertex set, reads the state values of the source vertices, performs calculations, and propagates the computed updated values to the target vertices (EDGEMAPDENSE). To improve system performance and resource utilization, Ligra uses parallel reading of vertices and parallel traversal of "out-edges" to optimize system performance when dealing with sparse active vertex sets, and uses parallel reading of vertices and sequential traversal of "in edges" when dealing with dense active vertex sets. Therefore, when dealing with smaller vertex subsets, the efficiency of EDGEMAPSPARSE is higher than that of EDGEMAPDENSE, while the opposite is true for larger vertex subsets.

The limited computational and storage resources of a stand-alone machine impose constraints on the scale of graph data that can be processed and the performance of the stand-alone graph computation systems. To expand the data scale that stand-alone systems can handle, it is necessary to expand the external storage space of the stand-alone system, such as using external storage devices (disks, SSDs, etc.) for storing large-scale graph data. However, this approach can cause performance degradation. To improve the performance of a stand-alone system, it is necessary to expand the memory space and improve the data locality in memory as much as possible. However, achieving compatibility between the performance and processing capabilities of out-of-core and in-memory computation engines in stand-alone systems is a challenging task. To vertically improve the performance and horizontally scale up the scale, MOSAIC adopts NVMs as its external storage extension, employs a graph data partitioning method based on Hilbert order, dividing the graph data into multiple subgraphs according to the Hilbert space-filling curve, and adopts a streaming processing approach to analyze and process the graph data. MOSAIC puts the memory-intensive operations (e.g., the edge-centric operation of the whole graph) on the fast main CPU at the host side and puts the computation- and I/O-intensive operations (e.g., the edge-centric operation of the whole graph) on the coprocessor. In addition, MOSAIC proposes a Pull-Reduce-Apply programming abstraction that uses selective scheduling to reduce data transfer volume and achieves load balancing between coprocessors in a single-machine multi-core environment and load balancing among single-core multi-threading environment. With this system, graph data analysis on the scale of 1×10^{12} edges can be completed on a single machine. When handling smaller-scale graph data, MOSAIC outperforms current state-of-the-art stand-alone graph computing systems. For larger-scale graph data, MOSAIC exhibits a performance improvement of 9.2× compared to the Chaos (disk-based) distributed graph computation system.

6.3.3 Graph Computation Accelerator

In addition to the aforementioned distributed graph computing systems and stand-alone graph computation systems, research on graph computing accelerators is also a hot topic in the field of graph computation. These accelerators can be categorized based on different acceleration platforms, including GPU-based graph computation accelerators, ASIC-based graph computation accelerators, and FPGA-based graph computation accelerators.

6.3.3.1 GPU-Based Graph Computation Accelerator

CuSha is a vertex-centric graph computation accelerator based on the GPU platform, developed by the research team at the University of California, Riverside [28]. It addresses the storage inefficiency issue in previous GPU-based graph computing accelerators that primarily use the CSR format for graph data storage, resulting in irregular memory access patterns. Therefore, CuSha optimizes the representation of graph data by employing G-Shards and Concatenated Windows (CW) for storage. The mapping between CuSha's GPU hardware resources and graph data enables CuSha to fully coalesce memory accesses, thereby improving GPU resource utilization. CuSha also leverages data parallelism in the graph data processing stage by employing multiple hardware units to concurrently process multiple subgraph data. Additionally, to alleviate the programming complexity, CuSha provides an accelerator programming framework for the GPU platform, allowing users to implement their vertex-centric graph algorithm applications through its interface.

Medusa [29] is a simplified version of a GPU-based graph computing accelerator developed by the research team at Nanyang Technological University. It provides a simplified programming framework for graph computation on the GPU platform, aiming to reduce the programming complexity and code verbosity. Additionally, Medusa designs a series of optimization strategies centered around subgraph data to enhance the performance of the accelerator. It introduces a novel graph computation programming model called

"Edge-Message-Vertex (EMV)." Medusa is capable of efficient message passing at runtime and automatically schedules user-defined algorithm programs to execute on different compute units within the same GPU or across multiple GPUs, which is transparent to the user. To improve Medusa's access efficiency, the accelerator is designed with a new graph data layout scheme to increase the coalescing of memory accesses. It also utilizes data reuse techniques to reduce data transfers and overlaps computation with communication to enhance the performance of the accelerator.

6.3.3.2 ASIC-Based Graph Computation Accelerator

Tesseract [33] is a scalable parallel graph computation accelerator based on in-memory computing, a collaboration between Seoul National University, Oracle Labs, and Carnegie Mellon University. As the scale of graph data continues to grow, traditional computer systems face limitations in performance due to memory bandwidth constraints. Consequently, the system's performance does not increase linearly with memory capacity. To address this issue, processing-in-memory has emerged as a viable solution. 3D stacking technology (stacking compute logic and storage wafers) has become a key enabler of in-memory computation, enabling a linear increase in system performance versus memory capacity. Using this technique, Tesseract proposes a novel graph computation hardware architecture that effectively utilizes memory bandwidth. Tesseract incorporates efficient communication mechanisms between different memory partitions during the accelerator design process. Additionally, Tesseract designs two dedicated hardware prefetching techniques based on the memory access patterns of graph data processing. To utilize the underlying customized hardware, Tesseract implements a set of programming interfaces. Experimental results demonstrate significant improvements over DDR3-based graph data processing systems, achieving a 10× acceleration ratio and reducing energy consumption by 87%. Graphicionado [31] is a high-performance and energy-efficient graph data analytics accelerator developed through a collaboration between Princeton University, UC Berkeley, and Intel Parallel Computing Lab. Graphicionado analyses the memory access and computation efficiencies on a stand-alone graph computation system. It reveals that in such systems, data interaction between the Cache and Memory is measured in terms of cache line (64 bytes), but graph algorithms often only utilize 4–8 bytes effectively within a cache line, resulting in low-memory-bandwidth utilization. Additionally, computational instructions, including arithmetic and logic operations, account for less than 6% of the total instructions in a stand-alone graph computation system. To address these inefficiencies, Graphicionado designs a dedicated data path tailored for graph computation to improve computational efficiency and a storage subsystem to enhance memory efficiency. Multiple pipelined parallel computing modes are implemented to mitigate pipeline conflicts and maximize parallelism in graph data processing. The experimental results show that Graphicionado has a speedup ratio of 1.76–6.54× and an energy efficiency ratio of 50–100× compared to GraphMat, a stand-alone graph computation system.

6.3.3.3 FPGA-Based Graph Computation Accelerator

Graph processing framework on FPGA (FPGP) [36] is an FPGA-based graph data processing framework designed by the National Laboratory of Information Science and Technology, Tsinghua University. It is a customized implementation of the stand-alone graph computation system, NXGraph [60], on the FPGA platform. FPGP adopts a vertex-centric computation model. The graph data is stored based on Interval-Shard, the vertices of the graph data are stored in the shared vertex storage area, and the edges are stored in the private edge set storage area. On each FPGA chip, multiple processing cores are available, and the read and write operations on the on-chip vertex data are separated to eliminate data conflicts arising from multiple cores accessing the same vertex data. This framework enables the mapping of various graph algorithms onto the FPGA platform. Furthermore, FPGP analyzes the performance bottlenecks of FPGA-based graph computation accelerators and establishes a performance model specifically for FPGA-based graph computation accelerators. Experimental results demonstrate that when processing data sets such as Twitter and Yahoo Web, FPGP achieves acceleration ratios of 1.22× and 3.86× compared to GraphChi, respectively. Zhou et al. [38] have proposed a high-throughput and energy-efficient FPGA-based graph computation accelerator, developed by the research team at the University of Southern California. Unlike FPGP, this accelerator adopts an edge-centric computation model for graph data processing, serving as a customized implementation of the X-Stream single-machine graph computation system on the FPGA platform. The accelerator's design optimizes the data layout based on X-Stream's graph data storage structure, reducing power consumption caused by accessing on-chip storage areas. Moreover, the accelerator incorporates a pipeline-based parallel graph computation architecture to maximize the exploitation of parallelism in graph data processing. Experimental results demonstrate that the accelerator achieves a throughput exceeding 600MTEPS (Million Traversed Edges per Second) and an energy efficiency surpassing 30MTEPS/W which is a 3.6× performance improvement and a 5.8× energy efficiency improvement over the comparator. The above design of an FPGA-based graph computation accelerator primarily focuses on optimizing the graph data layout and designing a pipeline structure for parallel computation. However, the investigation of using asynchronous computing for FPGA-based graph computation accelerators remains an unexplored research area. To address this gap, it is valuable to begin the study by evaluating and analyzing a stand-alone graph computation system based on general-purpose processors, considering its computational efficiency and memory access efficiency. By comparing synchronous and asynchronous computing approaches, it is possible to design an asynchronous and energy-efficient graph computation accelerator. Furthermore, leveraging the hardware accelerator as a foundation, a heterogeneous graph computation system can be constructed.

6.3.4 Graph Neural Network Accelerator

Currently, there have been numerous studies conducted both domestically and internationally on GNN accelerators, which are designed for dedicated processors for GNNs. Existing research can be broadly categorized into two types: two-stage processors and unified processors. In the case of two-stage processors, hardware architectures are separately designed for graph computation and neural network architecture, whereas unified processors adopt a unified hardware architecture for both graph computation and neural network architecture. In the following paragraphs, we will provide an introduction to these two categories of related work.

6.3.4.1 Two-Stage Processor

HyGCN [61] is an early proposal for a two-stage processor used for GNN inference. Its architecture, as shown in Figure 6.12, is designed with separate hardware architectures for the aggregation and combination stages. The aggregation stage focuses on irregular sparse computations and adopts an edge-parallel execution mode consisting primarily of a sparse elimination module and multiple single-instruction multiple-data (SIMD) execution units. Given the large size of graph data, it is necessary to be executed first for slicing, and then load the data into cache for aggregation operations. The

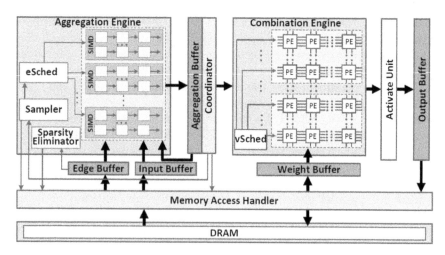

FIGURE 6.12
HyGCN architecture design.

sparse elimination module utilizes sliding and shrinking methods to select suitable fragments, which are then loaded onto the accelerator for processing, effectively reducing memory access. On the other hand, the combination stage targets regular matrix multiplication computations and employs a configurable systolic array. The term "configurable" here refers to the independent and collaborative modes of the systolic array. The aggregation and combination stages can be executed independently, and a pipelining optimization technique is applied between the two phases. However, there are still some issues that need to be addressed. First, the problem of load imbalance between SIMD units is not adequately discussed in the chapter, and specific optimization strategies are not provided. Second, due to the significant differences in computational requirements between the aggregation and combination phases on different graph data sets, further optimization is necessary to address the issue of load imbalance between these two stages.

The work presented in "Two-Stage Accelerator" [62] focuses on the design of a GNN accelerator implemented on an FPGA platform. It adopts a two-stage pipelined architecture, with dedicated computing units designed for sparse-matrix operations in the aggregation stage and dense matrix operations in the combination stage. The bottleneck in sparse operations occurs in memory storage, and the solution proposed in the chapter is to maximize the utilization of locality and improve on-chip cache reuse. On the other hand, the bottleneck in dense operations occurs in computation, which is executed by utilizing a systolic array. The on-chip cache on the FPGA employs a double-buffer structure to minimize pipeline stall overhead. Moreover, the chapter discusses the partitioning of input data to enable efficient utilization of FPGA resources by filling the slices on the FPGA. Furthermore, this study proposes two preprocessing algorithms: graph sparse partitioning and node reordering. Both methods are optimized for the topology of the adjacency matrix, allowing the partitioned input data to make better use of data locality, and the preprocessing algorithms, although time-consuming, can be done offline. Additionally, the chapter implements two kinds of data flows, corresponding to the first execution of the aggregation operation and the first execution of the combination operation, respectively. In practical applications, the choice between these two data flows can be made based on specific data sets and parameter configurations.

EnGN [63] is a dedicated accelerator implemented on ASIC. Its architecture, as shown in Figure 6.13, abstracts graph algorithms into three processing operations: feature extraction, aggregation, and update operations, to design a processor EnGN that supports various GNNs. The main computational unit is a two-dimensional array of processing engines (PEs). Each PE consists of feature extraction, aggregation, and update processing units, and each processing unit contains a multiply-accumulate unit, a feature cache and a weight cache for better data reuse. The data path between PEs is designed to be efficient. In terms of storage optimization, this study implements a multi-level memory structure. The research preprocesses the graph

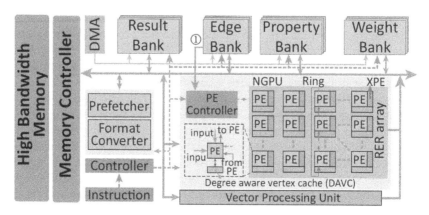

FIGURE 6.13
EnGN overall architecture design.

data to efficiently map it onto the processor, using static methods to address load-balancing issues. For input data, a slicing technique is employed to ensure contiguous access and minimize memory accesses. However, there will be dependencies between the sliced data, so a suitable scheduling strategy is required.

GRIP [64] abstracts the inference process of graph algorithms into four phases: Gather, Reduce, Transform, and Activate. The study implements computational units for the aforementioned phases, driving them through an instruction set to support the execution of multiple GNN models such as GCN, GraphSage, G-GCN, and GIN. The GRIP paper primarily focuses on three types of calculation units: Edge Unit, Vertex Unit, and Update Unit. In the Edge Unit, the graph model is abstracted as a Nodeflow structure, enabling the partitioning of graph data. This module includes multiple prefetch units to alleviate irregular memory access issues. The Vertex Unit consists of parallel multiply units and accumulation trees, optimizing memory hierarchy to enhance weight reuse. Lastly, the Update Unit implements support for activation functions.

6.3.4.2 Unified Processors

AWB-GCN [65] implements a column-major sparse processor architecture, as shown in Figure 6.14. Focusing on the execution characteristics of graph data in GNNs, this work adopts a co-design approach, combining software and hardware, to enhance dynamic load-balancing support on a sparse processor. At the algorithm scheduling level, three dynamic load-balancing algorithms are proposed: Distribution Smoothing (distributing to neighboring nodes, optimizing within the group), Remote Exchange (using neighbors as a group, optimizing between groups), and Special Row Remapping (for rows with excessive data). On the hardware

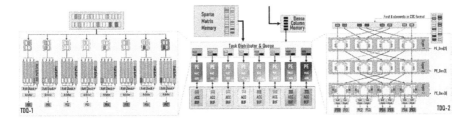

FIGURE 6.14
AWB-GCN architecture design.

architecture side, support for load redistribution is provided through task distribution queues. Compared to static load-balancing preprocessing algorithms, dynamic load-balancing methods do not require additional offline preprocessing. The architecture in this study supports both inter-layer and intra-layer pipelining. The experimental platform for this research is FPGA hardware, but it can be easily migrated to other hardware platforms for implementation.

The paper [66] presents a unified GNN processor called GCNAX. The authors first experimentally evaluate two data flows, (AX)W and A(XW), where A is a sparse adjacency matrix, X is a feature matrix, and W is a weight matrix. The study finds that the (AX)W mode can reduce computation by 32 times compared to the A(XW) mode. With the use of A(XW) data flow, the GNN algorithm is unified into two consecutive sparse multiplication operations, implemented using the outer product algorithm for sparse-matrix multiplication. The authors analyze the loop execution process of the two-stage sparse multiplication to improve on-chip data reuse and reduce off-chip memory accesses. They propose three optimization strategies: loop unrolling, loop swapping, and loop fusion, aiming to find suitable solutions using heuristic exploration methods. The hardware architecture of this research heavily relies on sparse processor implementation, comprising various cache modules and computation units, where the input and output caches can be used interchangeably. A software scheduler is used to implement loop optimization strategies and generate corresponding instructions for the control unit.

Based on our survey of previous related works, we have found that the two-stage architecture separates graph computation and neural network frameworks but does not consider the load-balancing issues brought about by the fusion of the two architectures. Its memory access and architecture implementation are also not optimized. On the other hand, the unified architecture implements a common core to support both graph computing and neural network phases, and focuses on how to schedule and distribute data to achieve load balancing but lacks an analysis of access memory optimization, which is worth further exploration.

6.4 Chapter Summary

With the rapid growth of big data, the scale of user data has increased significantly. As a result, large-scale graph data processing has gradually become a focus of attention in academia and industry at home and abroad presenting a significant research challenge. In today's context of advocating for sustainable development, system power consumption and energy efficiency have become important metrics in system design. This chapter provides a comprehensive introduction to the customized approaches for typical computation systems and accelerators used in graph processing algorithms. It is hoped that this information will serve as a valuable reference for researchers and practitioners engaged in related research work.

References

1. Howe D., Costanzo M., Fey P., et al. The future of biocuration. *Nature*, 2008, 455(7209): 47–50.
2. Hashem I. A. T., Yaqoob I., Anuar N. B., et al. The rise of "big data" on cloud computing: Review and open research issues. *Information Systems*, 2015, 47: 98–115.
3. Robinson I., Webber J., Eifrem E. *Graph Databases: New Opportunities for Connected Data*. Sebastopol, CA: O'Reilly Media, Inc., 2015.
4. Xu C., Zhou J., Lu Y., et al. Evaluation and trade-offs of graph processing for cloud services. *2017 IEEE International Conference on Web Services (ICWS)*. IEEE, Honolulu, HI, 2017: 420–427.
5. Zhou S., Chelmis C, Prasanna V K. Accelerating large-scale single-source shortest path on FPGA. *2015 IEEE International Parallel and Distributed Processing Symposium Workshop*. IEEE, Hyderabad, 2015: 129–136.
6. Gao Q., Abel F., Houben G. J., et al. A comparative study of users' microblogging behaviour on Sina Weibo and Twitter. *User Modeling, Adaptation, and Personalization: 20th International Conference, UMAP 2012*, Montreal, Canada, July 16–20, 2012. Proceedings 20. Springer, Berlin Heidelberg, 2012: 88–101.
7. Twitter usage statistics [EB/OL]. https://www.internetlivestats.com/twitter-statistics/.
8. Beamer S., Asanovic K., Patterson D. Locality exists in graph processing: Workload characterization on an Ivy bridge server. *2015 IEEE International Symposium on Workload Characterization*. IEEE, Atlanta, GA, 2015: 56–65.
9. Satish N., Sundaram N., Patwary M. M. A., et al. Navigating the maze of graph analytics frameworks using massive graph datasets. *Proceedings of the 2014 ACM SIGMOD International Conference on Management of Data*. Snowbird, UT, 2014: 979–990.
10. Dean J., Ghemawat S. MapReduce: Simplified data processing on large clusters. *Communications of the ACM*, 2008, 51(1): 107–113.

11. Hadoop A. Hadoop. Available: https://hadoop.apache.org/ [Accessed: 27 Dec 2017], 2009.

12. Nilakant K., Dalibard V., Roy A., et al. PrefEdge: SSD prefetcher for large-scale graph traversal. *Proceedings of International Conference on Systems and Storage*. Haifa, 2014: 1–12.

13. Malewicz G., Austern M. H., Bik A. J. C., et al. Pregel: A system for large-scale graph processing. *Proceedings of the 2010 ACM SIGMOD International Conference on Management of Data*. Indianapolis, IN, 2010: 135–146.

14. Gonzalez J. E., Low Y., Gu H., et al. PowerGraph: Distributed graph-parallel computation on natural graphs. *10th USENIX Symposium on Operating Systems Design and Implementation (OSDI 12)*. Hollywood, CA, 2012: 17–30.

15. Low Y., Gonzalez J., Kyrola A., et al. Distributed graphlab: A framework for machine learning in the cloud. arXiv preprint arXiv:1204.6078, 2012.

16. Xin R. S., Gonzalez J. E., Franklin M. J., et al. Graphx: A resilient distributed graph system on spark. *First International Workshop on Graph Data Management Experiences and Systems*. New York, 2013: 1–6.

17. Avery C. Giraph: Large-scale graph processing infrastructure on hadoop. *Proceedings of the Hadoop Summit*. Santa Clara, 2011, 11(3): 5–9.

18. Roy A., Bindschaedler L., Malicevic J., et al. Chaos: Scale-out graph processing from secondary storage. *Proceedings of the 25th Symposium on Operating Systems Principles*. Monterey, CA, 2015: 410–424.

19. Zhu X., Chen W., Zheng W., et al. Gemini: A computation-centric distributed graph processing system. *12th USENIX Symposium on Operating Systems Design and Implementation (OSDI 16)*. Savannah, GA, 2016: 301–316.

20. Sparka. Apache spark: Lightning-fast cluster computing. https://spark apache org, 2016: 2168–7161.

21. Kyrola A., Blelloch G., Guestrin C. GraphChi: Large-scale graph computation on just a PC. *10th USENIX Symposium on Operating Systems Design and Implementation (OSDI 12)*. Hollywood, CA, 2012: 31–46.

22. Roy A., Mihailovic I., Zwaenepoel W. X-stream: Edge-centric graph processing using streaming partitions. *Proceedings of the Twenty-Fourth ACM Symposium on Operating Systems Principles*. Farmington, PA, 2013: 472–488.

23. Zhu X., Han W., Chen W. GridGraph: Large-scale graph processing on a single machine using 2-level hierarchical partitioning. *2015 USENIX Annual Technical Conference (USENIX ATC 15)*. Santa Clara, CA, 2015: 375–386.

24. Shun J., Blelloch G. E. Ligra: A lightweight graph processing framework for shared memory. *Proceedings of the 18th ACM SIGPLAN Symposium on Principles and Practice of Parallel Programming*. Shenzhen, 2013: 135–146.

25. Cheng J., Liu Q., Li Z., et al. VENUS: Vertex-centric streamlined graph computation on a single PC. *2015 IEEE 31st International Conference on Data Engineering*. Seoul, IEEE, 2015: 1131–1142.

26. Cheng S., Zhang G., Shu J., et al. Asyncstripe: I/o efficient asynchronous graph computing on a single server. *Proceedings of the Eleventh IEEE/ACM/IFIP International Conference on Hardware/Software Codesign and System Synthesis*. Pittsburgh, PA, 2016: 1–10.

27. Maass S., Min C., Kashyap S., et al. Mosaic: Processing a trillion-edge graph on a single machine. *Proceedings of the Twelfth European Conference on Computer Systems*. Google, Belgrade, 2017: 527–543.

28. Khorasani F., Vora K., Gupta R., et al. CuSha: Vertex-centric graph processing on GPUs. *Proceedings of the 23rd International Symposium on High-Performance Parallel and Distributed Computing.* Pisa, 2014: 239–252.

29. Zhong J., He B. Medusa: Simplified graph processing on GPUs. *IEEE Transactions on Parallel and Distributed Systems*, 2013, 25(6): 1543–1552.

30. Wang Y., Davidson A., Pan Y., et al. Gunrock: A high-performance graph processing library on the GPU. *Proceedings of the 21st ACM SIGPLAN Symposium on Principles and Practice of Parallel Programming.* Barcelona, 2016: 1–12.

31. Ham T. J., Wu L., Sundaram N., et al. Graphicionado: A high-performance and energy-efficient accelerator for graph analytics. *2016 49th Annual IEEE/ACM International Symposium on Microarchitecture (MICRO).* IEEE, Taipei, 2016: 1–13.

32. Ozdal M. M., Yesil S., Kim T., et al. Energy-efficient architecture for graph analytics accelerators. *ACM SIGARCH Computer Architecture News*, 2016, 44(3): 166–177.

33. Ahn J., Hong S., Yoo S., et al. A scalable processing-in-memory accelerator for parallel graph processing. *Proceedings of the 42nd Annual International Symposium on Computer Architecture.* Portland, OR, 2015: 105–117.

34. Zhou J., Liu S., Guo Q., et al. Tunao: A high-performance and energy-efficient reconfigurable accelerator for graph processing. *2017 17th IEEE/ACM International Symposium on Cluster, Cloud and Grid Computing (CCGRID).* IEEE, Madrid, 2017: 731–734.

35. Nurvitadhi E., Weisz G., Wang Y., et al. GraphGen: An FPGA framework for vertex-centric graph computation. *2014 IEEE 22nd Annual International Symposium on Field-Programmable Custom Computing Machines.* IEEE, Boston, MA, 2014: 25–28.

36. Dai G., Chi Y., Wang Y., et al. FPGP: Graph processing framework on FPGA a case study of breadth-first search. *Proceedings of the 2016 ACM/SIGDA International Symposium on Field-Programmable Gate Arrays,* Monterey, CA, 2016.

37. Dai G., Huang T., Chi Y., et al. ForeGraph: Exploring large-scale graph processing on multi-FPGA architecture. *Proceedings of the 2017 ACM/SIGDA International Symposium on Field-Programmable Gate Arrays.* Monterey, CA, 2017: 217–226.

38. Zhou S., Chelmis C., Prasanna V. K. High-throughput and energy-efficient graph processing on FPGA. *2016 IEEE 24th Annual International Symposium on Field-Programmable Custom Computing Machines (FCCM).* Washington, DC, IEEE, 2016: 103–110.

39. Oguntebi T., Olukotun K. Graphops: A dataflow library for graph analytics acceleration. *Proceedings of the 2016 ACM/SIGDA International Symposium on Field-Programmable Gate Arrays.* Monterey, CA, 2016: 111–117.

40. Gtx N. G. 780. https://www nvidia com/gtx-700-graphics-cards/gtx-780.

41. Malicevic J., Dulloor S., Sundaram N., et al. Exploiting NVM in large-scale graph analytics. *Proceedings of the 3rd Workshop on Interactions of NVM/FLASH with Operating Systems and Workloads.* Monterey, CA, 2015: 1–9.

42. Hamilton W., Ying Z., Leskovec J. Inductive representation learning on large graphs. *Advances in Neural Information Processing Systems*, Long Beach, CA, 2017: 30.

43. Ying R., He R., Chen K., et al. Graph convolutional neural networks for web-scale recommender systems. *Proceedings of the 24th ACM SIGKDD International Conference on Knowledge Discovery & Data Mining.* London, 2018: 974–983.

44. Duvenaud D. K., Maclaurin D., Iparraguirre J., et al. Convolutional networks on graphs for learning molecular fingerprints. *Advances in Neural Information Processing Systems*, Montreal, 2015:28.
45. Wu Z, Pan S, Chen F, et al. A comprehensive survey on graph neural networks[J]. *IEEE transactions on neural networks and learning systems*, 2020, 32(1): 4–24.
46. Wu Z., Pan S., Chen F., et al. A comprehensive survey on graph neural networks. *IEEE Transactions on Neural Networks and Learning Systems*, 2020, 32(1): 4–24.
47. Zhou J., Cui G., Hu S., et al. Graph neural networks: A review of methods and applications. *AI Open*, 2020, 1: 57–81.
48. Wang M. Y. Deep graph library: Towards efficient and scalable deep learning on graphs. *Proceedings of the ICLR Workshop on Representation Learning on Graphs and Manifolds*, New Orleans, LA, 2019.
49. Fey M., Lenssen J. E. Fast graph representation learning with PyTorch Geometric. arXiv preprint arXiv:1903.02428, 2019.
50. Ma L., Yang Z., Miao Y., et al. NeuGraph: Parallel deep neural network computation on large graphs. *2019 USENIX Annual Technical Conference (USENIX ATC 19)*. Renton, WA, 2019: 443–458.
51. Chen T., Du Z., Sun N., et al. Diannao: A small-footprint high-throughput accelerator for ubiquitous machine-learning. *ACM SIGARCH Computer Architecture News*, 2014, 42(1): 269–284.
52. Chen Y., Luo T., Liu S., et al. Dadiannao: A machine-learning supercomputer. *2014 47th Annual IEEE/ACM International Symposium on Microarchitecture*. IEEE, Cambridge, 2014: 609–622.
53. Zhang S., Du Z., Zhang L., et al. Cambricon-X: An accelerator for sparse neural networks. *2016 49th Annual IEEE/ACM International Symposium on Microarchitecture (MICRO)*. IEEE, Taipei, 2016: 1–12.
54. Tian Y., Balmin A., Corsten S. A., et al. From "think like a vertex" to "think like a graph". *Proceedings of the VLDB Endowment*, 2013, 7(3): 193–204.
55. Yan D., Cheng J., Lu Y., et al. Blogel: A block-centric framework for distributed computation on real-world graphs. *Proceedings of the VLDB Endowment*, 2014, 7(14): 1981–1992.
56. Xie W., Wang G., Bindel D., et al. Fast iterative graph computation with block updates. *Proceedings of the VLDB Endowment*, 2013, 6(14): 2014–2025.
57. Yuan P., Xie C., Liu L., et al. PathGraph: A path-centric graph processing system. *IEEE Transactions on Parallel and Distributed Systems*, 2016, 27(10): 2998–3012.
58. Chen J., Ma T., Xiao C. Fastgcn: Fast learning with graph convolutional networks via importance sampling. arXiv preprint arXiv:1801.10247, 2018.
59. Chen R., Shi J., Chen Y., et al. Powerlyra: Differentiated graph computation and partitioning on skewed graphs. *ACM Transactions on Parallel Computing (TOPC)*, 2019, 5(3): 1–39.
60. Chi Y., Dai G., Wang Y., et al. Nxgraph: An efficient graph processing system on a single machine. *2016 IEEE 32nd International Conference on Data Engineering (ICDE)*. IEEE, Helsinki, 2016: 409–420.
61. Yan M., Deng L., Hu X., et al. Hygcn: A gcn accelerator with hybrid architecture. *2020 IEEE International Symposium on High-Performance Computer Architecture (HPCA)*. IEEE, San Diego, CA, 2020, 26: 15–29.

62. Zhang B., Zeng H., Prasanna V. Hardware acceleration of large scale gcn infer-ence. *2020 IEEE 31st International Conference on Application-specific Systems, Architectures and Processors (ASAP)*. IEEE, Univ Manchester, Dept Comp Sci, Manchester, 2020,31: 61–68.

63. Liang S., Wang Y., Liu C., et al. Engn: A high-throughput and energy-efficient accelerator for large graph neural networks. *IEEE Transactions on Computers*, 2020, 70(9): 1511–1525.

64. Kingham K., Levis P., Ré C. GRIP: A graph neural network accelerator architec-ture. *IEEE Transactions on Computers*, 2022, 72(4): 914–925.

65. Geng T., Li A., Shi R., et al. AWB-GCN: A graph convolutional network accel-erator with runtime workload rebalancing. *2020 53rd Annual IEEE/ACM International Symposium on Microarchitecture (MICRO)*. IEEE, Electr Network, 2020: 922–936.

66. Li J., Louri A., Karanth A., et al. GCNAX: A flexible and energy-efficient accelera-tor for graph convolutional neural networks. *2021 IEEE International Symposium on High-Performance Computer Architecture (HPCA)*. IEEE, Electr Network, 2021: 775–788.

7

Overview of Hardware Acceleration Methods for Neural Network Algorithms

7.1 Neural Network Algorithms and Their Hardware Acceleration Background

7.1.1 Principles of Neural Network Algorithms

Neural networks are derived from the simulation of the functioning of the human brain's nervous system and are large-scale computing models composed of basic computing units, that is, neurons. A neuron is shown in Figure 7.1, which can receive multiple signals from other neurons and transmit signals to other neurons. The computing process of a single neuron is shown in formula (7.1). x is the input, w is the weight, b is the offset, and f is the threshold or activation function.

According to the characteristics of biological neurons, each neuron has a threshold, and when the weighted effect of the input signal exceeds the threshold, the neuron is in an activated state. To model this process, artificial neural networks (ANNs) introduce activation functions. Typical activation functions include threshold functions, linear functions, and S-shaped functions.

$$y = f\left(\sum_{i=0}^{n} x_i {}^* w_i + b\right) \tag{7.1}$$

To model the chunked representation of information in a biological nervous system, neuronal connections are represented hierarchically on topological representations. This hierarchical representation results in three types of interconnections between neurons: intra-layer connections, cyclic connections, and inter-layer connections. Intra-layer connections are connections among neurons in this layer, which can be used to strengthen or compete for signals from neurons in the inner layer; cyclic connections are connections between neurons and themselves for strengthening the

DOI: 10.1201/9780429355080-7

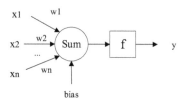

FIGURE 7.1
Neuronal computation process.

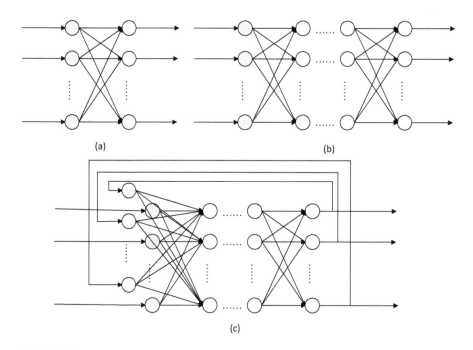

FIGURE 7.2
(a) Schematic diagram of a single-layer network. (b) Schematic diagram of a multi-layer network. (c) Schematic diagram of a recursive network.

neurons themselves and are a type of feedback connection; inter-layer connections are neuronal connections between different layers, this way to achieve inter-layer signal transmission, layer signal transmission can be forward or backward. Figure 7.2 shows three different network schematic diagrams.

In addition to working similarly, neural networks are similar to the human brain in two ways. First, the knowledge obtained by the neural network is learned from the external environment, and the formation of the network is a learning process. Second, the connection strength of neurons, or synaptic weights, is used to store the learned knowledge. We call the process of obtaining these synaptic weights the training process or the learning process. The process of processing data based on these synaptic weights is called the prediction process. The neural network training process utilizes the gradient descent and back propagation method, also known as supervised learning, where training is a learning process and the source of learning is the data set, which consists of values and labels. The values of the training data set are fed into the neural network for prediction, the labels are obtained, and the weight parameters of each layer are adjusted in turn by comparing the difference between the predicted labels and the true labels, which is a reverse computation from the output layer to the input layer [1,2]. Here we take the error back propagation algorithm as an example to introduce the computing process of the neural network in detail.

Step one: Initialize the weight parameters of the neurons in each layer, typically randomly in a range.

Step two: Make predictions based on the data of the training set and store the data values generated by the predictions of each layer, which are recorded as D_i.

Step three: Starting from the last layer of the network, compare the predicted values D_n with the real label values L, and the error value E_n of the output layer is computed, and the error can be computed in a variety of ways according to the actual situation; an example is shown in Equation 7.2. After obtaining E_n, update the weights according to gradient descent as in Equation 7.3.

$$E_n = D_n * (1 - D_n) * (L - D_n) \tag{7.2}$$

$$\Delta W_n = D_{n-1}^T * E_n \tag{7.3}$$

Step four: Based on the error value of the last layer, the error value of the local layer is computed backward, and then the weight is updated according to the error value. Loop along the neural network until you reach the input layer.

The process of building large network models with a deep number of layers is called deep learning, and common deep learning network topologies include deep neural networks (DNNs), convolutional neural networks (CNNs), recurrent neural networks (RNNs), attention mechanism models (Trans-former), and so on. Deep learning models have different structures and have achieved remarkable results in classification, image recognition, natural language understanding, and other fields.

7.1.2 Hardware Acceleration Background of Neural Network Algorithms

With the development of the information age and the Internet, the application range of neural networks has gradually expanded. However, to solve more abstract and complex learning problems, the scale of deep learning networks is increasing, and the complexity of computation and data is also increasing; behind the excellent results are complex and huge network models, massive data sets, and computations. At present, the parameter scale of a large-scale network model is hundreds of millions, with insufficient performance and high overhead on existing general-purpose computing devices. Implementing deep learning-related algorithms with high performance and low energy consumption has become a research hotspot in scientific research institutions. In addition, the researchers observed that the neural network computing process as a whole is regular, and a large amount of parallelism can be mined during computing, making it possible to accelerate it using parallel computing. On the other hand, there is a large amount of data reuse for computation, which can be mined for high reusability, and reducing the repeated access to data by some means can reduce the running overhead. Of course, everything requires the support of the underlying hardware. Therefore, hardware acceleration for neural network algorithms is a trend that has accumulated with development.

Hardware acceleration makes full use of parallelism in the computing process, minimizes redundancy in computing, and uses hardware computing modules to replace software algorithms running on general-purpose central processing units (CPUs) to obtain performance improvements and overhead reductions. Common hardware acceleration technologies are application-specific integrated circuit (ASIC), field programmable gate array (FPGA), and graphics processing unit (GPU). Performance, power, development cost, and cycle time need to be considered.

7.2 Architectures of Hardware Accelerators

7.2.1 The ASIC Heterogeneous Accelerators of Deep Learning

With the development of deep learning and neural networks, smart chips and ASIC accelerators have become the hotspots of the computer architecture domain. The representative research contains a series of related works including DianNao [3], DaDianNao [4], and PuDianNao [5]. These representative works include the heterogeneous accelerating chips of computer machine learning and neural networks that are proposed and developed by the Institute of Computing Technology Chinese Academy of Science and the

Cambrian, and Nervana and other artificial intelligent-specialized chips. Otherwise, lots of ASIC neural network accelerators have emerged in international conferences such as ISCA and MICRO. For example, CNVlutin [6] proposed a DNN accelerator that eliminates ineffective neurons. As the number of parameters is redundant for representing functions, neural networks have high sparsity. CNVlutin proposed an eliminating ineffective neurons method to design neural network accelerators, according to the value of operators. Instead of aiming at control flow, CNVlutin separates and recombines instructions that contain zero operators from the rest of the instructions, to decrease the usage of computing resources and accelerate memory access, and then optimize performance and energy. Cambricon [7] proposed a neural network instruction set when facing processing large scale of neurons and synapses; this means that one instruction can process a group of neurons, especially, supporting the transfer of neurons and synapses on the chip. EIE [8] proposed an efficient compressed DNN inference engine and compressed CNN hardware implementations. Due to the high information redundancy, the weights of the compressed CNN can be completely stored in SRAM, which greatly reduces the energy consumption of traditional CNN gas pedals accessing DRAM. Eyeriss [9] proposed a low-power data structure for CNNs. Although the SIMD GPU (single instruction, multiple data GPU) architecture satisfies the requirement of CNNs' massive computing, it brings much data transfer cost, especially the data transfer cost beyond data computing cost. As a result, Eyeriss made accelerators using modern data transfer mode to replace the accelerator with SIMD/SIMT GPU (single instruction multiple threads GPU) architecture. NeuroCube [10] proposed a programmable neural network accelerator architecture using 3D stacking storage. The accelerator adopts modern 3D stacking storage technology as the basis of memory computing architecture, adds computing units at the deep layer of 3D stacking memory (logical layer), and accelerates neural network computing by specific logical modules to eliminate unnecessary data transfer while utilizing large internal memory bandwidth. Minerva [11] is a low-power-consumption and high-accuracy DNN accelerator. Minerva proposes an accelerator and optimized flow based on design space exploration, which decreased data complexity and bandwidth by neural network pruning, and then lowered system power. Redeye [12] proposed an analog CNN image sensor architecture aiming at mobile vision, using the modularized column paralleling design idea to decrease the complexity of analog design and promote the reuse of physical design and algorithms. These studies fully demonstrate neural network accelerators become the hotspot and keystone in the computer architecture domain. A dataflow-based reconfigurable deep CNN hardware accelerator architecture in the paper [13] adopts a typical specialized CNN accelerating engine integrating Digital signal processing (DSP) general processors. Processing convolutional operations in neural networks takes up most of the operations, so accelerators accelerate convolution on the accelerating engine and DSP processors by mining parallelism.

DNPU [14] is an energy efficiency reconfigurable general DNN processor and implements two types of structures, the computing bottleneck of independent architecture for convolutional layers and the memory bottleneck of full-connected layers. The convolutional accelerating module CP and RNN-LSTM (long short-term memory) module FRP use distributed memory to ensure data requirements of processing elements and computing cores. The aggregation core collects data and communicates with recursive neural network computing modules. The paper [15] designs a chip-based accelerator for sparse neural networks, which adopts two measures to optimize the whole system. The one is using a sign-magnitude number format to store parameters and computing, which increases the bit-flipping rate of complement representation. The other is eliminating zero operators in computing. The paper [16] is a circuit using limited network width and quantified sparse weight matrices for automatic speech recognition and voice activity detection to improve precision, programmability, and scalability. enVision [17] is a dynamic voltage accuracy frequency scalable (DVAFS)-based adjustable CNN processor. With the requirements of computing and limited energy of embedded devices, enVision expands dynamic voltage accuracy scalable to a DVAFS method, optimizes multipliers, and finally implements frequency adjusted. DVAFS implements the increasing value of all configurable parameters, such as activity, frequency, and voltage. Through high-bit and low-bit multiplication, two 8-bit multiplication can run on a 16-bit array that has a significant improvement in throughput and resource utilization in different precision. The paper [18] proposed an always-on and Internet-of-Things (IoT) application scenario, which uses CMOS image sensor (CIS) and CNNs to realize an SoC of much lower face recognition. According to the energy requirements in variable application scenarios, the architecture is different. The specialized chip for accelerating IoT DNNs [19] has the main feature of four-level cache memory at various speeds and energy.

Aiming at improving performance and energy efficiency, and taking advantage of FPGAs, the University of Science and Technology of China (USTC) team has proposed FPGA-based accelerators for deep learning and big data applications. The work [20] presented a software-defined FPGA-based accelerator named SODA for big data. The accelerator could reconstruct and reorganize for various requirements of data-intensive applications by decomposing complex applications. Due to the layer-wise structure and the data dependency between layers, the paper [21] proposed a pipeline energy-efficient multi-FPGA-based accelerator PIE, which accelerates operations in DNNs by processing two adjacent layers in a pipeline. With the diversity and increasing size of deep learning neural networks for high accuracy, the works [22,23] design accelerator architectures to improve the performance and adapt to the scalability of various neural networks. The paper [22] presented a service-oriented deep learning architecture Solar, by various accelerators such as GPU and FPGA-based approaches. To facilitate programmers, Solar provides a uniform programming model that hides hardware design and scheduling. The paper [23] presented a deep learning accelerator unit (DLAU) to large-scale deep learning networks based on FPGA. To improve the throughput and take full use of data locality for applications, the accelerator uses three pipelined processing units.

7.2.2 The GPU Accelerators of Neural Networks

As the fixed circuit, the long design and verification cycles of ASIC, and the high speed of model iterators and optimizations in neural network algorithms and application development, designing a future neural network ASIC-specialized chips has much difficulty and risk. However, heterogeneous GPU accelerators with a short design period and high bandwidth are the widely used solution to build quick prototype systems in the industry. Otherwise, in academia, some neural network accelerators for GPU have existed. For instance, research focuses on CNNs' computing efficiency and neglects CNNs' internal memory efficiency [24], but the memory efficiency of different CNN layers can affect data layout and memory access mode to performance. The paper [25] proposed a high-efficiency GPU implementation of the large scale of recursive neural networks and demonstrated the scalability of this GPU implementation. Utilizing the potential parallel ability of recursive neural networks, this work proposed a fine-grained two-stage pipeline. The paper [26] suggests convolution operations during the executing time of DNNs and aims to improve the performance of advanced convolution algorithms (Winograd convolutions) on GPU. Generally, CNNs have lots of zero weights, and the research proposed a low-latency and high-efficiency hardware mechanism to pass zero inputs multiplication and give results 0 (ZeroSkip); Winograd convolutions with extra data conversions limit performance, but the data reuse optimizing of add operations (AddOpt) improves the utilization of local registers and then decreases the on-chip buffer accesses. The experiment results demonstrate that compared with the non-optimized one, the method proposed by this work has a 58% improvement in performance. The paper [27] compares open-source CNN GPU-based implementations and analyzes potential bottlenecks of system performance. The paper [28] proposed two scheduling strategies to optimize object detection tasks and improve the system performance. One is to accelerate the CNNs' forward process by utilizing an efficient image compositional algorithm; the other is a lightweight memory consumption algorithm to make it possible to train an arbitrary size CNNs model in limited memory conditions. Overall, the heterogeneous accelerating systems based on GPU are relatively mature and can quickly iterate neural network topology models and algorithms among GPU boards.

7.2.3 The FPGA Heterogeneous Accelerators of Neural Networks

Except for the ASIC and GPU, the FPGA is an important platform for implementing heterogeneous hardware accelerators. Compared to the ASIC and the GPU, the FPGA has higher flexibility and lower energy consumption. Besides, the current neural networks, such as DNNs and recursive neural networks, can rapidly evolve. For example, utilizing the sparsity (pruning) and simple data types (1 bit–2 bits) makes it highly efficient for algorithms. However, the innovations of customized data types introduce irregular parallelism, resulting in hardness for the GPU processing while adapting for the FPGA customizable features.

In recent years, there has been a series of representative heterogeneous FPGA-based accelerators, for instance, ESE [29] proposed a sparse LSTM efficient speech recognition engine by FPGA, which optimizes software and hardware simultaneously, not only compresses neural networks into small size in algorithms but also supports compressed deep learning algorithms in hardware. In software, ESE comes up with a load-balance aware pruning algorithm, which takes the load-balance problems among different cores into consideration, when multi-core accelerators compute in parallel ultimately; in hardware, ESE redesigns the hardware architecture supporting multi-user and recursive neural networks. Nurvitadhi et al. [30] evaluate the performance and power efficiency difference between the FPGA and the GPU when accelerating next-generation DNNs and conclude that the strong computing resources on GPU make it have a natural parallelism with regular neural networks, nevertheless, the pruning and compressing methods cause irregular neural networks, so that impact computing neural networks in parallel using GPU. To solve the above problem, the FPGA could use customized methods. With the increasing resources of the next-generation FPGA, the FPGA will become a choice as the next-generation DNNs' accelerating platform. Nurvitadhi et al. [31] research a variant of recursive neural networks named Gate Recurrent Unit (GRU) and propose an optimized storage means to avoid partial dense matrix-vector multiplication (SEGMV), in addition, evaluate implementations of the FPGA, the ASIC, the GPU, and the multi-core CPU. The results demonstrate that compared with the other implementations, the FPGA performs a higher energy efficiency. On the one hand, DnnWeaver [32] designs an accelerator for specific models and implements an auto-generated synthesizable accelerator framework according to the network topology and hardware resources.

From the optimizing perspective, loop unrolling, tiling, and switching or fine-tuning the fixed accelerator architecture and data flow are general ways to optimize neural networks. Yufei Ma [33] proposed a quantitative multi-variable-based analyzing and optimizing method to optimize convolution loops. The search design variables are configured to minimize memory accesses and data migration for a given dataflow in the hardware CNN accelerator, while maximizing resource efficiency for better performance of the dataflow. Similarly, Jialiang Zhang et al. [34] proposed a performance analysis model for deeply analyzing the resource requirements of classification kernels in CNNs and resources provided by state-of-the-art FPGAs. The critical bottleneck is the memory bandwidth on-chip. Therefore, a new core design is proposed, which efficiently orientates the bandwidth-limited problems to optimally balance the computing, the on-chip memory access, and the off-chip memory access.

All of the above works demonstrate constructing neural network hardware accelerators adopting the FPGA is feasible, while most of the researches are limited by the bandwidth of the FPGA, and could not fully solve optimizing memory access problems in computing. Hence, researching a computing and storing combination architecture should helpfully improve the FPGA hardware access bandwidth.

7.2.4 The Modern Storage Accelerators

In traditional computer systems, we adopt dynamic random-access memory (DRAM) as the system memory. Before processing, programs and data should be loaded into the main memory. As the increasing speed of the data scale is much faster than the main memory, and the capability of traditional main memory increasing could not improve its bandwidth concurrently, the challenge of "storage wall" will become serious. With the rapid development of modern storage technologies (such as 3D stacking technology [35]), researchers in China and abroad find, moreover, metal-oxide resistor random access memory (ReRAM), a spin transfer torque magnetoresistive random access Memory (STT-RAM), and phase change memory with the ability not only storing data but also executing logic and algorithm operations. Hence, researches on new storage neural network accelerators are becoming more and more widespread.

Prime [36] proposed a neural network memory computer architecture with the ReRAM. A partial ReRAM crossbar array could be an accelerator of neural network applications or expand the capability of the main memory. Additionally, the circuit, structure, and software interfaces of Prime make the ReRAM array have the ability of dynamical reconfiguration between the main memory and the accelerator. They also allow Prime to support more types of computation than just neural networks. Isaac [37] proposed a crossbar analog computation accelerator for CNNs. Isaac uses eDRAM as a data register between pipeline stages to implement accelerating computing of different layers in neural networks in the way organized in pipelines and designs analog data encoding types to decrease the overhead of analog-to-digital conversions. Although both Prime and Isaac use the ReRAM modern storage to accelerate neural network computing, they only accelerate the testing stage of neural networks, in the meanwhile, the training stage of neural networks adopts traditional methods as before.

Therefore, PipeLayer [38] proposed an accelerator supporting both the testing stage and the training stage. PipeLayer analyzes the data dependency and weight updating problems in the training stage and designs pipelines to implement parallel computing in layers; besides, PipeLayer suggests a highly parallel design and weights redundancy based on the conception of parallel granularity to support parallel between layers. Junwhan et al. [39] proposed an extensible accelerator named Tesseract, which computes in the main memory of graph data processing in parallel. It puts computing units in the 3D stacking HMC, each vault of the HMC is responsible for processing different subgraph data, and the message-passing communication mechanism is used between vaults. To improve the utilization of memory bandwidth, Tesseract designs and implements two-ways prefetching mechanism suitable to the memory access mode of graph data. Graphicionado [40] proposed a high-performance and energy-efficient graph data-analyzing accelerator with eDRAM. The accelerator processes graph data into two phases, which are the processing phase and the application phase implemented by pipelines. Additionally, Graphicionado designed a new graph data access mode to decrease the number of random access as far as possible. Oscar [41] adopts STT-RAM as the last-level cache to relieve cache conflicts in the CPU-GPU heterogeneous architecture. Oscar integrates the asynchronous batching scheduling mechanism and the priority-based allocation strategy to maximize the potential of STT-RAM-based last-level cache. The paper [42] proposed a memristor-based architecture for data-dense memory computing, which integrates storage and computing in a crossbar topology structure memristor. The paper [43] proposed a ReRAM-based crossbar accelerator for the forward processing of binary CNNs. In the ReRAM-based computing system, this work adopts the low bit-level ReRAM and low bit-level analog-to-digital converter (ADC)/digital-to-analog converter (DAC) interfaces to realize more quickly read and write operations and higher energy efficiency. When a crossbar is incapable of storing the total weights in a neural network layer, the accelerator designs two implementations, a matrix partition type and a pipeline type. Resparc [44] proposed a memristor-based crossbar accelerator for spiking neural networks, which is reconfigurable and efficient. Resparc utilizes a high-energy efficient crossbar to perform inner products and implements a layered reconfigurable design for (spiking neural network) SNN including a data flow model; Resparc can map the topology of spiking neural networks to the most optimal scale crossbars.

All of the aforementioned works are based on modern storage to implement heterogeneous accelerators for typical neural network applications; however, because the capacity of storage structures to realize logic is restricted, methods to integrate current GPUs, FPGAs, and other computing units into an integration framework are still a domain needed to do further researches.

7.3 Common Optimization Methods in Hardware Customization

The neural network is a computation-intensive and storage-intensive application. In the design of neural network accelerators, there are many contradictions, so in most of the related work in recent years, neural network accelerators have been designed from the perspective of optimizing calculation, optimizing storage, optimizing the area and power consumption, and some others apply the neural network to specific problems. Presumably, the following areas are covered.

7.3.1 Optimizing Calculation

Although the most advanced CNN accelerators can deliver high computational throughput, the performance is highly unstable. Once new networks with different model structures (e.g., layers and kernel size) emerge, the fixed hardware structure may no longer match new applications. Consequently, the accelerator will fail to deliver high performance due to the underutilization of either logic resources or memory bandwidth. To overcome this problem, C-Brain [45] proposes a novel deep-learning accelerator, which offers multiple types of data-level parallelism: inter-kernel, intra-kernel, and hybrid. When processing different layers in parallel, the parallel approach is part of the input with the feature map data. The inter-kernel parallelism is used to process different layers of the input feature map; intra-kernel parallelism is used to process the same layer of the feature map. The design can adaptively switch among the three types of parallelism and the corresponding data tiling schemes to dynamically match different networks or even different layers of a single network. No matter how we change the hardware configurations or network types, the proposed network mapping strategy ensures optimal performance and energy efficiency. Caffeine [46] first points out that the convolution layer of the neural network is computationally intensive, and the full-connected layer belongs to the memory-intensive. When CNN is accelerated on the FPGA, the convolution layer cannot be accelerated only. Otherwise, the operation of the full-connected layer will become a new bottleneck. Caffeine analyzes and studies the uniform representation of the neural network for the convolution layer and the full-connected layer (as shown in Figures 7.3 and 7.4) to reduce the amount of intermediate data generated. Finally, they design hardware and software co-designed library to accelerate the entire CNN on FPGAs efficiently and optimize the bandwidth of the accelerator.

Spiking neural network as the third generation of the ANN has appeared in more and more applications. When the network scale rises to the order of cells in the human visual cortex, the spiking neural network faces severe computational efficiency problems. AXSNN [47] applies the approximate

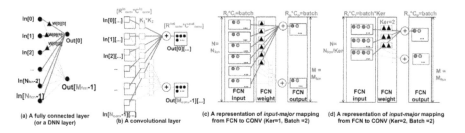

(a) A fully connected layer (or a DNN layer)   (b) A convolutional layer   (c) A representation of *input-major* mapping from FCN to CONV (Ker=1, Batch =2)   (d) A representation of *input-major* mapping from FCN to CONV (Ker=2, Batch =2)

FIGURE 7.3

Input–output mapping from each calculation layer to the CONV layer. (a) A fully connected layer. (b) A convolutional layer. (c) FCN layer. (d) FCN layer, kernel size=2.

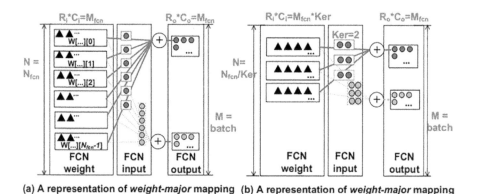

(a) A representation of *weight-major* mapping from FCN to CONV (Ker=1, Batch =2)   (b) A representation of *weight-major* mapping from FCN to CONV (Ker=2, Batch =2)

FIGURE 7.4

Multi-batch data mapping from the FCN layer to the CONV layer. (a) Kernel size=1. (b) Kernel size=2.

calculation method to select the neuron, based on the static and dynamic information of the neuron's average spiking frequency, the current internal state, and the connected synaptic weight in the calculation of the spiking neural network. And then selectively skip the pulse reception and pulse output that does not affect the output of these neurons, thereby reducing the redundancy calculation, and improving the calculation efficiency. In the experiment, the spiking neural network based on approximate calculation is implemented in software and hardware. Compared with the optimized network, the scalar computation is reduced by 1.4–5.5 times on average, and the energy consumption is 1.2–3.62 times and 1.26–3.9 times.

The computational process of convolution neural networks is complex; a huge amount of data movements between the computational processor core and memory hierarchy occupy the majority of the power consumption. Chain-NN [48] focuses on the hardware calculation process of the convolution operation concerning multiplexing the input data and designs the convolution neural network accelerator Chain-NN based on the one-dimensional chain architecture. Chain-NN consists of the dedicated dual-channel process engines; the overall structure can be configured according to the structural parameters of the network to improve the overall resource utilization. The experimental results show that the accelerator can achieve 84%–100% of the internal resource utilization rate when dealing with the commonly used convolution neural network. Under the TSMC 28 nm structure, it can reach 806.4GOPS throughput with 700 MHz operating frequency, and power efficiency is at least 2.5–4 times better than the state-of-the-art works. The paper [5] presents a novel method to improve the computation rate of CNN accelerators by packing two product operations and integrating the operation into one DSP block of an off-the-shelf FPGA. The same feature of the multiplier coincides with the computational model corresponding to the parallel processing of multiple output neurons, thus improving the computational efficiency and resource utilization of the network. The experimental results show that this approach not only increases the computation throughput of a CNN layer by twice with the same resource, but the network performance also improves by 14%–84% over a highly optimized state-of-the-art accelerator solution. The fact that a large number of zero values are in the convolution neural network severely degrades the computational efficiency of the network. The paper [6] proposes a novel hardware accelerator for CNNs exploiting zero weights and activations. Unlike most CNN accelerators that use a synchronous parallel computing model, the accelerator uses a finer granular program element (PE) internally, and each PE uses a weak synchronous mode of operation that can independently detect and skip zero values in the weights and activation output value. Besides, the authors also report a zero-induced load imbalance problem, which exists in zero-aware parallel CNN hardware architectures, and present a zero-aware kernel allocation as a solution. The simulation results show that the proposed architecture running two real deep CNNs pruned AlexNet and VGG-16, offers 4× speedup. The inherent approximation in neural network calculations can be used to simplify the computational process. LookNN [49] proposes a new simplified processing strategy, using the similarity idea and the fault-tolerant properties of the neural network. All the floating-point multiplication operations in the neural network are transformed into a query operation based on the look-up table. Then, the quick search operation in the calculation process is realized by adding the associated memory for the quick retrieval of the calculation result. The experimental results show that the strategy can reduce energy consumption by 2.2 times. Without additional calculation errors, performance is increased by 5 times, and energy consumption is reduced by 3 times.

7.3.2 Optimizing Storage

In the mobile device and other embedded devices to deploy the machine learning accelerator, due to power consumption and area and other factors, accelerator on-chip storage capacity is very limited. To avoid frequent off-chip access, the network weights need to be compressed, and the traditional sparse matrix compression method's random access and online coding and decoding will make the calculation logical throughput limited. To overcome this problem, the paper [9] proposes an efficient on-chip memory architecture for CNN inference acceleration. The K-means accelerator storage subsystem provides a fast mechanism for decoding encoded data to ensure the throughput of the computational logic while compressing the weights. At the same time, the storage subsystem encodes the intermediate results of the output between the layers in the network. By using a shorter index to replace the output of a large number of values 0, the cost of storing intermediate results is reduced. Besides, before storing data in the calculation logic, the storage subsystem can detect and skip the calculation of the operand of 0 to increase the computational speed. The results of the experiment show that the accelerator that uses the proposed storage subsystem can reduce the storage capacity by 8 times and energy consumption by 4 times, which makes it possible for mobile phones and other small embedded devices to use accelerators to perform efficient calculations of large-scale CNN. Large-scale ANNs have shown significant promise in addressing a wide range of classification and recognition applications However, their large computational requirements stretch the capabilities of computing platforms. The core of a digital hardware neuron consists of a multiplier, accumulator, and activation function. Multipliers consume most of the processing energy in the digital neurons. The paper [10] proposes an approximate multiplier that utilizes the notion of computation sharing and exploits the error resilience of neural network applications to reduce power consumption. The authors also propose multiplier-less artificial neurons for even larger improvement in energy consumption and adapt the training process to ensure minimal degradation in accuracy. The experiment results show a 35% and 60% reduction in energy consumption, for neuron sizes of 8 bits and 12 bits, respectively, with a maximum of ~2.83% loss in network accuracy, compared to a conventional neuron implementation. Neural networks require significant memory capacity and bandwidth to store a large number of synaptic weights. The paper [11] presents an application of JPEG image encoding to compress the weight matrix by exploiting the spatial locality and smoothness of the weights. To minimize the loss of accuracy due to JPEG encoding, the authors propose to adaptively control the quantization factor of the JPEG algorithm depending on the error-sensitivity (gradient) of each weight. With the adaptive compression technique, the weight blocks with higher sensitivity are compressed less for higher accuracy. The adaptive compression reduces memory requirement, which in turn results in higher performance and lower energy of neural network hardware. The simulation for inference hardware for multi-layer perceptron with the MNIST data set shows that with less than 1% loss of recognition accuracy, effective memory bandwidth has been increased by 3 times.

7.3.3 Optimizing the Area and Power Consumption

The emerging metal-oxide resistive random-access memory (RRAM) and RRAM crossbar have shown great potential in neuromorphic applications with high energy efficiency. However, the interfaces between analog RRAM crossbars and digital peripheral functions, namely ADCs and DACs, create significant overhead due to the large amount of intermediate data in CNN. RRAM-based CNN design would consume most of the area and energy. The paper [12] proposes an energy-efficient structure for RRAM-based CNN. Based on the analysis of data distribution, a quantization method is proposed to transfer the intermediate data into 1 bit and eliminate DACs. An energy-efficient structure using input data as selection signals is proposed to reduce the ADC cost for merging results of multiple crossbars. The experimental results show that the proposed method and structure can save 80% area and more than 95% energy while maintaining the same or comparable classification accuracy of CNN on MNIST. The paper [13] proposes using the metal-insulator-transition-based two-terminal device as a compact oscillation neuron to parallel read operation from the resistive synaptic array. The weighted sum is represented by the frequency of the oscillation neuron. Compared to the complex complementary metal–oxide–semiconductor (CMOS) integrate-and-fire neuron with tens of transistors, the oscillation neuron achieves significant area reduction, thereby alleviating the column pitch matching problem of the peripheral circuitry in resistive memories. Finally, through the comparison of the circuit-level benchmark, at the level of the single neuron node, oscillating neurons compared to CMOS neurons, the area decreased by 12%. At the array level of 128×128, the oscillating neurons are used to reduce the total area by 4%; the energy consumption is saved 5 times, and the leakage power is reduced by 40 times, demonstrating the advantages of oscillating neuron integration. Because the number of synapses in ANN is much greater than the number of neurons, synaptic read and write operations also occupy a large part of the power consumption, the paper [14] proposes to reduce the voltage to improve energy efficiency. However, the traditional 6T SRAM memory with the voltage drop shows instability, easily leading to reduced computational accuracy. In this paper, the memory structure is optimized, using a stable 8T SRAM to replace part of the traditional 6T SRAM (as shown in Figure 7.5). Storing the more important calculation data will ensure the accuracy of the calculation and further reduce the voltage, to achieve the purpose of improving energy efficiency. At the same time, to reduce the power consumption while minimizing the use of the area, according to the importance of different network layers on the calculation results, change the synaptic weights stored in 8T SRAM most significant bit number in different layers. To alleviate the computational energy efficiency problem in the neural network, the paper [15] proposes a technical scheme NNCAM, which can be used to calculate the neural network based on content addressable memory (CAM) for the GPU platform.

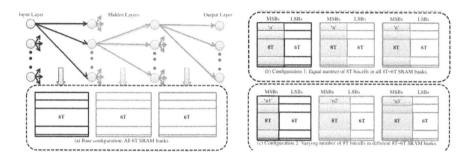

FIGURE 7.5
Synaptic memory configurations under study. (a) All 6T SRAM. (b) Significance-driven hybrid
8T-6T SRAM. (c) Synaptic-sensitivity driven hybrid memory architecture.

First of all, NNCAM stores and searches the process of pattern matching
which is used very frequently, achieving the reuse of the results, thus dig-
ging out the learning algorithm in the local. Second, layer-based associative update and selective approximation techniques are used in NNCAM
to improve computational efficiency and accuracy. The NNCAM module is
integrated into AMD's Southern Island GPU for experimental evaluation.
The results show that the new technology can reduce energy consumption
by 68%, and improve performance by 40%, at the cost of accuracy loss less
than 2%.

Neural associative memory (AM) is one of the critical building blocks for
cognitive workloads such as classification and recognition. One of the key
challenges in designing AM is to extend memory capacity while minimizing power and hardware overhead. However, prior arts show that memory
capacity scales slowly, often logarithmically or in root with the total bits of
synaptic weights. This makes it prohibitive in hardware to achieve large
memory capacity for practical applications. The paper [16] proposes a synaptic model called recursive synaptic bit reuse, which enables near-linear scaling of memory capacity with total synaptic bits. Also, the model can handle
input data that are correlated, more robustly than the conventional model.
The experiment is conducted in Hopfield neural networks (HNN) which contains the total synaptic bits of 5–327 kB and finds that the model can increase
the memory capacity as large as 30× over conventional models. The authors
also study hardware cost via very large scale integration (VLSI) implementation of HNNs in a 65 nm CMOS, confirming that the proposed model can
achieve up to 10× area savings at the same capacity over the conventional
synaptic model.

The standard CMOS-based artificial neuron designs to implement nonlinear neuron activation function typically consist of a large number of transistors, which inevitably causes large area and power consumption. There is a
need for a novel nanoelectronic device that can intrinsically and efficiently
implement such complex nonlinear neuron activation functions. The paper
[17] first proposes a threshold-tunable artificial neuron based on magnetic

Skyrmion. Meanwhile, the authors propose a Skyrmion Neuron Cluster (SNC) to approximate nonlinear soft-limiting neuron activation functions, such as the most popular sigmoid function. The device-to-system simulation indicates that the recognition accuracy is 98.74% in deep learning CNNs based on the MNIST handwritten digits data set. Moreover, the energy consumption of the proposed SNC is more than two orders lower than that of its CMOS counterpart.

7.3.4 Programming Framework

The FPGA-based hardware accelerator design process is complex; the upper application developers may lack understanding of the underlying neural network structure, resulting in accelerator design being more difficult. To simplify the design process, the paper [50] proposes a design automation tool, DeepBurning (as shown in Figure 7.6), which allows the application developers to build accelerators from scratch with custom configurations and operations for their specific network models for performance optimization. DeepBurning includes an Register-transfer-level (RTL) accelerator generator and a coordinated compiler that generates the control flow and data layout fixed constraints under User-SPE. The tool can be used to implement an FPGA-based NN accelerator or help generate chip design for the early design stage. In general, DeepBurning supports a large family of NN models and greatly simplifies the design flow of NN accelerators for the machine learning or AI application developers. The evaluation shows that the generated accelerators exhibit greater power efficiency compared to state-of-the-art FPGA-based solutions. The framework makes it possible

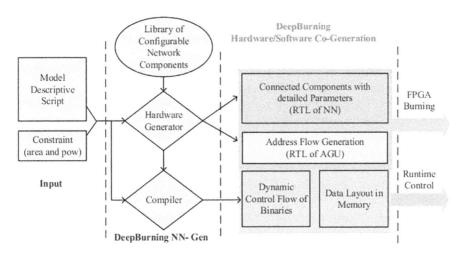

FIGURE 7.6
Neural network accelerator development framework – DeepBurning [50].

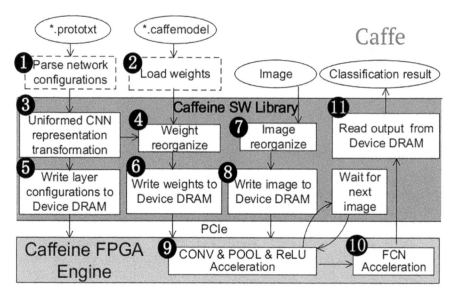

FIGURE 7.7
Caffeine FPGA architecture.

for the upper application designers to use FPGA to accelerate the computation of neural networks as easily as Caffe, which greatly improves the
applicability of FPGA in this field.

The paper [46] first analyzes and studies a uniformed convolutional
matrix multiplication representation for both computation-intensive convolutional layers and communication-intensive fully connected layers, then
designs and implements Caffeine (as shown in Figure 7.7), and provides
various hardware/software definable parameters for user configurations.
Finally, integrate Caffeine into the industry-standard software deep learning framework Caffe. Compared to traditional CPU and GPU, the accelerator has considerable performance and energy efficiency improvement. The
question of how to best design an accelerator for a given CNN has not been
answered yet. The paper [19] addresses that challenge, by providing a novel
framework that can universally and accurately evaluate and explore various architectural choices for CNN accelerators on FPGAs. The exploration
framework is more extensive than that of any previous work concerning
the design space and takes into account various FPGA resources to maximize performance including DSP resources, on-chip memory, and off-chip
memory bandwidth. The experimental results using some of the largest
CNN models including one that has 16 convolutional layers demonstrate
the efficacy of our framework, as well as the need for such a high-level
architecture exploration approach to finding the best architecture for a
CNN model.

7.3.5 The New Method Applied to Neural Networks

The paper [20] presents an efficient DNN design with stochastic computing (as shown in Figure 7.8). Pointing out that directly adopting stochastic computing to DNN has some challenges including random error fluctuation, range limitation, and overhead in accumulation, the authors address these problems by removing near-zero weights, applying weight-scaling, and integrating the activation function with the accumulator. Experimental results show that the approach outperforms the conventional binary logic in terms of gate area, latency, and power consumption. The paper [21] also simplifies the computation of deep convolution neural networks (DCNNs) by stochastic computing. In this paper, eight feature extraction designs for DCNNs in two groups are explored and optimized in detail from the perspective of calculation precision, where the authors permute two SC implementations for inner-product calculation, two down-sampling schemes, and two structures of DCNN neurons. Experimental results show that the accuracies of SC-based DCNNs are guaranteed compared with software implementations on CPU/GPU/binary-based ASIC synthesis, while area, power, and energy are significantly reduced by up to 776×, 190×, and 32,835×. The paper [22] develops a highly energy-efficient hardware implementation of a

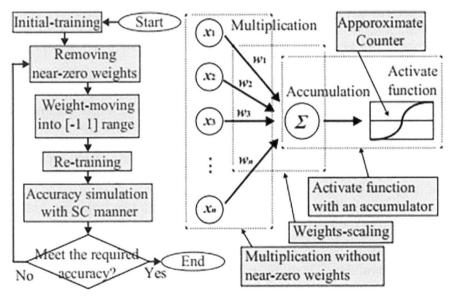

(a) Training procedures   (b) Testing with the SC neuron

FIGURE 7.8

(a) Training procedure for DNN using SC with 32-bit floating-point computation. (b) SC neurons are operated with SC exploiting the suggested solutions in the testing phase.

class of sketching methods based on random projections. At the same time, it shows how to explore the randomness of the mapping matrix to build efficient machine learning applications. The authors define a random matrix construction method to explore the special sparse structure, and thus efficiently make use of hardware to optimize the conversion on the FPGA. The proposed design can achieve up to 2× speedup with a 17% area reduction. Applying the transform to the problem of k-nearest neighbors (KNN) classification and principal component analysis (PCA) achieves up to 7× latency and energy improvement. More importantly, the ability to average accumulation error allows the design to use a 1-bit multiplier instead of the 4-bit used in the KNN algorithm, which results in a further 6% energy saving and 50% area reduction. The paper [23] proposes a robust and energy-efficient analog implementation of the spiking temporal encoder. The authors pattern the neural activities across multiple timescales and encode the sensory information using time-dependent temporal scales. The concept of iteration structure is introduced to construct a neural encoder that greatly increases the information processing ability of the proposed temporal encoder. Integrated with the iteration technique and operational-amplifier-free design, the error rate of the output temporal codes by the encoder is reduced to an extremely low level. Integrated with the iteration technique and operational-amplifier-free design, the error rate of the output temporal codes is reduced to an extremely low level. The simulation and measurement results show the proposed temporal encoder exhibits not only energy efficiency but also high accuracy DNNs have many convolutional layers with different parameters in terms of input/output/kernel sizes as well as input stride.

Design constraints usually require a single design for all layers of a given DNN. Thus a key challenge is how to design a common architecture, which can be quite diverse and complex. The paper [24] presents a flexible and highly efficient 3D neuron array architecture that is a natural fit for convolutional layers. The authors also present the technique to optimize its parameters including on-chip buffer sizes for a given set of resource constraints for modern FPGAs. The experimental results targeting a Virtex-7 FPGA demonstrate that the proposed technique can generate DNN accelerators that can outperform the state-of-the-art solutions, by 22% for 32-bit floating-point MAC implementations, and are more scalable in terms of computing resources and DNN size.

Memristor-based neuromorphic computing system provides a promising solution to significantly boost the power efficiency of the computing system. The system simulator can model the system and realize an early-stage design space exploration. The paper [51] develops a memristor-based neuromorphic system simulation platform (MNSIM, as shown in Figure 7.9). MNSIM proposes a general hierarchical structure for the memristor-based neuromorphic computing system and provides a flexible interface for users to customize the design. MNSIM also provides a detailed reference design for large-scale applications. MNSIM embeds estimation models of area, power,

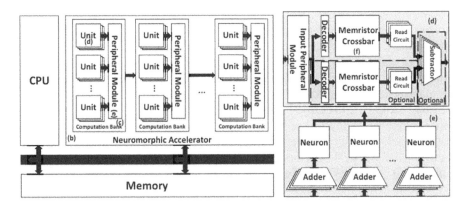

FIGURE 7.9
MNSIM architecture.

and latency to simulate the performance of the system. To estimate the computing accuracy, MNSIM proposes a behavior-level model between computing error rate and crossbar design parameters considering the influence of interconnect lines and non-ideal device factors. Experimental results show that MNSIM achieves more than 7,000 times speed-up compared with SPICE and obtains reasonable accuracy. Aiming at a large number of dot-product operations in neural network computation, the paper [52] presents and experimentally validates 3D-DPE, a general-purpose dot-product engine, which is ideal for accelerating ANNs. 3D-DPE is based on a monolithically integrated 3D CMOS–memristor hybrid circuit and performs a high-dimensional dot-product operation (a recurrent and computationally expensive operation in ANNs) within a single step, using analog current-based computing. 3D-DPE is made up of two subsystems, namely a CMOS subsystem serving as the memory controller and an analog memory subsystem consisting of multi-layer high-density memory. Crossbar arrays are fabricated on top of the CMOS subsystem. Their integration is based on a high-density area-distributed interface, resulting in much higher connectivity between the two subsystems. Compared to the traditional interface of a 2D system or a 3D system integrated using through-silicon-via, 3D-DPE's single-step dot-product operation is not limited by the memory bandwidth, and the input dimension of the operations scales well with the capacity of the 3D memristive arrays.

Recently, memristor crossbar arrays have been utilized in realizing spiking-based neuromorphic systems, where memristor conductance values correspond to synaptic weights. Most of these systems are composed of a single crossbar layer, in which system training is done off-chip, using computer-based simulations, and then the trained weights are pre-programmed to the memristor crossbar array. However, multi-layered, on-chip trained systems become crucial for handling the massive amount of data and to overcome the resistance shift that occurs to memristors over time. The paper [27] proposes a spiking-based multi-layered neuromorphic computing system capable of online training. The experimental results show that the overall performance of the system is improved by 42% while ensuring the accuracy of the calculation. The resistance variations and stuck-at faults in the memristor devices, however, dramatically degrade not only the chip yield but also the classification accuracy of the neural networks running on the RRAM crossbar. Existing hardware-based solutions cause enormous overhead and power consumption, while software-based solutions are less efficient in tolerating stuck-at faults and large variations. The paper [28] proposes an accelerator-friendly neural network training method, by leveraging the inherent self-healing capability of the neural network, to prevent the large weight synapses from being mapped to the abnormal memristors based on the fault/variation distribution in the RRAM crossbar. Experimental results show the proposed method can pull the classification accuracy (10%–45% loss in previous works) up close to the ideal level with less than 1% loss.

7.3.6 Applications Using Neural Network

ANNs provide a suitable mechanism for fault detection and fault-tolerance in critical domains like automotive systems. However, common ANNs are inherently computationally intensive, and the precision requirements in harsh automotive environments mean large networks are required, making software implementations impractical. The paper [29] presents a hybrid approach, based on the Xilinx Zynq platform, which integrates an ANN-based prediction system that doubles up as a replacement sensor in the case of persistent faults (as shown in Figure 7.10). The ANN network is completely contained within a partially reconfigurable region (PRR), integrated with parallel sensor acquisition interfaces, a fault detection system, a data processing engine, and a network interface. PRR allows seamless migration from the fault-detection ANN network (under normal operation) to the fault-tolerant mode with a larger, more complex, and accurate network that effectively replaces the faulty sensor. The proposed parallel architecture enables the ANN to be evaluated in a predictable short latency of under 1us, even for the larger prediction network.

Deep convolutional networks (ConvNets) are currently superior in benchmark performance, but the associated demands on computation and data transfer prohibit straightforward mapping on energy-constrained wearable platforms. The computational burden can be overcome by dedicated hardware accelerators, but it is the sheer amount of data transfer and level of utilization that determines the energy efficiency. The paper [30] presents the neuro vector engine, a SIMD accelerator of ConvNets for visual object classification, targeting portable and wearable devices. The proposed accelerator is very flexible due to the usage of VLIW ISA, at the cost of instruction fetch overhead. The authors show that this overhead is insignificant when the extra flexibility enables advanced data locality optimizations and improves

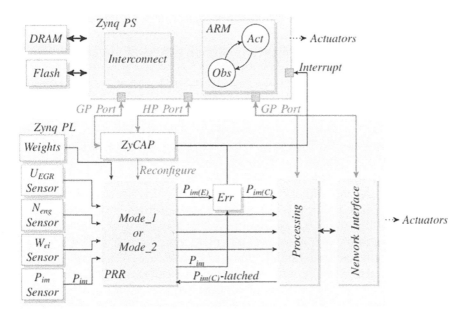

FIGURE 7.10
Proposed hybrid fault-tolerant ECU model on Zynq.

hardware utilization. Using ConvNet Vision and co-optimizing accelerator architecture and algorithm loop structure, 30Gops is achieved with a power of 54mW and TSMC 40nm technology, enabling high-end visual object recognition by portable and even wearable devices. Ideally, systems would employ near-sensor computation to execute these tasks at sensor endpoints to maximize data reduction and minimize data movement. However, near-sensor computing presents its own set of challenges such as operating power constraints, energy budgets, and communication bandwidth capacities. The paper [31] proposes a stochastic binary hybrid design that splits the computation between the stochastic and binary domains for near-sensor NN applications. In addition, the proposed design uses a new stochastic adder and multiplier that are significantly more accurate than existing adders and multipliers. The authors also show that re-training the binary portion of the NN computation can compensate for precision losses introduced by shorter stochastic bit-streams, allowing faster run times at minimal accuracy losses. The evaluation shows that the proposed hybrid stochastic-binary design can achieve 9.8× energy efficiency savings, which makes it possible to locally process the CNN at the sensor end. DNNs are generally difficult to deploy on resource-constrained devices, some existing attempts mainly focus on client-server computing paradigm or DNN model compression, which require either infrastructure supports or special training phases, respectively. The paper [53] proposes MoDNN – a locally distributed mobile computing system for DNN applications. MoDNN can partition already trained

DNN models onto several mobile devices to accelerate DNN computations by alleviating device-level computing costs and memory usage. Two model partition schemes are also designed by the authors to minimize non-parallel data delivery time, including both wakeup time and transmission time. Experimental results show that when the number of worker nodes increases from 2 to 4, MoDNN can accelerate the DNN computation by 2.17–4.28×.

Bidirectional long short-term memory neural networks have shown superior performance in character recognition concerning other types of neural networks. The paper [33] proposes the first hardware architecture of the bidirectional long short-term memory neural network with connectionist temporal classification for optical character recognition. Based on the new architecture, the authors present an FPGA hardware accelerator that achieves 459 times higher throughput than state-of-the-art. Visual recognition is a typical task on mobile platforms that usually uses two scenarios either the task runs locally on an embedded processor or offloaded. The authors show that computationally intensive visual recognition task benefits from being migrated to our dedicated hardware accelerator and outperforms high-performance CPUs in terms of runtime while consuming less energy than low-power systems with negligible loss of recognition accuracy.

7.3.7 Others

In addition to the above papers, there is some exploratory and optimized content that deserves our attention. Many neural networks are calculated using hardware units with different data bits at different energy consumption and precision requirements. However, there is a lack of comprehensive research on the required input data and weight data bits in the neural network. The paper [34] quantifies the impact of floating-point data and fixed-point data on network precision, memory footprint, power consumption, energy consumption, and design area for different bit widths in the network analysis. Under the same hardware resources, one can reduce the data bit width to deploy a more large-scale network, to achieve network accuracy, and to achieve energy consumption optimization. TrueNorth design has the issue of limited precision of synaptic weights. The current workaround is running multiple neural network copies in which the average value of each synaptic weight is close to that in the original network. The paper [35] theoretically analyzes the impacts of low data precision in the TrueNorth chip on inference accuracy, core occupation, and performance, and presents a probability-biased learning method to enhance the inference accuracy by reducing the random variance of each computation copy. The experimental results proved that the proposed techniques considerably improve the computation accuracy of the TrueNorth platform and reduce the computation quantity of the platform. To improve the performance as well as maintain the scalability, the paper [36] presents Solar, a service-oriented deep learning architecture using various accelerators like

GPU and FPGA-based approaches. Solar provides a uniform programming model to users so that the hardware implementation and the scheduling are invisible to the programmers. The paper [20] presents a software-defined FPGA-based accelerator for big data, named SODA, which could reconstruct and reorganize the acceleration engines according to the requirements of the various data-intensive applications. SODA decomposes large and complex applications into coarse-grained single-purpose RTL code libraries that perform specialized tasks in out-of-order hardware. The experiment results show that SODA can achieve up to 43.75× speedup at 128 node applications. The paper [38] uses FPGA to design a deep learning accelerator, which focuses on the implementation of the prediction process, data access optimization, and pipeline structure. To improve the performance as well as to maintain the low power cost, the paper [23] designs a DLAU, which is a scalable accelerator architecture for large-scale deep learning networks. The DLAU accelerator employs three pipelined processing units to improve the throughput and utilizes tile techniques to explore locality for applications. The experimental results on the state-of-the-art Xilinx FPGA board demonstrate that the DLAU accelerator can achieve up to 36.1× speedup. Compared to the Intel Core 2 processor, the performance is 1× higher, and power consumption is only 234 mW. After realizing two adjacent layers in different calculation orders, the data dependency between layers can be weakened. The paper [21] proposes a pipeline energy-efficient accelerator named PIE to accelerate the DNN inference computation by pipelining two adjacent layers. As soon as a layer produces an output, the next layer reads the output as an input and starts the parallel computation immediately in another calculation method. In such a way, computations between adjacent layers are pipelined.

7.4 Parallel Programming Models and the Middleware of Neural Networks

Although heterogeneous hardware accelerators have lots of advantages in performance, bandwidth, power, and other aspects, they often have problems with difficult programming and need to provide programming models to support development. For machine learning approaches, the different kinds of open-source deep learning frameworks at present have a good effect on computer vision, speech recognition, natural language processing, and other domains. Recently, there have been mainly common open-source frameworks to processing kinds of neural networks, such as Theano [54], Torch [55], TensorFlow [56], Caffe [57], CNTK [58], Keras [59], SparkNet [60], Deeplearning4J [61], ConvNetJS [62], MxNet [63], Chainer [64], PaddlePaddle [65], DeepCL [66], and PyTorch [67].

Theano is a Python library, developed by École Polytechnique de Montréal in 2008. Users could define, optimize, and evaluate mathematical formulas, especially multi-dimension arrays. Theano calls for GPU to realize large data problems compared to using C language, and this method can get better acceleration and performance. The subsequent significant open-source frameworks in academia and industry, such as Lasagne [68], Keras, and Blocks [69], are constructed by Theano. Keras is an advanced Python-based neural network library; it runs on TensorFlow or Theano frameworks and rapidly constructs prototype systems. This tool supports CNNs, recursive neural networks, and arbitrary connecting strategies running on the CPU and the GPU. Torch is a scientific computing framework, which invokes the GPU first to support machine learning algorithms widely. The framework developed by Lua language is the Facebook and Twitter mainly recommended open-source deep learning framework; it can build complex neural networks flexibly and utilize multiple CPUs and GPUs in parallel. TensorFlow is a digital calculating open-source software library employing data flow graphs, which is developed using C++ language by Google Company. Each node and edge in the data flow graph represent a mathematical operation and a multi-dimension array of data between nodes named tensor respectively. TensorFlow with the feasible architecture, which could migrate among variable platforms, supports multiple users to utilize different kinds of programming languages and develop on distributed platforms continually, and then be migrated to the Spark platform named TensorFlow on Spark. Caffe deep learning framework using modularization to realize, based on C/C++ language, is developed by Yangqing Jia at the University of California, Berkeley, and also provides Python interfaces at the top level. The advantages of Caffe are modular definition allocated from clusters to mobile devices and supporting distributed projects Caffe on Spark. CNTK is an open-source deep learning toolkit from Microsoft, and now it has changed its name to The Microsoft Cognitive Toolkit, which is developed by C++ programming language integrating Python interfaces for users. In the CNTK, a directed graph is used to describe a series of operation steps in neural networks. Leaf nodes and the other nodes represent input data or neural network parameters and matrix operations, respectively. SparkNet developed by AMPLab is a Spark-based framework for training DNNs, including a convenient interface to read data from Spark RDD, a Scala interface in Caffe deep learning frameworks, and a light-weight multiple dimensions tensor library using centralized parameter servers to implement. Deeplearning4J from Skymind Company, the first Java-based commercial open-source distributed deep learning library, integrates Hadoop and Spark and can be used on distributed CPUs and GPUs. The method through Keras interfaces imports neural network models from other deep learning frameworks, including TensorFlow, Caffe, Torch, and Theano. ConvNetJS is a browser plugin developed by Andrej Karpathy at Stanford University finally implemented on browsers totally. ConvNetJS supports general neural network modules, containing classification, logistical regression functions, and other essential structures without GPU's participation. MxNet, a lightweight, feasibly distributed, C++-based, and mobile deep learning framework, is developed by researchers in CXXNet, Minerva [11], and Purine2 [70]. It is embedded in host languages and integrates symbol representation and tensor computations. For users, the framework supplies automatic division to get gradients. The main features of the framework are computing and memory efficiency, running on variable heterogeneous platforms, and even mobile devices. Chainer is a software framework developed by Preferred Networks Company. Based on the principle that networks are defined in the running dynamically, Chainner provides feasible, visualized, and high-performance deep learning models, including models and changeable self-encoders at present. The C++ language-based PaddlePaddle is a Baidu Company deep learning framework, containing Python interfaces. Users configure a series of parameters to train traditional neural networks or more complex models. Then in emotion analysis, machine translations, image descriptions, and other domains, the frameworks perform the best performance. DeepCL is a Hugh Perkins-developed OpenCL library, which is used to train convolution neural networks. PyTorch, especially for training complex models, implements a machine learning framework Torch executing in Python language type, including running by the CPUs- and GPUs-based tensor operation library and the neural network library. The framework supports training models and shared-memory multi-thread concurrency, adopting dynamic computing graph structure to construct the whole neural networks rapidly.

7.5 Latest Developments and Conclusions

7.5.1 Summary of the Latest Developments

The survey on international conferences shows that neural networks especially DNNs and recursive neural networks have a feature of rapidly evolving. Meanwhile, sparsity, and simple data types and shorter data width can make these algorithms efficiency have significant leaps. The studies focus on accelerating deep learning algorithms whose structures are sparse and compressed in software and hardware and optimizing the results in load balance problems. Compared to performance and energy efficiency of GPUs and FPGAs, GPUs have significant advantages in processing regular neural networks in parallel, while FPGAs can customize and be reconfigured to process irregular pruned and compressed neural networks, which means the FPGA is a candidate for the next-generation DNN accelerating platform.

Another candidate for the next-generation DNN accelerating platform is specialized neural network chips. Using neural network chips to allocate convolution layers occupying most of the operations in neural networks on accelerating engines, the other operations such as ReLU function layers, pooling layers, and full-connected layers on another module (DSP or others) compute in parallel. Additionally, sparsity and other features should be taken into consideration.

7.5.2 Conclusions and Outlook

Analyzing the ASIC, the GPU-based, and the FPGA-based hardware neural network accelerators, the research of how to perform neural network applications has become a hot issue in industry and academia, and the related works concentrate on domains of optimizing memory access bandwidth, advanced storage devices, and programming models. However, the research of heterogeneous neural network accelerators still in the developing stages finally forms the mature large-scale application technology which needs scientists to do more creative literature. First, the critical problem of neural network applications is the need to describe neural network features and memory access. Second, a computing-memory-integrated architecture should be designed in accelerators. At last, tools supporting programming frameworks and code conversions are also one of the key issues.

Neural networks are widely used in a range of domains, such as computer vision, speech recognition, and natural language processing. More and more studies will develop new chips and software- and hardware-accelerating systems. Recently, the developments are not only in software applications, algorithms, programming models, and topology structures but also in constructing hardware architectures. All afore works are a firm foundation to promote the construction of new computer systems, artificial intelligence chips, and system industrialization.

References

1. LeCun Y., Boser B., Denker J., et al. Handwritten digit recognition with a back-propagation network. *Advances in Neural Information Processing Systems*, 1989, 2.
2. Chauvin Y., Rumelhart D. E. *Backpropagation: Theory, Architectures, and Applications*. Hove: Psychology Press, 2013.
3. Chen T., Du Z., Sun N., et al. Diannao: A small-footprint high-throughput accelerator for ubiquitous machine-learning. *ACM SIGARCH Computer Architecture News*, 2014, 42(1): 269–284.
4. Chen Y., Luo T., Liu S., et al. Dadiannao: A machine-learning supercomputer. *2014 47th Annual IEEE/ACM International Symposium on Microarchitecture*. IEEE, Cambridge, United Kingdom, 2014: 609–622.

5. Liu D., Chen T., Liu S., et al. Pudiannao: A polyvalent machine learning accelerator. *ACM SIGARCH Computer Architecture News*, 2015, 43(1): 369–381.

6. Albericio J., Judd P., Hetherington T., et al. Cnvlutin: Ineffectual-neuron-free deep neural network computing. *ACM SIGARCH Computer Architecture News*, 2016, 44(3): 1–13.

7. Liu S., Du Z., Tao J., et al. Cambricon: An instruction set architecture for neural networks. *ACM SIGARCH Computer Architecture News*, 2016, 44(3): 393–405.

8. Han S., Liu X., Mao H., et al. EIE: Efficient inference engine on compressed deep neural network. *ACM SIGARCH Computer Architecture News*, 2016, 44(3): 243–254.

9. Chen Y. H., Emer J., Sze V. Eyeriss: A spatial architecture for energy-efficient dataflow for convolutional neural networks. *ACM SIGARCH Computer Architecture News*, 2016, 44(3): 367–379.

10. Kim D., Kung J., Chai S., et al. Neurocube: A programmable digital neuromorphic architecture with high-density 3D memory. *ACM SIGARCH Computer Architecture News*, 2016, 44(3): 380–392.

11. Wang M., Xiao T., Li J., et al. Minerva: A scalable and highly efficient training platform for deep learning. *NIPS Workshop, Distributed Machine Learning and Matrix Computations*. Montreal, Quebec, Canada, 2014: 51.

12. LiKamWa R., Hou Y., Gao J., et al. Redeye: Analog ConvNet image sensor architecture for continuous mobile vision. *ACM SIGARCH Computer Architecture News*, 2016, 44(3): 255–266.

13. Desoli G., Chawla N., Boesch T., et al. 14.1 A 2.9 TOPS/W deep convolutional neural network SoC In FD-SOI 28nm for intelligent embedded systems. *2017 IEEE International Solid-State Circuits Conference (ISSCC)*. IEEE, San Francisco, CA, USA, 2017: 238–239.

14. Shin D., Lee J., Lee J., et al. 14.2 DNPU: An 8.1 TOPS/W reconfigurable CNN-RNN processor for general-purpose deep neural networks. *2017 IEEE International Solid-State Circuits Conference (ISSCC)*. IEEE, San Francisco, CA, USA, 2017: 240–241.

15. Whatmough P. N., Lee S. K., Lee H., et al. 14.3 A 28nm SoC with a 1.2 GHz 568nJ/ prediction sparse deep-neural-network engine with >0.1 timing error rate tolerance for IoT applications. *2017 IEEE International Solid-State Circuits Conference (ISSCC)*. IEEE, San Francisco, CA, USA, 2017: 242–243.

16. Price M., Glass J., Chandrakasan A. P. 14.4 A scalable speech recognizer with deep-neural-network acoustic models and voice-activated power gating. *2017 IEEE International Solid-State Circuits Conference (ISSCC)*. IEEE, San Francisco, CA, USA, 2017: 244–245.

17. Moons B., Uytterhoeven R., Dehaene W., et al. 14.5 Envision: A 0.26-to-10TOPS/W subword-parallel dynamic-voltage-accuracy-frequency-scalable convolutional neural network processor in 28 nm FDSOI. *2017 IEEE International Solid-State Circuits Conference (ISSCC)*. IEEE, San Francisco, CA, USA, 2017: 246–247.

18. Bong K., Choi S., Kim C., et al. 14.6 A 0.62 mW ultra-low-power convolutional-neural-network face-recognition processor and a CIS integrated with always-on haar-like face detector. *2017 IEEE International Solid-State Circuits Conference (ISSCC)*. IEEE, San Francisco, CA, USA, 2017: 248–249.

19. Bang S., Wang J., Li Z., et al. 14.7 a 288μw programmable deep-learning processor with 270kb on-chip weight storage using non-uniform memory hierarchy for mobile intelligence. *2017 IEEE International Solid-State Circuits Conference (ISSCC)*. IEEE, San Francisco, CA, USA, 2017: 250–251.

20. Wang C., Li X., Zhou X. SODA: Software defined FPGA based accelerators for big data. *2015 Design, Automation & Test in Europe Conference & Exhibition (DATE)*. IEEE, Grenoble, France, 2015: 884–887.
21. Zhao Y., Yu Q., Zhou X., et al. Pie: A pipeline energy-efficient accelerator for inference process in deep neural networks. *2016 IEEE 22nd International Conference on Parallel and Distributed Systems (ICPADS)*. IEEE, Wuhan, China, 2016: 1067–1074.
22. Wang C., Li X., Yu Q., et al. SOLAR: Services-oriented learning architectures. *2016 IEEE International Conference on Web Services (ICWS)*. IEEE, San Francisco, CA, USA, 2016: 662–665.
23. Wang C., Gong L., Yu Q., et al. DLAU: A scalable deep learning accelerator unit on FPGA. *IEEE Transactions on Computer-Aided Design of Integrated Circuits and Systems*, 2016, 36(3): 513–517.
24. Li C., Yang Y., Feng M., et al. Optimizing memory efficiency for deep convolutional neural networks on GPUs. *SC'16: Proceedings of the International Conference for High Performance Computing, Networking, Storage and Analysis*. IEEE, Salt Lake City, UT, USA, 2016: 633–644.
25. Li B., Zhou E., Huang B., et al. Large scale recurrent neural network on GPU. *2014 International Joint Conference on Neural Networks (IJCNN)*. IEEE, Vancouver, BC, Canada, 2014: 4062–4069.
26. Park H., Kim D., Ahn J., et al. Zero and data reuse-aware fast convolution for deep neural networks on GPU. *Proceedings of the Eleventh IEEE/ACM/IFIP International Conference on Hardware/Software Codesign and System Synthesis*. Pittsburgh, PA, USA, 2016: 1–10.
27. Li X., Zhang G., Huang H. H., et al. Performance analysis of GPU-based convolutional neural networks. *2016 45th International Conference on Parallel Processing (ICPP)*. IEEE, Philadelphia, PA, USA, 2016: 67–76.
28. Li S., Dou Y., Niu X., et al. A fast and memory saved GPU acceleration algorithm of convolutional neural networks for target detection. *Neurocomputing*, 2017, 230: 48–59.
29. Han S., Kang J., Mao H., et al. ESE: Efficient speech recognition engine with sparse LSTM on FPGA. *Proceedings of the 2017 ACM/SIGDA International Symposium on Field-Programmable Gate Arrays*. Monterey, CA, USA, 2017: 75–84.
30. Nurvitadhi E., Venkatesh G., Sim J., et al. Can FPGAs beat GPUs in accelerating next-generation deep neural networks? *Proceedings of the 2017 ACM/SIGDA International Symposium on Field-Programmable Gate Arrays*. Monterey, CA, USA, 2017: 5–14.
31. Nurvitadhi E., Sim J., Sheffield D., et al. Accelerating recurrent neural networks in analytics servers: Comparison of FPGA, CPU, GPU, and ASIC. *2016 26th International Conference on Field Programmable Logic and Applications (FPL)*. IEEE, Lausanne, Switzerland, 2016: 1–4.
32. Sharma H., Park J., Amaro E., et al. DnnWeaver: From high-level deep network models to FPGA acceleration. *2016 49th Annual IEEE/ACM International Symposium on Microarchitecture (MICRO)*. IEEE, Taipei, China, 2016: 1–12.
33. Ma Y., Cao Y., Vrudhula S., et al. Optimizing loop operation and dataflow in FPGA acceleration of deep convolutional neural networks. *Proceedings of the 2017 ACM/SIGDA International Symposium on Field-Programmable Gate Arrays*. Monterey, CA, USA, 2017: 45–54.

34. Zhang J., Li J. Improving the performance of OpenCL-based FPGA accelerator for convolutional neural network. *Proceedings of the 2017 ACM/SIGDA International Symposium on Field-Programmable Gate Arrays*. Monterey, CA, USA, 2017: 25–34.
35. Loh G. H., Xie Y., Black B. Processor design in 3D die-stacking technologies. *IEEE Micro*, 2007, 27(3): 31–48.
36. Chi P., Li S., Xu C., et al. Prime: A novel processing-in-memory architecture for neural network computation in ReRam-based main memory. *ACM SIGARCH Computer Architecture News*, 2016, 44(3): 27–39.
37. Shafiee A., Nag A., Muralimanohar N., et al. ISAAC: A convolutional neural network accelerator with in-situ analog arithmetic in crossbars. *ACM SIGARCH Computer Architecture News*, 2016, 44(3): 14–26.
38. Song L., Qian X., Li H., et al. PipeLayer: A pipelined ReRam-based accelerator for deep learning. *2017 IEEE International Symposium on High Performance Computer Architecture (HPCA)*. IEEE, Austin, TX, USA, 2017: 541–552.
39. Ahn J., Hong S., Yoo S., et al. A scalable processing-in-memory accelerator for parallel graph processing. *Proceedings of the 42nd Annual International Symposium on Computer Architecture*. Portland, OR, USA, 2015: 105–117.
40. Ham T. J., Wu L., Sundaram N., et al. Graphicionado: A high-performance and energy-efficient accelerator for graph analytics. *2016 49th Annual IEEE/ACM International Symposium on Microarchitecture (MICRO)*. IEEE, Taipei, China, 2016: 1–13.
41. Zhan J., Kayıran O., Loh G. H., et al. OSCAR: Orchestrating STT-RAM cache traffic for heterogeneous CPU-GPU architectures. *2016 49th Annual IEEE/ACM International Symposium on Microarchitecture (MICRO)*. IEEE, Taipei, China, 2016: 1–13.
42. Hamdioui S., Xie L., Du Nguyen H. A., et al. Memristor based computation-in-memory architecture for data-intensive applications. *2015 Design, Automation & Test in Europe Conference & Exhibition (DATE)*. IEEE, Grenoble, France, 2015: 1718–1725.
43. Tang T., Xia L., Li B., et al. Binary convolutional neural network on RRAM. *2017 22nd Asia and South Pacific Design Automation Conference (ASP-DAC)*. IEEE, Tokyo, Japan, 2017: 782–787.
44. Ankit A., Sengupta A., Panda P., et al. Resparc: A reconfigurable and energy-efficient architecture with memristive crossbars for deep spiking neural networks. *Proceedings of the 54th Annual Design Automation Conference 2017*. Austin, TX, USA, 2017: 1–6.
45. Song L., Wang Y., Han Y., et al. C-Brain: A deep learning accelerator that tames the diversity of CNNs through adaptive data-level parallelization. *Proceedings of the 53rd Annual Design Automation Conference*. New York, NY, USA, 2016: 1–6.
46. Zhang C., Sun G., Fang Z., et al. Caffeine: Toward uniformed representation and acceleration for deep convolutional neural networks. *IEEE Transactions on Computer-Aided Design of Integrated Circuits and Systems*, 2018, 38(11): 2072–2085.
47. Sen S., Venkataramani S., Raghunathan A. Approximate computing for spiking neural networks. *Design, Automation & Test in Europe Conference & Exhibition (DATE), 2017*. IEEE, Swisstech, Lausanne, Switzerland, 2017: 193–198.

48. Wang S., Zhou D., Han X., et al. Chain-NN: An energy-efficient 1D chain architecture for accelerating deep convolutional neural networks. *Design, Automation & Test in Europe Conference & Exhibition (DATE), 2017.* IEEE, Swisstech, Lausanne, Switzerland, 2017: 1032–1037.

49. Razlighi M. S., Imani M., Koushanfar F., et al. LookNN: Neural network with no multiplication. *Design, Automation & Test in Europe Conference & Exhibition (DATE), 2017.* IEEE, Swisstech, Lausanne, Switzerland, 2017: 1775–1780.

50. Wang Y., Xu J., Han Y., et al. DeepBurning: Automatic generation of FPGA-based learning accelerators for the neural network family. *Proceedings of the 53rd Annual Design Automation Conference.* New York, NY, USA, 2016: 1–6.

51. Xia L., Li B., Tang T., et al. MNSIM: Simulation platform for memristor-based neuromorphic computing system. *IEEE Transactions on Computer-Aided Design of Integrated Circuits and Systems*, 2017, 37(5): 1009–1022.

52. Lastras-Montano M. A., Chakrabarti B., Strukov D. B., et al. 3D-DPE: A 3D high-bandwidth dot-product engine for high-performance neuromorphic computing. *Design, Automation & Test in Europe Conference & Exhibition (DATE), 2017.* IEEE, Swisstech, Lausanne, Switzerland, 2017: 1257–1260.

53. Mao J. *Local Distributed Mobile Computing System for Deep Neural Networks.* Pittsburgh, PA: University of Pittsburgh, 2017.

54. Bergstra J., Breuleux O., Bastien F., et al. Theano: A CPU and GPU math compiler in Python. *Proceedings of the 9th Python in Science Conference.* 2010, 1: 3–10.

55. Collobert R., Kavukcuoglu K., Farabet C. Torch7: A Matlab-like environment for machine learning. *BigLearn, NIPS Workshop.* Granada, Spain, 2011 (CONF).

56. Abadi M., Agarwal A., Barham P., et al. TensorFlow: Large-scale machine learning on heterogeneous distributed systems. arXiv preprint arXiv:1603.04467, 2016.

57. Jia Y., Shelhamer E., Donahue J., et al. Caffe: Convolutional architecture for fast feature embedding. *Proceedings of the 22nd ACM International Conference on Multimedia.* Orlando, FL, USA, 2014: 675–678.

58. Seide F., Agarwal A. CNTK: Microsoft's open-source deep-learning toolkit. *Proceedings of the 22nd ACM SIGKDD International Conference on Knowledge Discovery and Data Mining.* San Francisco, CA, USA, 2016: 2135–2135.

59. Chollet F. Keras: Deep learning library for Theano and TensorFlow. 2015, 7(8): T1. https://keras.io/k.

60. Moritz P., Nishihara R., Stoica I., et al. Sparknet: Training deep networks in spark. arXiv preprint arXiv:1511.06051, 2015.

61. Team D. Deeplearning4j: Open-source distributed deep learning for the JVM. *Apache Software Foundation License*, 2016, 2(2). http://deeplearning4j.org/.

62. Karpathy A. ConvNetJS: Deep learning in your browser. 2014. https://cs.stanford.edu/people/karpathy/convnetjs.

63. Chen T., Li M., Li Y., et al. MXNet: A flexible and efficient machine learning library for heterogeneous distributed systems. arXiv preprint arXiv:1512.01274, 2015.

64. Tokui S., Oono K., Hido S., et al. Chainer: A next-generation open source framework for deep learning. *Proceedings of Workshop on Machine Learning Systems (LearningSys) in the Twenty-Ninth Annual Conference on Neural Information Processing Systems (NIPS).* Montreal, Quebec, Canada, 2015, 5: 1–6.

65. Ma Y., Yu D., Wu T., et al. PaddlePaddle: An open-source deep learning platform from industrial practice. *Frontiers of Data and Computing*, 2019, 1(1): 105–115.

66. Perkins H. DeepCL: OpenCL library to train deep convolutional neural networks. Accessed: Oct, 2015, 14

67. Paszke A., Gross S., Chintala S., et al. PyTorch: Tensors and dynamic neural networks in python with strong GPU acceleration. *PyTorch: Tensors and Dynamic Neural Networks in Python with Strong GPU Acceleration*, 2017, 6(3): 67.

68. Battenberg E., Dieleman S., Nouri D., et al. Lasagne: Lightweight library to build and train neural networks in Theano. 2015. https://github.com/Lasagne/Lasagne.

69. Van Merriënboer B., Bahdanau D., Dumoulin V., et al. Blocks and fuel: Frameworks for deep learning. arXiv preprint arXiv:1506.00619, 2015.

70. Lin M., Li S., Luo X., et al. Purine: A bi-graph based deep learning framework. arXiv preprint arXiv:1412.6249, 2014.

8

Customization of FPGA-Based Hardware Accelerators for Deep Belief Networks

8.1 Background and Significance

Artificial neural networks (ANNs) are proposed on the basis that the human brain perceives things in a layer-by-layer, step-by-step abstraction. ANNs with multi-layer structures can improve the prediction performance and at the same time reduce the dimensionality of disaster [1]. However, as the depth of neural networks deepens, the number of neural networks can be reduced. However, as the depth of the neural network deepens, the training process of ANNs has problems such as local optimality and gradient dispersion, which makes its performance inferior to that of shallow neural networks [2]. The performance of ANNs is not as good as that of shallow neural networks. In 2006, Geoffrey Hinton and his team proposed a new computational model, deep neural network (DNN), and proposed an efficient algorithm for this model [3]. In 2006, Geoffrey Hinton and his team proposed a new computational model—deep belief network (DBN)—and proposed an efficient training algorithm for the model, through layer-by-layer training and wake–sleep tuning algorithms instead of the traditional ANN training methods, to alleviate the problem of locally optimal solutions and to promote the hidden layer to seven layers, which has opened up the research of deep learning in the industrial world and the academic world, and Hinton has also been called the father of deep learning.

Deep belief networks (DBNs), as a basic network model in deep learning, have been used in image recognition [4,5], speech recognition [6–8], information retrieval [9], and other fields. In addition, a DBN is also a deep probabilistic generative model; by training its network weights, a DBN can generate training data according to the maximum probability.

DBNs are stacked by a set of restricted Boltzmann machine (RBM), and the unsupervised greedy layer-by-layer method is used to pre-train the weights of the generative model, which can optimize the weights of the network, and then probabilistically reconstruct its inputs, thus significantly reducing the training time and improving the efficiency of the training. The greedy

DOI: 10.1201/9780429355080-8

layer-by-layer training method of DBN can optimize the weights of the DBN, and using the configured DBN to initialize the weights of the deep neural network or multi-layer perceptron often gives better results than random initialization methods. Compared to another commonly used deep learning model, convolutive neural network (CNN), DBN can handle both labeled and unlabeled data and is equally effective in modeling one-dimensional data, making it more suitable for handling binary data with less localized features. With the increasing complexity of applications and the advent of the big data era, the development of DBNs is promising.

In the era of big data, deep learning is gradually applied to more and more complex computational problems, the amount of processed data is increasing, and the scale of neural networks is also expanding. The training process can meet the needs of general applications offline, while the prediction process needs to be carried out online, which requires higher real-time performance. Therefore, accelerating the prediction process has more practical significance and application market, and the high-performance implementation of the DBN prediction process has become one of the research hotspots in academia and industry.

8.2 Deep Belief Networks

8.2.1 Introduction to Deep Belief Networks

8.2.1.1 Basic Concepts

DBNs, also known as Deep Confidence Networks, was proposed by Geoffrey Hinton in 2006. DBNs are generative deep structures that not only recognize and classify data but also generate it. Figure 8.1 shows the process of recognizing handwritten digits using a DBN. At the bottom right of the figure is a black-and-white bitmap of the number to be recognized, above which there are three black rectangles representing the three hidden layers, and within each black rectangle there are several small rectangles representing the neurons, where the small black rectangles represent the neurons that are not activated, and the small white rectangles represent the neurons that are activated. After three hidden layers, the bottom left of the third hidden layer shows the recognition result, that is, the rightmost neuron in the first row is activated, and comparing it with the table on the top left of the screen, it can be seen that the number is correctly recognized as 4.

A classical DBN consists of several layers of RBM and one layer of ErrorBackPropagation (BP), as shown in Figure 8.2. Each layer of RBM contains two layers of neurons, the lower layer is explicit neurons, which are used for input computational data, and the higher layer is invisible neurons, referred to as hidden neurons, which are used for feature detection. In each layer of RBM, the features of the hidden elements are inferred from the input data of the

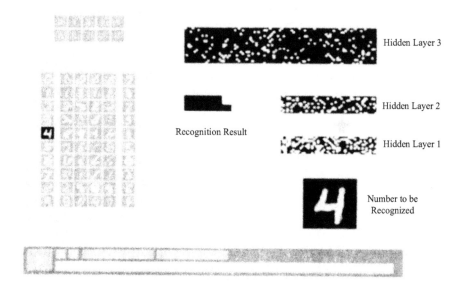

FIGURE 8.1
Example of a deep belief network recognizing handwritten numbers.

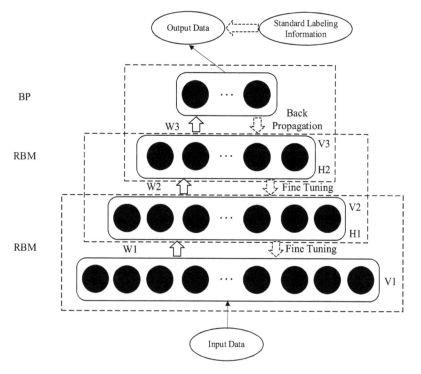

FIGURE 8.2
Basic structure of a deep belief network.

explicit elements, and the hidden elements of that layer of RBM are used as the data of the explicit elements of the neighboring high layer of RBM, which constitutes the structure of the DBN through the stacking of the multi-layer RBMs. The BP layer is responsible for the fine-tuning of the whole DBN network by propagating the error information from the top to the bottom of each layer of the RBMs after the completion of the pre-training. Depending on the application domain, the BP can also be replaced by other classifier models.

8.2.1.2 Introduction to Restricted Boltzmann Machines

The RBM was proposed by Smolensky [10]. Proposed by Smolensky, it is an optimized improvement of the Boltzmann machine (BM) [11]. The RBM is a component of a DBN consisting of a layer of dominant elements v and a layer of hidden elements h. There are no connections between neurons within the layers, which is where the term "restricted" comes from, and the inter-layer neurons are fully connected through synapse W, as shown in Figure 8.3. RBM was proposed by Boltzmann to describe the distribution of particles under the influence of an external force [12]. The activation states of the hidden elements are all independent of each other given the state of the explicit elements, and the activation states of the explicit elements are also independent of each other given the state of the hidden elements, which provides a good theoretical basis for the parallelization of the computational process, and the states of the neurons in the same layer can be computed in parallel.

The extensive research and application of RBM are due to the fast learning algorithm Contrastive Divergence (CD) proposed by Hinton in 2002 [13]. In the original RBM model, Gibbs sampling needs to be used several times [14] to sample explicit and hidden elements alternately, and after multiple sampling, random samples obeying the distribution defined by RBM are obtained. In contrast, Hinton proposes that only one step of Gibbs sampling is usually needed to obtain sufficient approximate samples. In the contrast scattering method, first the explicit element state is set as the training input data, the probability of the hidden element being switched on is calculated,

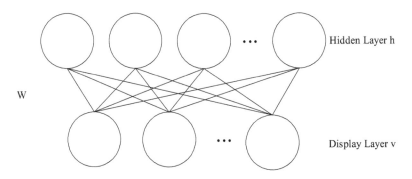

FIGURE 8.3
Graph model of the RBM.

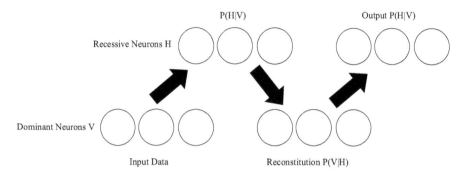

FIGURE 8.4
Schematic diagram of the contrast scatter approach.

then the explicit element state is reconstructed according to the hidden element state, then the reconstructed explicit element is used to calculate the probability of the hidden element being activated, and then the corresponding synaptic weights and bias parameters are updated to get the corresponding synaptic weights and bias parameters as shown in Figure 8.4.

8.2.2 Algorithm Analysis

8.2.2.1 Prediction Algorithms

The DBN adopts full connection between adjacent RBM layers, and the calculation of each hidden element in each layer is the same; first, read in the state of the explicit element and the corresponding weights for the weighting operation, and then the obtained results and the bias are added together, and then through the excitation function to get the final output results. Assuming that the input explicit element corresponding to a hidden element is $(x_1, x_2,...,x_n)$, the corresponding weights are $(w_1, w_2,..., w_n)$, the bias is b, the excitation function is f, and the output of the hidden element is Y, then the computation process in each hidden element can be abstracted as Equation (8.1):

$$y = f\left(\sum_{i=1}^{n} x_i * w_i + b\right) \qquad (8.1)$$

If the explicit data corresponding to a hidden element is regarded as a row vector and the corresponding weights as a column vector, then the computation within each hidden element can be regarded as the inner product of a row vector x and a column vector w, which is then summed up with the bias b and passed to the excitation function, then Equation (8.2) can be obtained:

$$y = f(\vec{x} \cdot \vec{w} + b) \qquad (8.2)$$

In this chapter, the sigmoid function is used as the excitation function f. The sigmoid function is calculated as shown in Equation (8.3):

$$f(x) = \frac{1}{1+e^{-x}} \qquad (8.3)$$

The prediction process of the DBN is a feed-forward computation, where the above operations are performed layer by layer from the bottom to the top, and the final recognition or classification result is obtained at the top layer. The algorithm for the DBN prediction process is shown in Algorithm 8.1. The inner loop in_for represents the computation process of a single hidden element, where each hidden element multiplies the input explicit data with the corresponding weights, and adds up the result of the product; the outer loop out_for represents the computation process of all the hidden elements in the complete layer of the RBM, where the result of the vector inner product is obtained through the in_for loop, then added with the bias value, and then obtained the final result of the hidden element through the activation function sigmoid. The final state of the hidden element is obtained by sigmoid; the outer loop layer_for represents the computation of multi-layer RBM corresponding to each sample data; the outermost loop data_for completes the computation of all sample data in the whole sample set.

Algorithm 8.1 Deep Belief Network Prediction Algorithm Pseudocode

    Module: Inference_of_DBN

    Input: DATA is the image data

    Input: weights is the weight coefficients

    Output: RES is the classification results

1.   **data_for: for**(int d=0; d<data_num; d++) **do**
2.   Neurons[d][0] = DATA[d];
3.   **layer_for: for**(int l=0; l<layer_num; l++) **do**
4.   **out_for: for**(int i=0; i<h_num[l]; i++) **do**
5.   energy_acc=0.0;
6.   **in_for: for**(int j=0; j<v_num[l]; j++) **do**
7.   energy_acc += neurons[d][l][j]*weights[l][j][i];
8.   **end_for**
9.   if(l == layer_num-1)
10.   **then** RES[d][i] = sigmod(energy_acc+bias);
11.   **else** neurons[d][l+1][i] = sigmod(energy_acc+bias);
12.   **end_for**
13.   **end_for**
14.   **end_for**

Suppose there are D input samples, the network depth of the DBN is L, that is, there are L layers of RBM, and there are N_{l-1} explicit elements and N_l hidden elements in the first layer of RBM, where the number of explicit elements, N_0, is equal to the dimension of the input samples when $l=1$, that is, in the first layer of RBM. Let the explicit element data in the layer 1 RBM be X_l, the hidden element data be Y_l, the synaptic weights be W_l, the corresponding bias be B_l, and the excitation function used be f. f still adopts the sigmoid function as shown in Equation (8.3), then the computation of each layer of the RBM can be abstracted as Equation (8.4):

$$Y_l = f\left(X_l * W_l + B_l\right), (l = 1, 2, \ldots, L) \tag{8.4}$$

included among these

$$Y_l = \begin{bmatrix} y_{11}^l & y_{12}^l & \cdots & y_{1N_l}^l \\ y_{21}^l & y_{22}^l & \cdots & y_{2N_l}^l \\ \vdots & \vdots & \ddots & \cdots \\ y_{D1}^l & y_{D2}^l & \cdots & y_{DN_l}^l \end{bmatrix} \tag{8.5}$$

$$X_l = \begin{bmatrix} x_{11}^l & x_{12}^l & \cdots & x_{1N_{l-1}}^l \\ x_{21}^l & x_{22}^l & \cdots & x_{2N_{l-1}}^l \\ \vdots & \vdots & \ddots & \cdots \\ x_{D1}^l & x_{D2}^l & \cdots & x_{DN_{l-1}}^l \end{bmatrix} \tag{8.6}$$

$$W_l = \begin{bmatrix} w_{11}^l & w_{12}^l & \cdots & w_{1N_l}^l \\ w_{21}^l & w_{22}^l & \cdots & w_{2N_l}^l \\ \vdots & \vdots & \ddots & \cdots \\ w_{N_{l-1}1}^l & w_{N_{l-1}2}^l & \cdots & w_{N_{l-1}N_l}^l \end{bmatrix} \tag{8.7}$$

$$B_l = \left(b_1^l, b_2^l, b_3^l, \ldots, b_{N_l}^l\right) \tag{8.8}$$

The calculation of each network layer can be divided into the following three steps: first, multiply the explicit matrix and the weight matrix, then add each column of the temporary matrix with the corresponding element in the bias vector, and finally input the matrix into the excitation function to get the final output of the layer, which is used as the explicit data of the next layer. Wherein, the number of rows of the hermit matrix is the number of samples in the original sample data set, and each row vector represents the state of the hermit element of the layer corresponding to the sample data; the number of rows of the hermit matrix is the number of samples in the original data set, and each row vector represents the state of the hermit element of the layer corresponding to the sample data, and each row vector in the hermit matrix in the first layer represents a sample data; the number of rows of the weight matrix is the number of hermit elements in the layer, and the number of columns is the number of hermit elements in the layer. The number of rows of the weight matrix is the number of explicit elements in the layer, and the number of columns is the number of hidden elements in the layer.

To further simplify the calculation process, the bias vector B_1 is moved to the weight matrix W_1, so that the calculation of each layer of neurons is simplified to two steps of matrix multiplication and excitation calculation, and the corresponding calculation formula is modified as follows:

$$Y_l = f\left(X_l' * W_l'\right), (l = 1, 2, \ldots, L) \tag{8.9}$$

included among these

$$X_l' = \begin{bmatrix} 1 & x_{11}^l & x_{12}^l & \cdots & x_{1N_{l-1}}^l \\ 1 & x_{21}^l & x_{22}^l & \cdots & x_{2N_{l-1}}^l \\ \vdots & \vdots & \vdots & \ddots & \cdots \\ 1 & x_{D1}^l & x_{D2}^l & \cdots & x_{DN_{l-1}}^l \end{bmatrix} \tag{8.10}$$

$$W_l' = \begin{bmatrix} b_1^l & b_2^l & \cdots & b_{N_l}^l \\ w_{11}^l & w_{12}^l & \cdots & w_{1N_l}^l \\ w_{21}^l & w_{22}^l & \cdots & w_{2N_l}^l \\ \vdots & \vdots & \ddots & \cdots \\ w_{N_{l-1}1}^l & w_{N_{l-1}2}^l & \cdots & w_{N_{l-1}N_l}^l \end{bmatrix} \tag{8.11}$$

8.2.2.2 Parallel and Streaming Calculations

After the previous subsection, the prediction process is abstracted into two parts: matrix multiplication and excitation function. Matrix multiplication contains a large number of computational operations that can be parallelized and streamlined, which are analyzed in the following sections: single-layer matrix multiplication and multi-layer matrix multiplication, respectively. Taking Figure 8.5 as an example, without loss of generality, matrix X and matrix W are ten-row and ten-column matrices, which are multiplied together to obtain matrix Y with ten rows and ten columns.

There are two different ways of calculating matrix multiplication, one is to decompose the calculation into the inner product of several sets of row and column vectors, and the result of each set of inner products corresponds to an element in the result matrix, as shown in Figure 8.6. The

Matrix X

x00	x01	x02	x03	x04	x05	x06	x07	x08	x09
x10	x11	x12	x13	x14	x15	x16	x17	x18	x19
x20	x21	x22	x23	x24	x25	x26	x27	x28	x29
x30	x31	x32	x33	x34	x35	x36	x37	x38	x39
x40	x41	x42	x43	x44	x45	x46	x47	x48	x49
x50	x51	x52	x53	x54	x55	x56	x57	x58	x59
x60	x61	x62	x63	x64	x65	x66	x67	x68	x69
x70	x71	x72	x73	x74	x75	x76	x77	x78	x79
x80	x81	x82	x83	x84	x85	x86	x87	x88	x89
x90	x91	x92	x93	x94	x95	x96	x97	x98	x99

*

Matrix W

w00	w01	w02	w03	w04	w05	w06	w07	w08	w09
w10	w11	w12	w13	w14	w15	w16	w17	w18	w19
w20	w21	w22	w23	w24	w25	w26	w27	w28	w29
w30	w31	w32	w33	w34	w35	w36	w37	w38	w39
w40	w41	w42	w43	w44	w45	w46	w47	w48	w49
w50	w51	w52	w53	w54	w55	w56	w57	w58	w59
w60	w61	w62	w63	w64	w65	w66	w67	w68	w69
w70	w71	w72	w73	w74	w75	w76	w77	w78	w79
w80	w81	w82	w83	w84	w85	w86	w87	w88	w89
w90	w91	w92	w93	w94	w95	w96	w97	w98	w99

=

Matrix Y

y00	y01	y02	y03	y04	y05	y06	y07	y08	y09
y10	y11	y12	y13	y14	y15	y16	y17	y18	y19
y20	y21	y22	y23	y24	y25	y26	y27	y28	y29
y30	y31	y32	y33	y34	y35	y36	y37	y38	y39
y40	y41	y42	y43	y44	y45	y46	y47	y48	y49
y50	y51	y52	y53	y54	y55	y56	y57	y58	y59
y60	y61	y62	y63	y64	y65	y66	y67	y68	y69
y70	y71	y72	y73	y74	y75	y76	y77	y78	y79
y80	y81	y82	y83	y84	y85	y86	y87	y88	y89
y90	y91	y92	y93	y94	y95	y96	y97	y98	y99

FIGURE 8.5
Schematic diagram of matrix multiplication.

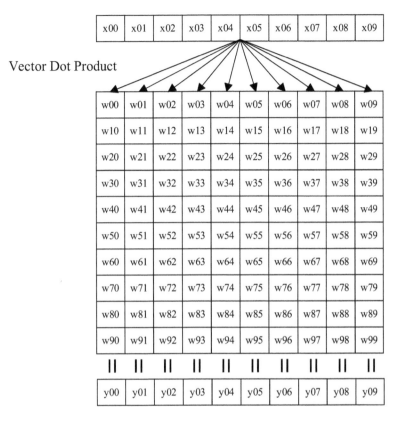

Vector Dot Product

FIGURE 8.6
Matrix products dominated by vector inner product forms.

same shading indicates the same set of calculations. Take the operation related to the first-row vector in matrix X for example. First X_0 performs inner product operation with column vectors in matrix W and W_0 to get the result Y_{00}, then X_0 performs vector inner product operation with column vectors in turn to get the values of Y_{01}, Y_{02},... respectively, that is, to get the first-row vector in matrix Y $y0$. Then take the second-row vectors in matrix X to perform the above operation, to get the second-row *vect*or in matrix Y, and then X performs the operation with column vectors, and so on. The corresponding pseudocode of the algorithm is shown in Algorithm 8.2. In this inner product-based matrix multiplication method, there are two parallelizable calculations: first, in the inner product of row vectors and column vectors, there is no data dependence on the product between the elements of the vectors, which can be executed in parallel; second, in the inner product of the same row vector and different column vectors, there is no data dependence on the product of the inner product, which can also be executed in parallel. At the same time, there is also a reuse of data, that is, the reuse of the same row vector to complete the inner product operation with different column vectors.

Algorithm 8.2 Matrix Multiplication Pseudocode for the Inner Product Calculation Algorithm

> **Module: Inner_Product**
>
> **Input**: X, W are the data matrices to multiply
>
> **Output**: Y is the result matrix after the inner product
>
> 1.　　**for** each row $\overrightarrow{x_i}$ in X **do**
> 2.　　　**for** each column $\overrightarrow{w_j}$ in W **do**
> 3.　　　　$y_{ij} = \overrightarrow{x_i} * \overrightarrow{w_j}$
> 4.　　　**end for**
> 5.　　**end for**
> 6.　　Output Y

Another way of computing matrix multiplication means that the computation is broken down into multiple sets of number multiplications between numbers and row vectors, where the result of each set of number multiplications corresponds to the intermediate value of one of the row vectors in the result matrix, and the corresponding intermediate values are then subjected to a vector addition operation to obtain the final result matrix as shown in Figure 8.7, where the same shading indicates the same set of computations.

Algorithm 8.3 Matrix Multiplication Pseudocode of the Algorithm for Calculating Number Multiplication

> **Module: Scalar_Product**
>
> **Input Matrix**: X, W are the data matrices to multiply
>
> **Output Matrix**: Y is the result matrix after the inner product
>
> 1.　　**Define Matrix**: temp
> 2.　　**for** each row $\overrightarrow{x_i}$ in X **do**
> 3.　　　**for** each row $\overrightarrow{w_j}$ in W **do**
> 4.　　　　row $\overrightarrow{temp_j} = x_{ij} * \overrightarrow{w_j}$
> 5.　　　**end for**
> 6.　　　**for** each element y_{ik} in $\overrightarrow{y_i}$ **do**
> 7.　　　　$y_{ik} = \sum_{jk} temp_{jk}$
> 8.　　　**end for**
> 9.　　**end for**
> 10.　Output Y

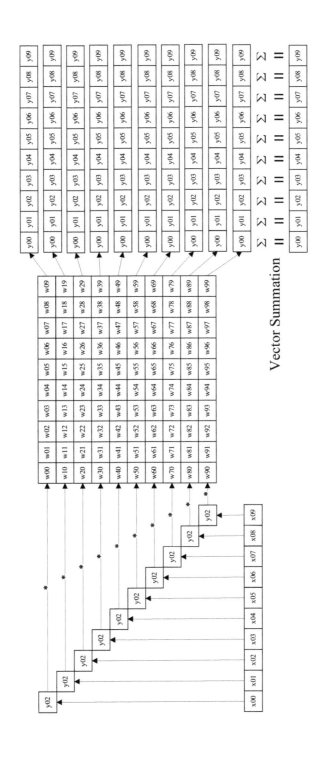

FIGURE 8.7
Matrix product dominated by vector number multiplication.

Take the first-row vector X_0 of matrix X as an example: first, the element X_{00} of X_0 performs a multiplication operation with the row vector W_0 of matrix W to get the temporary row vector y_0; then the element X_{01} of X_0 performs a multiplication operation with the row vector W_1 of matrix W to get the other temporary row vector y_1; then X_{02}, X_{03},... perform multiplication operation with the row vectors of matrix W to get the temporary row vectors y_2, y_3,...; all the temporary row variables are added two by two to get the first-row vector of matrix Y; next, take the second-row vector of matrix X, multiply its elements with the corresponding row vectors of matrix W, and then add the temporary row vectors to get the second-row vector of matrix Y, and so on. The corresponding pseudocode of the algorithm is shown in Algorithm 8.3. In this method of matrix multiplication operation based on number multiplication, two computations can be processed in parallel: first, in the number multiplication of an element with a row vector, there is no data dependency for the multiplication of that element with the elements in the row vector, but there is a storage read conflict so that the multiplication between the elements can be executed in parallel if multi-port reading of the elements can be realized; second, in the number multiplication of different elements with different row vectors, there is no data dependency and can be executed in parallel.

Based on the above excavation of parallelism in single-layer matrix multiplication, the next step is to analyze how to exploit the parallelism between multi-layer matrix multiplication. Without loss of generality, we analyze how to achieve parallelism between two layers of matrix multiplication, as shown in Figure 8.8, where matrix A is multiplied by matrix B to obtain matrix C and matrix C is multiplied by matrix D to obtain matrix E.

For the sake of clarity, the matrix to the left of the multiplication sign in a matrix multiplication is referred to as the matrix being multiplied, and the matrix to the right of the multiplication sign is referred to as the multiplying matrix. In a matrix multiplication based on vector inner product, each vector inner product operation requires a row vector of the matrix being multiplied and a column vector of the multiplying matrix, whereas, in a matrix multiplication based on vector counting, each vector counting operation requires an element of the matrix being multiplied and a row vector of the multiplying matrix. Therefore, if the first layer of matrix multiplication is based on vector inner product and the second layer of matrix multiplication is based on vector multiplication, the maximum overlap between the two layers of matrix multiplication can be achieved. The following is an example of the matrix in Figure 8.8, and a detailed description of this calculation is given in Figure 8.9.

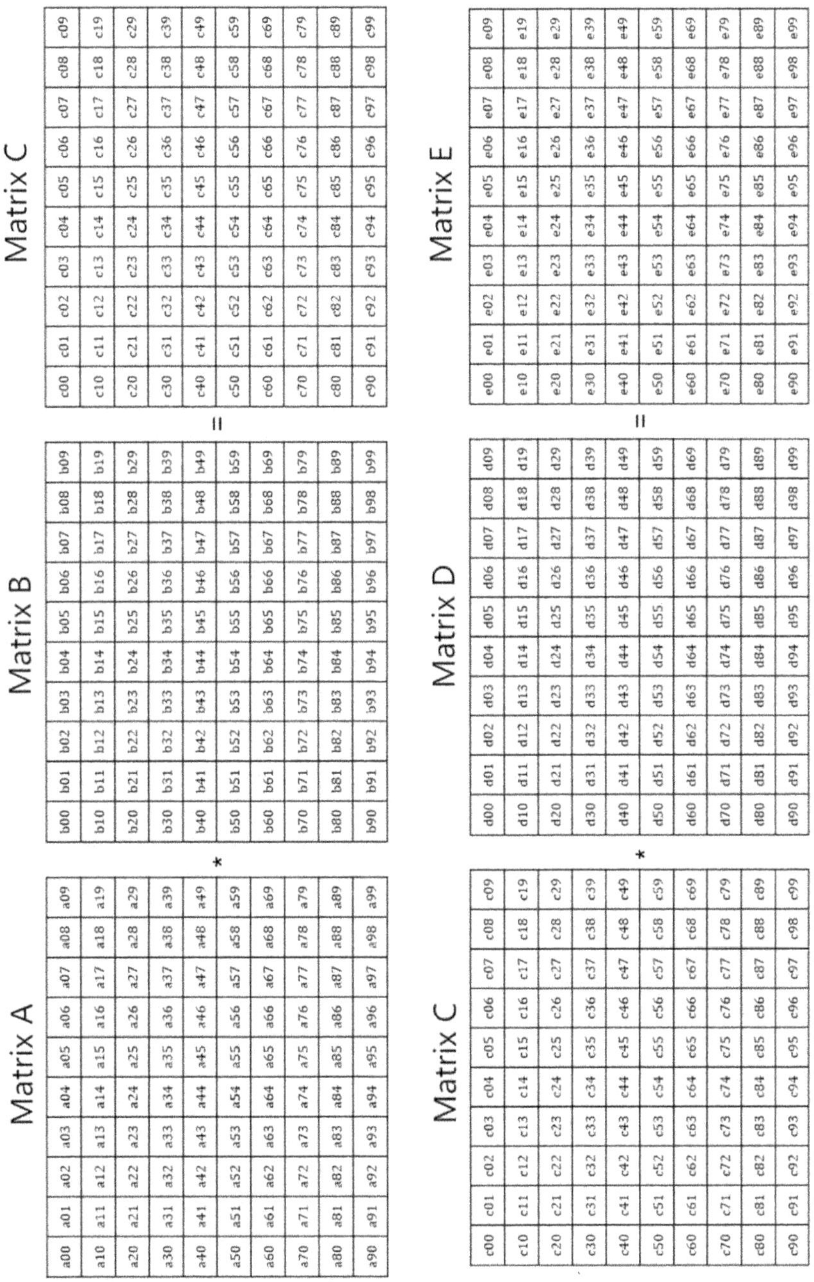

FIGURE 8.8
Two-layer matrix multiplication.

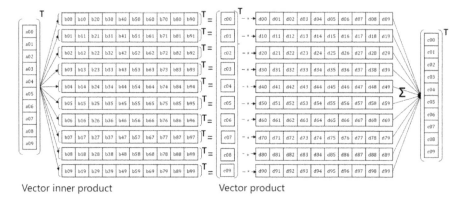

Vector inner product   Vector product

FIGURE 8.9
Schematic diagram of the two-layer matrix multiplication process.

Without loss of generality, as an example of the operations related to the first row of row vectors in matrix A, the vectors are transposed to represent the row vectors in column form and the column vectors in row form, identified by the superscript T, to make the picture more readable. In the multiplication of matrix A and matrix B, the inner product is used as the main calculation method, that is, a_0 performs the vector inner product operation with the column vectors b_0^T, b_1^T, ..., b_9^T in matrix B, and then obtains the elements c_{00}, c_{01}, ..., c_{09} in the row vector c_0 in matrix C. In the multiplication of matrix C and matrix D, vector multiplication is used as the main calculation method. In the multiplication of matrix C with matrix D, a vector-based multiplication is used, in which the elements c_0, c_{00}, c_{01}, ..., c_{09} are multiplied with the row vectors d_0, d_1, ..., d_9 of matrix D to obtain the temporary vectors for the row vectors e_0 of matrix E, and then the vector accumulation is used to obtain the row vectors e_0.

Every time the first-layer matrix multiplication obtains an element in the result matrix, the element can be immediately applied to the second-layer matrix multiplication to carry out the digital multiplication operation. Still take Figure 8.9 as an example, a_0 is first multiplied with b_0^T to get c_{00}, then c_{00} can be multiplied with d_0, at the same time, a_0 is multiplied with b_1^T to get c_{01}; c_{01} is multiplied with d_1, at the same time, the vectorial inner product of a_0 and b_2^T is started, and so on. The corresponding pseudocode of the algorithm is shown in Algorithm 8.4.

Algorithm 8.4 Pseudocode for Two-Layer Matrix Multiplication Flow Calculation Algorithm

Module: Pipeline_Matrix_Multiply

Input Matrix: A, B, D are the data matrices to multiply

Output Matrix: E is the result matrix after matrix multiply

1.   **Define Matrix:** C, temp

2.   **for** each row $\vec{a_l}$ in A **do**

3.   **for** each col $\vec{b_j}$ in B **do**

4.   //pipeline computing

5.   row $\overrightarrow{temp_j} = c_{ij} * \vec{d_j}$

6.   **end for**

7.   **for** each element e_{ik} in $\vec{e_l}$ **do**

8. $e_{ik} = \sum_j temp_{jk}$

9.   **end for**

10.   **end for**

11.   Output E

If a vector inner product or a vector multiplication is considered as a group of computations, the computation of the *i*-th group in the first layer and the *i*−1-th group in the second layer can be carried out at the same time. When multiplying matrices in multiple layers, alternating between inner product and digital multiplication can maximize the parallel pipelining of matrix multiplication in two layers, while ensuring the parallelization of calculations in each layer. It should be noted that, in the case of matrix multiplication based on digital multiplication, each set of calculations obtains a temporary vector, not a final vector, so the matrix multiplication in the next layer cannot be executed in parallel with the matrix multiplication in that layer.

Previous single FPGA acceleration systems for the prediction process [15,16], which only focuses on mining the parallelism in each layer of network computation, are dedicated to improving the performance of single-layer network computation, maximizing the throughput rate of a single layer, and thus improving the computational performance of the whole neural network. Take Deep Learning Accelerator Unit (DLAU) [16] for example, when implementing the computation of multi-layer neural networks, it is mainly done by reusing the computational structure of a single layer, which leads to two problems: (1) the multi-layer network computation can only be executed serially, and (2) the results need to be returned to the Central Processing Unit (CPU) side after the completion of the computation of each layer of the network, and then the computational results of the previous layer will be passed into the accelerator when starting the computation of the next layer. In this chapter, a new single FPGA acceleration system PIE (Pipeline Inference Engine) is proposed to ensure the performance of single-layer network computation while realizing the streaming computation between two layers of the network, which not only reduces the number of incoming and outgoing times of computation results of the intermediate network layer but also further improves the performance of the acceleration system.

8.3 Hardware Deployment/Acceleration Customization-Related Work

8.3.1 Single FPGA Acceleration System PIE

Based on the analysis of algorithm parallelization in Section 8.2, this subsection proposes PIE, a hardware acceleration system based on a single FPGA, and describes the optimizations that have been taken to improve the performance and scalability of the system.

8.3.1.1 Accelerated System Framework

Figure 8.10 illustrates the interconnections between the host CPU, storage, and accelerator in a PIE-based hardware acceleration system, as well as the interconnections between the components within the accelerator, where the dark gray arrows represent the data flow in the system and the light gray arrows represent the control flow in the system.

In the PIE acceleration system, the host controls the computational flow of the entire prediction algorithm, allocates computational data, and configures the accelerator. The data required for computation is stored in the Double Data Rate (DDR) memory and transferred to the on-chip buffer through direct memory access (DMA) according to the needs of the accelerator. The main reason for using DMA is to reduce the workload of data transfer at the host CPU side. There are three sets of buffers within the accelerator, which are responsible for buffering the synaptic weights matrix, the input manifolds, and the intermediate data useful in the computation process. Each group of buffers contains multiple small buffers, which are responsible for prefetching the data, reducing the computation stall time caused by communication, and ensuring that the communication and computation are executed in a streamlined manner. There are multiple processing units (processing element (PE)) inside the accelerator, and the PEs can read data and compute in parallel.

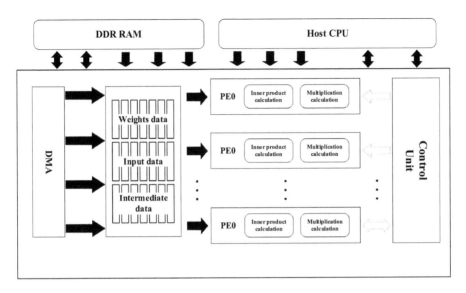

FIGURE 8.10
Schematic diagram of the PIE acceleration system structure.

Each PE can solidify the inner product computation unit, can solidify the number multiplication computation unit, and can also solidify multiple units at the same time. In the PE task division, a principle needs to be followed: the inner product computation unit and the number multiplication computation unit need to be laid out alternately to ensure that the adjacent two layers of network computation can be pipelined, and the specific design of pipelining will be described in detail in Section 8.3.1.3. Ideally, multiple PEs can be cured within the accelerator regardless of storage and computation resources and bandwidth constraints, thus increasing computation parallelism and system throughput. In reality, the number of units in the PEs and the number of PEs in the system should be reasonably designed to achieve better performance, taking into account the storage and computation resources, as well as the bandwidth limitation.

8.3.1.2 IP Core Design

This section introduces the design of the intellectual property (IP) core responsible for the forward prediction algorithm in the accelerator, which mainly includes the design of the inner product and multiplication modules. A parallel method of alternating inner product and multiplication is used to speed up the computation, and therefore the pipelining design between the two layers of computation is also presented in this section. Finally, the optimization of the IP core is presented.

1. Inner Product Calculation Module

As shown in Figure 8.11, the basic computation of the inner product calculation is three parts: multiplication of elements, accumulation of the multiplication result, and the excitation function, which will be introduced as one of the optimization tools in Section 8.1.4 since the excitation function has the same application in the number multiplication calculation module and is optimized accordingly for the excitation function to make it better mapped to the hardware implementation.

Parallel computation: In the inner product operation, the multiplication between different elements is independent, and the accumulation of the product result can be carried out by multiple two-by-two additions. Therefore, the structure of multiple multiplier-addition trees is used to achieve the parallel computation, that is, the multiplication is parallelized between multiplications, the addition at the same level, and the multiplication is parallelized between multiplications and additions, as well as the water flow is synchronized between the additions at different levels. Considering the characteristics of two-by-two addition in the adder tree, setting the parallelism degree to the nth power of 2 can make the most efficient use of computing resources. Combined with the transmission bandwidth and computational resource limitations, the parallelism is set to $P(=2^n)$, that is, P multiplication operations are processed at the same time, and the number of adders in the first layer of the addition tree

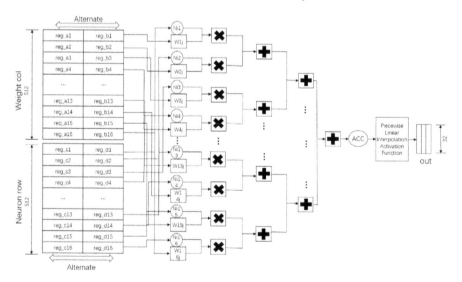

FIGURE 8.11
Inner product calculation module.

is half of the parallelism, that is, the first layer has $p/2$ adders, and the number of adders in the next layer is reduced by half in turn until the last layer has 1 adder to get the final result of the summation, and the total number of layers in the addition tree is n, requiring a total of $P-1$ adders. Between the multiplier and the first layer of the addition tree, there are registers to store the multiplication result for the adder to read, in the schematic diagram this type of registers are not indicated. The addition tree itself adopts a pipelined design, where the computations of the adders at each level are fully pipelined, and a pipelined design is also adopted between the multipliers and the adders at the first level of the addition tree. Therefore, the structure of the multi-multiplier-additive tree not only realizes the parallel execution of computations of the same group but also realizes the fully pipelined execution of computations of different groups, which greatly reduces the computation time. Assuming that a multiplication time is t_1 and an addition time is t_2, in the original serial computation, the time required to complete P multiplications and P accumulations of data is $P*t_1 +(P-1)*t_2$, and after adopting the structure of multi-multiplier-addition tree, it only requires $t_1 + t_2 * \log_2 P$, that is, $t_1 + n*t_2$.

On the other hand, considering the limited storage resources in the accelerator, the synaptic weights and explicit data cannot be completely stored in Block Random Access Memory (BRAM) in advance, and the required data must be continuously transferred into the accelerator according to the computational needs, so in addition to ensuring the parallelization and pipelined execution of the computational units, it is also necessary to ensure the parallel reading of the data, as well as the pipelined data communication and computation, to ensure that the data communication does not cause excessive time overhead. The data prefetching method is applied here. Here, a data prefetching method is applied, and a dedicated storage unit with double buffers is designed to cache the upcoming computation data in advance. The multiplier alternately reads the required data from one set of buffers, while the accelerator stores the required data for the next set of computations in the other set of buffers in advance for reading. The module needs to read P input data in parallel each time. Considering the limitation of transmission bandwidth, when determining the value of P, it is necessary to ensure that the time consumed for transmitting P data is less than the reading interval of P data, and the data communication will not become the performance bottleneck of the pipeline. No matter the reading of synaptic weights or explicit data, it is necessary to read P data in parallel, so the weight buffer and explicit buffer both contain two groups of buffers, each containing P *registers*, to ensure the parallel reading of P data.

Data processing and multiplexing: In vector inner product operations, the weight matrix is read and computed in columns. Therefore, to ensure that the weight matrices in the hardware accelerator are also read and computed in columns, the computed data need to be aligned in advance. Since this part of the work is not time-consuming and not computationally intensive, it is assigned to the software side. When the synaptic weights are transferred into the accelerator, the host CPU transfers the weights in the first dimension, with the parallelism P as the cyclic granularity, each time transferring P weights in a column to the accelerator buffer, and after one column is completed, the next column will start to transfer the data.

In matrix multiplication, there is a high data locality both for the input explicit matrix, and for the weight matrix, and the number of data transfers can be reduced by selecting the data with the shortest multiplexing distance to be present in the on-chip cache. From the perspective of the explicit element matrix, each row of explicit element data needs to be successively vectorized with the weights of the columns of the weight-value matrix for the inner product operation. From the perspective of the weight matrix, each column of weights needs to be inner-produced with different rows of explicit data after a certain period. The reuse distance of the explicit data is smaller than that of the weight matrix, so it is possible to cache a row of explicit data in the on-chip storage, reuse the row of data to perform operations with the weights of different columns until all the column weights have completed the inner product operation with the row of data, then replace it off-chip, and do not need to read it in again. On the other hand, the reuse distance of the weight data is larger, and after reusing the explicit data, it is necessary to read the corresponding weight data every time, and for different explicit data, the weight data of the same column may need to be read in again and again. To reduce the communication overhead caused by reading the weight data, if the network size is not large or the on-chip storage resources are sufficient, it can be considered that the weight matrix can be stored in the chip in advance, to reduce the time overhead and energy consumption overhead of reading it.

2. Multiplication module

As shown in Figure 8.12, the digital multiplication computation module also contains mainly multiplication and addition operations, so many of the designs are similar to the inner product computation module, such as the use of multiple multipliers to implement parallel multiplication and the use of double buffers to mask the data communication time. The following section highlights the differences from the inner product calculation module.

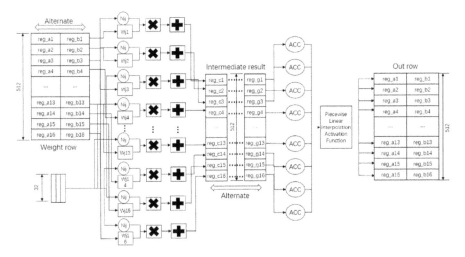

FIGURE 8.12
Multiplication calculation module.

Parallel computation: In the multiplication module, the multiplication of a constant and a vector is the multiplication of the elements of the constant and the vector, and the multiplication operations are independent of each other, so the multiplication can be done in parallel using multiple multipliers. Addition is the sum of two vectors, and the elements of vector addition are independent of each other, so multiple adders are used to complete the addition of two vectors in parallel. The parallelism of addition is the same as that of multiplication, which is P. In the flow calculation of multiplication and addition, each time after the multiplication of explicit data and weight data, the result is stored in the register, and the adder reads the result and starts to complete the vector addition in parallel, and at the same time the multiplier starts to calculate the next set of multiplication in the multiplier.

Data processing and multiplication: In this module, the weight matrix needs to be read by rows and multiplied with the explicit elements, so the host does not need to process the weight matrix but only reads it cyclically by rows. In addition, in the multiplication operation, the explicit data and the weight data are different from each other, and the explicit data and the weights of the corresponding rows can be replaced out of the slice after completing the multiplication operation, so there is no need to read them in again. The weight matrix needs to be read in again after a period when the corresponding explicit data of another sample data is obtained. Therefore, there exists data reuse for the weight matrix, but the reuse distance is large, and in the case of small storage resources or network size, it can be considered that the weight matrix is completely mapped into the on-chip storage resources.

8.3.1.3 Inter-Story Flow Design

Sections 8.3.1.2 and 8.3.1.3 implemented the inner product computation module and the number multiplication computation module, respectively, and both modules can fully flow water single-layer neural network computations. In this subsection, the inner product computation module and the number multiplication computation module are merged to optimize the prediction process of the DBN network by implementing the streaming computation between the two modules, which can simultaneously implement the single-layer intra-streaming computation and the multi-layer inter-streaming computation. In this chapter, the layer numbers of the bottom-up RBMs of the DBN are sequentially numbered from 1 and set so that in the odd-numbered layer RBMs of the DBN, the curing inner product calculation module completes the prediction calculation of the layer; in the even-numbered layer RBMs of the DBN, the curing number multiplication calculation module completes the prediction calculation of the layer. By alternating the two modules, the pipelined computation of adjacent network layers is achieved. The pipeline design is detailed in Figure 8.13. The whole pipeline is divided into five stages: (1) multiply-and-accumulate computation, abbreviated as MAC (Multiply and Accumulate), which mainly completes the vector inner product operation of the explicit element data and the synaptic weights in the odd-numbered layers of the RBM; (2) stimulus computation, which completes the processing of the inner product result by calling the stimulus function to get the corresponding hidden element's activation state; (3) number multiplication computation, completing the vector number multiplication operation of a dominant element and synaptic weights in the RBM of even-numbered layers; (4) vector summation, adding the temporary vectors obtained in stage (3) with the temporary vectors of the

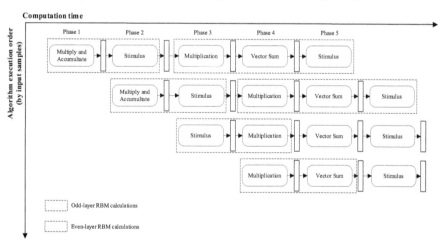

FIGURE 8.13
Schematic diagram of interflow water calculation.

previous iteration; (5) excitation computation, this stage is not computed at every moment, only when the final vector result is obtained in stage (4), the calculation is performed by calling the excitation function to get the cryptic element's activation state, and when the final vector result is not obtained in stage (4), and stage (5) is in the idle state. The thin rectangles between the stages represent registers that cache the computation results of the previous stage for timely reading in the next stage.

Each of the five phases corresponds to a part of the pipeline of the inner product module or the number multiplication module, and each phase is a fully pipelined, and the computations between different phases are also fully pipelined. Based on the above, it is possible to achieve the pipelined computation of two adjacent RBMs. Once the odd-numbered RBMs get the computation result of a hidden element, the even-numbered RBMs can immediately read the result as the value of the explicit element and start the corresponding computation of the even-numbered RBMs. However, it should be noted that, because the result of each computation in the even-layer RBM is the intermediate state of the hidden element, and its neighboring high-level RBMs need the final state of a neuron due to the MAC, so only after all the computations of the even-layer RBMs are completed, the neighboring high-level RBMs can start the relevant computations. That is to say, the pipeline can only realize the pipeline of low-level odd-level RBMs and high-level even-level RBMs, and the calculations of low-level even-level RBMs and high-level odd-level RBMs can only be executed serially.

8.3.1.4 Optimization Tools

1. Approximate implementation of the excitation function

   In this chapter, the sigmoid function is used as the excitation function. Sigmoid function contains exponential calculation and taking the inverse calculation, which is difficult to be perfectly implemented on the hardware and consumes a lot of resources. In this chapter, a segmented linear function is used to approximate the sigmoid function. The reasonableness of doing so has two points, one is that the DBN has a high degree of fault tolerance, as long as the segmented function is reasonably designed, the computational error can be controlled in a very small range; the second is that the computation of the segmented function is relatively simple, and the hardware implementation is easier to achieve a better performance, and the dependence on the sigmoid function is small, and when the sigmoid function is replaced by other S-type functions or linear functions, there is no need to change the hardware implementation of the segmented function. When the sigmoid function is changed to another S-type function or linear function, there is no need to change the hardware implementation of the segmented function and only need to modify the corresponding coefficient settings.

2. In this chapter, we refer to the literature [17]. In the implementation method in this chapter, the segmented linear function is calculated as shown in Equation (8.12). The sigmoid function is centrosymmetric at the point (0, 0.5), so when the input parameter X is less than 0, it is calculated according to $1-f(-x)$, which can achieve the reuse of hardware resources and reduce the computational resource overhead. When $x > 8$, the sigmoid value is infinitely close to 1 from 0.999665, so the value of $f(x)$ is set to be 1 when the input parameter X is larger than 8; accordingly, when $x < -8$, the value of $f(x)$ is 0. When X takes the value of (0, 8), the value of $f(x)$ is taken as $a_i * x + b_i$, and the parameters a_i and b_i are taken from the arrays of a and b with the length of $8/k$, and k is the segmentation interval size. k is the size of the segmented interval, according to the value of $[x/k]$, respectively, from the a and b arrays to read the value of the corresponding element, as a parameter of the linear function, to get the value of $f(x)$; when x takes the value of (−8, 0], using a similar method, according to the value of $[−x/k]$, respectively, to get the value of a_i and b_i, to calculate the value of $f(x)$.

$$f(x)=\begin{cases} 0,\ x\leq -8 \\ 1+a\left[-\dfrac{x}{k}\right]*x-b\left[-\dfrac{x}{k}\right],\ -8<x\leq 0 \\ a\left[\dfrac{x}{k}\right]*x+b\left[-\dfrac{x}{k}\right],\ 0<x\leq 8 \\ 1,\ x\geq 8 \end{cases}$$

(8.12)

After repeated tests, it was found that the error of the segmented linear function concerning the sigmoid is sufficiently small when k takes the value of 1, see Figure 8.14, and the FPGA implementation can avoid the division operation and achieve the best performance, so the size of the segmented interval was selected to be 1.

2. Slice computing

In the design of IP cores, due to the limited on-chip storage resources, it is not possible to store all the data required for computation on-chip, so it is necessary to continuously transfer data from the on-board memory into the chip, and due to the limitations of the transmission bandwidth and computational resources, it is only possible to compute p pieces of data in parallel at a time. When the size of the network is increasing, it is necessary to use slice computing to adapt to the hardware structure.

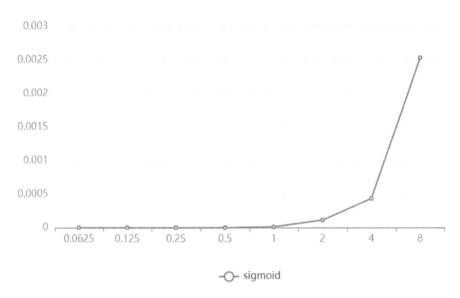

FIGURE 8.14
Segmented linear function error analysis.

Assuming that the slice size is *T*, the inner product calculation module is mainly the inner product operation of row vector and column vector, so the explicit data will be divided into data slices of size *T* by rows, and the weight matrix will be divided into data slices of size *T* by columns in a circular manner, and each time *T* data in the rows of the explicit data will be read and calculated with *T* data in the corresponding columns of the corresponding weights, as shown in Figure 8.15. The explicit matrix contains *N* explicit row vectors, and each row vector is divided into *k* sub-vectors of size *T*; the weight matrix contains *M* weight column vectors, and each column vector is divided into *k* sub-vectors of size *T*. The value of *k* depends on the length of the explicit row vector, *K*, and the size of the slice, *T*, and is $k = K/T$. In the slice calculation, first, the inner product operation is performed between the sub-vectors of row $_l$ and the sub-vectors with the same shading in the column vector col_l of the weight matrix, and the results of the inner product of the sub-vectors are summed up to get the result of the complete inner product calculation; then row_l performs the same slice inner product operation with other column vectors, such as col_2 in turn, and the slice calculation of the other row vectors of the manifold is carried out in the same way.

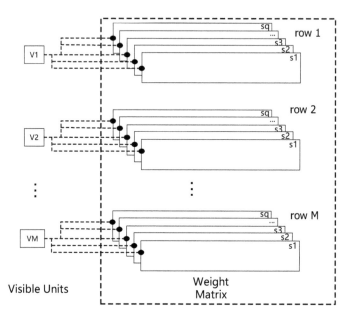

FIGURE 8.15
Schematic diagram of the slice calculation within the inner product module.

In the multiplication module, since only one explicit element is needed for each multiplication, there is no need to slice the explicit element but only to divide the weight matrix into slices containing T data by rows. As shown in Figure 8.16, there are M significant elements, and the weight matrix contains M weight row vectors, each of which is divided into q sub-vectors of size T. The value of q depends on the length of the weight row vectors, Q, and the size of the slices, T, with $q = Q/T$. The neuron v_1 performs the multiplication operation with the sub-vectors of the weight row vector row_1 in turn and connects the resultant sub-vectors to obtain a complete intermediate row vector; then the neuron v_2 performs the same calculation and connection operation with the sub-vectors of the weight row vector row_2 in turn, and so on.

To ensure high throughput, the slice size T should be equal to the granularity of the parallel computation in the module P. Although slice computation can improve the computational performance and scalability of the system, when the size of the network does not match the slice size, that is, the number of neurons in the network layer is not divisible by the size of the slice, it is necessary to fill in the data with zeros to make the granularity of the parallel computation in the last iteration still be P. The operation of filling up the zeros will

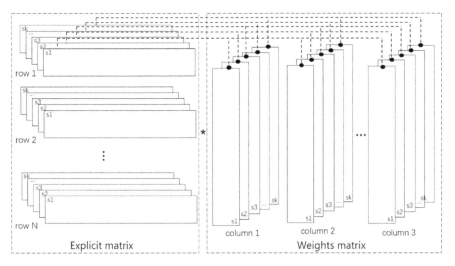

row 1

row 2

row N

Explicit matrix

column 1   column 2   column 3

Weights matrix

FIGURE 8.16
Schematic diagram of slice-and-dice calculations within the number multiplication module.

cause additional invalid computation, and the maximum number of zeros in each computation is $p-1$, which will affect performance. However, when the value of P *is* small compared to the number of neurons in the network layer, the performance impact is relatively small and negligible.

3. Redundant storage

In the multiplication module, a vector addition operation is performed on the intermediate vectors. Each vector addition is a summing operation between the result of the current computation and the result of the previous summation, so it is necessary to wait for the completion of the last addition operation before performing the current vector addition, that is, there is a data dependency. Ideally, if the operands are fixed-point numbers, the addition operation takes only one clock cycle, and the whole pipeline can be executed completely in a stream. However, considering floating-point operations, floating-point addition may consume multiple clock cycles. For example, in the system implementation of this chapter, the floating-point addition operation is realized by the DSP48E soft core encapsulated in the FPGA, and at a system frequency of 100 MHz, each floating-point addition takes five clock cycles. The multiplier sends a vector element result to the adder every other clock cycle, and the vector addition becomes the performance bottleneck of the whole pipeline, which greatly reduces the throughput rate and computational performance of the pipeline.

To eliminate this data dependency, the space-for-time method is used to set up multiple intermediate result caches, where the result of the multiplication is added with the vector elements in different buffers, and the result of the addition is then stored in the cache. The number of intermediate result caches is decided according to the number of additional clocks. In this chapter, floating-point addition is used, and each floating-point addition takes five clock cycles, so five intermediate result caches are set up. The number of intermediate result caches depends on the number of iterations of the calculation. Taking Figure 8.17 as an example, there are five caches from IRB1 to IRB5. Assuming that the number of iterations is i, that is to say, the i-th intermediate vector is obtained, and the value of i%5 is the number of the selected cache, the intermediate vector will be added with the vectors in this cache and the result of the addition will be stored back to this cache for the next time of addition. Until all the number multiplication and vector accumulation operations on the hidden metadata are completed, each cache is summed up through a small, addition tree (log5 depth) to obtain the final vector result, which is passed to the next activation unit for the next computation. Since the data are read from different caches in every five iterations, there is no data dependency between them, and the next time the data are read from a certain cache, the addition operation of the corresponding cache is just completed, so there is no data dependency. The method is highly portable; although the addition time varies with different hardware platforms, system frequencies, or data bit widths, the number of intermediate result caches can be

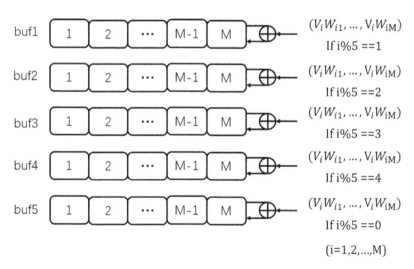

FIGURE 8.17
Schematic diagram of redundant storage.

modified according to the difference in the addition time. Assuming that the addition time is t, setting t intermediate result buffers can still be used to eliminate the data dependency in this type of addition operation.

4. Structural reuse

The PIE acceleration system can only realize the streaming computation of the adjacent two layers of RBM, while every two layers are still serial computations, so only the computational structure of the two-layer RBM is cured on the FPGA. When the network depth of the DBN is greater than 2, the prediction process of multi-layer RBM is completed by reusing the computational structure of these two layers of RBM, which maximizes the resource-saving while ensuring that there is no degradation in the performance.

8.3.2 Multi-FPGA Acceleration System

Using multiple FPGAs to accelerate the prediction algorithm of DBNs can provide higher computational parallelism and can also alleviate the problems of storage and computational resource constraints caused by large-scale neural network computation, so based on Section 8.3.1, this subsection extends the accelerator design to multiple FPGAs. This subsection introduces the detailed design of the multi-FPGA acceleration system and introduces two schemes for distributing the network computation to multiple FPGAs, namely, layer-by-layer and intra-layer.

8.3.2.1 System Framework

The multi-FPGA acceleration system designed in this chapter is shown in Figure 8.18. On one accelerator card, multiple FPGA chips are cured as independent processing units, communicating with the CPU processor through the PCIe interface, and completing the algorithms in collaboration with the CPU processor. The CPU processor is responsible for data storage, communication, and algorithmic control. The hardware accelerator integrates one control FPGA, which is responsible for transmitting data and control signals with the CPU and other FPGAs, and undertaking part of the computation work, playing the role of control and computation intermediary in the multi-FPGA system, avoiding the frequent communication between the CPU and the multi-FPGAs. The hardware acceleration card also integrates multiple computational FPGAs, which are mainly responsible for the hardware acceleration of the prediction algorithm. Each FPGA is equipped with dedicated off-chip private storage and on-chip cache to store the neurons, weights, and intermediate results used in the computation, and communicates with other FPGAs through the interconnection network. The computational modules

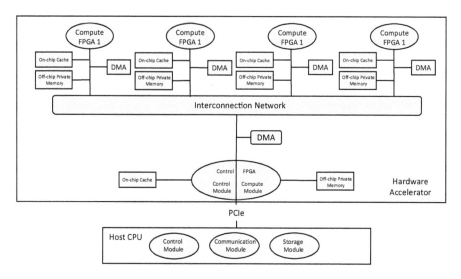

FIGURE 8.18
Multi-FPGA system architecture diagram.

within the control FPGA and compute FPGA differ according to the network partitioning scheme. Section 8.2.2 describes in detail the multi-FPGA acceleration system DBL (Division Between Layers), which is implemented using a layer-by-layer scheme, and Section 8.2.3 describes in detail the multi-FPGA acceleration system DIL (Division Inside Layers), which is implemented using an intra-layer partitioning scheme, and its internal design of computational modules, data paths, etc.

The interconnect topology between the FPGAs is a one-dimensional bidirectional ring array, as shown in Figure 8.19. Each FPGA node communicates bi-directionally with only two neighboring nodes, while each computation node is connected to the control FPGA to ensure that it can obtain the computation results from the control FPGA side and write the results back to the control FPGA.

In a multi-FPGA system, FPGAs send control and data information to each other via packets, which are defined in the format shown in Figure 8.20. The data packet is divided into two parts, the header and the data. The header is in the front, accounting for the first 8 bytes of the packet, and the data part is in the back. The following describes the fields of the packet header in detail.

1. Operation instruction, 4 bits, is the control field of the packet, indicating the type of the packet and the corresponding operation type. 0×0 means divide by layer and execute the corresponding calculation process; 0×1 means calculation round; 0×2 means divide by layer and execute the corresponding calculation process; 0×3 means data write-back; and 0×4 means the data in the packet is explicit

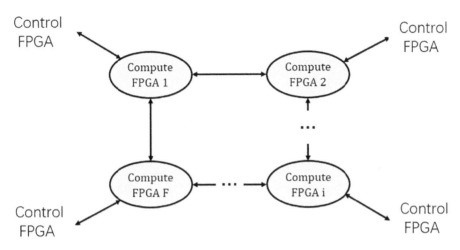

FIGURE 8.19
Interconnection topology.

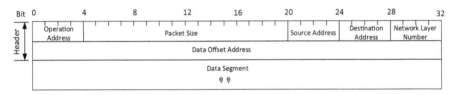

FIGURE 8.20
Schematic diagram of the packet format.

data and no calculation operation is carried out. Among them, 0×0 and 0×1 are only applicable to the layer-by-layer scheme, 0×2 is only applicable to the intra-layer scheme, and 0×3 and 0×4 apply to both schemes.

2. Packet size, 16 bits, indicates the size of the packet: the sum of the size of the header and the data, the maximum decimal value that can be expressed is 65,535, the unit of the number expressed in this field is byte, so the maximum packet size is 65,535 bytes, the header is fixed to account for 8 bytes, so the packet can carry up to 65,527 bytes of data.

3. Source address and destination address, each occupying 4 bits, indicate the source and destination address of the packet.

4. Network layer number, 4 bits, indicates the data in this packet which corresponds to the data of the RBM of the layer, counting from $1, 0\times0$ is an invalid value.

5. Data Offset Address, 32 bits, indicates the starting offset position of the data in this packet for this network layer calculation and is expressed in bytes as the offset unit. This field is often used with

the network layer number for data alignment to ensure calculation accuracy and synchronized calculations between FPGAs.

8.3.2.2 System DBL by Layer

1. Delineation of ideas

Layer by layer means that the computation of a multi-layer neural network is distributed to each FPGA by layer, and each FPGA is responsible for the prediction computation of a certain layer of neural network. To make the computation process among FPGAs overlap as much as possible, the FPGA responsible for the RBM computation of odd layers (hereinafter referred to as odd FPGA) is designated to complete the matrix computation in the form of vector inner product, and the FPGA responsible for the RBM computation of even layers (hereinafter referred to as even FPGA) completes the matrix computation in the form of vector multiplication, drawing on the method of double-layer streaming computation in the single FPGA acceleration system. As shown in Figure 8.21, once the odd FPGA gets the

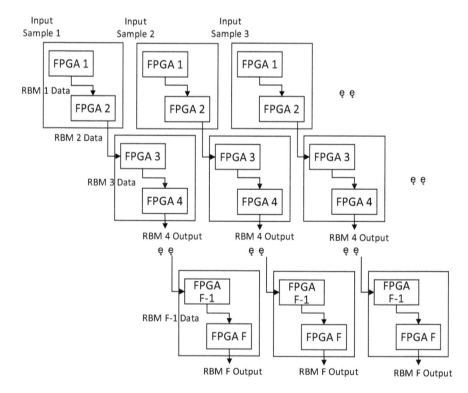

FIGURE 8.21
Schematic diagram by layer.

state of the first hidden element, the adjacent even FPGA node can read in the neuron state as the explicit element input and start the computation of the RBM of the even-numbered layers, realizing the streaming computation of the two FPGAs under a single task. This method can only achieve single-task pipelined computation between two FPGAs, if the neighboring odd FPGA and even FPGA are computed as a group, the single-task computation is still executed serially when the FPGA group completes the single-task computation between them.

When the network depth is less than or equal to the number of computational FPGAs, the FPGA group can achieve inter-multi-task pipelined computation. When the network depth is greater than the number of computational FPGAs, if all RBM layer computations for one sample data are completed first and then all RBM layer computations for the next data are started, the computational FPGAs are unable to realize the streaming computation among multi-tasks, which will greatly reduce the system performance. Assuming that the number of computational FPGAs in the system is F, in order to maximize the system performance, the system first completes the RBM pipelining computation of the first F layers of the sample data and caches all the results of the Fth layer of the RBM: after completing the computation of the first F layers of the RBM for all the sample data, FPGA1 reads in the results of the Fth layer of the RBM in the cache sequentially, and then starts the pipelining computation of the RBMs for the layers from $F+1$ to $2F$, and so on, until all the RBM layer calculations are completed and the final prediction result is obtained. When the depth of the network cannot be calculated by the number of FPGA nodes divisible, the last set of F-layer RBM calculations, the excess computation FPGA turn empty, is responsible only for the transmission of data, and the final prediction results are still output by the FPGA F output. For example, if there are a total of 4 computational FPGAs and the network depth is 14, the prediction computation is divided into 4 (=14/4) groups of streaming computations, in the last group of streaming computations, FPGA 1 completes the computation of the 13th layer RBM, FPGA 2 completes the computation of the 14th layer RBM, while FPGA 3 and FPGA 4 take the role of transmitting the data only and do not carry out any computation, and FPGA 4 reads the computation results from FPGA 2 sent by FPGA 3 and transmits them back to the control FPGA.

In the DBL system, the control FPGA only communicates data with FPGA 1 and FPGA F. It is responsible for encapsulating the incoming input sample data from the CPU into data packets and sending them to FPGA 1, and reading the data packets from FPGA F, as well as calibrating and extracting the calculation results of the final neural network.

2. Calculation module design

The computation of the odd FPGA is based on the vector inner product, and its computational module is similar to the inner product computational module in the PIE acceleration system. As shown in Figure 8.22a, the parallel computation also uses a multiple multiplier-addition tree structure, masks the time overhead of data communication through multiple buffers, and also supports piecewise computation, none of which are described in detail here. The computation in the even FPGA is based on vector multiplication, so its computational module is similar to the multiplication computational module in the PIE acceleration system. As shown in Figure 8.22b, the parallel computation also adopts a multi-multiplier and multi-adder structure. As shown in Figure 8.22b, the parallel computation also adopts the structure of multiple multipliers and multiple adders, masks the data communication time overhead through multiple buffers, adopts redundant storage to eliminate the data dependency in vector addition, and also supports the slice computation, which is not described in detail here.

Synchronized computation: A synchronization unit is embedded in each FPGA to ensure the accuracy of the calculation results. Although the odd FPGA and even FPGA have different calculation methods, the overall calculation process is the same, so the same state machine is used to control the overall calculation process. In this chapter, a finite state machine is used to solve the problem of synchronization between FPGAs, and the state transition diagram of the state machine is shown in Figure 8.23. The starting state of FPGA is idle state and polls whether the input FIFO is empty or not, if the input FIFO is empty, it will keep idle state, if the input FIFO is not empty, that is, the superior node passes in new data, then it jumps to the read data state; in the read data state, the FPGA reads the packet in the input FIFO and reads the relevant information in the header, verifies whether the source address and the

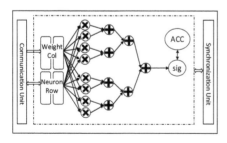
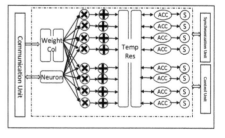

a) Odd FPGA On-chip IP Core Design for DBL System   b) Even FPGA On-chip IP Core Design for DBL System

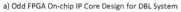

FIGURE 8.22

DBL system IP core design. (a) Odd FPGA On-chip IP Core Design for DBL System. (b) Even FPGA On-chip IP Core Design for DBL System.

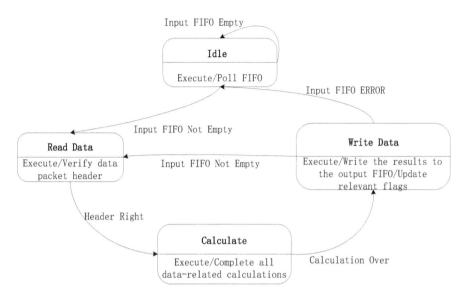

FIGURE 8.23
DBL system calculating FPGA state transitions.

destination address are correct, combines the two fields of network
layer number and data offset, and compares the verification with
the local information of the computation stage, if the information is
wrong, jump back to the idle state and continue to wait for the new
data; if the information in the first part is not wrong, jump to the
computation state; in the computation state, the FPGA completes all
the operations related to the read data, and after the computation is
completed, it transfers to the write data state; in the write data state,
the FPGA writes the computation results into the output First In
First Outs (FIFOs) of the lower nodes and updates the local information in the output FIFOs of the lower nodes. FIFO updates the local
information of the relevant calculation flags and judges whether the
input FIFO is empty; if it is empty, it will be transferred to the idle
state; if the FIFO is not empty, it will be transferred to the read data
state. Since the control FPGA is only responsible for data transfer
and has no computational tasks, it is relatively simple, so no state
machine is designed.

8.3.2.3 Delineation within Layers System DIL

1. Delineation of ideas
   Intra-layer division means that the computation of each RBM layer
   is evenly distributed on multiple FPGAs, and the computation of
   the same RBM layer is completed by multiple computing FPGAs in

parallel. In this scheme, the single instruction stream multiple data stream SIMD calculation method is used, where the control FPGA divides the input explicit data into several data blocks and distributes them to different computational FPGAs, and each piece of computational FPGA is responsible for part of the computation of a certain layer of the RBM and completes the same computational operation on the received different explicit data blocks, respectively, and since each piece of computational FPGA is only responsible for a part of the computation of the RBM, they can only get the partial computation results of the RBM layer, the computing FPGA passes the results back to the control FPGA, and then the control FPGA integrates the partial results of the computing FPGA to get the complete computation results of the RBM of that layer, and sends the results to the computing FPGA as the explicit metadata of the next layer of the RBM, respectively, as shown in Figure 8.24. In this scheme, there is data communication between the control FPGA and each computational FPGA, and it is not only responsible for distributing the incoming data from the CPU to each computational FPGA and recycling the results from the computational FPGAs, but it also undertakes a part of the computational task, that is, it is responsible for the integrated computation of the local results.

Data distribution: The DIL system divides the explicit data matrix and the weight matrix by blocks, and each computing FPGA is responsible for the computation of one matrix sub-block, and the matrix multiplication adopts the vector inner product mode. Take the matrix multiplication in Figure 8.25 as an example, different shades represent neurons and weights data of different computing

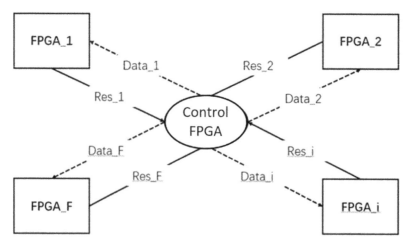

FIGURE 8.24
Schematic diagram of intra-story division.

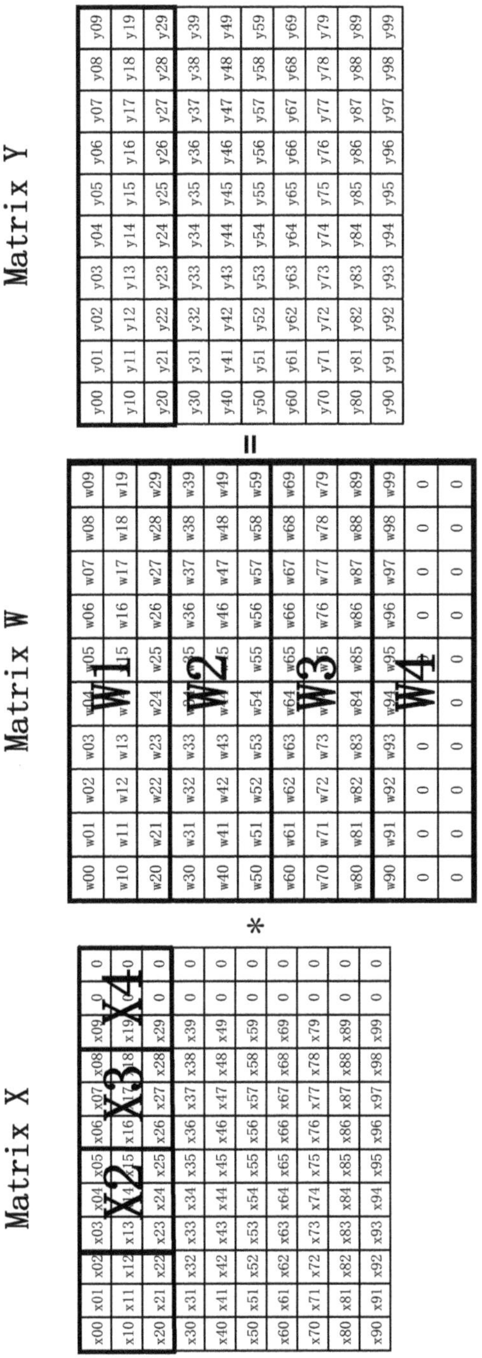

Matrix X

x00	x01	x02	x03	x04	x05	x06	x07	x08	x09	0
x10	x11	x12	x13	x14	x15	x16	x17	x18	x19	0
x20	x21	x22	x23	x24	x25	x26	x27	x28	x29	0
x30	x31	x32	x33	x34	x35	x36	x37	x38	x39	0
x40	x41	x42	x43	x44	x45	x46	x47	x48	x49	0
x50	x51	x52	x53	x54	x55	x56	x57	x58	x59	0
x60	x61	x62	x63	x64	x65	x66	x67	x68	x69	0
x70	x71	x72	x73	x74	x75	x76	x77	x78	x79	0
x80	x81	x82	x83	x84	x85	x86	x87	x88	x89	0
x90	x91	x92	x93	x94	x95	x96	x97	x98	x99	0

(overlay labels: X1, X2, X3, X4)

*

Matrix W

w00	w01	w02	w03	w04	w05	w06	w07	w08	w09
w10	w11	w12	w13	w14	w15	w16	w17	w18	w19
w20	w21	w22	w23	w24	w25	w26	w27	w28	w29
w30	w31	w32	w33	w34	w35	w36	w37	w38	w39
w40	w41	w42	w43	w44	w45	w46	w47	w48	w49
w50	w51	w52	w53	w54	w55	w56	w57	w58	w59
w60	w61	w62	w63	w64	w65	w66	w67	w68	w69
w70	w71	w72	w73	w74	w75	w76	w77	w78	w79
w80	w81	w82	w83	w84	w85	w86	w87	w88	w89
w90	w91	w92	w93	w94	w95	w96	w97	w98	w99
0	0	0	0	0	0	0	0	0	0
0	0	0	0	0	0	0	0	0	0

(overlay labels: W1, W2, W3, W4)

=

Matrix Y

y00	y01	y02	y03	y04	y05	y06	y07	y08	y09
y10	y11	y12	y13	y14	y15	y16	y17	y18	y19
y20	y21	y22	y23	y24	y25	y26	y27	y28	y29
y30	y31	y32	y33	y34	y35	y36	y37	y38	y39
y40	y41	y42	y43	y44	y45	y46	y47	y48	y49
y50	y51	y52	y53	y54	y55	y56	y57	y58	y59
y60	y61	y62	y63	y64	y65	y66	y67	y68	y69
y70	y71	y72	y73	y74	y75	y76	y77	y78	y79
y80	y81	y82	y83	y84	y85	y86	y87	y88	y89
y90	y91	y92	y93	y94	y95	y96	y97	y98	y99

FIGURE 8.25
Chunked matrix multiplication.

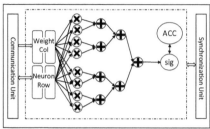

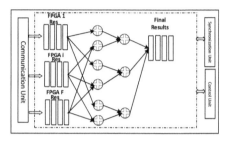

a) DIL system computation FPGA on-chip IP core design   b) DIL system control FPGA on-chip IP core design

FIGURE 8.26
DIL system IP core design. (a) DIL system computation FPGA on-chip IP core design. (b) DIL system control FPGA on-chip IP core design.

FPGAs, such as the pure gray-shaded 3×3 explicit sub-block of matrix X and the four 3×3 weights sub-blocks of pure gray-shaded matrix W are stored in the computing FPGA1, first, the row vectors (X_{00}, X_{01}, X_{02}) and the column vectors (W_{00}, W_{10}, W_{20}) perform the vector inner product operation to get the local result about Y_{00}. Then the row vector and column vectors (W_{01}, W_{11}, W_{21}), (W_{02}, W_{12}, W_{22}) in turn perform inner product operations to get the local result about Y_{01}, Y_{02}, and then the row vector (X_{10}, X_{11}, X_{12}) performs inner product operation with the column vectors (W_{00}, W_{10}, W_{20}), and so on. Each FPGA completes the computation of the corresponding local data block in this order, obtains the local computation result of the same result block in the Y matrix, and passes it back to the controlling FPGA. As can be seen in Figure 8.26, to ensure load balancing on each computational FPGA, the matrix chunking operation will bring additional 0 data and 0 computation. Similar to the chunking computation, the 0-filling operation introduces additional invalid operations but has a greater side effect on system performance.

2. Calculation module design

In the DIL acceleration system, the computation within the computational FPGA is the same, both for vector inner product operation and excitation function computation, and the design of its on-chip IP core is shown in Figure 8.26a, which is the same as that of the IP core of the odd FPGA in the DBL system and will not be repeated here.

The design of the control FPGA's on-chip port core is relatively simple, mainly through the parallel addition tree to complete the accumulation operation of each matrix block, as shown in Figure 8.26b. The control FPGA reads the local result vector in the F-slice computing FPGA in parallel and each time divides the vector elements into multiple data groups according to the offset position of the elements in the vector. Each data group contains the element values of the same position from different FPGAs in the F-slice, and adds the F elements in each data group in parallel by the depth of the 1092 F addition tree two by two, to get the final result value of the position.

Synchronous computing: The DIL acceleration system also has synchronous units within the compute FPGA and the control FPGA for synchronous computation. The finite state machine design in the computational FPGA is consistent with the state machine design of the computational FPGA in the layer-by-layer scheme and will not be repeated here. The control FPGA plays the role of communication and control intermediary between the CPU and the computational FPGA, and has relatively more states, and the state machine state transition diagram is shown in Figure 8.27. The initial state of the control FPGA is idle and constantly polls the data FIFO connected to the CPU to see if it is empty, waiting for incoming sample data from the CPU side, and if this FIFO is empty, it remains in the idle state, and if the FIFO is not empty, then it jumps into the data distribution state; in the data distribution state, the control FPGA processes the incoming sample data from the CPU in chunks and encapsulates them into packets, and sends the individual. In the data distribution state, the FPGA is controlled to process the incoming sample data

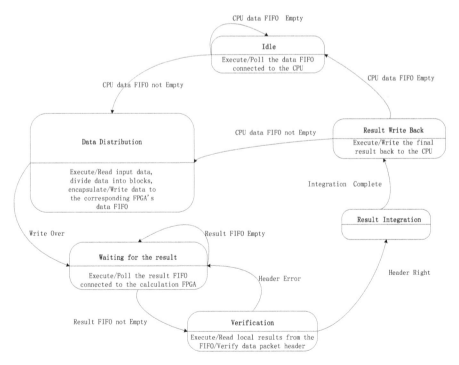

FIGURE 8.27
Schematic of DIL system control FPGA state transitions.

from the CPU in chunks and encapsulate them into data packets, and then send the data packets to the corresponding data FIFOs of the computation FPGA, and then jump into the waiting for result state; in the waiting for result state, the FPGA is controlled to poll the F result FIFOs connected to the computation FPGA continuously, and then wait for the computation FPGA to complete, and then keep the FPGA in the present state if the FIFOs are empty, and jump into the verification state if the FIFOs are not empty: in the verification state, the FPGA is controlled to read the In the check state, the FPGA is controlled to read the result packet returned by the computation FPGA and check the first part of the packet, if the first part is wrong, it jumps back to the waiting result state, if the first part is correct, it jumps into the result integration state; in the result integration state, the FPGA is controlled to carry out the accumulation operation on the received local result to get the final output result, and it jumps into the result writing back state; in the result writing back state, the FPGA is controlled to write the final result of the computation into the result FIFO connected to the CPU, which is connected to the result FIFO. In the result write-back state, the FPGA is controlled to write the final calculation result into the result FIFO connected to the CPU and judge whether the CPU data FIFO is empty; if it is empty, it jumps into the idle state; if it is not empty, it jumps into the data distribution state.

8.4 Chapter Summary

At present, deep learning has demonstrated its unique advantages in many fields such as image recognition, speech recognition, and so on. A DBN is a commonly used basic neural network in deep learning, which is composed of multiple layers of constrained BM superposition. Considering that DBNs are computation-intensive and data-intensive operations, and the scale of processed data and network size are also expanding, high-performance and low-power computing has become one of the research hotspots for DBNs. In this chapter, FPGA is used as an implementation platform to accelerate the prediction process of DBNs by taking advantage of FPGA reconfigurability, high performance, and low power consumption. Considering that the resources of single FPGA are limited and the network scale is too large, this chapter gives a square method of how to implement the accelerator customization for neural networks on multiple FPGAs while optimizing the single FPGA acceleration system and proposes two network division schemes, namely, layer-by-layer and intra-layer division. The related methods are hoped to provide a reference for carrying out related research work.

<hr>

References

1. Wang S. C. *Interdisciplinary Computing in Java Programming*. Berlin: Springer Science & Business Media, 2003.
2. Bengio Y, Delalleau O. On the expressive power of deep architectures. *International Conference on Algorithmic Learning Theory*. Berlin, Heidelberg: Springer, 2011: 18–36.
3. Hinton G. E., Osindero S., Teh Y. W. A fast learning algorithm for deep belief nets. *Neural Computation*, 2006, 18(7): 1527–1554.
4. Nair V., Hinton G. E. 3D object recognition with deep belief nets. *Advances in Neural Information Processing Systems*, 2009, 22.
5. Lee H., Grosse R., Ranganath R., et al. Convolutional deep belief networks for scalable unsupervised learning of hierarchical representations. *Proceedings of the 26th Annual International Conference on Machine Learning*, Montreal, QC. 2009: 609–616.
6. Mohamed A., Dahl G., Hinton G. Deep belief networks for phone recognition. *NIPS Workshop on Deep Learning for Speech Recognition and Related Applications*, Vancouver, BC. 2009, 1(9): 39.
7. Mohamed A., Sainath T. N., Dahl G., et al. Deep belief networks using discriminative features for phone recognition. *2011 IEEE International Conference on Acoustics, Speech and Signal Processing (ICASSP)*, Waikoloa, HI. IEEE, 2011: 5060–5063.
8. Sainath T. N., Kingsbury B., Ramabhadran B., et al. Making deep belief networks effective for large vocabulary continuous speech recognition. *2011 IEEE Workshop on Automatic Speech Recognition & Understanding*, Waikoloa, HI. IEEE, 2011: 30–35.
9. Demirli K. Selected papers from NAFIPS 2006, 2006 annual conference of the North American fuzzy information processing society. *International Journal of Approximate Reasoning*, 2009, 50(1): 62–62.
10. Smolensky P. Information processing in dynamical systems: Foundations of harmony theory. MIT Press, 1986: 194–281.
11. Ackley D. H., Hinton G. E., Sejnowski T. J. A learning algorithm for Boltzmann machines. *Cognitive Science*, 1985, 9(1): 147–169.
12. Freund Y., Haussler D. Unsupervised learning of distributions on binary vectors using two layer networks. *Advances in Neural Information Processing Systems*, 1991, 4. https://dl.acm.org/doi/10.5555/2986916.2987028
13. Hinton G. E. Training products of experts by minimising contrastive divergence. *Neural Computation*, 2002, 14(8): 1771–1800.

14. Liu J. S., Liu J S. *Monte Carlo Strategies in Scientific Computing*. New York: Springer, 2001.
15. Yu Q., Wang C., Ma X., et al. A deep learning prediction process accelerator based FPGA. *2015 15th IEEE/ACM International Symposium on Cluster, Cloud and Grid Computing*, Shenzhen. IEEE, 2015: 1159–1162.
16. Wang C., Gong L., Yu Q., et al. DLAU: A scalable deep learning accelerator unit on FPGA. *IEEE Transactions on Computer-Aided Design of Integrated Circuits and Systems*, 2016, 36(3): 513–517.
17. Le Ly D., Chow P. High-performance reconfigurable hardware architecture for restricted Boltzmann machines. *IEEE Transactions on Neural Networks*, 2010, 21(11): 1780–1792.

9

FPGA-Based Hardware Accelerator Customization for Recurrent Neural Networks

9.1 Background and Significance

Nowadays, artificial intelligence, as a booming discipline in the field of computer science, has achieved many remarkable results in both scientific research and practical applications [1]. Among them, machine learning is an important method to realize artificial intelligence, which enables computer systems to "learn" unprogrammed functions by parsing data, to make corresponding predictions for specific problems in reality [2]. In machine learning models, artificial neural networks (ANNs) [3] have gained widespread application in practical tasks due to their high predictive accuracy. They are utilized in various domains such as facial recognition [4], speech recognition [5], disease diagnosis [6], and more.

In the late 1980s, with the introduction of the backpropagation training algorithm and the development of computer technology, the research of neural networks reached a new peak and gave birth to the most popular neural network structures such as convolutional neural networks (CNNs) and recurrent neural networks (RNNs). However, the high computational demands of neural networks have hindered their further development. Until around 2010, with the emergence of cloud computing and GPUs, computing resources were no longer a limiting factor, and scientific research based on neural networks once again ushered in springtime. In 2012, Alex Krizhevsky from the University of Toronto designed a deep neural network called AlexNet [7], which achieved remarkable success in the ImageNet Large Scale Visual Recognition Challenge (ILSVRC) of the same year. AlexNet significantly reduced the error rate of ImageNet image classification [8] from 26% to 16%, surpassing the accuracy limitations of traditional machine learning algorithms in this field. This breakthrough demonstrated the value of neural networks and caught the attention of researchers worldwide. Nowadays, research based on neural networks is still on the rise, and the artificial

DOI: 10.1201/9780429355080-9

intelligence Alpha Go [9] designed by Google's DeepMind team based on neural network technology has successively defeated the world's top human players such as Lee Sedol and Ke Jie in Go; in the industrial field, neural network technology is also used in various products, such as image recognition-based image search technology [10], AI-powered conversational systems based on speech recognition [11], and machine translation software based on natural language processing [12], which increasingly reflect the value of the neural network.

Although neural networks have achieved great success in both the scientific research and industrial communities, the growing demand for practical applications has posed new challenges. Neural networks are now required to tackle more complex learning problems, leading to an increase in network size, parameters, and computational complexity. Large-scale neural networks face challenges in terms of performance, storage, and energy consumption. Therefore, realizing neural network algorithm applications with high performance and low energy consumption while meeting storage requirements has become one of the current research hotspots [13].

Indeed, the field of neural networks encompasses various models, and currently, two widely applied models are CNNs and RNNs. Among them, CNNs are mostly used in the field of image recognition, while RNNs are generally used in speech recognition [14], and language processing [15], and of course can also be used in the field of image processing [16]. A complete neural network algorithm consists of two essential components: the backward part and the forward part. The backward part, also known as the training stage, involves training the parameters of the neural network using a data set to achieve the desired learning outcome. On the other hand, the forward part, also known as the prediction stage, utilizes the fully trained neural network to perform actual prediction operations. In this chapter, we focus on the long short-term memory (LSTM) of RNNs. We will mainly introduce the acceleration and low-power implementation of its forward algorithm, and use compression to solve the storage bottleneck problem of large-scale neural networks.

9.2 Recurrent Neural Networks

9.2.1 Introduction to Recurrent Neural Networks

9.2.1.1 Basic Concepts

Recurrent neural networks, also known as recursive neural networks, abbreviated as RNNs, originated from the Hopfield network [17] proposed by John Hopfield in 1982 which was replaced by fully connected neural networks due to difficulties in implementation and failure to find suitable application scenarios at that time. However, with the increasing demand for real-world applications, numerous tasks involving temporal dependencies emerged. Traditional fully connected neural networks were unable to leverage the temporal aspects of input data. Therefore, RNN structures, which are more effective in temporal applications, have been explored and continue to evolve with the emergence of new variants.

RNNs are widely used in applications related to sequence processing. From Figure 9.1a, it can be observed that in conventional neural networks, the hidden layer neurons are only connected to nodes in the input and output layers, without any connections among the neurons within the hidden layer. In contrast, RNNs have connections among hidden layer neurons, enabling the propagation of information within the same layer. Figure 9.1b illustrates that the RNN allows information to be passed inside the hidden layer at every moment due to the presence of loops in the hidden layer. Figure 9.2 displays the temporal unfolding of an RNN network, where each moment in time can be seen as a "copy" of the network topology from the previous moment, transmitting messages to the network at the next time step. It can be

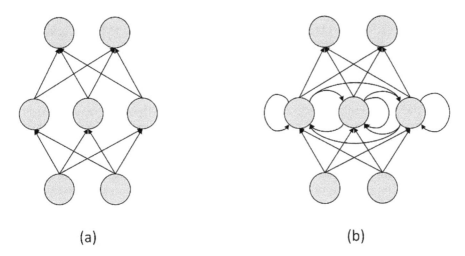

(a)   (b)

FIGURE 9.1
(a) Conventional neural network and (b) recurrent neural network.

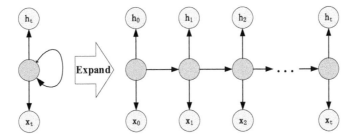

FIGURE 9.2
RNN unfolding according to timeline.

observed that compared to DNN networks, which can only transmit information in space, RNNs have the ability to transmit information over time, thereby retaining a certain level of "memory" of the previous time steps [18]. Based on the characteristics of RNN, it is generally used in speech recognition, machine translation, image analysis, stock prediction, and so on.

9.2.1.2 Introduction to Long Short-Term Memory Networks

RNNs rely on past information to infer the current task. If the time gap between the relevant past information and the current task is not too long, traditional RNNs are sufficient to handle such short-term dependencies effectively. However, in practical applications, it is often necessary to consider a larger context to infer the current task effectively. As depicted in Figure 9.3, when there is a significant time gap between relevant information, the issue of long-term dependencies arises [19]. Traditional RNN models struggle to capture such distant connections in the time dimension [20]. To solve this problem, the LSTM was born [21].

The LSTM neural network was proposed by Sepp Hochreiter and Jürgen Schmidhuber in 1997 [22]. As can be seen in Figure 9.4, LSTM networks are based on traditional RNN networks where the hidden layer neurons are replaced by specialized LSTM units, and each LSTM unit has three additional "gate" structures compared to traditional neurons: input gate (i), forget gate (f), and output gate (o). The LSTM relies on these gate structures to allow the input information to selectively influence the state of the neural network at each moment. The structure of each gate consists of a multiplicative weighting operation of the incoming information and the connection weights, and an activation function operation using a sigmoid. The sigmoid function takes values in the range [0,1] and is used in the gate structure to determine the amount of information that can pass through the gate: when the sigmoid function calculates to 0, no information can pass through the gate, which is equivalent to the gate being completely closed; when the value

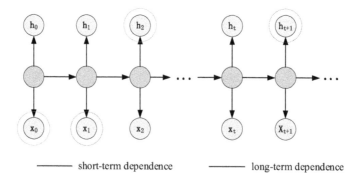

FIGURE 9.3
Short-term dependence and long-term dependence in RNNs.

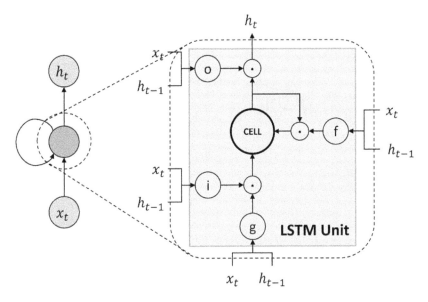

FIGURE 9.4
Hidden layer unit of LSTM network.

of the sigmoid function is 1, all the information can pass through, which is equivalent to the door being completely open. In addition, the LSTM unit includes a cell component that is responsible for storing the current state of the LSTM unit. After each time step, the state value of the cell gets updated.

The gate structures play a crucial role in LSTM networks as they enable the network to maintain long-term memory. Since an LSTM neural network cannot retain all previous information in memory, it is necessary to determine what information needs to be memorized and what information needs to be forgotten at each time step. The role of forgetting gates is to determine what information needs to be memorized and what information needs to be forgotten through synthesizing the inputs at the current moment x_t and the output of the previous moment h_{t-1} and state value c_{t-1} to comprehensively determine which memorized information is not very important and should be forgotten. While forgetting unimportant memories, LSTM also needs to incorporate new information based on the current input. This is where the input gate comes into play, determining which information should be written into the new state. The combination of the forgetting gate and the input gate of the LSTM unit ensures that the necessary information is retained and the unimportant information can be discarded more effectively. After updating the current state, the output gate structure is also needed to decide the output at the current moment. Compared to the conventional ANNs introduced previously, the forward propagation algorithm of the LSTM neural network involves a more intricate computation process. It encompasses not only the recursive loop process for output values but

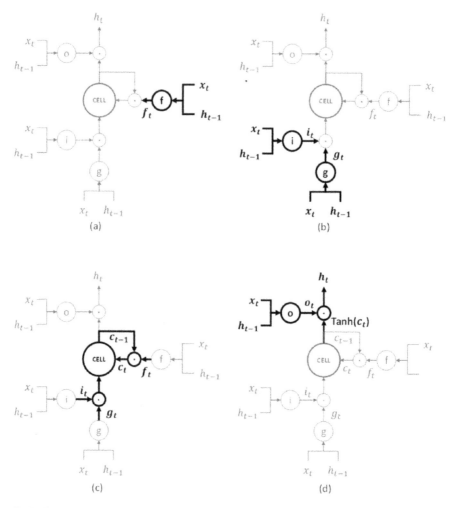

FIGURE 9.5
(a) Oblivion gate operation, (b) input side operation, (c) cell state value update operation, and
(d) Output gate operation.

also the manipulation of three gate vectors. As illustrated in Figure 9.5, the
execution flow of each LSTM unit is as follows:

1. The first step in an LSTM network involves determining which
   information to forget from the cell component. At this stage, the forget gate reads inputs x_t and h_{t-1}, and outputs a number ranging from
   0 to 1 using the sigmoid function to control the degree of information
   forgetfulness. The corresponding equation for this step is as follows:

$$f_t = \text{sigmoid}\left(W_{xf}x_t + W_{hf}h_{t-1} + b_f\right) \tag{9.1}$$

2. Subsequently, the determination of which information to retain in the cell state value follows. This involves a multi-step implementation process: on the one hand, the input gate decides which values to update, and on the other hand, the new candidate value g_t is received and incorporated into the state. The subsequent update of the cell state requires the simultaneous involvement of these two values. The corresponding equation for this step is as follows:

$$i_t = sigmoid\left(W_{xi}x_t + W_{hi}h_{t-1} + b_i\right) \tag{9.2}$$

$$g_t = tanh\left(W_{xg}x_t + W_{hg}h_{t-1} + b_g\right) \tag{9.3}$$

This step involves updating the cellular state, where the cellular state at the previous time moment is denoted as $c\_(t-1)$. First, it is multiplied by f_t to discard the information that needs to be forgotten. Additionally, the values obtained from the previous step, i_t and g_t, are multiplied together to obtain the new update value, which is then added to the cellular state. This process can be represented by the following equation:

$$c_t = f_t \odot c_{t-1} + i_t \odot g_t \tag{9.4}$$

3. Finally, the computation of the output value is required. The output value is not solely based on the cellular state but also involves a filtering step, which is governed by the output gate. The output gate utilizes a sigmoid function to determine the portion of the cellular state that needs to be output. Subsequently, the cellular state is passed through a hyperbolic tangent (tanh) function, resulting in a value ranging from −1 to 1. This value is then multiplied by the output gate's value to obtain the output component. This process can be represented by the following equation:

$$o_t = sigmoid\left(W_{xo}x_t + W_{ho}h_{t-1} + b_o\right) \tag{9.5}$$

$$h_t = tanh\left(c_t\right) \odot o_t \tag{9.6}$$

9.2.2 Algorithm Analysis

9.2.2.1 Analysis of LSTM Prediction Algorithms

First, we delve into a comprehensive analysis of the characteristics of the forward propagation algorithm in the LSTM neural network. In a step-by-step manner, we meticulously examine the distinctive features of each component involved in the computational process and thoroughly analyze the computational and storage costs associated with them.

LSTMs, like other RNN-type neural networks, in addition to the current input value x_t, also receive the output of the layer h_{t-1} from the previous time step. Moreover, in addition to the regular inputs, there are three additional gate structures, and each gate connection also has its value. Thus, the LSTM layer consists of a total of eight weight matrices corresponding to the input sides (i.e., i, f, o, g) for different input vectors (i.e., x_t and h_{t-1}): W_x, W_{xg}, W_{xf}, W_{xo}, W_h, W_{hg}, W_{hf}, W_{ho}. This part of the computation is a multiplication of the input vectors with the corresponding weights matrices thus obtaining the new vector values.

Since the operations between each weight matrix and vector are performed independently, it is possible to merge x_t and h_{t-1} into a single long vector. Similarly, the eight weight matrices can also be combined into a single matrix. After the matrix-vector multiplication, the resulting vectors are divided into four separate vectors, which participate in the subsequent activation function operations for the four input sides of the LSTM. This process yields the vectors i_t, g_t, f_t, and o_t, as depicted in Figure 9.6.

The process of matrix-vector multiplication: First, each element in the input vector is multiplied with the corresponding weight value in the matrix. Since

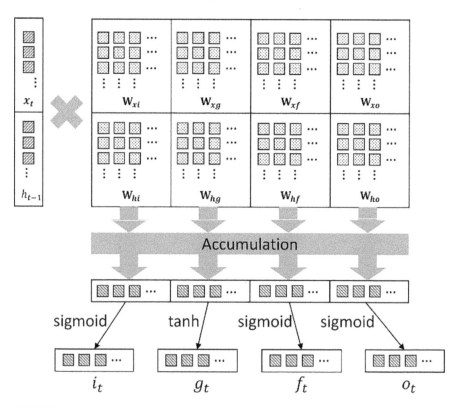

FIGURE 9.6
Matrix-vector multiplication computation process in LSTM neural networks.

each element in the weight matrix represents a connection in the neural network, this multiplication process exemplifies the transmission of information between neurons. Furthermore, to obtain the elements in the resulting vector, a summation operation is performed by accumulating the intermediate values obtained from the element-wise multiplications within each column of the matrix.

The pseudocode for the matrix-vector multiplication in LSTM is presented in Algorithm 9.1. Assuming the input layer size (i.e., the length of the vector x_t) is *INPUT_SIZE* and the LSTM hidden layer size is *HIDDEN_SIZE*, the merged vector length becomes (*INPUT_SIZE* + *HIDDEN_SIZE*). Similarly, the merged weight matrix size becomes (*INPUT_SIZE* + *HIDDEN_SIZE*) * (4 * *HIDDEN_SIZE*), and the merged bias vector length becomes (4 * *HIDDEN_SIZE*). The lengths of i_t, g_t, f_t, o_t and the cell state vector are all *HIDDEN_SIZE*.

Algorithm 9.1: Matrix-Vector Multiplication in Forward Computation for LSTM Networks

Input: x_t and h_{t-1}

Output: i_t , g_t , f_t , o_t

1 inputs = merge(x_t , h_{t-1});

2 weights = merge((W_{xi} , W_{xg} , W_{xf} , W_{xo}), (W , W_{hihg} , W_{hf} , W_{ho}));

3 biases = merge(b_i , b_g , b_f , b_o);

4 for $i = 0$; $i < 4 * HIDDEN\_SIZE$; $i = i + 1$ **do**

5   tmp[i] = 0.0;

6   **for** $j = 0$; $j < IINPUT\_SIZE + HIDDEN\_SIZE$; $j = j + 1$ **do**

7   tmp[i] = tmp[i] + inputs[j]*weights[j][i];

8   **end**

9   tmp[i] = tmp[i] + biases[i];

10 end

11 for $i = 0$; $i < HIDDEN\_SIZE$; $i = i + 1$ **do**

12 i_t [i] = sigmoid(tmp[i]);

13 g_t [i] = tanh(tmp[i+HIDDEN_SIZE]);

14 f_t [i] = sigmoid(tmp[i+2*HIDDEN_SIZE]);

15 o_t [i] = sigmoid(tmp[i+3*HIDDEN_SIZE]);

16 end

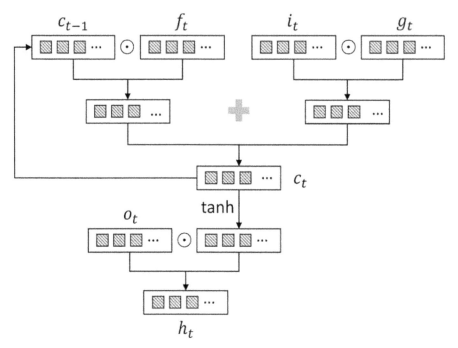

FIGURE 9.7
Element-wise calculation process.

After obtaining the vectors corresponding to the four input sides (one input and three gates) of the LSTM network through the matrix-vector calculation module, the next step involves computing the cell state vector and the output vector, as depicted in Figure 9.7. The type of computation in this part is Element-wise, which means that the elements at corresponding positions in the vectors are subjected to multiplication or addition operations. Additionally, this step involves the update operation of the cell state vector.

The pseudocode for the element-wise computation is presented in Algorithm 9.2. The four input vectors, i_t, g_t, f_t, and o_t, are the results of the matrix-vector multiplication operation.

Algorithm 9.2: Element-Wise Operations

> **Input:** i_t, g_t, f_t, o_t
>
> **Output:** h_t
>
> **1 for** $i = 0$; $i < HIDDEN\_SIZE$; $i = i + 1$ **do**
>
> 2   cell[i] = cell[i] * f_t[i] + i_t[i] * g_t[i];
>
> 3   h[i] = o_t[i] * tanh(cell[i]);

Considering the characteristics of LSTM, in addition to storing the weight values and offset parameters of the neural network itself, it is also necessary to store the state of the recording cell at the current moment and the current output value for the next moment of calculation.

In addition, the activation function serves to introduce nonlinearities in the neural network. In the LSTM cell, the input gate employs the hyperbolic tangent (tanh) activation function, while the other three gates utilize the sigmoid activation function. Additionally, when processing the output value in an LSTM unit, the cell state is also passed through the tanh activation function.

In the following, we analyze the computational intensity distribution of the LSTM neural network when performing a single forward propagation operation, where a single addition, subtraction, multiplication, and division of a floating-point number or an activation function operation is one computation. Suppose that the size of the input layer of the LSTM network is *INPUT_SIZE*, and the size of the hidden layer is *HIDDEN_SIZE*, then the number of times that the corresponding elements of the matrix and the vector are multiplied in the process of computation of this layer is *(INPUT_SIZE + HIDDEN_SIZE) * (HIDDEN_SIZE * 4)*. Afterward, *(INPUT_SIZE + HIDDEN_SIZE)* intermediate multiplication values of each column need to be summed to obtain one element of the resulting calculation vector. Based on the LSTM formula, the element-wise computation can be determined to be (HIDDEN_SIZE * 4) floating-point operations. The calculation count for the activation functions encompasses the operations on the input, the three LSTM gates, and the cell state value. Therefore, the total number of computations is (HIDDEN_SIZE * 5). Table 9.1 presents the computation counts required for each component when the number of LSTM units in the hidden layer is set to 32, 64, and 128 (with input vector size equal to the hidden layer dimension).

Based on the above analysis, it can be seen that the most computationally intensive operation during the forward operation of the LSTM network is the matrix-vector operation, which contains the multiplication of the corresponding elements as well as the accumulation of the multiplicative

TABLE 9.1

Number of Floating-Point Operations in Each Part of the LSTM Neural Network

LSTM Hidden Layer Scale	32	64	128
Matrix-vector multiplication of corresponding elements	8,192	32,768	131,072
Accumulation of multiplicative intermediate values	8,064	32,512	130,560
Bias vector summation	128	256	512
Element-wise multiply/add operations	128	256	512
Activation function operation	160	320	640
Total number of operations	16,672	66,112	263,296

intermediate values. Considering the content of Table 9.1, when the LSTM hidden layer size is 32, the proportion of matrix-vector operations in the computation is (8,192 + 8,064)/16,672 = 97.5%. When the hidden layer size is 64, the proportion of matrix-vector operations in the computation is 98.7%. Similarly, when the hidden layer size is 128, the proportion of matrix-vector operations in the computation is 99.4%. The matrix-vector operation is not only the most computationally intensive in LSTM forward pass but also its proportion increases with the growth of the LSTM network size. Therefore, if this part of the computation can be efficiently accelerated, it can lead to a significant improvement in the overall speed of the LSTM neural network.

For the consumption of storage resources in LSTM neural networks, the parameters mainly contain the weights matrix and bias vectors, plus buffers for storing the cell state value vectors as well as the output vectors. Assuming that the input size of a single layer of LSTM is *INPUT_SIZE* and the number of hidden layer cells is *HIDDEN_SIZE*, then the size of the weight matrix is *(INPUT_SIZE + HIDDEN_SIZE) * (HIDDEN_SIZE * 4)*, the size of the bias vector is *(HIDDEN_SIZE * 4)*, and the buffer size of both the cell state value and output vectors has *HIDDEN_SIZE*. Table 9.2 presents the storage resource requirements for various components of an LSTM neural network when the hidden layer sizes are set to 32, 64, and 128 (with input vector size equal to the hidden layer size).

According to Table 9.2, when the size of the LSTM hidden layer is 32, the weight matrix accounts for 97.3% of the storage resources; when the size of the hidden layer is 64, the weight matrix consumes 98.7% of the storage; and when the size of hidden layer reaches 128, the storage resources occupied by the weight matrix also reaches 99.3%. It can be seen that the weight matrix consumes most of the storage resources, and the amount of storage grows with the increase of the LSTM network size and should be the first target of compression. The pruning technique targets the connections in the neural network, that is, the weight matrix, so the pruning method is subsequently used to realize the compression of LSTM neural networks.

TABLE 9.2

Size of Storage Resources Occupied by Each Component in the LSTM Neural Network

LSTM Hidden Layer Scale	32	64	128
Input cache size	32	64	128
Weight matrix size	8,192	32,768	13,1072
Bias vector size	128	256	512
Cell state value size	32	64	128
Output cache size	32	64	128
Total storage capacity	8,416	33,216	131,968

9.2.2.2 Parameter Compression in LSTM Neural Networks

Based on the analysis from the previous section, the weight matrix, composed of connection weights, is the most storage-consuming component in LSTM neural networks. Therefore, pruning techniques are highly suitable for compressing LSTM neural networks. As shown in Figure 9.8, the main steps for pruning-retraining compression of LSTM neural networks are as follows:

1. First, employ conventional neural network training methods to obtain an initial LSTM neural network model.
2. Set the pruning rate. It is advisable not to set a pruning rate that is too large at once, as it may result in significant information loss in the neural network model, requiring a higher cost for retraining. Larger pruning rates can be achieved using multiple pruning-retraining iterations that increase the pruning rate one at a time.
3. Create an array consisting of the absolute values of all elements in the weight matrix. In this absolute value array, based on the pruning rate, identify the threshold value corresponding to the desired magnitude. In Figure 9.8, for illustrative purposes, the array is sorted in ascending order, but in practice, it is not necessary to sort the entire

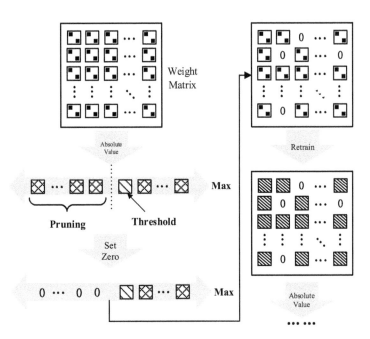

FIGURE 9.8
Pruning-retraining process for neural network models.

array. Only finding the threshold value is sufficient. This chapter uses the idea of the Quicksort algorithm to find the corresponding threshold.

4. Iterate through the weight matrix and set all elements with absolute values smaller than the threshold value to zero (setting a weight to zero can be considered as removing that connection). After this pruning step, some connections in the neural network are pruned, transforming the original dense network model into a sparse network model.

5. Retrain the pruned neural network to achieve optimal prediction accuracy for the sparse network. During the training process, when weight adjustments are required, only modify the non-zero elements in the weight matrix. The 0 elements in the matrix are not changed because they represent that the connection no longer exists.

6. Determine whether the current pruning rate has reached the desired requirement. If not, increase the pruning rate. However, as mentioned in Step 2, it is important not to increase the pruning rate too much at once.

7. Repeat steps 3 to 6 until the desired pruning rate is achieved, at which point the sparsity of the LSTM neural network meets the requirements and also maintains the prediction accuracy as much as possible.

Additionally, in basic pruning algorithms, pruning is performed on all elements of the weight matrix based on a certain percentage. As a result, the connections that are ultimately pruned are completely random, which can lead to an uneven distribution of remaining connections, as illustrated in Figure 9.9a. In the FPGA hardware implementation of sparse networks, if the weight matrix has an uneven data distribution, it can result in a significant imbalance in the number of element-wise multiplications and accumulations required for computing each result vector element in the matrix-vector operation. This can be detrimental to the parallel efficiency of FPGA implementations. Therefore, adjustments can be made to the traditional pruning scheme to maintain a certain degree of uniformity, which can be achieved through row-wise uniformity (equal number of elements per row) or column-wise uniformity (equal number of elements per column), as shown in Figure 9.9b. Indeed, the process of uniform pruning does not differ significantly from the aforementioned steps. The difference lies in steps 3 and 4. Instead of selecting a single threshold value for the entire weight matrix, each column is individually assigned a threshold value based on a certain percentage for pruning operations. By adopting this approach, it is possible to achieve uniformity in the values of each column.

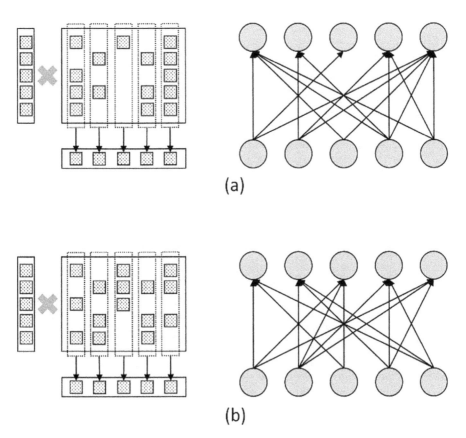

FIGURE 9.9
(a) Conventional pruning scheme and (b) uniform pruning scheme by columns.

9.3 Hardware Deployment/Acceleration Customization Related Work

Based on the algorithm analysis in Section 9.2.2, this section presents a customized FPGA hardware accelerator system for RNNs. We will first introduce the overall architecture of the system and then provide individual module descriptions.

9.3.1 The Overall Implementation Architecture

The design of this chapter adopts a collaborative mode of software and hardware, as illustrated in Figure 9.10. In the software part of the system, input data and the required LSTM parameters are stored in external

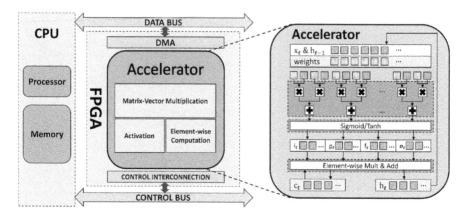

FIGURE 9.10
The overall system architecture.

memory. The software code is executed by the CPU, which uploads the task of LSTM forward computation to the FPGA hardware. The CPU can control the intellectual property (IP) cores of the hardware part through the control bus, upload the parameters and the input data through the data bus, and transmit the execution results of the hardware side back to the software side. The hardware component of the system, namely the FPGA accelerator, encompasses three main computational modules: the matrix-vector multiplication module, the element-wise computation module, and the activation function module. Additionally, the accelerator requires a cache to store neural network parameters, LSTM cell state values, and current output values [23].

The computational modules of the hardware can be designed and generated as IP cores using Vivado HLS. An IP core, as a logical module, can be ported to other semiconductors for reuse and implementation.

In the Vivado tool, the generated IP cores can be interconnected to create a hardware bitstream. Subsequently, the bitstream can be programmed into the FPGA using Vivado SDK. In the SDK, control programs can be written to facilitate the operations of the software part and enable data transfer between the software and hardware components.

For different data transmission modes, this chapter provides two design approaches:

1. Hardware Implementation with Single DMA Mode: Single Direct Memory Access (DMA) mode is used to transfer data. First, all the neural network parameters are transferred to the Block RAM (BRAM) of the FPGA. Subsequently, the input data is transmitted, and the forward computation of the neural network is performed. The matrix-vector operation part is realized by the single DMA mode matrix-vector operation module.

2. Hardware Implementation with Dual DMA Mode: Two DMA ports are used to transmit the input data and some of the required neural network parameters in parallel, respectively. The corresponding forward computation is then performed. The matrix-vector operation part is realized by the dual DMA matrix-vector operation module.

9.3.2 Matrix-Vector Multiplication Module

In this section, we will first introduce the parallel optimization strategies and hardware module design for the matrix-vector multiplication operation. Most of the operations in LSTM neural networks are concentrated in the matrix-vector multiplication part. Therefore, it is crucial to accelerate this operation using pipeline techniques and employ various optimization methods to enhance pipeline efficiency. In the matrix-vector multiplication operation, the involvement of weight matrices introduces a significant storage requirement. However, considering the limited on-chip storage resources of the FPGA, this chapter proposes three design options based on different LSTM network sizes: for smaller LSTM neural networks where the on-chip storage resources of the FPGA are sufficient to accommodate all the parameters, the design utilizes a single DMA mode FPGA computation module; for larger LSTM networks that exceed the storage limitations of the FPGA, two alternative computation module designs are provided: a double DMA parallel transmission mode arithmetic module and a single DMA mode sparse network operation module.

9.3.2.1 *Optimization Techniques for Matrix-Vector Operations*

In this section, we will first introduce the optimization techniques that can be employed in the matrix-vector multiplication operation. This particular computation involves computationally intensive operations, and its throughput can be enhanced by utilizing a pipeline approach. Additionally, the efficiency of parallel computation can be improved through the following optimization methods [24].

1. Parallel reading and writing
   The cache of an FPGA is composed of a large number of BRAM blocks. Each BRAM block can perform only one read or write operation within a clock cycle. However, in the matrix-vector multiplication operation, to achieve parallel multiplication of corresponding elements, it is necessary to simultaneously read the input vector and the weight matrix data in parallel. If the weight matrix is stored in the conventional sequential manner, it may result in multiple data reads from a single BRAM during the multiplication operation between the vector and a specific column of the matrix. This would increase the clock cycle required for the parallel computation, as illustrated

in Figure 9.11a. However, by partitioning the weight matrix and distributing the data across different BRAMs in a specific manner, it is possible to ensure that each BRAM is accessed only once during each vector-matrix column operation. This allows the computation to be completed within a single clock cycle, as depicted in Figure 9.11b.

2. Shard multiplexing

Based on the previous analysis, it is evident that partitioning the parameters and storing them in different BRAMs facilitate parallel read and write operations. However, due to the limited resources of BRAM and lookup tables in an FPGA, it is not feasible to partition and store each row of the weight matrix in separate BRAMs. Therefore, it is necessary to adopt a sharding approach, as illustrated in Figure 9.12. Due to the limitations in the number of floating-point

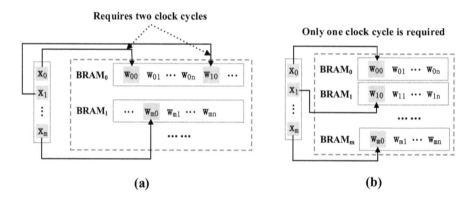

(a)   (b)

FIGURE 9.11
(a) Sequential storage of weight matrices and (b) split storage of weight matrices on different BRAMs.

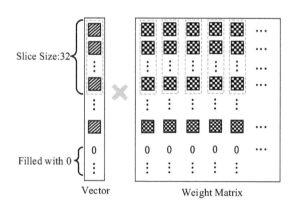

FIGURE 9.12
Piecewise multiplication.

multipliers, adders, and lookup tables available on the FPGA, this chapter employs a sharding method with a size of 32. For the parts that are less than 32, they are padded with zeros to ensure alignment. In this manner, both the vector and the matrix involved in the computation are divided into shards of length 32, and each shard in the vector can be reused multiple times. During the computation process, each time, a shard of the input vector is multiplied with the corresponding shard of the weight matrix, and the results are accumulated.

By employing the sharding approach, the process of parallel reading of weight parameters from BRAM for computation is depicted in Figure 9.13. (This section adopts a shard size of 32, i.e., $k=32$.) Although it does not enable the entire vector-matrix column operation to be completed within a single clock cycle, it ensures that the multiplication computation for each vector shard and matrix column shard is completed within one clock cycle.

3. Parallel accumulation

To fully utilize the parallel computing resources on an FPGA, an addition tree can be employed to accumulate the intermediate values obtained by multiplying corresponding elements in each shard. As shown in Figure 9.14a, for n multiplicative intermediate values, if the cyclic accumulation is performed, $n-1$ serial addition operations need to be performed, resulting in a time complexity of $O(n-1)$. Conversely, when utilizing a binary addition tree as shown in Figure 9.14b, the time complexity is reduced to $O(\log n)$. The size of the addition tree depends on the limitations of the computational units in the FPGA. For instance, when using 32-sized fragments for parallel element multiplication and addition tree accumulation, 32 floating-point multiplication units as well as 31 floating-point addition units are required.

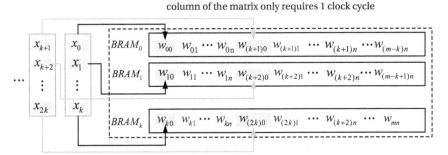

FIGURE 9.13
Partition storage of weights matrix using sharding method.

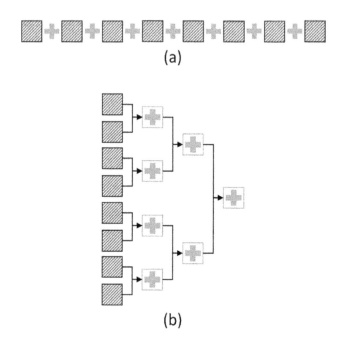

FIGURE 9.14
(a) Cyclic accumulation method and (b) addition tree parallel accumulation.

4. Double buffer

During the computation process of a neural network, due to the adoption of shard operations, when performing the multiplication and addition operations between each vector shard and the matrix, it is necessary to first read the entire content of that shard. The dependency between the memory access and computation stages results in prolonged pipeline cycles, limiting the efficient utilization of FPGA's parallel computing advantages. Therefore, this study adopts a double-buffering technique, alternating between memory access and computation operations, as illustrated in Figure 9.15. At a given time, while the data in buffer a is being multiplied with the matrix, buffer b simultaneously retrieves the content of the second shard. After the computation of the shard in buffer a is complete, the content of the third fragment is read, while simultaneously the shard data in buffer b is multiplied with the matrix. Since the time required for shard participation in multiplication and addition operations is much greater than the time taken to read the shard data, and there is no dependency between the data read by one buffer and the currently involved shard data in computation, it is possible to effectively overlap the shard reading and computation parts. By alternating between the two buffers for data reading and computation, the pipeline interval is minimized, leading to the highest computational efficiency.

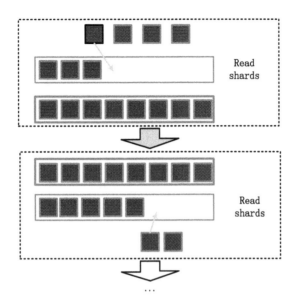

FIGURE 9.15
Double buffers alternately read data/participate in operations.

9.3.3.2 The Single DMA Mode Matrix-Vector Operation Module

When FPGA storage resources are relatively abundant for neural networks, it is possible to store all the neural network parameters in BRAM before performing computations with input data. Therefore, only one DMA is needed for data transfer. The computation process begins by using the DMA to transfer and store the parameter values, such as the weight matrix and bias vector, into the FPGA's BRAM. Subsequently, the input vectors are sequentially transferred for computation in the designated order. By utilizing a pipeline approach, it is possible to effectively reduce computation time. Additionally, the optimization techniques described in Section 9.3.2.1 can be employed to achieve the desired pipeline efficiency.

By combining the optimization techniques described in Section 9.3.2.1, the process of the single DMA mode matrix-vector multiplication operation module is shown in Figure 9.16, where the weights and bias parameters of the neural network are first transferred to the cache before the prediction task is performed, and then the input vectors are read in to perform the computation. Since this module is an implementation of the LSTM neural network, at each moment both the input vector of that moment and the output vector of the previous moment are read into the cache to form a long vector. This concatenated vector is then divided into shards and then these shards are read and multiplied with the corresponding elements of the weight matrix in the cache using double buffering. The intermediate multiplication results are accumulated using a binary addition tree to obtain the fragment computation result. Finally, the results of all the shard calculations in each column are summed up. The implementation algorithm is shown in Algorithm 9.3,

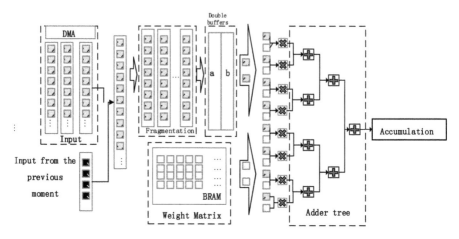

FIGURE 9.16
Single DMA mode matrix-vector multiplication module.

where the input size is *INPUT_SIZE*, the hidden layer size is *HIDDEN_SIZE*, the shard size is 32, and the double buffers are *tile1* and *tile2*, respectively. The addition tree algorithm for the single DMA mode operation module (Adder_Tree_1DMA) is presented in Algorithm 9.4.

Algorithm 9.3: Single DMA Mode Matrix-Vector Multiplication Implementation Algorithm

Input: x_t , h_{t-1}

Output: result_vector$_t$

1 input_vector = merge(x_t , h_{t-1});

2 for $i = 0; i < 32; i = i + 1$ **do**

3   tile1[i] = input_vector[i];

4 end

5 tile_flag = 0;

6 for $i = 0; i < INPUT\_SIZE + HIDDEN\_SIZE; i = i + 32$ **do**

7   **for** $j = 0; i < 4 * HIDDEN\_SIZE; i = i + 32$ **do**

8   (PIPELINE)

9   **if** $j < 32 and k < INPUT\_SIZE + HIDDEN\_SIZE - 32$ **then**

10   **if** *tile_flag* == 0 **then**

11   tile2[j] = input_vector[i + j + 32];

12 **else**

13 tile1[j] = input_vector[i + j + 32];

14 **if** *tile_flag* == 0 **then**

15 accum = Adder_Tree_1DMA(tile1, weights, i, j), tile_flag = 1;

16 **else**

17 accum = Adder_Tree_1DMA(tile2, weights, i, j), tile_flag = 0;

18 **if** *i* == 0 **then**

19 result_vector[j] = bias[j] + accum;

20 **else**

21 result_vector[j] = result_vector[j] + accum;

22 **end**

23 **end**

The advantage of the single DMA mode matrix-vector multiplication module is that, with sufficient storage resources, all neural network parameters can be transferred to the FPGA cache at one time, and the subsequent computation process only needs to transfer the input vectors without doing any further parameter transfers, which saves bandwidth. On the other hand, the neural network parameters stored in the cache exhibit locality, which enhances the efficiency of fragment reuse in multiplication operations. However, the single DMA mode matrix-vector multiplication module also has its limitations. It is highly sensitive to storage resources, and when the number of neural network parameters exceeds the storage capacity of the FPGA, it becomes impossible to store all parameters in BRAM at once. If the neural network parameters that are to be used are repeatedly transmitted in the single DMA mode, the transmission of the input vectors will be seriously affected, which will reduce the efficiency of the operation.

Algorithm 9.4: Addition Tree Algorithm in Single DMA Mode Adder_Tree_1DMA

Input: tile, weights, i, j

Output: accum

1 **for** $k = 0; k < 16; k = k + 1$ **do**

2 (UNROLL)

3 $accum_k = (tile[2 * k] * weights[i + 2 * k][j])$

4 $+ (tile[2 * k + 1] * weights[i + 2 * k + 1][j]).$

5 end

6 $accum_{16} = (accum_0 + accum_1) + (accum_2 + accum_3);$

7 $accum_{17} = (accum_4 + accum_5) + (accum_6 + accum_7);$

8 $accum_{18} = (accum_8 + accum_9) + (accum_{10} + accum_{11});$

9 $accum_{19} = (accum_{12} + accum_{13}) + (accum_{14} + accum_{15});$

10 $accum = (accum_{16} + accum_{17}) + (accum_{18} + accum_{19});$

9.3.2.3 Dual DMA Mode Matrix-Vector Arithmetic Module

In cases where the FPGA's storage resources are sufficient to accommodate all neural network parameters, the single DMA mode matrix-vector multiplication module is suitable for processing. However, when the scale of neural network parameters exceeds the storage limitations of the FPGA, it is no longer possible to store all weights and other parameters in the on-chip cache at once. Therefore, this chapter also introduces a dual DMA operation module, where one DMA is responsible for transferring input vector values, while the other DMA simultaneously transfers the corresponding weight parameters for computation with the input vector values.

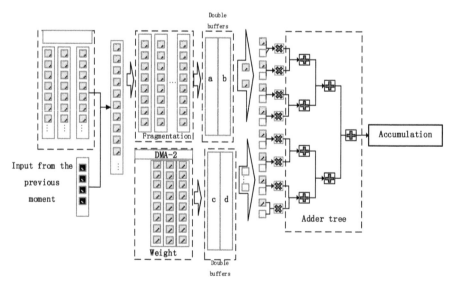

FIGURE 9.17
Dual DMA matrix-vector multiplication module.

Similar to the single DMA mode operation module, the dual DMA operation module also adopts 32 as the shard size, as shown in Figure 9.17. Initially, one DMA transfers the input vector of the current time step and stores it, along with the output vector of the previous time step, in a long vector cache. Subsequently, the long vector is sliced and read in shards using double buffering. At the same time, the other DMA is responsible for transferring the weights shard, and the weights shard is also read and multiplied with the vector shard using double buffers. Similar to the single DMA mode module, the multiplication intermediate values are also added in an additive tree manner to realize parallel accumulation calculation.

Due to the calculation sequence of this module, where each vector shard is computed with the corresponding position of the matrix before moving on to the next vector shard, the transmission order of the weight matrix needs to be adjusted based on the adjacent shard. This part of the work needs to be done off-chip on the software side, where the weight matrix is rearranged in units of 32-size shards, following the order of vector chunk reuse for multiplication. This ensures that the input vector shards on the FPGA are computed with their corresponding weight shards. Please refer to Algorithm 9.5 for the reordering process. The addition tree algorithm used in the dual DMA mode module differs slightly from the algorithm used in the single DMA mode. Please refer to Algorithm 9.6 for the specific details.

The dual DMA matrix-vector multiplication module eliminates the need for FPGA to consume a substantial amount of storage resources for caching neural network parameters. Additionally, the design of dual DMA enables parallel transmission of input data and weight data, further enhancing the efficiency of the system. However, the dual DMA operation module also has its limitations, as it requires continuous reading of weight parameter shards. The time required for one vector chunk and weight chunk dot product calculation is $O(1+\log 32)=O(6)$, while the time needed to read the next weight chunk is $O(32)$. This results in the reading of weight chunks taking more time than the computation itself, which affects the efficiency of the pipeline.

Algorithm 9.5: Double DMA Matrix-Vector Multiplication Implementation Algorithm

    Input: x_t , h_{t-1} , weights_values_tile

    Output: result_vector

    1 input_vector $=$ merge(x_t , h_{t-1}); **for** $i=0; i<32; i=i+1$ **do**

    2   tile1[i] $=$ input_vector[i];

    3 end

```
4 tile_flag=0, weight_flag=0;
5 for i=0; i<INPUT_SIZE+HIDDEN_SIZE; i=i+32 do
6      for j=0; i<4*HIDDEN_SIZE; i=i+32 do
7      ( PIPELINE )
8          if weight_flag == 0 then
9          if tile_flag == 0 then
10         if j<32andk<INPUT_SIZE+HIDDEN_SIZE - 32 then
11         tile2[j]=input_vector[i+j+32];
12         accum=Adder_Tree_2DMA(tile1, w_tile1), tile_flag=1;
13         else
14         if j<32andk<INPUT_SIZE+HIDDEN_SIZE - 32 then
15         tile1[j]=input_vector[i+j+32];
16         accum=Adder_Tree_2DMA(tile2, w_tile1), tile_flag=0;
17         w_tile2=next weights_values_tile, weight_flag=1;
18         else
19         if tile_flag == 0 then
20         if j<32andk<INPUT_SIZE+HIDDEN_SIZE - 32 then
21         tile2[j]=input_vector[i+j+32];
22         accum=Adder_Tree_2DMA(tile1, w_tile2), tile_flag=1;
23         else
24         if j<32andk<INPUT_SIZE+HIDDEN_SIZE - 32 then
25         tile1[j]=input_vector[i+j+32];
26         accum=Adder_Tree_2DMA(tile2, w_tile2), tile_flag=0;
27         w_tile1=next weights_values_tile, weight_flag=0;
28         if i == 0 then
29         result_vector[j]=bias[j]+accum;
30         else
31         result_vector[j]=result_vector[j]+accum;
32         end
33 end
```

Algorithm 9.6: Addition Tree Algorithm in Dual DMA Mode Adder_Tree_2DMA

Input: tile, weights_tile

Output: accum

1 for $k = 0; k < 16; k = k + 1$ **do**

2   (UNROLL)

3     $accum_k = (tile[2 * k] * weights\_tile[2 * k])$

4     $+ (tile[2 * k + 1] * weights\_tile[2 * k + 1]).$

5 end

6 $accum_{16} = (accum_0 + accum_1) + (accum_2 + accum_3);$

7 $accum_{17} = (accum_4 + accum_5) + (accum_6 + accum_7);$

8 $accum_{18} = (accum_8 + accum_9) + (accum_{10} + accum_{11});$

9.3.2.4 Single DMA Mode Sparse Matrix-Vector Arithmetic Module

When the neural network parameters exceed the storage capacity of the FPGA, in addition to using dual DMA for parallel transmission of weight and input data, another solution is to prune and compress the parameters of the neural network and design a sparse matrix-vector operation module in single DMA mode for this model. After pruning, the storage space occupied by the parameters will be greatly reduced by adopting the appropriate storage method.

Pruning in neural networks primarily focuses on the weight matrix. After pruning, the weight matrix of the neural network contains a large number of zeros, allowing for storage in sparse matrix format. Common sparse network storage formats include COO (Coordinate Format), CSR (Compressed Sparse Row Format), and CSC (Compressed Sparse Column Format). Among them:

1. The advantages of the COO storage method are its flexibility and simplicity. It only requires storing the non-zero elements of the matrix along with their row and column positions. It offers flexibility in computations. However, because it requires three arrays of equal length to store the non-zero elements, their row positions, and their column positions, it may not achieve the same level of compression efficiency as the CSR and CSC formats.

2. The CSR storage method also requires three arrays to store the data. Two of these arrays, of equal length, store the non-zero elements and their column indices in the matrix, while the third array stores the

row offsets. The row offsets indicate the starting offset position of the first element in each row in the non-zero elements array. As a result, the length of the row offsets array is much shorter than simply storing the row indices of each element, making it more efficient in terms of compression compared to the COO format.

3. The CSC storage method is very similar to CSR. Its three arrays store the non-zero elements of the matrix, their row indices, and the column offsets. Thus, it also achieves higher compression efficiency compared to the COO format.

The choice of storage format for the weight matrix in a sparse neural network should consider the computational process. In Figure 9.18, which illustrates the calculation of a sparse matrix and a vector, if the CSR storage format is used, the access pattern for the weight matrix would be non-continuous and has varying stride lengths, which is not conducive to data locality. However, using the CSC storage format allows for accessing continuous memory when calculating the results of chunk-wise operations. Therefore, in this chapter, the CSC format is used to store the sparse weight matrix.

Due to the uneven data distribution of the sparse network weight matrix caused using the traditional pruning method, which affects the efficiency of parallel computation, the pruning algorithm is modified to ensure that the number of elements in each column of the weight matrix is the same, to

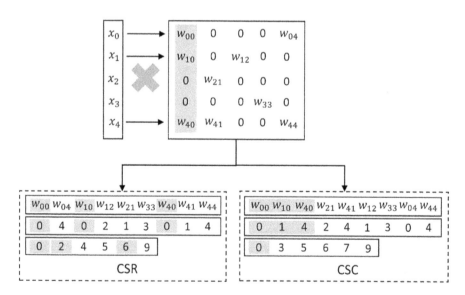

FIGURE 9.18
Access location of sparse matrices in operations using CSR and CSC storage forms.

ensure that the data is uniform to a certain extent. Furthermore, the design of the single DMA mode sparse matrix-vector operation module in this section is based on the sparse weight matrix that has undergone uniform pruning. As can be seen in Figure 9.19, since each column of the uniformly pruned sparse matrix has the same length, there is no longer a need to store column offset values, and both the non-zero elements and their corresponding row numbers can be stored in a two-dimensional array.

During the calculation process, because the elements in each column of the sparse weight matrix no longer correspond one-to-one with the output vector, but rather require column numbers as indices, the slicing and reuse methods used for dense matrices are no longer applicable in the sparse matrix operation module. In this chapter, the design of this module involves dividing the sparse weight matrix into shards of size 32 and multiplying the corresponding elements of the vector with the weight shard using indexing. The summation operation is then achieved through an addition tree, and computational efficiency is improved through pipelining. Please refer to Algorithm 9.7 for further details.

It is evident that the sparse weight matrix model obtained through pruning training significantly reduces the parameter size, resulting in a notable decrease in the FPGA storage resources required. The adoption of uniform pruning has also contributed to a certain level of reduction in the parallel complexity of the FPGA implementation of the LSTM neural network. However, due to the challenges in implementing certain hardware optimization techniques designed for dense network models in the sparse network setting, the throughput may be affected to some extent.

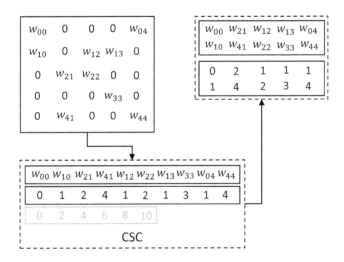

FIGURE 9.19
Sparse matrices after uniform pruning can be stored in a new way.

Algorithm 9.7: Algorithm for Implementing Sparse Matrix-Vector Multiplication in Single DMA Mode (with Addition Tree)

Input: x_t, h_{t-1}

Output: result_vector$_t$

1 input_vector = merge(x_t, h_{t-1}); **for** $i = 0$; $i < COL\_SIZE$; $i = i + 32$ **do**

2   **for** $j = 0$; $i < 4 * HIDDEN\_SIZE$; $i = i + 32$ **do**

3   (PIPELINE)

4   **for** $k = 0$; $k < 16$; $k = k + 1$ **do**

5   (UNROLL)

6   index$_{2*k}$ = indices[$i + 2 * $k][j];

7   index$_{2*k+1}$ = indices[$i + 2 * $k +1][j];

8   accum$_k$ = (input_vector[index$_{2*k}$] * sparse_weights[$i + 2 * $k][j])

9   + (input_vector[index$_{2*k+1}$] * sparse_weights[$i + 2 * $k + 1][j]).

10   **end**

11   accum$_{16}$ = (accum$_0$ + accum$_1$) + (accum$_2$ + accum$_3$);

12   accum$_{17}$ = (accum$_4$ + accum$_5$) + (accum$_6$ + accum$_7$);

13   accum$_{18}$ = (accum$_8$ + accum$_9$) + (accum$_{10}$ + accum$_{11}$);

14   accum$_{19}$ = (accum$_{12}$ + accum$_{13}$) + (accum$_{14}$ + accum$_{15}$);

15   accum = (accum$_{16}$ + accum$_{17}$) + (accum$_{18}$ + accum$_{19}$);

16   **if** $i == 0$ **then**

17   result_vector[j] = bias[j] + accum;

18   **else**

19   result_vector[j] = result_vector[j] + accum;

20   **end**

21 **end**

9.3.3 Element-Wise Module

The element-wise computation part is one of the important factors that differentiate the LSTM neural network from other neural networks. After computing the input vector and the three gate vectors unique to LSTM through the matrix-vector multiplication, the element-wise calculation is performed

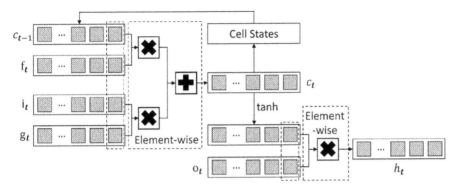

FIGURE 9.20
Element-wise calculation process.

to apply a filtering effect on the input–output vectors and the cell state values using the gate vectors. The calculations in this section are all multiplication and addition operations of the corresponding elements between the vectors, as shown in Figure 9.20.

The element-wise calculation module can be accelerated using a pipelining approach and the algorithm for this implementation can be found in Algorithm 9.8. In this algorithm, the *result_vector* is the computed output of the matrix-vector operation module. It is divided into four parts, and each part is processed separately using the corresponding sigmoid or tanh activation function to obtain the input vector g_t and the three gate vectors i_t, f_t, and o_t. In this chapter, the element-wise module integrates the activation function module to facilitate parallel acceleration of the overall computation. The implementation details of the activation function module are discussed in Section 9.3.4.

Algorithm 9.8: Element-Wise Implementation of the Algorithm

Input: result_vector$_t$

Output: h$_t$

1 i_vector, g_vector, f_vector, o_vector = split(result_vector$_t$); **for**
   $i = 0; i < HIDDEN\_SIZE; i = i + 1$ **do**

2   (PIPELINE)

3   gate_i = sigmoid(i_vector[i]);

4   gate_f = sigmoid(f_vector[i]);

5   gate_o = sigmoid(o_vector[i]);

6   g = tanh(g_vector[i]);

7   cell[j] = (cell[j] * gate_f) + (gate_i * g);

8   h_t [j] = gate_o * tanh(cell[j]);

9   **end**

9.3.4 Activation Function Module

The sigmoid and tanh nonlinear activation functions needed in LSTM neural networks are difficult to realize directly using logic gate units in FPGA hardware, but they can be realized in hardware by linear approximation. The method used in this chapter is the segmented linear computation method [25].

The principle of linear segmented approximation of nonlinear functions (sigmoid as well as tanh) is shown in Figure 9.21. When a certain value, x, is used as input for the activation function calculation, the first step is to determine the interval in which x is located. Let's assume that x belongs to the interval $[x_i, x_{i+1}]$. The slope of the linear segmentation function corresponding to this interval is a_i and the offset is b_i. By performing the appropriate multiplication and addition operations with x, an approximate value of the activation function can be obtained. The adoption of linear approximation for implementation is mainly based on the following factors:

1. In neural network computations, a certain degree of precision loss does not significantly impact the final prediction results. Furthermore, by continuously refining the segmented intervals, the accuracy of linear approximation can be improved. Although each segmented interval requires storage resources for the corresponding coefficients a and b, this requirement is negligible compared to the storage space occupied by the neural network parameters.

2. The sigmoid and tanh functions required for LSTM can both be implemented using linear approximation. The only difference lies in the corresponding values of coefficients a and b.

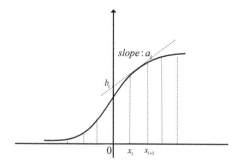

FIGURE 9.21
Linear piecewise approximation of nonlinear functions.

3. The computation result of the sigmoid function falls within the range of [0, 1], for example, when $x \in [-\infty, -6]$, sigmoid$(x)=0$, and when $x \in [6, \infty]$, sigmoid$(x)=1$. Therefore, only a segmented approximation is needed in the bounded interval [−6,6], and the number of segments is also finite after determining the interval between segments. The tanh function, being monotonically increasing and producing results within the range of [−1, 1], follows the same principle.

For code implementation, a suitable segment interval k can be selected, and then the slope value a and offset b corresponding to the linear approximation of the activation function for each segment interval can be computed separately. Then, the computed parameter values are pre-stored in the BRAM of the FPGA. The computational flow is illustrated in Figure 9.22. The activation function computation of the linear approximation can be accelerated by pipelining.

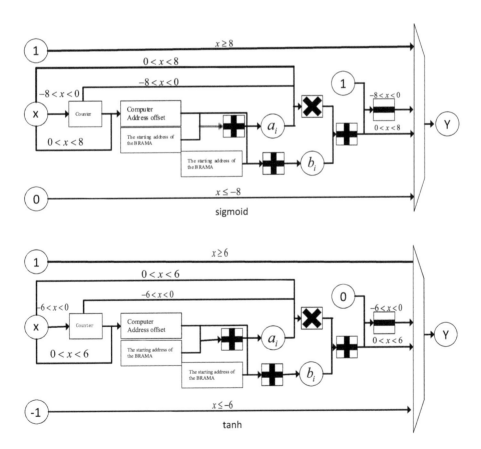

FIGURE 9.22
Linear approximation computation process.

9.4 Chapter Summary

Machine learning has become one of the hottest fields of research in computer science and has been widely adopted in industry. As one of the most effective machine learning models, neural networks have been used in countless products, changing people's daily lives. Among the wide variety of neural network models, LSTM is widely used in speech recognition, machine translation, image recognition, and other real-world tasks due to its outstanding performance in timing-related applications. Since LSTM network topology is characterized by a large number of connections and its computational process is both computationally intensive and data-intensive, achieving high performance and low power consumption in its algorithm implementation has become a research focus in the present time. On the other hand, due to the large parameter size of LSTM neural networks, the consumption of storage resources is also a non-negligible problem. Hardware acceleration is currently the most common approach for speeding up neural network computations. Among mainstream hardware acceleration technologies, FPGA is widely used in hardware logic design due to its high performance, low power consumption, and programmability. Therefore, in this chapter, we propose the hardware implementation of the forward computation process of an LSTM neural network based on FPGA. The ultimate goal is to achieve a relatively high-performance LSTM accelerator with low power consumption.

References

1. Russell S. J. *Artificial Intelligence a Modern Approach*. London: Pearson Education, Inc., 2010.
2. Alpaydin E. *Introduction to Machine Learning*. Cambridge, MA: MIT Press, 2014.
3. Schmidhuber J. Deep learning in neural networks: An overview. *Neural Networks*, 2015, 61: 85–117.
4. Rowley H. A., Baluja S., Kanade T. Neural network-based face detection. *IEEE Transactions on Pattern Analysis and Machine Intelligence*, 1998, 20(1): 23–38.
5. Graves A., Mohamed A., Hinton G. Speech recognition with deep recurrent neural networks. *2013 IEEE International Conference on Acoustics, Speech and Signal Processing*. Vancouver, BC. IEEE, 2013: 6645–6649.
6. Temurtas H., Yumusak N., Temurtas F. A comparative study on diabetes disease diagnosis using neural networks. *Expert Systems with Applications*, 2009, 36(4): 8610–8615.
7. Krizhevsky A., Sutskever I., Hinton G. E. Imagenet classification with deep convolutional neural networks. *Advances in Neural Information Processing Systems*, 2012, 25(1): 1097–1105.
8. Deng J., Dong W., Socher R., et al. Imagenet: A large-scale image database. *2009 IEEE Conference on Computer Vision and Pattern Recognition*. Miami, FL. IEEE, 2009: 248–255.

9. Moyer C. How google's alphago beat a go world champion. *The Atlantic*, 2016, 28.
10. Widrow B., Aragon J. C., Percival B M. Cognitive memory and auto-associative neural network based search engine for computer and network located images and photographs: U.S. Patent 7,333,963[P]. 2008-2-19.
11. Serban I., Sordoni A., Bengio Y., et al. Building end-to-end dialogue systems using generative hierarchical neural network models. *Proceedings of the AAAI Conference on Artific*ial *Intelligence*, Phoenix, AZ. 2016, 30(1).
12. Devlin J., Zbib R., Huang Z., et al. Fast and robust neural network joint models for statistical machine translation. *Proceedings of the 52nd Annual Meeting of the Association for Computational Linguistics* (Volume 1: Long Papers), Baltimore, MD. 2014: 1370–1380.
13. Yu D., Seltzer M. L. Improved bottleneck features using pretrained deep neural networks. *Twelfth Annual Conference of the International Speech Communication Association*, Florence. 2011.
14. Sak H., Senior A., Beaufays F. Long short-term memory based recurrent neural network architectures for large vocabulary speech recognition. arXiv preprint arXiv:1402.1128, 2014.
15. Cho K., Van Merriënboer B., Gulcehre C., et al. Learning phrase representations using RNN encoder-decoder for statistical machine translation. arXiv preprint arXiv:1406.1078, 2014.
16. You Q., Jin H., Wang Z., et al. Image captioning with semantic attention. *Proceedings of the IEEE Conference on Computer Vision and Pattern Recognition*, Las Vegas, NV. 2016: 4651–4659.
17. Hopfield J. J. Neural networks and physical systems with emergent collective computational abilities. *Proceedings of the National Academy of Sciences*, 1982, 79(8): 2554–2558.
18. Mandic D., Chambers J. *Recurrent Neural Networks for Prediction: Learning Algorithms, Architectures and Stability.* Hoboken, NJ: Wiley, 2001.
19. Lin T., Horne B. G., Tino P., et al. Learning long-term dependencies in NARX recurrent neural networks. *IEEE Transactions on Neural Networks*, 1996, 7(6): 1329–1338.
20. Bengio Y., Simard P., Frasconi P. Learning long-term dependencies with gradient descent is difficult. *IEEE Transactions on Neural Networks*, 1994, 5(2): 157–166.
21. Greff K., Srivastava R. K., Koutník J., et al. LSTM: A search space odyssey. *IEEE Transactions on Neural Networks and Learning Systems*, 2016, 28(10): 2222–2232.
22. Hochreiter S., Schmidhuber J. Long short-term memory. *Neural Computation*, 1997, 9(8): 1735–1780.
23. Zhang Y., Wang C, Gong L, et al. A power-efficient accelerator based on FPGAs for LSTM network. *2017 IEEE International Conference on Cluster Computing (CLUSTER)*. Honolulu, HI. IEEE, 2017: 629–630.
24. Zhang Y., Wang C., Gong L., et al. Implementation and optimization of the accelerator based on FPGA hardware for LSTM network. *2017 IEEE International Symposium on Parallel and Distributed Processing with Applications and 2017 IEEE International Conference on Ubiquitous Computing and Communications (ISPA/IUCC)*, Guangzhou. IEEE, 2017: 614–621.
25. Storace M., Poggi T. Digital architectures realizing piecewise-linear multivariate functions: two FPGA implementations. *International Journal of Circuit Theory and Applications*, 2011, 39(1): 1–15.

10

Hardware Customization/Acceleration Techniques for Impulse Neural Networks

10.1 Background of Impulse Neural Network Application

In recent years, with the continuous improvement of artificial intelligence (AI) theory, neural network models have been more and more widely used in various scenarios, especially in image processing, natural language processing, and audio and video processing. In specific tasks, the accuracy of artificial neural networks even exceeds human performance. In order to further improve the accuracy of artificial neural network recognition, over the past few years, neural networks are constantly moving toward deeper network hierarchies and more complex topologies so as to enable the network to abstract feature signals of higher dimensions. Higher hierarchies and more complex topologies allow neural networks to perform better and better in tasks. However, the complex network structure, with its large number of parameters, has brought the current computers more and more to the fore. One of the problems brought by a large number of computations is that, in order to complete a complete computation, the energy consumption consumed by the computer is also unbearable, especially for many embedded applications, so the problem of how to reduce the energy consumption of neural networks is a hot research issue in the previous two years. Another problem brought by a large number of computations is that in order to complete the computation, it is necessary to frequently access the parameters in the storage and frequently access to the storage of two aspects (the storage wall problem): one is that it will cause serious energy consumption problems and the other is that it will lead to serious delays, which is also unacceptable for real-time applications.

The bottleneck of artificial neural networks has not only led hardware researchers to try to get rid of the limitations of von Neumann architectures but also pushed the development of pulsed neural networks (SNNs) [1,2]. Impulse neural networks, as a typical representative of brain-like computing, have been hailed as the third generation of neural networks [3]. The birth of impulse neural networks is inspired by the biological brain. The brain

DOI: 10.1201/9780429355080-10

is a complex system with various advanced capabilities such as cognition, recognition, memory, and emotional expression. Biologists estimate that the number of neurons in the human brain is about 100 billion. Each neuron is connected to thousands of surrounding synapses. However, in the brain with such a large-scale neural network, the power when thinking is only 20w, equivalent to a low-power incandescent lamp. Because of this advantage of the brain and the high power consumption of current artificial neural networks, brain-like neural computation has gained more and more attention over the years.

Pulsed neural networks have numerous advantages over artificial neural networks. First, impulse neural networks are characterized by low energy consumption. Artificial neural networks perform weighted summation operations, which require the use of weights and multiplication of data. Pulse neural network input and output are single-bit, so the operation becomes an addition operation, eliminating a large number of multiplication operations in traditional neural networks, and the reduction in energy consumption it brings is extremely significant. In addition, each neuron in the same layer of an artificial neural network needs to transmit its output to the neurons in the subsequent layer. In contrast, a pulsed neural network needs to ensure that the current membrane voltage is greater than a certain threshold, that is, locally activated, before transmitting a pulse, which results in a very small number of neurons in an active state in each cycle, with a lower amount of data transmission and naturally lower power consumption. If combined with asynchronous design, an event-driven approach is used to design the pulsed neural network; its power consumption can be further reduced; and then the pulsed neural network is highly fault-tolerant. Pulsed neural networks have complex connectivity, and individual errors have a low impact on the results. In addition, the membrane voltage and threshold need to be compared before firing the pulse, small noise and small rise and fall are not enough for a neuron to send a pulse signal to the downstream neuron, so the effect of noise on the pulsed neural network is also relatively small.

In view of the structural characteristics of the pulse neural network, with the continuous improvement of its algorithm, the pulse neural network breaks through the bottleneck of the artificial neural network that requires huge data samples, and computational resources are greatly expected. At present, many countries in the world are advancing the research work of brain-like computing [4–8], and a lot of simulation work is also being carried out. However, as in the case of artificial neural networks, the energy consumption for deploying the execution of neuromorphic computation on conventional computer architectures is difficult to meet the application requirements, so it is particularly important to build new hardware acceleration architectures.

The research of pulsed neural network gas pedals or brain-like computing chips has gained a lot of attention from many countries around the world. In 2004, Stanford University started the research of Neurogrid, a brain-like chip, and in 2005, the United States and the European Union carried out the SyNAPSE project and FACETS program, respectively, which aimed to support the research of brain-like research. In 2011, the EU-funded BrainScaleS program began to implement the research and development of an Analog-digital Mixed Simulation (AMS) brain-like supercomputer, and in 2013, the EU carried out a comprehensive "human brain program". In recent years, the United States IBM, Intel, Microsoft, and so on have carried out research work on pulse neural networks. As a key technology to break through the bottleneck of traditional artificial neural network development, brain-like computing has attracted the attention of many colleges and research institutes in China. In 2015, Zhejiang University released the first pulse neural network chip "Darwin", and in the next few years, it took the lead in designing and realizing "Darwin 2" and "Darwin 3", and in 2019, Tsinghua University in China designed a brain-like chip "Tianmachine core" published in the journal *Nature*. In 2021, China's brain program was finalized, and pulse neural networks, known as the "third generation of neural networks", will be used in the next 10 years as the first chip to support both types of neural networks.

10.2 Details of the Impulse Neural Network Algorithm

There are many similarities and differences between impulse neural networks and artificial neural networks. These similarities and differences are mainly reflected in four aspects, which are the neuron model computation process, the neural network topology, the information encoding method, and the neural network learning algorithm. In the following, we will introduce the details of the algorithm of impulse neural network from these four aspects.

10.2.1 Impulse Neuron Model

Operational units or "nodes" in a neural network are called neurons. The behavioral actions of neurons directly affect the functional characteristics of the network. Different neuron models reflect different functions of the network. Artificial neuron models can be uniformly described as four phases, the input acquisition phase, the weighted summation phase, the nonlinear transformation phase, and the output result phase. The differences between different artificial neurons are reflected in the nonlinear transformation phase. Similarly, the impulse neuron model computational process can be divided into four phases: the obtaining input phase, the updating neuron state phase, the computing output phase, and the output release phase. The main difference between different impulse neuron models is reflected in the

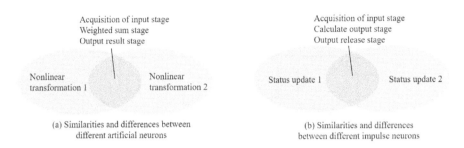

Acquisition of input stage
Weighted sum stage
Output result stage

Nonlinear transformation 1

Nonlinear transformation 2

(a) Similarities and differences between different artificial neurons

Acquisition of input stage
Calculate output stage
Output release stage

Status update 1

Status update 2

(b) Similarities and differences between different impulse neurons

FIGURE 10.1
Neuron model differences. (a) Similarities and differences between different artificial neurons. (b) Similarities and differences between different impulse neurons.

TABLE 10.1

Differences between the Two Types of Neuron Models

Points of Difference	Artificial Neurons	Pulsed Neurons
Neuron input/ output	Format Continuous real values	Single-bit pulse
Neuron activation state	Neuron activation state Definitely activated, output exists	Rarely activated, small probability of output
Output process	Directly passes output to next layer of neurons	There is a time delay in firing the pulse, and the delay varies from neuron to neuron

updating neuron state stage. Figure 10.1 reflects the stage in which the differences between different artificial neurons and different impulse neurons are reflected.

While there are some differences in the computational process between different artificial neuron models and different impulse neuron models, similar models can be divided into the same stages. However, there is a gulf in stages between the impulse neuron model and the artificial neuron model, which leads to the two classes of neurons exhibiting significant differences. Table 10.1 summarizes the differences between the two classes of neuron models.

Over the past decades, due to the different perceptions of biological neurons and needs among fields, brain scientists as well as brain-like sciences have proposed dozens of pulsed neuron models, and here we briefly introduce the three most commonly used neuron models, which are the HH neuron model, the LIF neuron model, and the IF neuron model.

10.2.1.1 The HH Neuron Model

The HH model [8] is a neuron model proposed by Alan Hodgkin and Andrew Huxley in 1952. As the most bionic neuron model, the HH model is able to

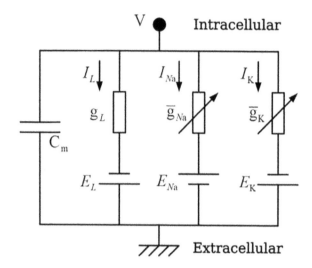

FIGURE 10.2
Schematic diagram of the HH model circuit structure [9].

accurately characterize the biological features of membrane potentials. In the HH model, the membrane potential is affected by the three dimensions: Na ion channels, K ion channels, and leak channels, and its corresponding circuit diagram is shown in Figure 10.2, where C_m denotes the membrane capacitance, I_L, I_{Na}, and I_K denote the current of the corresponding ion channel, and g and E denote the conductance value and reversal potential of the corresponding channel, respectively. On the one hand, the resistance of different ion channels possesses independent dynamic properties at different membrane potentials; on the other hand, each channel has corresponding turn-on and turn-off rates at a given membrane potential. Therefore, the HH model needs to use four ordinary differential equations and dozens of variables to represent the computational process, which makes it only suitable for smaller neural network fitting, difficult for large-scale simulation, and unfavorable for hardware implementation.

10.2.1.2 The LIF Neuron Model

The LIF model [10], as one of the simplest impulse response models, has been proposed as early as 1907. The LIF model simplifies the influencing factors of neuronal membrane potential into two, which are the input current channel and the leakage channel. In the LIF model, the neuronal state can be described as "charging", "discharging", and "resetting" as shown in Equations (10.1)–(10.3), respectively, where V_t denotes the neuron mode voltage, X_t denotes the voltage gain, H_t denotes the hidden state of the neuron, I_t denotes the neuron current input, S_t is the current moment pulse output,

V_{thrd} denotes the mode voltage threshold, V_{rst} denotes the reset voltage, and τ denotes the time constant.

$$H_t = V_{t-1} + X_t = V_{t-1} + \frac{1}{\tau}(I_t - V_{t-1}) \tag{10.1}$$

$$S_t = \begin{cases} 0, H_t < V_{\text{thrd}} \\ 1, H_t \geq V_{\text{thrd}} \end{cases} \tag{10.2}$$

$$V_t = \begin{cases} S_t V_{\text{rst}} + (1 - S_t) H_t, (\text{hard} - \text{reset}) \\ H_t - S_t V_{\text{thrd}}, (\text{soft} - \text{reset}) \end{cases} \tag{10.3}$$

The "charging" process is responsible for updating the hidden state of the neuron. The hidden state of a neuron is the sum of the neuron's membrane potential at the previous moment and the membrane potential gain at the current moment. The membrane potential gain comes from the input of the input current channel on one hand and the leakage of the leakage channel on the other hand. The "discharge" process is used to determine whether the neuron fires an impulse signal or not. If and only if the hidden state of the neuron exceeds the membrane potential threshold, the neuron is activated and emits a pulse signal to the postsynaptic neuron. The "reset" process is responsible for updating the neuron's membrane potential. When the neuron is activated, the neuron's membrane potential will regress from the hidden state to a new membrane potential level. There are two types of membrane potential reset, soft reset and hard reset. The final membrane potential of a soft reset neuron depends on the hidden state and the pulse firing threshold. Hard reset, on the other hand, regresses the neuron membrane potential to the resting potential.

10.2.1.3 The IF Neuron Model

The IF model [11,12] is a further simplification of the LIF model. Figure 10.3 shows the equivalent circuit diagram of the IF neuron model, where C_m and R_m represent the membrane capacitance and membrane resistance, respectively, V_{reset} and V_{thrd} represent the resting potential and pulse release threshold, respectively, and I represent the current gain. Like LIF neurons, the computational process of IF neurons is also divided into three processes: "charging", "discharging", and "resetting", and the difference between the two is in the "charging" process.

Equation 10.4 shows the "charging" process of the IF neuron, where there is a constant that represents the amount of membrane potential leakage.

$$H_t = V_{t-1} + X_t = V_{t-1} + \frac{1}{\tau} I_t - A \tag{10.4}$$

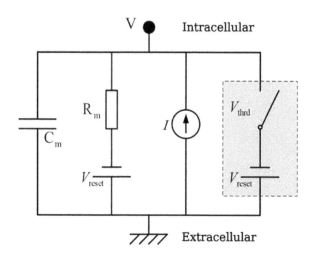

FIGURE 10.3
Schematic diagram of IF model circuit structure [9].

Comparing Equations (10.1) and (10.4), it is easy to find that the leakage of the membrane potential of the IF neuron is fixed at each moment, whereas the leakage of the LIF neuron is proportional to the state of the membrane potential at the previous moment. Therefore, the membrane potential of IF neurons leaks linearly in the time dimension, while the membrane potential of LIF neurons exhibits exponential leakage in the time dimension. The IF model and the LIF model greatly simplify the process of action potential changes, making neurons a compromise between biological accuracy and efficient computation, and they are the two neuron models most commonly used in the field of brain-like computation at present. Many subsequent studies have derived many variants of neuronal models based on these two models, such as the adaptive LIF model [13], IZHIKEVICH [14], and SRM [15].

10.2.1.3 SRM Neuron Modeling

The SRM model, or impulse response model, is a variant of the LIF model, which introduces the simulation of an undesired period on the basis of LIF. After activation, a biological neuron will regress its membrane potential to its resting potential, and at the same time, it will not respond to the impulse signals sent by the presynaptic neuron for a period of time, which is called the off-phase period. The SRM adopts the form of a filter to describe the process of its membrane potential change, and Equation (10.5) is the general form of expression of the SRM.

$$u_i(t) = F\left(t - t_i^f\right) + \sum_{j \in S_i} w_{ij} \sum_{t \in S_i} G\left(t - t_j^f\right) + \int_0^\infty H(s) I(t - s) ds \qquad (10.5)$$

In Equation (10.5), F, G, H, and I are the four functions. t denotes the current moment, t_i^f denotes the moment when neuron i fires a pulse signal, w_{ij} denotes the strength of the connection between neuron i and neuron j, $u_i(t)$ denotes the level of neuron's membrane potential at the moment t, and S_i denotes the set of presynaptic neurons for neuron i.

The SRM expression form contains three parts in total, of which the first part is the F function. This part is used to portray the process of membrane potential change after a neuron fires a pulse signal, and its standard potential change is shown in Figure 10.4. It should be noted that the here denotes the time when neuron I itself fires the impulse signal.

$$\sum_{j \in S_i} w_{ij} \sum_{t \in S_i} G\left(t - t_j^f\right)$$ is the second part of the SRM expression, which expresses the membrane potential gain to the postsynaptic neuron resulting from the firing of a pulse signal by the presynaptic neuron. Figure 10.5 depicts the change in membrane potential after a neuron receives a stimulus, where t_j^f denotes the time at which the presynaptic neuron fires a pulse signal.

The third item $\int_0^\infty H(s)I(t-s)ds$ is used to portray the changes in neuronal modal potentials after receiving a pulse signal in the period of ineligibility.

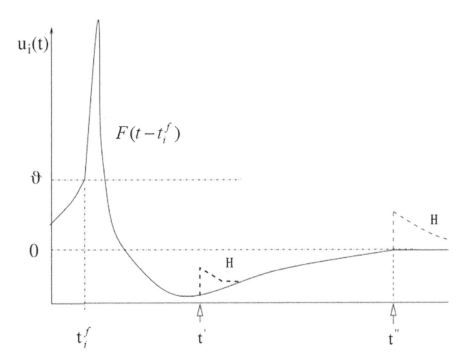

FIGURE 10.4
Schematic diagram of membrane potential change after SRM firing pulse [16].

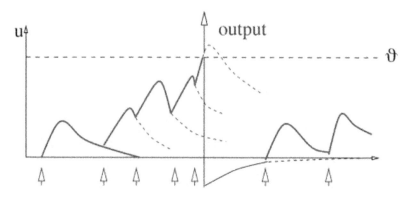

FIGURE 10.5
Schematic diagram of SRM response to pulsed membrane potential changes [16].

This part is designed to better match the laws of biological neuronal refractory periods. The membrane potential of a biological neuron is less affected by the pulse signal during the period of ineligibility, but it is not completely unresponsive to the pulse signal. The SRM is designed to consider setting a sensitivity function to describe the period of ineligibility. During the period of inappropriateness, the neuron is affected by external stimuli within one percent of the normal condition. The sensitivity of the neuron increases exponentially with time, eventually bringing the sensitivity back to normal (end of the period of inappropriateness).

10.2.2 Impulse Neural Network Topology

The connections between biological neurons are very complex, and as a product of brain-like research, pulsed neural networks also have complex connections. However, in practice, most of the pulsed neural networks and artificial neural networks have similar topologies. There are three types of impulse neural network topologies [17], which are feed-forward topology, cyclic topology, and graph connectivity topology.

10.2.2.1 Feed-Forward Topology

Feed-forward topology is the most common type of structure in impulse neural networks. The neurons of a feed-forward impulse neural network are arranged and interconnected in a hierarchical relationship, and any two neurons in the same layer are not connected. During operation, the output of the neuron in the previous layer will be used as the output of the neuron in the next layer, and the result of the operation of the neuron in the output layer will be used to express the output of the neural network. The most common structures of feed-forward impulse neural networks are multi-layer fully connected impulse neural networks and convolutional impulse neural networks, which are illustrated in Figure 10.6.

In traditional feed-forward artificial neural networks, neurons contain at most one connectivity relationship with each other, whereas pulsed neural networks can contain multiple connectivity relationships (multiple connectivity edges between two neurons) in both the former layer of neurons and the latter layer of neurons at the same time. In addition, because of the synaptic delay in the output signal of the impulse neuron, the output of the first layer of the neural network can be transmitted to the second layer of the neuron at different times, which is also different from the artificial neural network. The multiple synapses of the pulsatile neuron and the synaptic delays between neurons allow it to influence the membrane potential state of the postsynaptic neuron over a longer time scale.

10.2.2.2 Cyclic Topology

Unlike feed-forward topologies, loop-type topologies have loop relationships. The impulse signals output by the neurons of a loop-type impulse neural network can not only act on other neurons but also stimulate changes in their own membrane potentials. This feedback mechanism allows neural networks to model more complex time-varying systems. Recurrent impulse neural networks are categorized into two main types, namely, global recurrent impulse neural networks and local recurrent impulse neural networks, which can be applied to the solution of many complex problems, such as the field of natural language processing, the field of speech processing, and the field of image processing. Figure 10.7 illustrates a recurrent topology.

10.2.2.3 Graph Connection Topology

The graph-connected topology is the most bionic topology, which abstracts the connectivity of neural networks to ordinary graphs and therefore can describe all neural networks with irregular connectivity. Graph-connected impulse neural networks are often used in biological simulations to study the mechanism of biological brain operation. In the field of brain-like computing, irregular graph-connected impulse neural networks are not really common due to the limitations of impulse neural network programming tools and learning algorithms for irregular impulse neural networks. However, in order to realize the universality, there are still some brain-like chips that can realize the support of graph-connected impulse neural networks at this stage.

10.2.3 Impulse Coding Approach

Unlike artificial neural networks, impulse neural networks use discrete impulse signals as the vehicle for information transfer. Representing

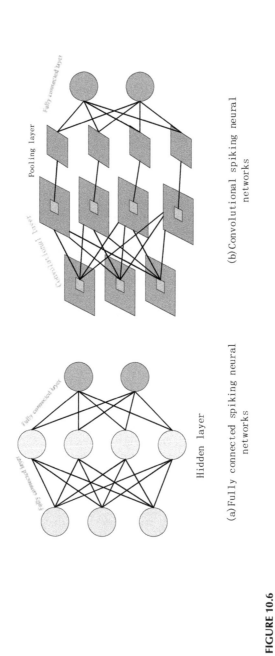

(a) Fully connected spiking neural networks

(b) Convolutional spiking neural networks

FIGURE 10.6
Feed-forward topology impulse neural network [4]. (a) Fully connected spiking neural networks. (b) Convolutional spiking neural networks.

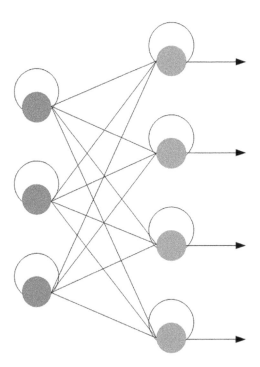

FIGURE 10.7
Recurrent topology impulse neural network.

the complex input data in neural networks with single-bit pulse signals is a much-discussed topic in the field of brain-like research. Currently, there are two main types of pulse coding methods for input data, namely frequency-domain coding and time-domain coding.

10.2.3.1 Frequency-Domain Coding of Pulses

Frequency-domain coding [18] is the most widely used coding method in impulse neural networks (see Figure 10.8a). This type of coding represents the data passed between neurons as impulse signals of different frequencies, usually using a Poisson pulse train. For the same input data, frequency-domain coding ensures that the total frequency at which the pulse sequence is issued is the same for a given time domain, but the timing of pulse issuance in the sequence is randomized.

The frequency-domain coding approach is simple and efficient, can express complex data information, and is widely used in impulse neural networks. However, it has two obvious drawbacks: (1) representing input data with several pulse signals significantly increases the number of signals in the network, which makes the impulse neural network unable to benefit from pulse sparsity and makes it difficult to reduce the computational power

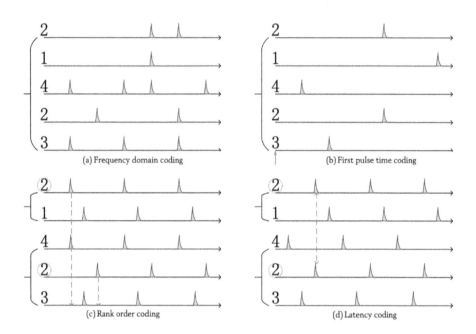

FIGURE 10.8
Pulse coding method. (a) Frequency domain coding. (b) First pulse time coding. (c) Rank order coding.(d) Latency coding.

consumption; (2) in order to ensure the temporal relationship of pulse signals, the impulse neural network is no longer equipped with a low-latency
property; and (3) it ignores the temporal semantic information of the pulse
signals, which is considered to be incompatible with the biological neuron
information transfer process.

10.2.3.2 Impulse Frequency-Domain Coding

The implausibility of frequency-domain coding has led brain-like scientists to propose alternative ways of encoding pulses, which mainly cover
time-domain coding. In contrast to pulse frequency-domain coding,
which ignores information about the internal intervals of the pulse signal,
time-domain coding pays sufficient attention to differences in the temporal
structure of the pulse signal.

Time-to-first-pulse coding [19] (see Figure 10.8b) is the most typical
time-domain coding. Time-to-first Spike (TTFS) coding encodes the input data
as a pulse signal over the entire time domain, and the larger the input data,
the earlier the pulse signal is issued. Time-to-first-pulse coding can explain
the brain's rapid response to visual stimuli but severely limits the computational power of neurons. Rank-ordered encoding [20] (see Figure 10.8c) dis-
cards the precise timing of the release of the pulse signals and focuses on the

order in which the pulse signals are released. This type of coding encodes each input data into multiple pulse signals (multiple batches) throughout the time domain. The larger the data within the same group, the earlier in each batch the pulse signals are emitted. Even if the data in different groups are the same, the pulse signals may be emitted at different times in the corresponding batches. Delayed coding (see Figure 10.8d) is also concerned with the order of pulse signal emission, and this type of coding ensures that the sequence of pulse signals is fixed for the same input data and that the stronger the stimulus, the earlier the pulse signals are emitted from the input data. Although time-domain coding has gained a lot of attention, it adds difficulty to the training process of impulse neural networks and therefore is not as widely used as frequency-domain coding.

10.2.4 Pulsed Neural Network Learning Algorithm

Learning of artificial neural networks is the process of continuously adjusting the network parameters based on the data set for a specific task. The back propagation (BP) algorithm combined with the gradient descent (GD) algorithm is the theoretical core of modern artificial neural network model optimization. In addition, tools such as batch-normalized training and distributed training have made it possible to train and deploy large artificial neural network models in practice. Unlike artificial neural networks, for which there are specific learning models, learning algorithms for impulse neural networks have not yet been finalized in the academic community. Currently, there is no recognized learning algorithm that can unify the approval of researchers. The research on learning algorithms for impulse neural networks is still in the stage of competition, but in general, the algorithms can be categorized into two groups, supervised learning algorithms and unsupervised learning algorithms. Supervised learning algorithms are highly accurate but have high hardware overhead. Unsupervised learning algorithms are slightly less accurate than supervised learning, but their learning process is simple, and massive unlabeled data exist in practice scenarios, so it is more appropriate to integrate unsupervised learning algorithms in hardware modules.

10.2.4.1 Supervised Learning Algorithms

There are many supervised learning algorithms for impulse neural networks, which can be categorized into three main groups, as shown in Table 10.2.

The core idea of gradient descent-based learning algorithms is to use the difference between the network prediction results and the neuron's real target output to solve the error, and then use the error back propagation process to update the synaptic connection weights between neurons. Three gradient descent learning algorithms are introduced here: (1) Spikeprop algorithm: This algorithm is suitable for multi-layer feed-forward impulse neural networks. When impulse neural networks operate, the issuance of impulse

TABLE 10.2

Pulsed Neural Network Supervision Algorithm

Classes of Supervised Algorithms for Impulse Neural Networks	Example
Gradient descent-based learning algorithm	Spikeprop algorithm [21]
	Multi-spikeprop algorithm [22]
	Tempotron algorithm [23]
Synaptic plasticity-based learning algorithm	Remote supervised learning algorithm [24]
	Synaptic weight association training algorithm [25]
Impulse convolution-supervised learning algorithm	Impulse pattern association training algorithm [26]
	Precision impulse-driven plasticity algorithm [27]

signals may lead to uncertainty in the internal state of neurons. To avoid this problem, the spikeprop algorithm restricts all neurons in all layers of the network to emit only one pulse signal during the whole computation process. (2) Multi-spikeprop algorithm: This algorithm alleviates the limitation of the spikeprop algorithm to a certain extent by not restricting the number of pulses emitted by neurons in the input layer and the hidden layer of the impulsive neural network. There is no restriction on the number of firing times, but the algorithm restricts the output layer neurons to fire at most one pulse signal during the computation process. (3) Tempotron algorithm: This algorithm achieves the optimization of neuron synaptic connectivity weights by minimizing the pulsed neuron membrane potential error. The Tempotron algorithm is only applicable to single neurons.

Synaptic plasticity [28] is a hypothesis for updating the strength of neuronal synaptic connections first proposed by Hebb, which is a network learning algorithm with biological interpretability. The more well-known supervised learning algorithms based on synaptic plasticity are remote supervised learning algorithms and synaptic weight association training algorithms. (1) The remote supervised learning algorithm is a combination of the impulse timing-dependent plasticity algorithm and the inverse impulse timing-dependent plasticity algorithm. The algorithm can be adapted to various types of impulse neuron models. Its limitation is that it can only be applied to single-layer feed-forward impulse neural networks. (2) The synaptic weight association training algorithm combines the impulse timing-dependent plasticity algorithm and the Bienenstock–Cooper–Munro (BCM) learning rule and can be applied to the training process of multi-layer feed-forward impulse neural networks. The synaptic weight association training algorithm uses the hidden layer of the impulse neural network as a frequency filter for extracting input features, and the weights of this filter are fixed. Only the corresponding connection weights of the neurons in the output layer are changed during training, and the BCM is used to stabilize the weight adjustment process controlled by the impulse timing-dependent plasticity algorithm.

The impulse convolution-supervised learning algorithm utilizes a specific kernel function to transform the impulse sequence into a time function. The time function of the target sequence and the time function of the true output sequence are then subjected to an inner product operation to quantitatively analyze the two sequences. Finally, the training of the network is then completed based on this quantitative computation. (1) The impulse pattern joint training algorithm is a typical impulse convolution-supervised learning algorithm that uses the widrow-hoff rule to adjust the synaptic connection weights between neurons. The limitation of the impulse pattern joint training algorithm is that it can only be applied to a single-layer impulse neural network based on LIF neurons. (2) The precise pulse-driven plasticity algorithm uses the error between the pulse output sequence and the target sequence to adjust the synaptic connection weights, which consist of both positive and negative errors, which lead to long-range enhancement and long-range inhibition, respectively. The accurate pulse-driven plasticity algorithm has high computational efficiency and can achieve high model accuracy when coded correctly.

10.2.4.2 Unsupervised Learning Algorithms

Unsupervised learning algorithms for impulse neural networks have gained wider attention in academia. The impulse timing-dependent plasticity algorithm [29] (STDP) and the impulse-driven synaptic plasticity algorithm [30] (SDSP) are two typical unsupervised learning algorithms for impulse neural networks.

The core idea of the STDP algorithm is based on the synaptic plasticity hypothesis, and its learning rule is specifically that if a presynaptic neuron fires a pulse signal, the postsynaptic neuron is activated within a certain time window, which belongs to the long-range reinforcement, and then the connection weights between the two should be strengthened. If the postsynaptic neuron reflects a pulse, and within a certain time window, the presynaptic neuron also fires a pulse, which is a long-duration inhibition, then the weights between the two should be weakened. Figure 10.9 shows a schematic diagram of the amount of change in STDP weights, where Δw is the amount of change in weights and Δt is the time difference between the time when the presynaptic neuron fires a pulse signal and the time when the postsynaptic neuron fires a pulse signal. The Δw absolute value decays exponentially with the absolute value of Δt, which is calculated as Equation 10.6.

$$\Delta w = \begin{cases} \alpha e^{\frac{|\Delta t|}{\tau}}, \ \Delta t \leq 0 \\ -\alpha e^{\frac{|\Delta t|}{\tau}}, \ \Delta t > 0 \end{cases}$$

(10.6)

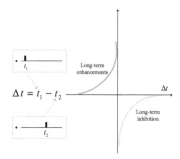

FIGURE 10.9
Schematic diagram of STDP weight update.

The SDSP algorithm is not only based on the theory of synaptic plasticity but also realizes synapses with memory properties. Synapses with memory properties were proposed by J. Brader, who argued that the adjustment of synaptic connection weights is a continuous process rather than a single moment in time. The SDSP algorithm implements synapses with memory properties by introducing Ca ion channels. The Ca ion concentration of the neuron is used as a measure of impulse delivery, and the update of the calcium ion concentration is correlated with its own impulse delivery history; if the neuron has delivered impulse signals multiple times in a recent period of time, the Ca ion concentration is boosted, and vice versa.

A schematic of the synaptic update of the SDSP algorithm is given in Figure 10.10. As shown in the figure, the SDSP algorithm is given two Ca ion concentration ranges φ_1, φ_2 and a membrane potential cutoff point θ. When the postsynaptic neuron Ca ion concentration is at φ_2, and the neuron membrane potential is above the cutoff point, the synaptic connection strength is enhanced. When the postsynaptic neuron Ca ion concentration is at φ_1, and the neuron membrane potential is lower than the cutoff point, the synaptic connection strength is weakened. The SDSP algorithm does not need to take into account the difference in the time of the neuron's pulse release before and after the synapse, and it only needs to make a corresponding judgment based on the neuron's own situation, which is more in line with the biological characteristics and is easier to be realized.

10.3 Hardware Deployment/Acceleration Customization-Related Work

Pulsed neural network acceleration hardware or neuromimetic chips are typically composed of both gas pedal cores and routing components. Each gas pedal core can physically implement a certain number of pulsed neuron

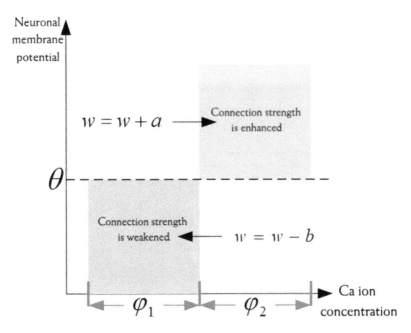

FIGURE 10.10
Schematic diagram of STSP weight update.

functions. Multiple gas pedal cores are implemented to support large-scale neural networks through the routing component. The gas pedal cores can be implemented using digital circuits or through analog circuits. Since the routing component requires long time-range data transfer, which is difficult to accurately characterize by analog-electric circuits, this difference is usually implemented by digital circuits. In general, impulse neural acceleration hardware implementations fall into two categories: hybrid digital–analog implementations and purely digital circuit implementations.

10.3.1 Impulse Neural Network Number Hybrid Implementation

In 2014, Neurogrid, a hybrid digital–analog implementation of pulsed neural networks, was proposed at Stanford University [31]. Neurogrid utilizes the subthreshold analog electrical properties of silicon transistors to simulate membrane potential changes in neurons. Neurogrid implements support for neuronal calcium–potassium ion circuits and can run a wide range of complex neuronal models (e.g., HH models). The Neurogrid can support up to 64K pulsed neurons per compute core, with pulse routing between multiple cores via a tree routing grid, which in turn enables support for networks of millions of pulsed neurons. The Neurogird has an overall power consumption of 3.1 watts, and a schematic of its board is shown in Figure 10.11.

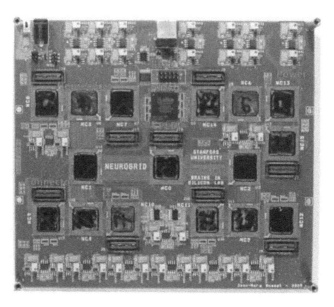

FIGURE 10.11
Schematic of the Neurogird board.

In 2017, the University of Zurich, Switzerland, also designed Dynaps, a hybrid digital–analog neural network computing chip [32]. The Dynaps single board contains nine chips with four computing cores in each chip. Dynaps implements 256 neurons in each core so that it can support networks with up to 9K pulsed neurons. Dynaps is characterized by its use of heterogeneous storage. Dynaps features heterogeneous storage for pulse routing. Nine chips of Dynaps use a 3*3 grid architecture for pulse routing, while the intra-chip computational cores route pulses through a common parent node. The heterogeneous storage routing architecture of Dynaps has two advantages: (1) the intra-chip pulse signals can be delivered to the destination neurons quickly and with low latency, and (2) the inter-slice pulse signals can take full advantage of the low bandwidth requirement of the 2D mesh, although sacrificing some transmission efficiency. Figure 10.12 shows the system schematic of Dynaps.

10.3.2 Pure Digital Circuit Implementation of Impulse Neural Networks

In 2013, the University of Manchester released the neuromorphic system SpiNNaker [33]. SpiNNaker integrates 48 processor chips on board and 18 ARM cores in each processor chip, each ARM core implements 1000 neurons, and thus SpiNNaker implements a total of 864,000 neurons. SpiNNaker in each neuron supports up to 1024 synaptic inputs, and the whole system supports a pulsed neural network with up to 880 million synaptic connections. Figure 10.13 shows the hardware architecture of each processor node

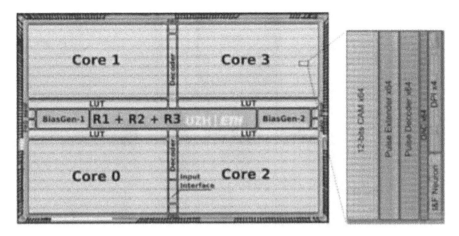

FIGURE 10.12
Schematic diagram of the Dynaps system.

of SpiNNaker. The SpiNNaker neuromorphic system has two main features: (1) it supports STDP online learning, which greatly enhances the system's capability; and (2) the topology of the on-chip network uses a 2D triangular ring structure, which is highly fault-tolerant and supports multi-casting.

In 2014, Daniel Neil's team implemented an event-driven pulsed neural network gas pedal, Minitaur, using FPGAs [34]. The gas pedal focused on optimizing memory access, simplifying the neuron model, and reducing power consumption. To reduce power consumption and connectivity queries in the graph structure, the gas pedal is designed for regular impulse neural networks. The Minitaur gas pedal can support 65K neurons and 19M synaptic connections and consumes only 1.5 W. Tested on the Handwritten Digit Recognition MNIST data set, the system achieves a classification accuracy of 92%. An experimental accuracy of 71% was achieved on 20 sets of classification data. Figure 10.14 shows the overall structure of the Minitaur.

In 2015, IBM released TrueNorth, a pulsed neural network processing chip [35]. The TrueNorth chip is designed with digital logic and implements a non-Von Neumann architecture. The chip is integrated with 4096 processing cores, each of which contains 256 neurons, each of which in turn can remain connected to 256 surrounding neurons. Overall, the chip implements 1 million digital neurons and 256 million synapses. Figure 10.15 shows the architecture of the TrueNorth chip. The TrueNorth chip is mainly used in image vision processing, feature extraction, and so on, and is typically characterized by low power consumption, high parallelism, and high scalability. The TrueNorth consumes only 65mW of power. It not only achieves better performance, but also consumes two orders of magnitude less power than other chips when running similar algorithms.

In 2015, Zhejiang University developed the first brain-like computing chip "Darwin" [36]. "Darwin" is a single-core, embedded platform-oriented

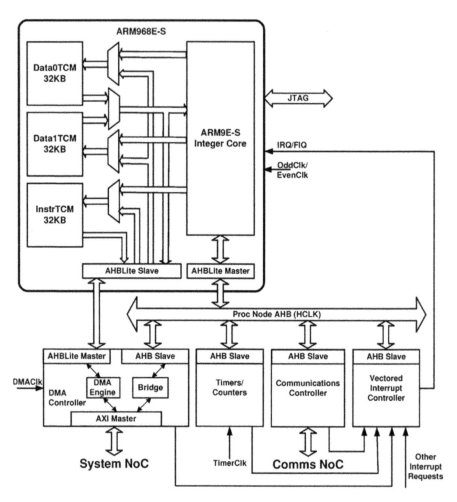

FIGURE 10.13
Schematic diagram of Spinnaker structure.

impulse neural network processor. The processor supports the operation of impulse neural networks with up to 2048 neurons and 4 million synaptic connections. There are 16 output queues in Darwin to store the impulse signals at different moments, so the maximum synaptic delay of the impulse neural network supported by it cannot exceed 16-time steps. Figure 10.16 shows the architecture of the Darwin chip. Darwin is implemented in a 180 nm CMOS process with an area of 5×5 mm² and a minimum clock frequency of 70 MHz. The power consumption of the chip is about 0.84 mW/MHz during operation.

In 2019, Intel manufactured the pulsed neural network chip Loihi [37], which integrates 124 processing cores and contains a total of about 130,000 neurons as well as 130 million synapses. In July of the same year, Intel implemented a neuromorphic system, Pohoiki Beach, which used 64 Loihi chips

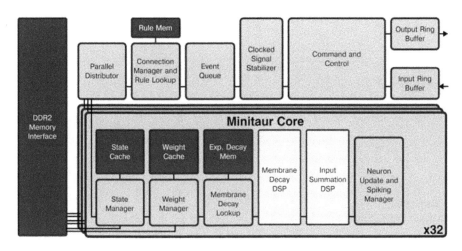

FIGURE 10.14
Schematic of Minotaur's structure.

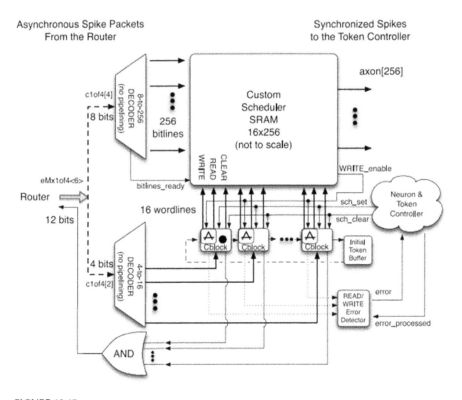

FIGURE 10.15
Schematic diagram of TrueNorth structure.

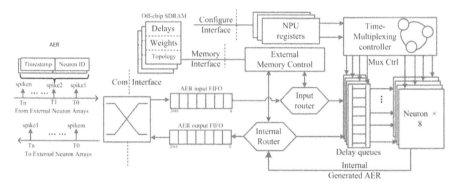

FIGURE 10.16
Schematic of the "Darwin" structure.

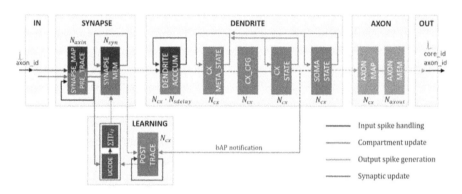

FIGURE 10.17
Schematic of the Loihi architecture.

to support impulsive neural network simulations with fewer than 8 million neurons and fewer than 8 billion synapses. Loihi was fabricated in a 14 nm process and consumed only a fraction of the latency of conventional chips when running locally competitive algorithms in the form of impulsive convolution. It consumes only a few thousandths of the latency of conventional chips when running localized competitive algorithms in the form of pulsed convolutions. Subsequent work has been done to design a toolchain for running impulse neural networks specifically for the Loihi chip (Figure 10.17).

In 2019, Tsinghua University's brain-like chip "TENCENT" [38] was published in the journal *Nature*. The "SkyCore" is a heterogeneous neural network chip, which is composed of 156 impulse processor cores Fcore. Each Fcore has 256 fan-ins and fan-outs, which means that each core realizes 256 neurons, and each neuron is connected to at most 256 neurons. Therefore, the chip supports a total of 40,000 neurons and 10 million synaptic connections. The "SkyMachine" core is realized using a 28 nm process with an area

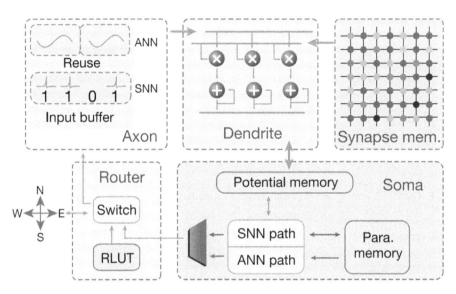

FIGURE 10.18
Diagram of the structure of the "SkyChip".

of only $3.8 \times 3.8\,mm^2$. Figure 10.18 shows the SkyMachine heterogeneous fusion brain-like computing architecture. In order to verify the chip's computational capability, the Tsinghua University research team built a balanced car system. Experiments show that compared with the TrueNorth chip, the "Tianmachine" increases the computing speed by 10× and the data transmission bandwidth by 100×.

The "SkyMachine" pioneered the heterogeneous integration of artificial neural networks and pulse neural networks, which allows the deployment of multiple neural network applications using one chip. By configuring the module, it can not only simply support these two types of networks but also realize the hybrid mode of impulse neural network and artificial neural network. The significance of "SkyCore" is that it provides a good cross-research platform for AI and neural system academics, which not only promotes the joint progress of computer science modeling and neuroscience modeling but also lays a certain foundation for the arrival of artificial general intelligence.

References

1. Roy K., Jaiswal A., Panda P. Towards spike-based machine intelligence with neuromorphic computing. *Nature*, 2019, 575(7784): 607–617.
2. Diehl P U, Cook M. Unsupervised learning of digit recognition using spike-timing-dependent plasticity. *Frontiers in Computational Neuroscience*, 2015, 9: 99.

3. Maass W. Networks of spiking neurons: The third generation of neural network models. *Neural Networks*, 1997, 10(9): 1659–1671.
4. Taherkhani A, Belatreche A, Li Y, et al. A review of learning in biologically plausible spiking neural networks[J]. *Neural Networks*, 2020, 122: 253–272.
5. Navaridas J., Furber S., Garside J., et al. SpiNNaker: Fault tolerance in a power-and area-constrained large-scale neuromimetic architecture. *Parallel Computing*, 2013, 39(11): 693–708.
6. Benjamin B. V., Gao P., McQuinn E., et al. Neurogrid: A mixed-analog-digital multichip system for large-scale neural simulations. *Proceedings of the IEEE*, 2014, 102(5): 699–716.
7. Ma D., Shen J., Gu Z., et al. Darwin: A neuromorphic hardware co-processor based on spiking neural networks. *Journal of Systems Architecture*, 2017, 77: 43–51.
8. Qu P., Zhang Y., Fei X., et al. High performance simulation of spiking neural network on GPGPUS. *IEEE Transactions on Parallel and Distributed Systems*, 2020, 31(11): 2510–2523.
9. Hodgkin A. L., Huxley A. F., Katz B. Measurement of current-voltage relations in the membrane of the giant axon of Loligo. *The Journal of Physiology*, 1952, 116(4): 424.
10. Yamazaki K, Vo-Ho V K, Bulsara D, et al. Spiking neural networks and their applications: A review[J]. *Brain Sciences*, 2022, 12(7): 863.
11. Dayan P., Abbott L. F. *Theoretical Neuroscience: Computational and Mathematical Modeling of Neural Systems*. Cambridge, MA: MIT Press, 2005.
12. Abbott L. F. Lapicque's introduction of the integrate-and-fire model neuron (1907). *Brain Research Bulletin*, 1999, 50(5–6): 303–304.
13. Brette R., Gerstner W. Adaptive exponential integrate-and-fire model as an effective description of neuronal activity. *Journal of Neurophysiology*, 2005, 94(5): 3637–3642.
14. Izhikevich E. M. Which model to use for cortical spiking neurons?. *IEEE Transactions on Neural Networks*, 2004, 15(5): 1063–1070.
15. Jolivet R., Gerstner W. The spike response model: A framework to predict neuronal spike trains. *International Conference on Artificial Neural Networks*. Berlin, Heidelberg: Springer, 2003: 846–853.
16. Gütig R. To spike, or when to spike?[J]. *Current opinion in neurobiology*, 2014, 25: 134–139.
17. Ghosh-Dastidar S, Adeli H. Spiking neural networks[J]. *International journal of neural systems*, 2009, 19(04): 295–308.
18. Adrian E. D. The impulses produced by sensory nerve endings: Part I. *The Journal of Physiology*, 1926, 61(1): 49.
19. VanRullen R., Guyonneau R., Thorpe S. J. Spike times make sense. *Trends in Neurosciences*, 2005, 28(1): 1–4.
20. Thorpe S., Gautrais J. Rank order coding. *Computational Neuroscience: Trends in Research*. Boston, MA: Springer US, 1998: 113–118.
21. Bohte S. M., Kok J. N., La Poutre H. Error-backpropagation in temporally encoded networks of spiking neurons. *Neurocomputing*, 2002, 48(1–4): 17–37.
22. Ghosh-Dastidar S., Adeli H. A new supervised learning algorithm for multiple spiking neural networks with application in epilepsy and seizure detection. *Neural Networks*, 2009, 22(10): 1419–1431.
23. Gütig R., Sompolinsky H. The tempotron: A neuron that learns spike timing-based decisions. *Nature Neuroscience*, 2006, 9(3): 420–428.

24. Ponulak F., Kasiński A. Supervised learning in spiking neural networks with ReSuMe: Sequence learning, classification, and spike shifting. *Neural Computation*, 2010, 22(2): 467–510.

25. Wade J. J., McDaid L. J., Santos J. A., et al. SWAT: A spiking neural network training algorithm for classification problems. *IEEE Transactions on Neural Networks*, 2010, 21(11): 1817–1830.

26. Mohemmed A., Schliebs S., Matsuda S., et al. Span: Spike pattern association neuron for learning spatio-temporal spike patterns. *International Journal of Neural Systems*, 2012, 22(04): 1250012.

27. Caporale N., Dan Y. Spike timing-dependent plasticity: A Hebbian learning rule. *Annual Review of Neuroscience*, 2008, 31: 25–46.

28. Hebb D. O. *The Organization of Behavior: A Neuropsychological Theory*. New York: Psychology press, 2005.

29. Caporale N., Dan Y. Spike timing-dependent plasticity: A Hebbian learning rule. *Annual Review of Neuroscience*, 2008, 31: 25–46.

30. Fusi S. Hebbian spike-driven synaptic plasticity for learning patterns of mean firing rates. *Biological Cybernetics*, 2002, 87(5): 459–470.

31. Benjamin B. V., Gao P., McQuinn E., et al. Neurogrid: A mixed-analog-digital multichip system for large-scale neural simulations. *Proceedings of the IEEE*, 2014, 102(5): 699–716.

32. Moradi S., Qiao N., Stefanini F., et al. A scalable multicore architecture with heterogeneous memory structures for dynamic neuromorphic asynchronous processors (DYNAPs). *IEEE Transactions on Biomedical Circuits and Systems*, 2017, 12(1): 106–122.

33. Wei X., Yu C. H., Zhang P., et al. Automated systolic array architecture synthesis for high throughput CNN inference on FPGAs. *Proceedings of the 54th Annual Design Automation Conference 2017*, Austin, TX. 2017: 1–6.

34. Ham T. J., Jung S. J., Kim S., et al. A^3: Accelerating attention mechanisms in neural networks with approximation. *2020 IEEE International Symposium on High Performance Computer Architecture (HPCA)*, San Diego, CA. IEEE . 2020: 328–341.

35. Wang X., Wang C., Cao J., et al. WinoNN: Optimizing FPGA-based convolutional neural network accelerators using sparse Winograd algorithm. *IEEE Transactions on Computer-Aided Design of Integrated Circuits and Systems*, 2020, 39(11): 4290–4302.

36. Ma D., Shen J., Gu Z., et al. Darwin: A neuromorphic hardware co-processor based on spiking neural networks. *Journal of Systems Architecture*, 2017, 77: 43–51.

37. Painkras E., Plana L. A., Garside J., et al. SpiNNaker: A 1-W 18-core system-on-chip for massively-parallel neural network simulation. *IEEE Journal of Solid-State Circuits*, 2013, 48(8): 1943–1953.

38. Pei J., Deng L., Song S., et al. Towards artificial general intelligence with hybrid Tianjic chip architecture. *Nature*, 2019, 572(7767): 106–111.

11

Accelerators for Big Data Genome Sequencing

11.1 Background on Group-Based Sequencing and Its Hardware Acceleration

At present, the acceleration work for gene sequencing has a variety of developments [1–3]. There are a variety of acceleration algorithms for the algorithm, and the acceleration platform is diverse. In this section, we will begin by providing an overview and analysis of the different hardware platforms that are widely employed in gene sequencing applications.

11.1.1 Distributed Systems

The distributed system relies on the computer network [4] and is composed of multiple computers. With the increase of the system scale, the number of computers involved can reach significant levels, making managing and maintaining distributed systems more challenging.

The concept of cloud also originates from distributed systems [5]. Unlike traditional independent work, distributed systems are multiple machines working together. For the user, a distributed system is not only a set of computer collections but also a separate object. After receiving a task, the distributed system partitioned the whole task to different machines, and then all the computers deal with the task in parallel. This differs from parallel work on a single machine. Typically, these processes are parallel but similar tasks, yet a distributed system needs to consider which machine resources can handle a specific task, rather than a simple partitioning. Compared to parallel computing, a distributed system has a higher degree of freedom and can handle larger tasks [6]. Additionally, the distributed system also has a higher tolerance. After all, a distributed system contains many machines, and when a machine fault occurs, the distributed system loses only one of the local machine node tasks, and all processes will be affected in parallel [7].

DOI: 10.1201/9780429355080-11

From the characteristics of distributed systems, it can be observed that they are well-suited for the task of processing large-scale data with distributed tasks. The study of gene sequencing aligns perfectly with this type of problem.

The acceleration of gene sequencing through the utilization of distributed systems can begin with task partitioning. Based on the types of tasks involved in the gene sequencing process, they can be categorized into two groups: computational tasks and storage tasks. Accelerating gene sequencing can be approached from these two aspects.

In terms of computing, we can make full use of the resources of each computing node to improve the granularity and parallelism of computing. Storage plays a significant role in distributed systems, which offer various storage structures including structured and unstructured storage. By analyzing the data attributes, optimizing the storage approach based on data consistency becomes a direction for system optimization.

11.1.2 GPU Platforms

The GPU is an integrated processor designed for image processing. Initially, GPUs were primarily used to enhance the image performance of CPUs by rendering screens to meet the increasing demands for higher image quality. Images contain a large number of pixels, the higher the level of the image, the more points there are. To handle such pixel-intensive tasks, GPUs require exceptional data processing capabilities. With the development of GPU [8], people are not only focused on image processing, the powerful data processing ability gradually lets people attempt to accelerate the algorithm by making use of GPU resources [9].

The simplest GPU acceleration is to turn part of the CPU calculation independently of the GPU to complete, which was the initial purpose of GPU acceleration [10]. Then the GPU gradually developed into the GPGPU, equipped with multiple general-purpose computing units that enable highly parallel data processing, thereby accelerating the execution of computing [11].

11.1.3 FPGA Platforms

Through the development of GPU, we can see that the custom hardware circuit [12] has a good effect on accelerating calculation [13], the current mainstream hardware circuit design is divided into FPGA and application specific integrated circuit (ASIC) design, and the advantages are briefly narrated in the previous section.

FPGA stands for Field Programmable Gate Arrays [14], which are programmable logic devices that have evolved from simple logic devices like PROM and EPROM to slightly complex PLD and then more complex CPLD. FPGA experienced continuous progress in adapting to the design of large-scale circuits gradually. The computing resources of FPGA are more abundant, programming is more flexible, the development cycle of FPGA is shorter, and the cost is lower.

The principle of FPGA is table look-up [15]. The look-up table is also a RAM when we use the hardware description language to design the hardware circuit. FPGA development tool will integrate all the possible results into a look-up table when we enter data to find the output FPGA just need to search the table. All this makes full use of the hardware resources of FPGA and improves the efficiency [16].

11.1.4 Conclusion

Through the above description, the current popular acceleration methods primarily include cloud computing platforms, GPU acceleration, and FPGA hardware acceleration [17–19]. To summarize these three platforms, we can organize them into a table, as shown in Table 11.1.

Currently, most of the research on gene sequencing is carried out for a single gene sequencing algorithm, and its versatility and universality are very limited. There is no general framework for a variety of gene sequencing algorithms. Additionally, current hardware accelerators require improvements in performance and power optimization. Based on the above problem, this chapter implements a hardware accelerator framework of gene sequencing algorithm based on FPGA.

In this chapter, two gene sequencing algorithms are accelerated on the FPGA platform and then analyzed the performance of FPGA acceleration. At last, we compared it with other acceleration methods to evaluate the advantages of FPGA acceleration. The main works are as follows:

TABLE 11.1

The Analysis of Three Different Platforms

Platform	Distributed	GPU	FPGA
Speedup rate	The overall has a good acceleration effect, but it is the result of many nodes. A single node remains to be improved	Integrated with high speed up, but the acceleration of a single computing unit—the effect of FPGAs	Has a good acceleration effect
Power cost	Essentially, CPU processing calculates the power consumption as a normal power level	Too many computing units in the GPU cause high power consumption	Extremely low power
Maintain and design	Cluster maintenance requires a lot of costs, and the parallel of the task partitioning data set needs careful consideration	The development is harder than the other platforms	Short development cycle, easy to modify, easy maintenance, easy to achieve large-scale design and implementation

1. Design and analysis of gene sequencing algorithm. Two algorithms are designed, the modules in the algorithms are sorted out, and then the module design is carried out. The main modules of the algorithm are the displacement calculation module of KMP (Knuth–Morris–Pratt) and the conversion module of BWA (Burrows–Wheeler Alignment).
2. The design of the accelerator. To achieve accelerated performance, the powerful computational capabilities of FPGA can be leveraged to accelerate the core modules of the algorithm. It is essential to organize each module in a balanced manner to ensure optimal efficiency.
3. Driver writing. Drive design under the Linux system.
4. According to the results, analyze the performance of the accelerator and evaluate the resource occupancy and power consumption. Analyze and evaluate the advantages and disadvantages of the FPGA platform.

11.2 Genome Sequencing Algorithms and Their Hardware Acceleration Principles

11.2.1 Gene Sequencing

Gene sequencing, a combination of bioinformatics, computer science, statistics, and other disciplines, is a hot direction of contemporary research. Its significance lies in its ability to shed light on the mechanisms underlying human behavior, thus enabling a deeper understanding of ourselves. The target of gene sequencing is a large number of gene fragments. Like most animals, humans use DNA as genetic material. DNA consists of four bases composed of A, T, C, and G, respectively. Within the human body, DNA exists as a double helix, with the two strands connected to form base pairs. These base pairs, which follow a specific pattern (A-T and C-G), exhibit distinct genetic information based on their arrangement. According to the matching rule of base pair, we can measure the base sequence of a DNA single chain and achieve the purpose of gene sequencing. Gene sequencing is gradually improved, and it is generally believed that gene sequencing has three main stages. The first stage is basic chemical sequencing, the second stage is high-throughput sequencing, and the third stage is molecular sequencing.

The first stage of sequencing is mainly based on the degradation of DNA. Through chemical means, the double-stranded DNA is broken down into individual nucleotide molecules and then the DNA base sequence is obtained by observing the permutation sequence of the denatured nucleotide molecules. The main methods of this stage are chemical degradation, terminal termination method, etc. According to the principle of sequencing, these methods have a high accuracy point to a single base, but the sequencing speed is not so ideal. The gradual degradation of DNA and the efficiency of subsequent electrophoresis separation need to be further improved.

The first stage of the limitations is the inability to deal with large-scale DNA sequencing, and the second phase of the sequencing approach involves high-throughput [20] sequencing of a large number of sequences. Thanks to the development of PCR technology, we can copy multiple DNA from a given DNA at this stage and then sequence the DNA at the same time. When thousands of sequences are parallel, it will greatly improve the efficiency of sequencing. The gene sequencing at this stage needs to consume a lot of DNA samples for synchronous analysis to improve efficiency and increase the cost. The final result is synthesized through the analysis of all the DNA samples, so the accuracy is decreased.

In the face of decreasing accuracy and high costs of sequencing technology, the third stage of the gene sequencing method is gradually born. The previous sequencing method is to study the result after the end of the DNA reaction. The third stage of sequencing can be synchronized in the DNA replication process which greatly enhances the efficiency, while not losing accuracy and there is great space for development. During this period, what limits sequencing efficiency is the DNA replication rate, and DNA sequencing is performed in vitro, which poses challenges to PCR technology. These three sequencing methods are collaborative work in gene sequencing.

11.2.2 KMP and BWA

The whole function of KMP is composed of two parts, namely, KMP-Match and Prefix, as shown in Figure 11.1. The KMP-Match is the main part of the function. At first, we need two input strings called pattern string and source string. Then we do a Prefix for the pattern string.

We have explained that the difference between KMP and traditional pattern match is the KMP moves as far as it can when the mistake of match happens. How to know the right step is what the Prefix function does. The Prefix function deals with the input string according to the attribute of the string. It will generate a Prefix array which helps us to know how many steps we should move. As Algorithm 11.1 shows, at the beginning of each time in the loop, we set $k = F[q-1]$. When the cycle runs for the first time the condition by line 2 to line 3, and line 9 ensure that the conditions in each iteration. Lines 5–8 adjust the value of K and make it become the correct value for $F[q]$. The 5–6 line search all eligible k, until we find a value that makes $P(k+1) = P(q)$. At this point, we can think of that $F[q] = k+1$. If we can't find the k, in line 7 we set $k=0$; if $P = P[q]$, we set $k=1$ and $F[q]$ is set to 1, otherwise just make $F[q] = 0$. Lines 7–9 complement the set of the value of k and $F[q]$.

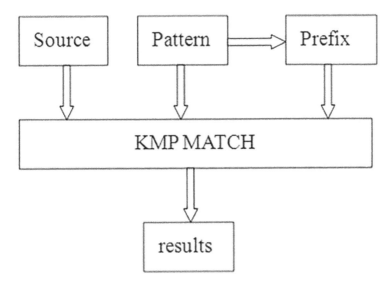

FIGURE 11.1
The process of KMP.

Algorithm 11.1 PREFIX

1. m← Length[P]

2. F[1] ←0

3. k←0

4. for q←2 to m

5.   do while k>0 and P[k+1]!=P[q]

6.   do k← F[k]

7.   if P[k+1]=P[q]

8.   k=k+1

9.   F[q] ←k

10. return F

The pattern string is ATCATG, and with this algorithm, we will generate a table like Table 11.2.

Since we have the Prefix array, how can arrays assist us in finding the maximum number of steps we can take? Here, the KMP-Match will, according to the array, give us the answer. As Algorithm 11.2 shows, we define the value of q as the number of characters which have a right match at first. Then we find the first matched character and judge the next character. If the next

TABLE 11.2

Example of the Next Table

i	1	2	3	4	5	6
P[i]	A	T	C	A	T	G
F[i]	0	0	0	1	2	0

character is also matched, we set $q = q + 1$, which means we have a more character matched. Otherwise, if the next is not matched, we will use the generated array $F[]$ to set q as $F[q]$.

Algorithm 11.2 KMP-Match

1. n ← length[S]

2. m ← length[P]

3. F ← prefix(P)

4. q ← 0

5. for i←1 to n

6.   do while q>0 and P[q+1]!=S[i]

7.   do q←F[q]

8.   if P[q+1]=S[i]

9.   q=q+1

10.   if q=m

11.   print "match."

12.   q←F[q]

The essence of the KMP-Match is to find how many steps are the right steps. Algorithm 11.2 just shows us that the right step is the value of $q - F[q]$. Take Table 11.2 as an example, at the first time of the cycle, we find that just three characters are matched. So we set $q = 3$, according to Table 11.2, we know $F[3] = 0$. Then we are sure that the next step should be three steps. As Figure 11.2 shows, if we move three steps we will have the second cycle. In the second cycle, all the characters are matched. To find a new match, we set $q = 0$ to repeat the algorithm.

The process of BWA [21–23] is similar to KMP. The difference between the two algorithms is that the KMP does preprocess with pattern data, but the BWA does with the source data. After the B-W switch [24], we get an array

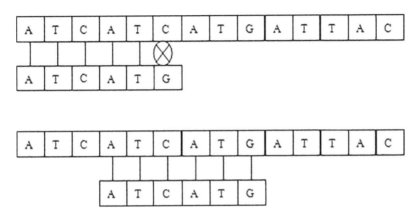

FIGURE 11.2
KMP search.

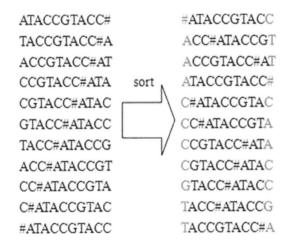

FIGURE 11.3
BW switch.

that contains all the information of the source data [25]. The whole process of the BW switch is shown in Figure 11.3, where the first row of the matrix represents the array we require.

Since we get the array, how can we search pattern string [26]? As we see, the matrix is composed of all the suffixes of the source string [27], and we put all the suffixes in a tree and build a tree. The depth of the tree is the length of the source string. When we want to search a pattern we just need to search the tree. If we put the suffix in an alphabetical order, it will save lots of time.

Algorithm 11.3 BWA Search

1.   c←P[p], i←p;

2.   top←C[c]+1, bot←C[c+1];

3.   **while**((top<=bot) and i>=2) **do**

4.   c← P[i-1];

5.   top← C[c]+OCC(c, 1, top-1)+1;

6.   bot← C[c]+OCC(c, 1, bot);

7.   i=i-1;

8.   **if**(top<bot) **then**

9.   **return** " cannot find";

10. **Else**

11. Return "find(bot-top+1)";

11.2.3 The Principle of the Accelerate Base on Hardware

Hardware acceleration, as the name suggests, refers to the use of hardware to enhance performance. Program computations and calculations take place within the processor. Because the task of the processor is not a single task, the processor is designed more universally, and so the processing speed may not be satisfied. To achieve optimal efficiency, specific hardware architectures can be employed to handle these data-intensive operations. In essence, hardware acceleration is to transfer the relatively complex operations to the hardware during the processor processing program. The efficient processing of these data through specific hardware structures can reduce the burden of the processor and accelerate the efficiency of the whole system.

The typical representative of the processor is the CPU. Designed to handle a variety of tasks, the CPU exhibits excellent versatility and is capable of processing diverse user instructions with flexibility and precision. But its flexibility and universality are limitations. GPU is an image processor; its development is driven by the limitations of CPU universality. An image contains a lot of pixels, and with the complexity of various image attributes, the amount of data contained in the image becomes more and larger. It seems the CPU that deals with these data will be weak. To address this challenge, the GPU relies on its finer granularity and parallel processing performance compared to the CPU. While the GPU demonstrates greater specificity than the CPU, its applicability is relatively limited—though this limitation is inconsequential. The GPU stretched out by the CPU is good for image processing, which is also a hardware acceleration application. Moreover, with the ongoing advancement of technology, the GPU has transcended its initial confinement to image processing. Leveraging its powerful floating-point data processing capabilities and high degree of parallelism, the GPU has gradually found long-term development prospects in various other domains. The development of GPU raises people's thinking about whether we can design more targeted processors to deal with some special tasks to reduce the efficiency of the system. FPGA is a programmable logic gate array, which has rich computing resources and powerful computing power. Because of its strong performance in data processing, people began to try using FPGA to customize the processor to adapt to a special direction and improve the efficiency of the system.

In summary, the FPGA application in hardware acceleration is a result of technological advancement and the need for processor personalization and specialization.

From the above, we know that hardware acceleration is essentially the transfer of data processing to dedicated hardware for processing. However, the question remains: how do we determine which portion of the code should be transferred to the hardware? Our first idea is to transfer the most time-consuming and resource-intensive parts. We call this code hot code. At the initial stage of hardware acceleration, we need to find the hot code first. There are many ways to find the hot code; we select instrumentation as a method to find the hot code. Instrumentation has inserted a marker at a certain point of the program code as a wooden pile, through many running programs to analyze the code between two adjacent piles, the code cost most of the time is hot code. Furthermore, the hotspot code must be compatible with the chosen hardware acceleration architecture.

After finding the hot code, and then we can take our second step, and analyze the code structure to find the appropriate speedup. There are many hardware acceleration methods, and we need to choose the appropriate structure. The common methods are parallel computing, pipeline processing [26], and storage structure optimization; all these will be explained in this section. Parallel computing is a commonly used acceleration method that can save a significant amount of processing time for data handling, such as the correlation between the source string and pattern string in our string matching algorithm. Each processing module can be seen as an independent process, through parallel we can efficiently perform source string and pattern strings to save time expenditure. Pipeline technology is a classical accelerating method and a method of high efficiency. The pipeline [27] is widely used in various fields, by dividing a complete production process into different flow segments, each segment running the same segment independently to achieve high efficiency. Take a three-stage process as an example, the processing time is assumed to be 1, and if we don't take any action to complete these processes, we can significantly improve efficiency and then start our second process after the first flow of the first process without waiting for the first process to complete. As we increase the number of pipelines and refine the pipeline structure at each time point, we can achieve even higher efficiency gains. However, it is important to note that this increased efficiency comes at the cost of additional resource utilization, which involves trade-offs in terms of space and time. Additionally, optimizing storage structures is another viable approach to enhance operational efficiency. Optimizing storage structures is indeed a valuable approach to improve operational efficiency. One classic method involves selecting the appropriate storage location and accessing data through processors. The process of searching and retrieving data through processors can consume a significant amount of time during interaction with the processor. At the same time, the storage of data can be reasonably planned, reducing the frequency of interaction with memory can also speed up the running efficiency of the program.

Finally, you can build the acceleration system to select the appropriate method of code acceleration for hot code, which will be described in detail later.

11.3 The Design of Accelerator

11.3.1 System Analysis

The system is designed as a system of hardware acceleration for the string matching algorithm of gene sequencing. The overall framework of the system is as follows: Firstly, our design focuses on a user-oriented system design. Users directly interact with the application program to accelerate two algorithms. The system serves as an underlying hardware acceleration system. To fulfill the users' requirements, an intermediate stage of support needs to be added, consisting primarily of library functions, application programming interfaces (APIs), and driver programs corresponding to our underlying design [28].

The main contents of our design are as follows:

a. Design of string matching algorithm
   The string algorithms employed in our system include the KMP and BWA algorithms. Our primary objective is to design and implement these two algorithms, both of which are renowned for their excellence in string processing. These algorithms have significantly improved upon traditional string algorithms, offering substantial enhancements in terms of efficiency and performance.

b. On the board realization of the algorithm

This chapter uses a ZedBoard-based development board.

c. IP core

The package of the algorithm requires the tools of Xilinx using the Vivado design suite. Vivado is an integrated design environment released by xilinx2012, including a highly integrated design environment and a new generation from the system to IC tools. Vivado design suite can quickly synthesize and verify c language, enabling the generation of IP cores for encapsulation.

d. The implementation of intermediate-stage support

With the implementation of the IP core, we need to write the appropriate driver to support its operation. This mainly includes our two IP cores: the driver of KMP and BWA and the related driver of DMA.

11.3.2 IP Core

The generation of IP core, shown in Figure 11.4, needs the corresponding tool, with Vivado's HLS functionality being the primary choice. HLS is a high-level synthesis, which refers to the process from the computational description to register transport layer description. The task goal of HLS is to find a hardware structure that not only meets the specified constraints and objectives but also minimizes costs. It has the advantage of increasing design speed and shortening the design cycle while being easy to understand. HLS is generally composed of the following steps:

1. Compilation and conversion of calculating description
2. Scheduling (leaving the operation to control step)
3. Allocation of data paths (each operation is assigned to the appropriate functional unit)
4. Controller synthesis (integrated controller of data-driven routing driver)
5. Generating (generating a low-level physical implementation)

After several steps, we can get an IP core.

11.3.3 The Implement of the Accelerator

Our design framework is built on the above development board, adopting the software and hardware co-design design framework. According to the above description, we can see that the overall design of this system is divided into multiple modules, namely the software module design at the algorithmic level and the hardware design of the accelerator module. Traditional system design methods often separate the entire system into software and hardware design, with a primary focus on low-level hardware design, followed by

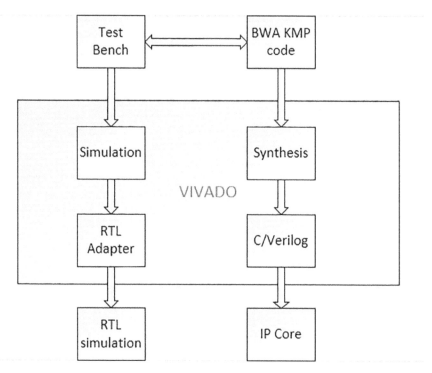

FIGURE 11.4
HLS and IP core.

software development on the hardware platform. However, these two processes are often independent and loosely connected, making it challenging to meet the requirements of software module design. Due to the independent design, there is a lack of thorough analysis of software requirements in the early stages, which can lead to issues due to a lack of understanding of the overall structural mechanism and software operation analysis. Figure 11.5 shows the flow of the traditional design process.

The design process outlined above reveals the lengthy duration of the entire system design cycle. The resolution of conflicts between software and hardware system design consumes a significant amount of time, with numerous modifications further extending the overall design timeframe. Additionally, unforeseen issues arise, necessitating substantial time investment for their resolution. The hardware and software co-design is the improvement of system design for this problem. It takes the entire system design as a unified entity, allowing for parallel design of software and hardware components, thereby identifying optimal points of integration. This approach ultimately enhances design efficiency. Its design cycle is different from traditional design, as shown in Figure 11.6.

The primary advantage of software–hardware co-design is its ability to establish a connection between software and hardware at the beginning of

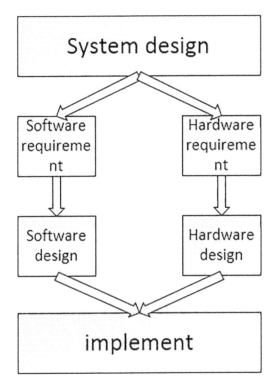

FIGURE 11.5
The traditional design ways.

development. By focusing on software–hardware resources at an early stage, significant reductions in time investment can be achieved. This proactive approach enables identifying and resolving issues during the design phase. In the following section, we will provide a detailed description of the design process, following the flow of software–hardware co-design.

First is the overall system design. This process mainly uses the system-level description language to transform the system design into the system function performance and aspects of the digital circuit. Then according to the description, we organize function modules and establish the system model. After the completion of the system modeling, we began to design the hardware and software modules. At the beginning, we need to have a clear understanding of hardware modules and software modules. The hardware part is characterized by high efficiency, programmability, and strong programmable capability. It is primarily used to solidify certain relatively fixed general computing components. On the other hand, the software modules are responsible for the computation of other parts. The entire design possesses the advantages of flexibility, ease of modification, and maintenance. In the design, the hardware implementation can also be a software implementation, so we need to analyze further and find the most suitable way. This design phase will

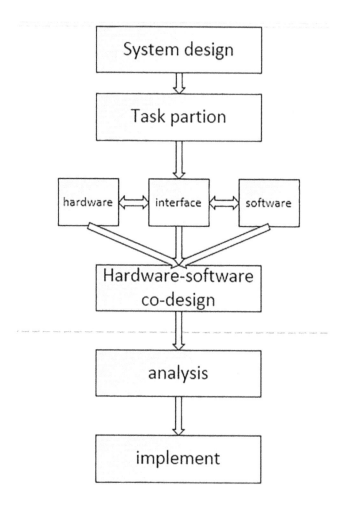

FIGURE 11.6
The process of co-design.

occupy a significant period of our design cycle. During this stage, we conduct a detailed division of the software and hardware functions, and subsequent functional module designs are based on this foundation. Therefore, caution is necessary at this stage. After the completion of the system module division, we have to do the interface design to complete the mapping of the whole system. This primarily involves the layout process, including the selection of various hardware modules, data transmission paths, and communication methods. Finally, we can complete the software and hardware co-design. Following the completion of the system's functional design, it is necessary to analyze and verify the system, modify its performance, and improve the system. This is not just validation of the accuracy of the system, but also a holistic improvement of our design system. In this process, we found the combination of hardware and software problems and modified it to avoid the final system meeting various problems. When we complete the above process, we can get a molding design. For the system design of this chapter, we organize the whole design process according to the hardware and software co-design, as follows:

1. Build the basic model of the system and analyze the system.
2. Selecting the accelerated algorithm and analyzing the hot code.
3. Design the hardware code that needs acceleration into the design of the hardware circuit, including the selection of hardware resources and the data transmission path between hardware resources.
4. Synthesize hardware code, judge whether its function is correct, and analyze its performance.
5. The IP core is generated according to the designed hardware module, and the layout routing of this accelerator is simulated and verified.
6. Generate the hardware bitstream file and transform it to board.
7. Finish all the above, we begin to package the whole system and do the support between the system and our hardware accelerator.

The whole software and hardware co-design system framework is divided into two parts: PS (program system) and PL (program logic). As shown in Figure 11.7, the frame of the co-design, PS as the control terminal of the whole system is located in the host, including the processor and storage unit to

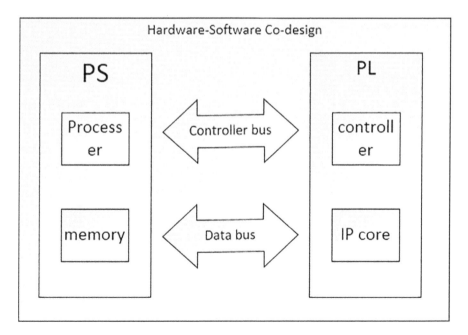

FIGURE 11.7
The frame of the co-design.

complete the operation of the server-side software code and the control of the hardware part. On the other hand, PL is the programmable logic unit of the FPGA part, serving as the hardware acceleration component of the system. It can accommodate various IP core designs and incorporate the corresponding IP cores to achieve our desired tasks, enabling highly parallel operation within the PL.

11.4 Conclusion

In this chapter, we proposed an accelerator based on the FPGA platform to accelerate the algorithm of gene sequencing. We put up two algorithms of gene sequencing, namely KMP and BWA. During the process, we design the two algorithms and implement the two algorithms in a digital circuit.

The experimental result showed that our accelerator could achieve a high speedup rate. For KMP, the speedup rate can reach 5.1X, and it will increase with the data. As to BWA, it also can reach a speedup rate of 3.2X; if the pattern string is large, the speedup rate will reach a higher speedup rate. What is more, the accelerator costs less power and it only needs 0.10 W to support the accelerator.

References

1. Owens J. D., Houston M., Luebke D., et al. GPU computing. *Proceedings of the IEEE*, 2008, 96(5): 879–899.
2. Armbrust M., Fox A., Griffith R., et al. A view of cloud computing. *Communications of the ACM*, 2010, 53(4): 50–58.
3. Mahajan A., Soewito B., Parsi S. K., et al. Implementing high-speed string-matching hardware for network intrusion detection systems. *2008 International Conference on Parallel and Distributed Processing Techniques and Applications*, Las Vegas, NV. 2008: 157–163.
4. Schatz M C. CloudBurst: Highly sensitive read mapping with MapReduce. *Bioinformatics*, 2009, 25(11): 1363–1369.
5. Wang C., Li X., Chen P., et al. Heterogeneous cloud framework for big data genome sequencing. *IEEE/ACM Transactions on Computational Biology and Bioinformatics*, 2014, 12(1): 166–178.
6. Dharmapurikar S., Krishnamurthy P., Sproull T., et al. Deep packet inspection using parallel bloom filters. *11th Symposium on High-Performance Interconnects, 2003. Proceedings*, Stanford, CA. IEEE, 2003: 44–51.
7. Guo X., Wang H., Devabhaktuni V. A systolic array-based FPGA parallel architecture for the BLAST algorithm. *International Scholarly Research Notices*, 2012. doi: 10.5402/2012/195658.

8. Manavski S. A., Valle G. CUDA compatible GPU cards as efficient hardware accelerators for Smith-Waterman sequence alignment. *BMC Bioinformatics*, 2008, 9: 1–9.

9. Thambawita D., Ragel R., Elkaduwe D. To use or not to use: Graphics processing units (GPUs) for pattern matching algorithms. *7th International Conference on Information and Automation for Sustainability*, Colombo. IEEE, 2014: 1–4.

10. Huang N. F., Hung H. W., Lai S. H., et al. A GPU-based multiple-pattern matching algorithm for network intrusion detection systems. *22nd International Conference on Advanced Information Networking and Applications-Workshops (aina workshops 2008)*, Gino-wan, Okinawa. IEEE, 2008: 62–67.

11. Lin C. H., Liu C. H., Chien L. S., et al. Accelerating pattern matching using a novel parallel algorithm on GPUs. *IEEE Transactions on Computers*, 2012, 62(10): 1906–1916.

12. Cho Y. H., Navab S., Mangione-Smith W. H. Specialized hardware for deep network packet filtering. *International Conference on Field Programmable Logic and Applications*. Berlin, Heidelberg: Springer, 2002: 452–461.

13. Ahmed G. F., Khare N. Hardware-based string matching algorithms: A survey. *International Journal of Computer Applications*, 2014, 88(11). doi: 10.5120/15396-3898.

14. Brown S. FPGA architectural research: A survey. *IEEE Design & Test of Computers*, 1996, 13(4): 9–15.

15. Kuon I., Tessier R., Rose J. FPGA architecture: Survey and challenges. *Foundations and Trends(r) in Electronic Design Automation*, 2008, 2(2): 135–253.

16. Chen P., Wang C., Li X., et al. A FPGA-based high-performance acceleration platform for the next generation long read mapping. *2013 IEEE 10th International Conference on High-Performance Computing and Communications & 2013 IEEE International Conference on Embedded and Ubiquitous Computing*, Zhangjiajie. IEEE, 2013: 308–315.

17. Chen P., Wang C., Li X., et al. Accelerating the next generation of long read mapping with the FPGA-based system. *IEEE/ACM Transactions on Computational Biology and Bioinformatics*, 2014, 11(5): 840–852.

18. Chen P., Wang C., Li X., et al. Acceleration of the long read mapping on a PC-FPGA architecture. *Proceedings of the ACM/SIGDA International Symposium on Field Programmable Gate Arrays*, Monterey, CA, 2013: 271–271.

19. Wang C., Li X., Zhou X., et al. Big data genome sequencing on zynq-based clusters. *Proceedings of the 2014 ACM/SIGDA International Symposium on Field-Programmable Gate Arrays*, Monterey, CA, 2014: 247–247.

20. Schatz M. C., Trapnell C., Delcher A. L., et al. High-throughput sequence alignment using Graphics Processing Units. *BMC Bioinformatics*, 2007, 8(1): 1–10.

21. Homer N., Merriman B., Nelson S. F. BFAST: An alignment tool for large scale genome resequencing. *PloS one*, 2009, 4(11): e7767.

22. Langmead B., Trapnell C., Pop M., et al. Ultrafast and memory-efficient alignment of short DNA sequences to the human genome. *Genome Biology*, 2009, 10(3): 1–10.

23. Tang W., Wang W., Duan B., et al. Accelerating millions of short reads mapping on a heterogeneous architecture with FPGA accelerator. *2012 IEEE 20th International Symposium on Field-Programmable Custom Computing Machines*, Toronto. IEEE, 2012: 184–187.

24. Lippert R. A. Space-efficient whole genome comparisons with Burrows-Wheeler transforms. *Journal of Computational Biology*, 2005, 12(4): 407–415.

25. Li H., Durbin R. Fast and accurate short read alignment with Burrows-Wheeler transform. *Bioinformatics*, 2009, 25(14): 1754–1760.
26. Pao D., Lin W., Liu B. A memory-efficient pipelined implementation of the aho-corasick string-matching algorithm. *ACM Transactions on Architecture and Code Optimization (TACO)*, 2010, 7(2): 1–27.
27. Mahram A., Herbordt M. C. FMSA: FPGA-accelerated ClustalW-based multiple sequence alignment through pipelined prefiltering. *2012 IEEE 20th International Symposium on Field-Programmable Custom Computing Machines*, Toronto. IEEE, 2012: 177–183.
28. Lei S., Wang C., Fang H., et al. SCADIS: A scalable accelerator for data-intensive string set matching on FPGAs. *2016 IEEE Trustcom/BigDataSE/ISPA*, Tianjin. IEEE, 2016: 1190–1197.

12

RISC-V Open Source Instruction Set and Architecture

12.1 RISC-V Architecture Principles

In this section, we first provide an introduction to the RISC-V architecture and then describe in detail the characteristics of the RISC-V architecture compared to traditional instruction set architectures. Finally, we investigate and summarize the current research status of RISC-V in industry and academia.

12.1.1 Introduction to RISC-V

RISC-V ("RISC five") – the fifth generation of the Reduced Instruction Set Architecture – is an open-source, general-purpose processor instruction set that allows any company, university, research organization, or individual in the world to develop processors compatible with the RISC-V instruction set and to be integrated into the software and hardware ecosystems built on it, without having to pay a cent for the instruction set. Unlike almost all older architectures, its future is not subject to the whims or whims of any single company, and it belongs to an open, non-profit foundation whose goal is to maintain the stability of RISC-V, to develop it slowly and cautiously for technical reasons only, and to make it as popular for hardware as Linux is for operating systems.

The reason why RISC-V is being developed as a new Instruction Set Architecture (ISA), rather than inherited from the mature x86 or Advanced RISC Machine (ARM), is that these instruction set architectures have become complex and redundant over the years, and there are high patent and architecture licensing issues. Since RISC-V is different from traditional ISAs in its simplicity, open source, and modularity, more and more companies and projects are adopting processors based on the RISC-V architecture, and there is reason to believe that the RISC-V software ecosystem will grow and become popular.

12.1.2 RISC-V Instruction Set Features

The design of the RISC-V architecture draws on the lessons learned from the design of instruction sets such as ARM, MIPS, and x86. Therefore, compared with traditional instruction sets, RISC-V has such distinctive features as simple architecture, modular instruction set composition, configurable general-purpose registers, regular instruction encoding, simple memory access, efficient branch jumping, and dedicated reserved instruction space.

12.1.2.1 Simplicity of Infrastructure

The number of RISC-V integer instruction levels is just over 40, a mandatory instruction set for all RISC-V-compatible processors, and even with other standard modular extensions, it is just under a hundred instructions. Compared to the thousands of pages of architecture documentation for x86, RISC-V is only about 200 pages, which shows its indirectness.

12.1.2.2 Modular Instruction Set

RISC-V employs a modular architecture that allows different parts to be organized in a modular way, thus allowing a unified set of architectures to fit different domains in a way that x86 and ARM architectures do not.

Each module of RISC-V is represented by a letter of the alphabet, and the most basic and only mandatory part of the instruction set to be implemented in RISC-V is the subset of basic integer instructions represented by the letter I, which is used to implement a complete software compiler. The rest of the instruction subset is optional, and representative modules include M/A/F/D/C, as shown in Figure 12.1.

To increase code density, the RISC-V architecture also offers an optional subset of "compressed" instructions, denoted by the letter C. Compressed instructions have an instruction code length of 16 bits, while normal uncompressed instructions have a length of 32 bits. The compressed instructions have an instruction code length of 16 bits, compared to 32 bits for normal uncompressed instructions, and the RISC-V architecture also offers an "embedded" architecture, denoted by the letter E. This architecture is

Base ISA	Number of instructions	Description
RV32I	47	Integer instructions, 32-bit address space, 32 general registers
RV32E	47	RV32I subset, only supports 16 general integer registers
RV64I	59	Integer instruction, 64-bit address, support for some 32-bit instructions
RV128I	71	Integer instruction, 128-bit address, support for some 32/64-bit instructions
Standard Extension ISA	Number of instructions	Description
M	8	Integer Multiply and Division Instructions
F	26	Single-precision floating-point instructions (32-bit)
D	26	Double precision floating-point instruction (64-bit), must support F extension
C	46	Compression instruction, instruction length 16
A	11	Memory atomic operation, Load-Reserved/Store-conditional instructions

FIGURE 12.1
Modular instruction set composition.

intended for deeply embedded scenarios where very low area and power consumption are desired. This architecture is primarily used in deep embedded scenarios where very low area and power consumption are desired. This architecture needs to support only 16 general-purpose integer registers, compared to 32 general-purpose integer registers for the normal non-embedded architecture.

In addition to those mentioned above, there are several other modules including L, B, P, V, and T, among others. Most of these extensions are currently undergoing refinement and definition and have not yet been finalized, so this chapter will not deal with them in detail.

12.1.2.3 Configurable General-Purpose Register Set

The RISC-V architecture supports either 32-bit or 64-bit architectures, denoted by RV32 and RV64, respectively.

The integer general-purpose register set for the RISC-V architecture contains 32 (I-architecture) or 16 (E-architecture) general-purpose integer registers, of which integer register 0 is reserved as a constant 0, and the other 31 (I-architecture) or 15 (E-architecture) are normal general-purpose integer registers.

If a floating-point module (F or D) is used, a separate floating-point register set containing 32 general-purpose floating-point registers is required. Each general-purpose floating-point register is 32 bits wide if only the floating-point instruction subset of the F module is used or 64 bits wide if the floating-point instruction subset of the D module is used.

12.1.2.4 Regular Command Codes

The RISC-V instruction set is very well coded, and the indexes of the general-purpose registers required by the instructions are placed in fixed locations (as shown in Figure 12.2). Therefore, the Instruction Decoder can easily decode the register index and read the Register File (Regfile).

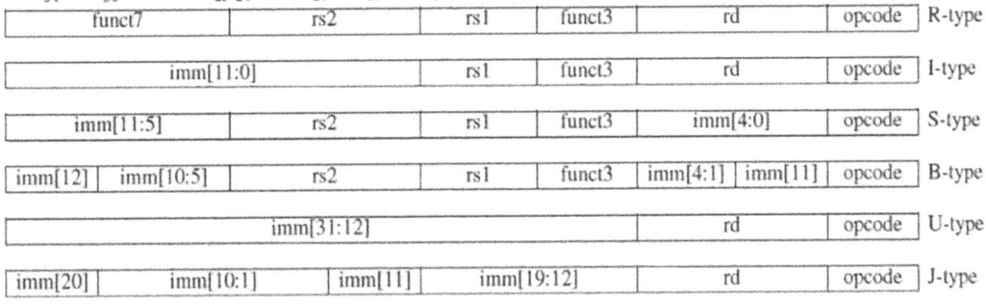

31	30	25	24	21	20	19	15	14	12	11	8	7	6	0	
funct7			rs2			rs1		funct3		rd			opcode		R-type
imm[11:0]						rs1		funct3		rd			opcode		I-type
imm[11:5]			rs2			rs1		funct3		imm[4:0]			opcode		S-type
imm[12]	imm[10:5]		rs2			rs1		funct3		imm[4:1]	imm[11]		opcode		B-type
imm[31:12]										rd			opcode		U-type
imm[20]	imm[10:1]			imm[11]		imm[19:12]				rd			opcode		J-type

FIGURE 12.2
Basic instruction format [1].

12.1.2.5 Simple Memory Accesses

Like all RISC processor architectures, the RISC-V architecture uses dedicated memory read and store instructions to access memory, which cannot be accessed by other common instructions. The RISC-V memory read and memory write instructions support memory read and write operations in units of one byte (8-bit), halfword (16-bit), and single word (32-bit), and in the case of 64-bit architectures, they can also support memory read and write operations in units of one double word (64-bit).

The memory access instructions of the RISC-V architecture also have the following notable features:

1. To improve the performance of memory reads and writes, the RISC-V architecture recommends the use of address-aligned memory read and write operations, but address-unaligned memory operations are also supported by the RISC-V architecture (either through software or hardware).

2. Since the mainstream applications today are in Little-Endian format, the RISC-V architecture only supports Little-Endian format.

3. The memory read and memory write instructions of the RISC-V architecture do not support the address self-increment and self-decrement modes.

4. The RISC-V architecture uses the Relaxed Memory Model, which does not require the execution order of memory read and write instructions to access different addresses unless they are masked by explicit memory barrier (Fence) instructions.

12.1.2.6 Efficient Branch Jumping

The RISC-V architecture has six Conditional Branch instructions, which use two integer operands directly like normal arithmetic instructions, then compare them and jump if the conditions of the comparison are met. Therefore, this kind of instruction puts two operations of comparison and jumps into one instruction, which reduces the number of instructions.

For low-end Central Processing Units (CPUs) that are not equipped with hardware branch predictors, to ensure their performance, the RISC-V architecture explicitly requires them to use the default static branch prediction mechanism, that is, if it is a conditional jump instruction that jumps backward, it is predicted to "jump"; if it is a conditional jump instruction that jumps forward, it is predicted to "not jump". The RISC-V architecture requires the compiler to compile assembly code according to this default static branch prediction mechanism, which allows low-end CPUs to get good performance.

| Inst[4:2] | 000 | 001 | 010 | 011 | 100 | 101 | 110 | 111 |
Inst[6:5]								(>32b)
00	LOAD	LOAD-FP	*custom-0*	MISC-MEM	OP-IMM	AUIPC	OP-IMM-32	48b
01	STORE	STORE-FP	*custom-1*	AMO	OP	LUI	OP-32	64b
10	MADD	MSUB	NMSUB	NMADD	OP-FP	*reserved*	*custom-2/rv128*	48b
11	BRANCH	JALR	*reserved*	JAL	SYSTEM	*reserved*	*custom-3/rv128*	≥80b

FIGURE 12.3
RISC-V basic opcode mapping table, inst[1:0]=11.

12.1.2.7 Support for Third-Party Extensions

RISC-V reserves dedicated instruction space for more customized accelerators, allowing for self-customizing instructions. Any RISC-V processor must support a basic integer ISA (RV32I or RV64I) with optional support for standard extensions (MAFD, where M is the Integer multiplication and division; A is the atomic instructions; F is the single precision floating point; and D is the double precision floating point). We have made the basic integer ISA instruction space and the standard instruction space into G, which is reserved for custom instructions as shown in Figure 12.3. The extended instructions can be standard, or non-standard, the former does not conflict with any standard extension, and the latter is a highly specialized extension that may conflict with other standard extensions, but not with the base integer instruction space.

12.1.3 Status of RISC-V Research

12.1.3.1 Academia

UCB (Berkeley) is the place where RISC-V was initiated. To promote RISC-V and make it easier for users to learn, UCB has set up the Rocket-Chip Generator project on GitHub [2], which includes Chisel (an agile open-source hardware programming language designed by UCB), GCC, the Rocket processor, as well as a series of bus units, peripherals, caches, etc., around the Rocket. A parameterized configuration methodology is used to make it easy to create SoCs based on the Rocket processor with different performance requirements, where Rocket is a 64-bit, five-stage pipelined, single-fire sequential execution processor. It supports an MMU with page-based virtual memory, a non-blocking data cache, and a front-end with branch prediction. Branch prediction is configurable and is provided by a branch target buffer (BTB), a branch history table (BHT), and a return address stack (RAS). Rocket can also be viewed as a library of processor components. Several modules originally designed for Rocket were reused by other designs, including functional units, caches, Translation Look-aside Buffers (TLBs), page table walkers, and privileged architecture implementations (i.e., control and status register files). In addition, Rocket has a custom co-processor interface (RoCC) designed to facilitate decoupled communication between the processor and attached co-processors.

In addition to this, UCB has implemented the superscalar disorder processor BOOM (the Berkeley Out-of-Order RISC-V Processor) [3], the vector processor Hwacha [4], the Z-scale/V-scale [5] for embedded environments, and the Sodor [6] for educational purposes.

Yungang Bao, a researcher at the Institute of Computing, Chinese Academy of Sciences (ICC, CAS), proposed a labeled Von Neumann architecture LvNA, and the team has implemented a RISC-V-based FPGA prototype, and the team proposed a labeled RISC-V [7]. ICC, CAS, has a team of Yuantao Wang, a researcher, and Lei Zhang, an associate researcher, who are working on a RISC-V-based smart IoT chip and made breakthroughs by successively twice presenting the progress and releasing the results in the RISC-V workshop. Wang et al. designed a fast network packet processing system using a RISC-V processor. The goal of this processing system is to provide faster network packet processing for upper-layer SDN and NFV applications using lower power consumption and lower prices.

ETH Zurich (ETHzurich) has designed and implemented the low-power, high-performance IoT edge computing device, PULpino [8], designed to allow next-generation edge devices to process data from more information-rich sensors (images, video, audio, and multi-directional movement). PULPino is an open-source, single-core microcontroller system based on the ETH Zurich-developed 32-bit RISC-V core PULP developed at ETH Zurich. PULpino features low power consumption and a small area and can be configured to use either a RISCY or a zero-risky core. Of these, RISCY is an ordered single core with four pipeline stages with IPC (Instructions Per Clock) close to 1 and full support for the basic integer instruction set (RV32I), compressed instructions (RV32C), and multiply instruction set extensions (RV32M). It can be configured to have a single-precision floating-point instruction set extension (RV32F). It implements several ISA extensions such as hardware loops, post-incremental load and store instructions, bit manipulation instructions, MAC (Multiply Accumulate) operations, support for fixed-point operations, packed SIMD instructions, and dot product. It is designed to improve energy efficiency in ultra-low-power signal processing applications. RISCY implements a subset of the 1.9 privileged specification.

Clarvi [9] is a simple RISC-V implementation based on SystemVerilog. It is intended to be clear and easy to understand while maintaining good performance and can be used for teaching purposes. The implementation is a subset of RV32I instructions. It provides the minimum implementation of the v1.9 RISC-V privileged specification, including full support for interrupts and exceptions. Only machine mode is implemented and only partial support for catching invalid instructions. The full v2.1 user-level specification is also supported. It passes all RV32I user-level tests and the associated RV32I machine mode tests (but not those assuming support for user mode, virtual memory, etc.).

f32c [10] is a redirectable, scalar, pipelined 32-bit processor core that supports RISC-V and MIPS instruction sets. It is implemented in parameterized VHDL, and synthesis allows trade-offs between space and speed. In addition, f32c includes a branch predictor, an exception-handling control block, and an optional direct-mapped cache. f32c also includes SoC modules such as multi-port SDRAM and SRAM controllers, video frame buffers with composite (PAL), HDMI, DVI and VGA outputs, simple 2D acceleration with windowing, floating-point vector processors, SPI, UART, PCM audio, GPUs, and VGAs. UART, PCM audio, GPIOs, PWM outputs, and timers, as well as glue logic tailored to many popular FPGA development boards from a variety of manufacturers.

12.1.3.2 Industry

1. Microprocessors

   Andes Technology Corporation, a founding member of the RISC-V Foundation, joined the consortium in 2016 and is dedicated to developing innovative 32/64-bit processor cores and related development environments. The company introduced the V5 architecture for designing embedded microprocessors with 64-bit architectures, becoming the industry's first mainstream architecture to adopt RISC-V 32/64-bit technology, and formally launched the 32-bit N25 and 64-bit NX25 based on the V5 in the fourth quarter of 2017. Andes Technology is actively promoting the RISC-V ecosystem and expects to release several new RISC-V products.

2. SoC

   SiFive is a leading provider of rapid development processor core IP based on the RISC-V instruction set architecture. Founded by the RISC-V R&D team, SiFive enables SoC designers to reduce time-to-market and cost savings through customized open-architecture processor cores and the in-house development of silicon-based on the RISC-V architecture. HiFive1, the world's first commercial SoC based on the open-source instruction set RISC-V architecture, was launched in June 2018 as the development board for the Freedom E310-G000, the world's first commercial SoC based on the RISC-V architecture. HiFive1 is the world's first commercial SoC Freedom E310-G000 development board based on the open-source instruction set RISC-V architecture, and in June 2018, SiFive launched its E2 Core IP family of configurable, small-area, low-power microcontroller (MCU) cores designed for embedded device use.

3. ASIC

   Codasip offers leading processor IP and advanced design tools that provide ASIC designers with all the benefits of the RISC-V open standard instruction set architecture, as well as the unique ability to automatically optimize the processor IP. Codasip is a leading supplier of RISC-V processor IP, having launched its first RISC-V processor in November 2015. Codasip is unique in providing advanced tools for its processors that enable you to modify RISC-V cores, automate the creation of design kits, and configure software. Codasip provides a verification environment that ensures correctness and compliance with the RISC-V ISA specification.

There is a steady stream of RISC-V-based research efforts in academia and industry, and we summarize here a representative selection of RISC-V processor cores, as shown in Table 12.1.

12.2 RISC-V–Based Accelerator Customization Solutions

In this section, we first provide an introduction to related work on custom computational acceleration based on the RISC-V architecture and through the design of extension instructions. Then, by analyzing the related work, we draw out our design principles and specific examples in designing extended instruction sets for convolutional neural networks.

12.2.1 Related Work

The Luca Benini research team at ETH Zurich proposed in 2017 an open-source RISC-V processor kernel designed for multicore clusters with ultra-low power consumption, introducing a series of instruction extensions and microarchitectural optimizations [11]. The kernel implements the RV32 IM standard instruction set and extends it with instructions for bit manipulation, MAC, dot product, and so on. Microarchitecture optimizations such as prefetching, hardware loops, and tightly coupled data storage have been added. In a low-power 65 nm CMOS process, the peak performance of a cluster containing four of these optimized cores can reach 67 MOPS/mW. The extended instructions dotp and shuttle can effectively accelerate 2D convolutional operations. By testing 3×3, 5×5, and 7×7 convolutional cores on 64×64 input images, respectively, the results show that the extended adopt and shuttle instructions can bring 2.2×–6.9× performance enhancement on average. In 2018, the team proposed an SoC for IoT end-user smart applications, GAP-8 [12], based on the four-core version as shown in Figure 12.4. The chip contains eight instruction-extended RISC-V cores and a hardware convolutional engine (HWCE) accelerator in the L1 shared memory. Experiments show that the chip can achieve a peak computation of up to 10 GMAC/s when executing a four-bit CNN inference process at 90 MHz, 1.0V.

Liang Yun's research team at Peking University has developed a heterogeneous system E-LSTM [13] for accelerating the long short-term memory (LSTM) inference process in embedded environments, which contains a Rocket general-purpose CPU and an LSTM accelerator, and the instruction and data transfer between the two is carried out through the RoCC interface (shared Dcache), as shown in Figure 12.5. Due to the limited data bandwidth of RoCC, a novel sparse compression method, eSELL is proposed in this

TABLE 12.1

Comparison of Typical Open-Source RISC-V Processor Cores

Nucleus	Rocket	BOOM	Sodor	Clare	PULPino	f32c	Hummingbird
Development language	Chisel	Chisel	Chisel	SV	SV	VHDL	Verilog
Research organization	UCB	UCB	UCB	Cambridge	ETH	Zagreb	Wick
Supported standard instruction sets	RV64G	RV64G	RV32I	RV32I	RV32 ICMF	RISC-V/MIPS	RV32I/E/A/M/C/F/D
Cache	Encompass	Encompass	Not have	Not have	Not have	Encompass	Not have
Branch forecasting mechanism	BTB BHT RAS	NLP BPD	-	-	-	Have	Simple-BPU
Ordered/messy	Successive	Disorder	Successive	Successive	Successive	Successive	Successive
DMIPS/MHZ	1.72	3.91	-	-	2.6–2.7	1.63/1.81	1.352
FPGA support model number	Xilinx ZC706 ZC702	Xilinx zc706	Xilinx pink-z1	-	Xilinx ZC702	Spartan6 Cyclone 4 Artix-7	Xilinx Artix-7
Benchmark product	Cortex-A5	Cortex-A9	-	-	Cortex-M4	-	Cortex-M0
Open-source protocol	BSD	BSD	-	BSD	SolderPad	BSD	Apache Licence 2.0
Whether or not the film is flowing	Successfully flowed the film	Successfully flowed the film	-	-	Successfully flowed the film	-	Successfully flowed the film

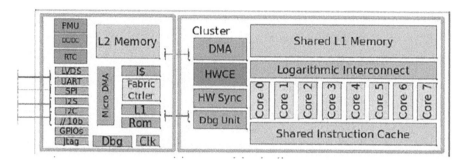

FIGURE 12.4
GAP-8 Architecture.

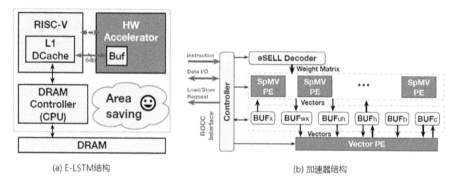

(a) E-LSTM结构   (b) 加速器结构

FIGURE 12.5
E-LSTM structure.

work, and layer fusion is applied to effectively increase the data computation efficiency. The experiments are based on the RISC-V toolchain and the Spike simulator (a cycle-level simulator in the RISC-V ecosystem), and the combination of sparse processing and layer fusion can bring an average of 1.4×–2.2× performance improvement through three sets of Benchmark tests.

Luk et al. from Imperial College London have proposed a RISC-V softcore optimized for custom SIMD instruction scaling – Simodense [14]. To maximize the performance of SIMD instructions, Simodense's memory system is optimized for streaming bandwidth, with ultra-wide blocks for the last level of cache, as shown in Figure 12.6. This LLC structure provides 256 bits of bandwidth per cycle, matching the width of the vector registers it is set up with. The base instruction implementation of the softcore is single cycle, with a separate pipeline for vector instructions and a conflict detection mechanism. The approach is tested on sample memory-intensive applications with custom instructions and achieves good acceleration results. In addition, this research pair presents insights into the effectiveness of adding FPGA resources in the form of reconfigurable SIMD instructions in general-purpose processors.

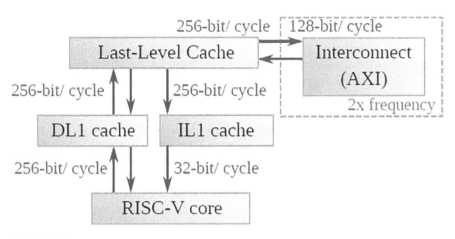

FIGURE 12.6
Data buffer optimization.

12.2.2 RISC-V Extended Instruction Design

It is evident from related work that designing dedicated hardware for a specific computation and encapsulating it as instructions can effectively accelerate CPU processing. However, the granularity of the design extension instructions varies, and the way the extension instructions are coupled to the CPU varies. In the following, we present our design guidelines for computation- and access-intensive CNN applications.

12.2.2.1 RISC-V Extensions

In the past, CNN hardware accelerators usually work as peripherals, and the host side reads and writes to the accelerators through drivers. Considering the large amount of data being copied between user space and kernel space, the time and resource overhead at the OS level in this process is unavoidable. However, the emergence of the RISC-V architecture has brought more options for the accelerator's mode of operation. This instruction set architecture consists of a base instruction set and other optional instruction sets that are open source and instruction customizable, providing users with the possibility of customizing the processor microarchitecture with the scope to design dedicated instructions. Therefore, designing dedicated instructions to control the execution of acceleration units based on RISC-V architecture is also more concise and efficient. Based on the above two analyses, we finally chose RISC-V as the target ISA and extended it with CNN-specific instructions while keeping the basic core and each standard extension unchanged. The final dedicated instructions can work with the scalar and logic control instructions that RV32 has to complete the inference process of CNN.

12.2.2.2 Data-Level Parallelism

There are many factors involved in designing a CNN-specific instruction set, but it is the part involving performance bottlenecks that should be the focus of attention. Considering the layer-by-layer stacked topology of CNNs and the independence of the weighted data in different layers, it is more efficient to design matrix instructions to exploit the data-level parallelism in its operation rather than mining its instruction-level parallelism. Studies have shown that the consumption for computation in Intel Xeon processor cores accounts for only 37% of the overall core energy consumption, and the rest of the energy consumption is an architectural cost and is not necessary for computation [15]. Therefore, when designing dedicated instructions, increasing the granularity of instructions, and spreading the overhead of instruction fetching, decoding and control over multiple elements of computation can effectively improve execution efficiency. In addition, when dealing with computations involving a large amount of data, matrix instructions can explicitly specify the independence between data blocks and reduce the size of the data dependency detection logic compared to traditional scalar instructions. Moreover, matrix instructions also have high code density, so we focus on data-level parallelism here.

12.2.2.3 Scratchpad Memory

Vector register banks are typically found in vector architectures where each vector register contains a vector of fixed length and allows the processor to operate on all elements of the vector at once. Sticky note memories are high-speed internal memories used on-chip to store temporary computational data with direct addressing access, low cost, and variable-length data access. Because of the low cost of implementing sticky note memories, larger sizes of sticky note memories with integrated direct memory access (DMA) controllers are often deployed for fast data transfers. In addition, given that dense, sequential, variable-length data accesses often occur in CNNs, we choose here to use sticky note memories instead of traditional vector register sets.

12.2.3 RISC-V Instruction Set Extensions

Based on the above design principles, we design an extended instruction set for CNNs, RV-CNN [16]. In this section, we first introduce its instruction format and generation process and then describe its comparison with typical instruction sets.

12.2.3.1 Introduction to the Extended Instruction Set

The composition of the RV-CNN instruction set is shown in Table 12.2, which contains data transfer instructions, logic instructions, and computation instructions. Together with part of the underlying RV-32I instruction set

TABLE 12.2

Overview of the RV-CNN Instruction Set

Instruction Type	Typical Example
Data transmission instruction	MLOAD/MSTORE
Calculation class instruction	MMM/MMA/MMS/MMSA
Logical class of instructions	MXPOOL/MNPOOL/APOOL/MACT

31 27	26 22	21 17	16 12	11 7	6 0
Reg3	Reg2	Reg1	00000	Reg0	opcode
Stride	Mat_size	Mat_addr	MLOAD	Dest_addr	

FIGURE 12.7
Matrix load instruction format.

(not described here), this instruction set can perform typical CNN-like computations. The RV-CNN instruction set architecture remains consistent with the RISC-V architecture, which is a load-store architecture, with data transfers performed only through dedicated instructions. Moreover, the instruction set still uses the 32 32-bit general-purpose registers in RV-32 for storing scalar values as well as indirect addressing of registers in the sticky note memory. In addition, we set up a vector-length register (VLR) to specify the length of the vectors processed at runtime. The instructions are described in detail below.

To flexibly support matrix operations, the data transfer instruction accomplishes the transfer of variable-sized blocks of data between off-chip main memory and on-chip sticky note memory. Figure 12.7 illustrates the format of the matrix load instruction (MLOAD).

In Figure 12.7, Reg0 specifies the on-chip destination address, and Reg1, Reg2, and Reg3 specify the source address of the matrix, the size of the matrix, and the span of adjacent elements, respectively. Specifically, the instruction transfers data from the main memory to the memo memory, where the step field of the instruction can specify the span of adjacent elements, thus avoiding "expensive" matrix transposition operations in memory. In contrast, the Matrix Store (MSTORE) instruction performs data transfers from sticky note memory to main memory and is similar in format to MLOAD, although the stride field is often omitted to avoid discontinuous off-chip access.

After mapping the 2-D convolution to the matrix multiply operation, it is natural to use the MMM (matrix-multiply-matrix) instruction to operate. The format of the instruction is shown in Figure 12.8, where Reg0 specifies the destination address in the sticky note memory of the matrix output; bits 16–12 are the function fields of the instruction, indicating the matrix multiplication operation. reg1 and reg2 specify the source addresses in the sticky note memory of matrix 1 and matrix 2, respectively. The four bytes in reg3

31	27	26	22	21	17	16	12	11	7	6	0
Reg3		Reg2		Reg1		00010		Reg0		opcode	
I|W|K|S		Mat2_addr		Mat1_addr		MMM		Dest_addr			

FIGURE 12.8
Matrix-multiply-matrix instruction format.

represent the height (H), width (W), convolution kernel size (K), and convolution step size (S). Considering the use of slicing techniques in practical execution, it is sufficient to use a single byte to store the corresponding information here. Therefore, the parameter information for the execution of the convolution operation is packed into 32'b {H, W, K, S} and specified by Reg3. Also, since the data is loaded in slices, the intermediate results it produces often need to be accumulated. Instead of a specific matrix addition instruction, the MMS instruction is designed here. This instruction, after completing the matrix multiplication calculation, accumulates some of the results when writing them to the target address with the original value of the address before storing them, making it possible to reduce data reloading while completing the accumulation. The format of this instruction and the meaning of each field are the same as that of the MMM instruction, which is specified by the function field, so it is not shown again. In addition, to take greater advantage of data locality and to reduce concurrent read/write requests to the same address, we chose to perform matrix multiplication using a dedicated MMM instruction, rather than breaking it down into finer-grained instructions (e.g., matrix-vector multiplication and vector dot product).

The fully connected layer is usually at the end of the entire convolutional neural network to map the features learned in the previous layers for classification. The computation of the fully connected layer can be represented by matrix-vector multiplication, and the MMM instruction can also represent the computation of the fully connected layer under different parameters so that the convolutional layer and the fully connected layer can reuse the same computational units.

Fusion, a common technique used in the design of current DNN accelerators minimizes bandwidth constraints by fusing some of the layers, thus replacing the data input and output operations of individual layers with a single data load and store. The advantages of the fusion operation, as well as the fact that the activation layer is usually immediately after the convolutional or fully connected layer in current CNNs, make it very suitable to design the corresponding coarse-grained instructions to perform the fusion of the two. Moreover, the excitation layer does not change the size of the input tensor and the activation function performs the activation operation element by element, which requires fewer parameters. Therefore, we design the MMMA instruction so that the partial final result of the convolutional or fully connected layer obtained by matrix multiplication can be output after the activation operation, and its instruction format and the meaning of each

31	27	26	22	21	17	16	12	11	7	6		0
00000		Reg2		Reg1		00110		Reg0		opcode		
ReLU		Mat_size		Mat_addr		Activate		Dest_addr				

FIGURE 12.9
Matrix activation command format.

31	27	26	22	21	17	16	12	11	7	6		0
Reg3		Reg2		Reg1		00100		Reg0		opcode		
H|W|K|S		Mat_size		Mat_addr		MXPOOL		Dest_addr				

FIGURE 12.10
Matrix pooling instruction format.

field are the same as that of the MMM instruction, which is specified by the function field. However, we still retain the activation instruction to complete the activation operation on the input data, its instruction format is shown in Figure 12.9, and bits 31–27 of its instruction are used to decide the choice of activation function, such as ReLU()/sigmoid()/Tanh().

The pooling layer reduces the size of the input image by downsampling each window sub-sampling of the input data to a single pool output. The remaining layers in a convolutional neural network contain very little computation and are limited by data access time compared to the convolutional and fully connected layers. In some CNN models, it is also effective to use fusion techniques for pooled and neighboring layers. However, unlike the activation layer, which has a relatively fixed position in the CNN and operates on an element-by-element basis, the pooling layer still has some flexibility, for example, pooling after stacking three convolutional layers. Thus, here we still treat the pooling layer as a separate layer. The instruction format of MXPOOL for performing maximum pooling is shown in Figure 12.10. Reg0, Reg1, and Reg2 denote the destination address of the output data, the source address of the input data, and the length of the input data, respectively. Drawing on the idea of designing MMM instructions, it is observed that pooling windows are usually of small sizes such as 2×2, 3×3, and 5×5 and that slicing techniques are usually used to process the input data, so the use of a single byte to denote the height (H), the width (1W), the size of the pooling window (K), and the step size (S), respectively, of the input matrix that can be processed in one slicing is sufficient. This necessary information is in turn packed into 32-bit values, as specified by Reg3.

12.2.3.2 Extended Instruction Generation Flow

The RV-CNN instruction generation flow is shown in Figure 12.11. Among them, the CNN model description file can be a description file under popular frameworks such as Caffe, TensorFlow, or Pytorch, which are familiar to deep

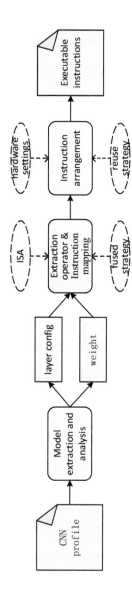

FIGURE 12.11
RV-CNN instruction generation flow.

learning engineers. This description file is parsed by the model analyzer to generate parameter information for model construction and weight information after rearrangement. On this basis, a data flow graph should be constructed and operators should be extracted based on the network parameter information, and then the extracted operators should be mapped to different instructions in the instruction pool (RV-CNN instruction set) under different fusion strategies. Since the instructions we designed are coarse-grained instructions, here the operators with suitable granularity should be extracted to be mapped to the target instruction set. After the dedicated instructions are extracted, the slice size should be decided based on the parameter information of the hardware, such as the size of the on-chip sticky note memory and the size of the hardware computational resources. The instructions should also be programmed according to the multiplexing strategy, such as input multiplexing or weight multiplexing, to generate the final code. In this, the RV32 base instruction set should be used to load the parameter information into the registers and complete the loop control.

12.2.3.3 Comparison of RV-CNN and Dedicated Instruction Sets

1. Scope of application

   The RV-V instruction set was built to take advantage of data-level parallelism in applications such as scientific computing, data signal processing, and machine learning, while the Cambricon [17] instruction set was designed for more than 10 network models in the neural network domain, such as Convolutional Neural Networks (CNN), recurrent neural networks(RNN), and LSTMs. In contrast, the RV-CNN instruction set is designed to focus on CNNs in the neural network domain, which involves fewer types of operations. As a result, the former two target a broader domain and are more difficult to design, which is also reflected in the type and number of instructions included in the instruction set. The RV-V instruction set already contains more than 60 instructions (draft version 0. 8), the Cambricon instruction set contains 47 instructions, and the RV-CNN instruction set contains only 10 instructions.

2. Coarse and fine particle size

   The RV-V and RV-CNN instruction sets contain vector and matrix instructions, respectively, while the Cambricon instruction set contains three different types of instructions: scalar, vector, and matrix. Cambricon contains scalar instructions because it is conceptually a complete neural network instruction set, but it is the vector and matrix instructions that are used to accelerate computation. Therefore, at the level of instruction granularity, the RV-CNN instruction set has the largest instruction granularity of the three, followed by the Cambricon instruction set, which has the smallest granularity in comparison because the RV-V instruction set is all vector instructions. This is also related to the scope of application of the instruction set, as the RV-V instruction set was designed to target the widest range of application domains, thus requiring common parts to be extracted from a wide range of computational operations. Considering the limitations of hardware size and energy consumption, this process often requires the combination of algorithmic characteristics, and the different computational processes are continuously split down to seek commonalities, to improve the expressive ability of the instruction set, and thus the instruction granularity of the RV-V instruction set is the smallest compared to the previous two.

3. Code mapping mechanism

The code mapping of the Cambricon instruction set is based on the framework, which provides adapted machine learning high-performance libraries and software runtime support for popular programming frameworks, upwards to provide the framework with a rich set of arithmetic and computational graphical methods for constructing the entire network and downwards to generate instructions for controlling the hardware through calls to the built-in driver. Unlike Cambricon, which modifies the framework, RV-CNN only analyzes the model description file under the framework to extract the model structure and weight information, then works with the fusion strategy to establish the mapping between operators and instructions in the model, then arranges the instructions according to the reuse strategy, and then assembles them to form an executable file. The RV-V instruction set is currently in a work-in-progress state and does not yet provide a compiler that can be used to complete the automatic vectorization process of the code, which still requires the user to write the assembly instructions by hand. The RV-V instruction set is currently in a work-in-progress state and does not yet provide a compiler that can be used to automate the vectorization process of the code, which still requires the user to write the assembly instructions by hand.

12.2.4 Examples

This section samples the use of RV-CNN and describes the corresponding hardware design support and final acceleration results.

12.2.4.1 Assembly Code Examples

To illustrate the usage of the proposed dedicated instruction set, we enumerate two representative parts of the CNN constructed using the RV-CNN, that is, the convolutional layer and the pooling layer. In this case, the implementation of the convolutional layer contains the operations of the excitation layer through fusion instructions. The code implementation of the fully connected

```
layer {                            //$1:input mat1 address, $2:input mat2 address
  type: "data"                     //$3:temp variable address, $4:output size
  name: "data"                     //$6:mat1 address, $7:mat1 size, $8:mat2 address,
  top: "data"                      //$9:mat2 size, $10:output matrix address
  input_param: {                   //$11,$12:loop counter
    shape: {
      dim: 512              LI      $5,    0x0E0E_0301 //H=14,W=14,k=3,s=1
      dim: 14               LI      $VLR,0x10          //set vector length(16)
      dim: 14}              LI      $6,   0x30000
    }                       LI      $8,   0x50000
}                           LI      $10, 0x70000
                            LI      $11,0x1E            //set c loop counter(30)
layers {                    LI      $12,0x20            //set kernel loop counter(32)
  bottom: "data"      L0: MLOAD   $1, $6, $7           //load tiled weights
  top: "conv1"            MLOAD   $2, $8, $9           //load tiled activations
  name: "conv1"           MMM     $3, $2, $1, $5       //mat1 x mat2
  type: CONVOLUTION       ADD     $8, $8, $9           // update address
  convolution_param {  L1: MLOAD   $2, $8, $9           //load new activations
    num_output: 512        MMMS    $3, $2, $1, $5       //mat2 x mat2 & accumulate
    pad: 1                 ADD     $8, $8, $9           //update mat2 address
    kernel_size: 3}        SUB     $11, $11, #1         // cnt--
}                          BGE     $11, #0,  L1         // if(loop counter>0) goto label1
                           MLOAD   $2, $8, $9           //load new activations
layers {                   MMSA    $3, $2, $1, $5       //mat2 x mat2 & accumulate&relu
  bottom: "conv1"          MSTORE  $3, $10, $4          //store  results to address($10)
  top: "conv2"             SUB     $12,$12, #1          // cnt--
  name: "relu1"            ADD     $6,  $6,  $7         //update mat1 address
  type: RELU               ADD     $10, $10, $4         //update output address
}                          BGE     $12, #0, L0          // if(loop counter>0) goto label0
```

FIGURE 12.12
Example of convolutional layer code for RV-CNN implementation.

layer is similar to that of the convolutional layer, with only slight differences in the configuration parameters, so we do not enumerate them.

The convolutional layer code for the RV-CNN implementation is shown in Figure 12.12, where on the left side is the convolutional layer code written in the Caffe framework (for illustrative purposes), which completes the process of feature extraction using 512 sets of convolutional kernels of size 3×3 with a step size of 1 on the input feature map ($14\times14\times512$). On the right side of the figure is a schematic code that performs the same function using dedicated instructions, assuming sufficient hardware on-chip resources and proper data ordering.

Since the instruction takes parameter information from the registers, we first need to load the necessary information into the registers. Here we first load the immediate 0x0E0E0301 to $5 registers. According to the description of the instruction format in the previous section, the four bytes of this 32-bit data from high to low represent the height (14), the width (14), the convolution kernel size (3), and the step size (1) of the input data, respectively. Afterward, the vector register VLR is set to 16, which represents the length of the vector to be processed at a time is 16. Due to the slicing technique, the loop counters

$11 and $12 are set here to complete the traversal of the depth direction and different convolutional kernels. Subsequently, the actual address of the data in the off-chip DDR is loaded by loading it in registers $6, $8, and $10 to complete the data transfer through MLOAD/MSTORE. The information in the above registers should be generated by the instruction generator or by the user based on the network model as well as the hardware parameter information. Based on this, the actual calculation process begins. Firstly, the data is loaded from off-chip 0×30000 and 0×50000 to the on-chip destination address specified by $1 and $2, respectively. After the data is loaded, the calculation is completed by executing the MMM instruction. The intermediate results of the computation are saved in the on-chip sticky note memory. Subsequent computations are completed by using the MMMS instruction to accumulate the computation with the on-chip intermediate results to reduce unnecessary off-chip accesses. Finally, the activation of some of the final results is completed by executing the MMMSA instruction and the results are transferred off-chip by the MSTORE instruction.

The pooling layer code for the RV-CNN implementation is shown in Figure 12.13. On the left-hand side, the pooling layer code written in the Caffe framework is still used to illustrate the functionality, which indicates that for the input feature map (14×14×512), the maximum value is sampled using a pooling window of 2×2 with a step size of two. On the right side of the figure, the same functionality is illustrated using dedicated instructions, which still assume sufficient on-chip hardware resources and proper data ordering.

Since the pooling layer does not contain weight data and does not accumulate in the depth direction, the code for its RV-CNN implementation is more concise than that of the convolutional layer code when the input image size is appropriate. After loading the parameters into the corresponding registers, the data to be processed is loaded from off-chip 0×10000 ($6) to the on-chip

```
                                      //$1:input mat address, $2:feature map size
                                      //$3:loop counter, $5:temp variable address
layers {                              //$6:mat address, $7:output mat address, $8:output size
  name: "pool"
  type: POOLING              LI       $4,    0x0E0E_0202  //H=14,W=14,k=2,s=2
  bottom: "data"             LI       $VLR,0x10          //set vector length(16)
  top: "pool"                LI       $3,    0x20         //set loop counter(32)
  pooling_param {            LI       $6,    0x10000
    pool: MAX                LI       $7,    0x40000
    kernel_size: 2       L0: MLOAD    $1,    $6,  $2      //load partial activations
    stride: 2               MXPOOL    $5,    $1,  $2, $4  //subsample
  }                         MSTORE    $5,    $7,  $8      //store mat to address($7)
}                           ADD       $7,    $7,  $8      //update address
                            ADD       $6,    $6,  $2      //update address
                            SUB       $3,    $3,  #1      // cnt --
                            BGE       $3,    #0,  L0      // if(loop counter>0) goto label0
```

FIGURE 12.13
Example of pooling layer code for RV-CNN implementation.

destination address $1 using the MLOAD instruction. After the input data is loaded, the MXPOOL instruction is used to downsample and store the result at the on-chip temporary address of $5. When the sampling is finished, the result is transferred to the off-chip address 0x40000 ($7) by MSTORE, and the outputs are not accumulated on-chip during this process. The cyclic counter in the code is designed to traverse the input data in the depth direction, with a single load, pool, and load-out completing the sampling of one slice of data, followed by updating the load and load-out addresses and the counter value.

12.2.4.2 Overall Structure

There can be various ways of choosing the hardware logic and the processor core for adding different instructions to the CPU, we list here the tightly coupled and loosely coupled approaches as shown in Figure 12.14. Designing SIMD instruction vectors to take a tightly coupled approach usually requires the addition of vector register pages in the processor core, and vector functional components, whose load/store components are shared with scalars. Thus the tightly coupled approach, the acceleration unit communicates directly with the processor core but has an impact on the timing of the processor core. In contrast, taking a loosely coupled approach, the acceleration unit typically uses SPM instead of Cache and integrates DMA in it to fetch data from the DDR, with synchronization and management between the data controlled by the user-programmed display. The benefits of using SPMs are variable-length data accesses lower power consumption and simpler control than Cache, but SPMs specific to the acceleration unit still add area overhead.

By analyzing the above two approaches, we designed an approach between tight and loose coupling, that is, the matrix unit has its SPM and integrates DMA for fast off-chip accesses, and its configuration information is still controlled by the CPU core, but it is not through the bus but directly embedded in the pipeline architecture. Figure 12.15 shows the main functional components of a RISC-V processor core containing the RV-CNN extension and a simplified pipeline architecture. It can be seen that it contains the five basic pipeline stages: fetch, decode, execute, access, and write back. The matrix computation unit is in the execution phase of the pipeline and is used to complete the execution of matrix instructions. After the finger fetching and

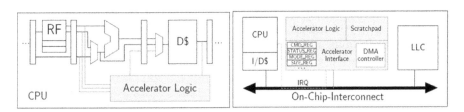

FIGURE 12.14
Tightly and loosely coupled approaches to acceleration logic and CPU cores.

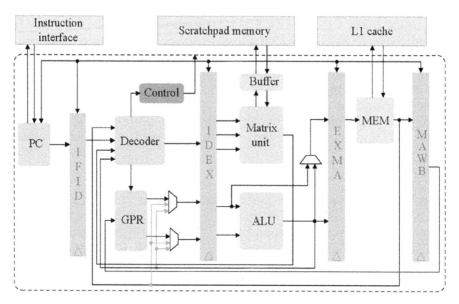

FIGURE 12.15
Simplified block diagram of a processor core containing RV-CNN extensions.

decoding stage, the instructions in the base instruction set will enter the ALU and then proceed to the next stage. When the decoding stage resolves that the current instruction is a matrix instruction, the decoder obtains the corresponding information from the registers and saves it to be fed into the matrix unit in the next cycle. The matrix unit determines whether or not to execute based on the received instruction information and detects the status of the corresponding functional components. Since the address space of the on-chip sticky note registers is visible to the user, the matrix unit can interact with the memory through the matrix data transfer instructions; therefore, the matrix instructions do not go through the two stages of access and write back after entering the matrix unit, while the rest of the instructions do not pass through the matrix unit, and their access is still through the cache (cache). This avoids unnecessary data dependency detection and automatic data swapping in and out by the hardware. In addition, since the matrix unit contains a large number of computation units, it has its internal pipeline structure, and the decoder decides whether or not to stop the pipeline based on whether or not the matrix unit can accept matrix instruction information. Given the continuous and large number of data accesses of matrix instructions, we integrate a DMA controller outside the sticky note memory to meet the data access requirements of the matrix unit. It is important to note that the data involved in the completion of computation and logic-type instructions by the matrix unit needs to be already present on the chip, which requires tight control by the program.

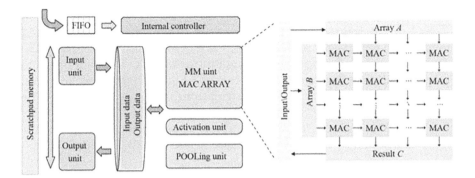

FIGURE 12.16
Schematic diagram of the structure of the matrix unit.

12.2.4.3 Matrix Unit Design

The overall structure of the matrix unit is shown in Figure 12.16, which contains mainly an input–output unit, a matrix multiplication unit, an activation unit, a pooling unit, and an internal controller, where the orange and gray arrows denote the control flow and the data flow, respectively. The matrix unit receives incoming instruction information as well as register information and stores it in a queue. The internal controller (as a finite state machine) is the control center of the matrix unit, which based on the control information will wake up the subcomponents (if available) to complete the corresponding tasks. Otherwise, it will generate a feedback signal to indicate that the corresponding functional unit is busy. The buffer module is essentially an on-chip memory from which the computational cores in the matrix unit fetch data and write the resulting results. The computational units correspond roughly one-to-one to the coarse-grained instructions, except for fusion instructions, which start multiple computational cores at the same time. Finally, the input–output module is responsible for transferring data between the matrix unit and the on-chip sticky note memory based on valid addresses.

Since the matrix multiplication unit is shared by the convolutional and fully connected layers and it carries out most of the computation, the implementation of this unit is crucial for performance. Here we have used a matrix multiplication implemented in a pulsating matrix structure, which is shown in the right part of Figure 12.16. Pulsating arrays are an efficient and simple implementation of matrix multiplication, where the MAC units are bound together by a two-dimensional grid, and the computational units take inputs from their neighbors, except for the computational units in the outermost layers of the array (in this case, the leftmost and uppermost), which are directly connected to the on-chip buffers to obtain data. This approach will significantly reduce the fan-in and fan-out of on-chip buffers as the MAC array becomes larger. Also, the fact that data is passed fluidly between MAC units increases data reuse. For example, when the MAC array is 12 x 16, the elements in matrix B are passed through the array by rows from left to right at different moments, and the data is reused 16 times at the time of output; similarly, the elements in matrix A are passed through the array by columns from top to bottom at different moments and are reused 12 times at the time of output. In this process, together with pipelining optimization, only 28 inputs to the array are required per cycle for 192 MAC operations. In addition, the short local interconnections reduce the difficulty of layout wiring, so here we have chosen to use pulsed arrays as an implementation of matrix multiplication.

12.2.4.4 Optimization Details

1. Instruction-level parallelism
   Although the extended instructions we design here are coarse-grained instructions that primarily explore data-level parallelism, inter-instruction parallelism is still necessary. Since matrix instructions often take thousands of cycles to complete, we here perform idle, busy, and conflict detection on subcomponents to parallelize computation and access to achieve the effect shown in Figure 12.17.
2. Quantification of data
   CNNs are inherently robust to limited numerical precision, and the use of floating-point computation in the prediction phase is not necessary. Instead, low bit-width representations of weights and activations help avoid expensive floating-point computations while significantly reducing bandwidth requirements and memory footprint. The loss of accuracy due to the use of fixed-point numbers for prediction is negligible (less than 1%) using retraining and specific fine-tuning. Therefore, the data types of the matrix cells are all of the INT16 data type.

12.2.4.5 Experimental Evaluation

To verify the effectiveness of the proposed dedicated instructions, we have constructed a processor core based on RISC-V architecture containing the extension of this instruction set on an FPGA platform. Its resource consumption is shown in Table 12.3.

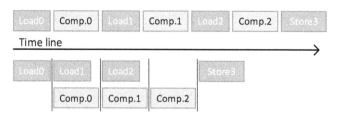

FIGURE 12.17
Execute, calculate instruction execution overlap.

TABLE 12.3

Hardware Resource Utilization for Deployments on the Xilinx ZC702
Platform

Resource	DSP	BRAM	LUT	FF	Power (W)
Total amount	220	280	53,200	106,400	
Used	200	181	26,177	30,665	
Utilization	91%	65%	49%	29%	2.12

It can be seen that this resource consumption is much larger than that consumed by a typical RISC-V base core, and since we are mainly concerned here
with the acceleration effect of the extended instructions on CNNs, the main
resource consumption is in the matrix unit. The Vivado power consumption
is reported to be 2.12 W. Based on this, the simulation is carried out by writing assembly instructions and using two different sizes of convolutional neural networks, AlexNet and VGG16. Simulations are performed for evaluation.
The peak performance of this prototype system can reach 10.27GOPS/w and
16.96GOPS/w, respectively, which is a significant energy-efficiency improvement over general-purpose CPUs.

12.3 Chapter Summary

The simplicity, efficiency, and open-source nature of the RISC-V architecture have attracted a lot of attention from industry and academia. Due to the
open-source nature of RISC-V, the design of low-power as well as high-performance chips will no longer be subject to high licensing fees. Therefore, the
industry is mainly oriented toward embedded chip architecture design, IoT AI
chips and development execution environments to get rid of the constraints of
ARM and Intel chip licensing fees and designs. Among them, embedded chip
design mainly includes microprocessor, SoC, and ASIC architecture design,
and IoT chip is mainly oriented to low-power, wearable end-measurement, and
other fields. The development execution environment mainly includes processor tracking technology, simulators, software toolchain, and trusted execution
environment. Academic research is even more extensive, involving work on
RISC-V-based optimization of general-purpose processor cores for low power
and high performance or work on extended instruction design for specific
scenarios or specific applications, and so on. By analyzing the work related
to RISC-V-based accelerator customization schemes, this section describes the
idea of extended instruction design and designs a coarse-grained instruction
set based on it, taking the current popular CNN application acceleration as
an example. The instruction set aims to accelerate convolutional operations in

CNN using data-level parallelism, so the acceleration unit is loosely coupled to the processor. Through prototyping on FPGAs, a good energy-efficiency ratio is achieved compared to general-purpose processors.

References

1. The RISC-V Instruction Set Manual, Volume I: User-Level ISA, Document Version 20191213", Editors A. Waterman and K. Asanovi´c, RISC-V Foundation, December 2019.
2. Asanović, K., Avižienis, R., Bachrach, J., Beamer, S., Biancolin, D., Celio, C., Cook, H., Dabbelt, P., Hauser, J., Izraelevitz, A., Karandikar, S., Keller, B., Kim, D., Koenig, J., Lee, Y., Love, E., Maas, M., Magyar, A., Mao, H., Moreto, M., Ou, A., Patterson, D., Richards, B., Schmidt, C., Twigg, S., Vo, H., Waterman, A. *The Rocket Chip Generator*, Technical Report UCB /EECS-2016-17, EECS Department, University of California, Berkeley, April 2016.
3. Zhao J., Korpan B., Gonzalez A., et al. Sonicboom: The 3rd generation berkeley out-of-order machine. *Fourth Workshop on Computer Architecture Research with RISC-V*. 2020, 5.
4. Lee Y., Schmidt C., Ou A., et al. The Hwacha vector-fetch architecture manual, version 3.8. 1. EECS Department, University of California, Berkeley, Tech. rep. ucb/eecs-2015-262, 2015.
5. Lee Y., Ou A., Magyar A. Z-scale: Tiny 32-bit RISC-V systems. *2nd RISC-V Workshop*, Denver, CO. 2015.
6. Ucb-Bar (2023a) UCB-Bar/RISCV-sodor: Educational microarchitectures for RISC-V ISA, GitHub. Available at: https://github.com/ucb-bar/riscv- sodor (Accessed: 14 August 2023).
7. Bao Y. G., Wang S. Labeled von Neumann architecture for software-defined cloud. *Journal of Computer Science and Technology*, 2017, 32: 219–223.
8. Traber A., Zaruba F., Stucki S., et al. PULPino: A small single-core RISC-V SoC. *3rd RISCV Workshop*, Redwood Shores, CA. 2016.
9. Ucam-Comparch. Ucam-comparch/clarvi: Clarvi simple RISC-V processor for teaching, GitHub. 2017. Available at: https://github.com/ucam-comparch / clarvi.
10. f32c. F32C/F32c: A 32-bit RISC-V / MIPS ISA retargetable CPU Core & SOC, 1.62 DMIPS/MHz, GitHub. 2023. Available at: https://github.com/f32c/ f32c (Accessed: 14 August 2023).
11. Kurth A., Vogel P., Capotondi A., et al. HERO: Heterogeneous embedded research platform for exploring RISC-V manycore accelerators on FPGA. arXiv preprint arXiv:1712.06497, 2017.
12. Flamand E., Rossi D., Conti F., et al. GAP-8: A RISC-V SoC for AI at the Edge of the IoT. *2018 IEEE 29th International Conference on Application-specific Systems, Architectures and Processors (ASAP)*, Milan. IEEE, 2018: 1–4.
13. Shi R., Liu J., So H. K. H., et al. E-LSTM: Efficient inference of sparse LSTM on embedded heterogeneous system. *Proceedings of the 56th Annual Design Automation Conference 2019*, Las Vegas, NV. 2019: 1–6.

14. Papaphilippou P., Kelly Paul H. J., Luk W. Simodense: A RISC-V softcore optimised for exploring custom SIMD instructions. *2021 31st International Conference on Field-Programmable Logic and Applications (FPL)*, Virtual, Dresden. IEEE, 2021: 391–397.
15. Cong J., Ghodrat M. A., Gill M., et al. Accelerator-rich architectures: Opportunities and progresses. *Proceedings of the 51st Annual Design Automation Conference*, San Francisco, CA. 2014: 1–6.
16. Lou W., Wang C., Gong L., et al. RV-CNN: Flexible and efficient instruction set for CNNs based on RISC-V processors. *Advanced Parallel Processing Technologies: 13th International Symposium, APPT 2019*, Tianjin, China, August 15-16, 2019, Proceedings 13. Springer International Publishing, 2019: 3–14.
17. Liu S., Du Z., Tao J., et al. Cambricon: An instruction set architecture for neural networks. *ACM SIGARCH Computer Architecture News*, 2016, 44(3): 393–405.

13

Compilation Optimization Methods in the Customization of Reconfigurable Accelerators

13.1 High-Level Integrated Tools and Hardware Customization

The demand for computing power has been growing over the past few decades. However, the technological developments that drove Moore's Law have slowed significantly [1]. However, the technology that drives Moore's Law has been slowing down significantly, and the "power wall" caused by heat dissipation has been limiting the growth of parallel computing. Another important limiting factor is the "memory wall" due to the speed at which memory performance scales [2]. This is because memory performance scales more slowly than processor performance. The communication between the computing units and the memory system becomes a performance bottleneck in many application areas. As a result, domain-specific customization is increasingly being adopted due to its highly customizable microarchitecture and the high power efficiency and memory utilization that comes with customization. Due to their reconfigurability, field programmable gate arrays (FPGAs) have played a vital role in rapidly adopting customizable accelerators in data centers [3–5]. At the same time, recent advances and the adoption of C-based high-level synthesis (HLS) technology [6–9] have greatly improved the development efficiency of FPGA accelerators, bringing "hard-to-program" FPGA accelerators to a broader community.

However, creating efficient accelerators is still not an easy task for programmers. Current C-based HLSs are highly dependent on compiler directives ("pragmas") inserted by the programmer to achieve good quality of results (QoR). Using these compiler directives requires background knowledge of the underlying microarchitecture, which can take a long time for every application domain expert. To make matters worse, even for experienced FPGA programmers, C-based HLS is typically less productive than high-level software languages, especially for applications requiring design space exploration and optimization beyond the memory constraints provided by the compiler directives.

DOI: 10.1201/9780429355080-13

This chapter will first introduce the background of FPGA accelerator design based on HLS and then submit the direction of exploration for FPGA accelerator design and optimization based on HLS compilation and optimization techniques from four aspects: source code to register-transfer-level (RTL) optimization, source code to source code optimization, domain customization language, and intermediate expression to accelerator template mapping.

13.2 Source Code to RTL Optimization

13.2.1 High-Level Synthesis (HLS) Principles

An FPGA is an integrated circuit that contains reprogrammable building blocks. Typically, such building blocks include look-up tables, flip-flops, digital signal processors (DSPs), and block random access memories. The functionality of each module, as well as their interconnections, is reprogrammable so that individual circuits can be customized into accelerators for different applications. This hardware reconfiguration gives complete control over computation and data paths without the overhead of general-purpose instructions, thus reducing the "power wall" and "memory wall" of widely used cores.

However, a significant drawback of FPGA accelerators, poor programmability, has prevented their widespread adoption for decades. The conventional programming abstraction for FPGA devices is the RTL description, which requires the programmer to design and optimize the program's functionality and forces the programmer to manually disaggregate and schedule the functionality into several pipeline stages. In contrast, software programmers only need to specify the program's behavior, with few details of hardware abstraction, making software programs' development and iteration cycles significantly shorter than those of hardware accelerators. As a result, FPGA researchers and vendors have adopted HLS technology over the past decade [8], eliminating the need for programmers to plan and optimize circuit design timing manually. A typical HLS compilation flow is shown in Figure 13.1. First, the user input program is compiled into an Low Level Virtual Machine (LLVM) intermediate representation (IR), and its control data flow graph is constructed. Then, IR to HDL (hardware description language) code conversion is performed to map the IR to an RTL design with scheduling optimizations. This completes the HLS process of mapping the behavioral description

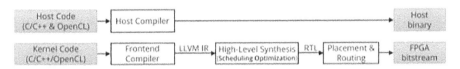

FIGURE 13.1
Typical HLS compilation flow.

of the design to its RTL description. Subsequently, a traditional FPGA design automation flow is initiated to generate a bitstream file of the invention containing configuration data for the FPGA logic and RAM blocks. Reports containing resource consumption and performance estimates are typically generated along with the RTL code to guide QoR evaluation and optimization.

Programmers using HLS can achieve faster development cycles (Figure 13.2b) compared to the traditional RTL paradigm (Figure 13.2a), where programmers often spend tens of minutes verifying the correctness of code changes. Programmers can write code in C and use fast software simulation to verify the correctness of the functionality. Such a correctness verification cycle may take as little as 1 second, allowing for rapid iteration of functionality. Once the HLS code is functionally correct, the programmer can generate RTL code, evaluate the QoR based on the developed performance and resource reports, and modify the HLS code accordingly. Such a QoR tuning cycle typically takes only a few minutes. Thanks to the HLS scheduling algorithm [9–13], timing optimization [7,14,15], and recent clock frequency [7] advances, HLS can not only shorten the development cycle but also generate programs that are often competitive in terms of cycle counts [16]. In addition, FPGA vendors provide HLS [17,18] cores designed in HLS with host drivers and communication interfaces, further easing the programmer's burden of integrating and offloading workloads to FPGA accelerators.

Over the years, more than 30 HLS tools have been implemented [19], as shown in Table 13.1. However, some of them are no longer in use for various reasons (e.g., abandoned by the community or purchased by commercial companies).

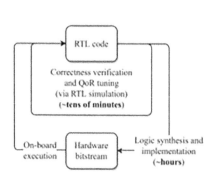

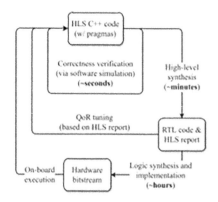

(a) FPGA accelerator development flow without HLS. Programmers often spend tens of minutes after code modification to evaluate the correctness and quality of result.

(b) FPGA accelerator development flow with HLS. Programmers spend seconds after code modification to verify the correctness. Quality of result can usually be obtained in less than 10 minutes from the HLS report.

FIGURE 13.2
Deployment flow of an FPGA accelerator (a) without and (b) with HLS.

TABLE 13.1

Existing HLS tools

License	Application Domain	Compiler	Owner	Input	Output	Year	Test Bench	FP	FixP
Commercial	All	VivadoHLS	Xilinx	C/C++/SystemC	VHDL/Verilog/SystemC	2013	Yes	Yes	Yes
		FPGA SDK for OpenCL	Intel	C	VHDL/Verilog/System-Verilog	2013	Yes	Yes	Yes
		LegUp	LegUp Computing Inc.	C	Verilog	2015	Yes	Yes	No
		Cyber Work Bench	NEC	BDL	VHDL/Verilog	2011	Cycle/Formal	Yes	Yes
		eXCite	Y Explorations	C	VHDL/Verilog	2001	Yes	No	Yes
		Catapult-C	Calypto Design Systems	C/C++/SystemC	VHDL/Verilog/SystemC	2004	Yes	No	Yes
		Stratus	Cadence	C/C++/SystemC	Verilog	2004	Yes	Yes	Yes
	DataFlow	BluSpec	BluSpec Inc.	BSV	System-Verilog	2007	No	No	No
		MaxCompiler	Maxeler	MaxJ	RTL	2010	No	Yes	No
	DSP	Symphony	Synopsys	C/C++/SystemC	VHDL/Verilog/SystemC	2010	Yes	No	Yes
Academic	Streaming	DK Design Suite	Mentor Graphics	Handle-C	VHDL/Verilog	2009	No	No	No
	DSP	GAUT	U.Bretagne	C/C++	VHDL	2008	Yes	No	Yes
	Streaming	ROCCC	UC.Riverside	C subset	VHDL	2010	No	Yes	No
	ALL	LegUp	U.Toronto	C	Verilog	2011	Yes	Yes	No
		Bambu	PoliMi	C	Verilog	2012	Yes	Yes	No
		DWARV	TU.Delft	C subset	VHDL	2012	Yes	Yes	Yes

LegUp [20], first released at the University of Toronto in 2011, has been updated to the latest version, 4.0, which is dedicated to the Altera FPGA family and supports Pthreads and OpenMP to synthesize software threads into hardware modules operating in parallel automatically. LegUp supports most C syntax except memory allocation and recursion. Based on bitmask analysis and variable scope at static compile time, LegUp can automatically narrow data path widths to reduce bit width and support register removal and multi-cycle path analysis. Register removal eliminates registers in multiple cycles on specific paths, generating constraints conforming to the tool flow's back end.

GAUT [21] is an open-source HLS tool for DSP applications. The potential parallelism of the application is first extracted before scheduling, assigning, and binding tasks. A possible pipeline architecture is generated, including processing and memory modules and communication units with GALS/LIS interfaces. Throughput and clock cycles are mandatory during synthesis, and I/O timing maps and memory mapping are optional.

AutoESL originally developed Vivado HLS under the name AutoPilot [8]. Xilinx acquired AutoPilot in 2011 and released the first LLVM-based Vivado HLS in 2013. Vivado HLS inputs C, C++, and System-C and generates HDL descriptions in Verilog, Very-High-Speed Integrated Circuit Hardware Description Language (VHDL), and System-C. The generation process can be fine-tuned through the integrated design environment and the rich set of features provided by Vivado HLS. Vivado HLS proposes various optimization options, such as loop pipelining, loop unrolling, operation linking, and memory mapping, and supports streaming and shared memory type interfaces to simplify integration between accelerators.

Altera originally released the FPGA SDK for OpenCL. It provides a heterogeneous parallel programming environment based on the enhanced OpenCL standard [22]. In October 2018, Intel released the Intel FPGA SDK for OpenCL™ Pro Edition 3. The FPGA SDK for OpenCL divides the application into two main parts: the host program that manages the application and the FPGA accelerator, and FPGA programming bitstream [23]. During compilation, the OpenCL compiler compiles the OpenCL kernel into an image file that the host application uses to program the FPGA. The host-side C compiler compiles the host program and links it to the Intel FPGA SDK for the OpenCL runtime library. If the automatic unfolding result is unsatisfactory, the FPGA compiler automatically unfolds the loop or manually with instructions.

Catapult-C is a commercially available HLS tool that provides the flexibility to select target technologies and libraries, set cycle frequencies, and map function parameters to stream interfaces, registers, RAM, or ROM. Now, it focuses on low-power FPGA solutions.

Max Compiler is a dataflow-oriented tool that accepts the Java-based language MaxJ as input. It generates synthesizable HDL descriptions for dataflow engines running on the Maxeler hardware platform. Max Compiler divides the application into the kernel, the manager configuration, and the

CPU application. The first component is responsible for the computational part of the application on the FPGA. The second component connects the kernel to the CPU, engine RAM, other cores, and other dataflow engines through MaxRing. The last part communicates with the data flow engine to transfer data to the kernel and engine RAM.

The DK Design Suite uses Handel-C as an input language. Handel-C is a subset of C and extends hardware-specific constructs. However, designers must specify timing specifications and code concurrent and synchronous components. In addition, users must manually map data to different storage elements. Therefore, due to these additional features, designers need advanced hardware knowledge.

Riverside Optimizing Compiler for Configurable Computing (ROCCC) focuses on parallelizing applications with high computational density and little control. This limits its application to streaming applications. And only a subset of C is accepted as a design language. For example, only integer array operations and perfectly nested loops with fixed step sizes are allowed.

13.2.2 Summary

In programming general-purpose processors (e.g., CPUs and GPUs), high-level languages gradually replace assembly language as software grows in size and complexity. Using this as a reference, the FPGA community sees HLS as a promising approach to solving FPGA design problems. However, research challenges remain.

First, high-level languages are designed for process descriptions of processors with instruction systems, whereas FPGA design is a description of circuit structures. This means designers still need to understand the rules of hardware design and learn how to describe hardware structures in high-level languages. Most designers start by learning high-level languages for process description, and their habits of mind are hard to change.

Second, unlike compilers for regular processors, HLS compilers cannot completely take over the optimization of a design. Most HLS tools provide the user with instructions to manually guide the optimization process, which makes it time-consuming and highly dependent on the designer's hardware experience. To make matters worse, the designer must refactor the program to match the rescheduling rules, which helps the synthesizer perform better during feature extraction. Due to the lack of rule files, the program refactoring again translates into a DSE problem.

According to our survey of the literature, the HLS community has contributed a lot to the performance optimization of HLS tools, e.g., making design space exploration faster and more automated, building libraries to improve code reuse, increasing the efficiency of verification and debugging, exploring better parallel methods, and providing predefined programming templates.

Based on the research on HLS and FPGA design, there is still some work to be done on HLS tools for future optimization.

First, the performance optimization of HLS tools should not only focus on the performance of the generated circuits, such as area, latency, throughput, and so on, but also take into account the ease of use of the HLS tools, e.g., automated code generation, automatic test frame generation, and more intuitive debugging. After all, programming takes up most of the HLS design.

Second, to reduce the required hardware knowledge designers, it is best to analogize the HLS design process with the embedded system design process. Embedded system design tools typically integrate hardware operations into open-source application programming interface (API) packages. Designers specify functionality through the API without regard to the hardware architecture so that they can focus on algorithms. For fine-grained operations, designers can manipulate the hardware directly through instructions or modify the library's source code to match functionality and performance requirements. A similar idea is available in the next generation of HLS tools. The API package is available through open-source libraries. Designers with less hardware knowledge can complete FPGA designs at a lower time cost. The API should be implemented in an RTL language to ensure performance. If performance optimization is required, designers can perform the underlying operations and resource management through the open source of the library. This will provide more resilient HLS tools.

Finally, FPGA virtual machines can offer a unified programming model. A virtual machine should be a higher-level abstraction of the FPGA processing power, consisting of customizable parallelized or pipelined processing units. With a virtual machine, designers focus on a unified programming model and implement algorithms from a parallel or heterogeneous computing perspective. FPGA template mapping is considered a type of FPGA virtual machine. However, the level of abstraction is not enough. The kernel must still be pre-designed by the designer.

13.3 Source Code to Source Code Optimization

13.3.1 Merlin Compiler

To alleviate heavy code refactoring efforts when improving HLSC programs, the Merlin compiler [24] is an FPGA-accelerated source-to-source conversion tool based on the CMOST compilation flow [25]. The Merlin compiler provides a set of pragmas with the prefix "#pragma ACCEL" to represent optimizations from an architectural design perspective. Based on the user-specified Merlin pragma, the compiler applies the corresponding architecture constructs to the program by invoking Abstract Syntax Tree (AST) analysis, vendor pragma insertion, and source-to-source conversion.

Figure 13.3 illustrates the execution flow of the Merlin compiler. It utilizes the ROSE compiler infrastructure [26] and the polyhedral framework [27]

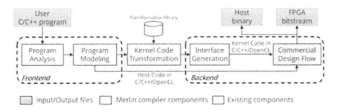

FIGURE 13.3
Merlin compiler execution flow.

to perform AST analysis and transformation. The front-end phase analyses the user program and separates the host and computational kernels. Then, the kernel code transformation phase applies multiple code transformations based on user-specified pragmas. The Merlin compiler performs all the necessary code refactoring to validate the changes. For example, when completing loop unrolling, the Merlin compiler unrolls the loop and performs memory partitioning to avoid repository conflicts [28]. The Merlin compiler performs loop unrolling and memory partitioning to avoid library conflicts. Finally, the backend stage takes the converted kernel and generates the FPGA bitstream using the HLS tool.

While the Merlin pragma eliminates manual code refactoring, designers must still manually search for the best options for each pragma, including location, type, and factors. This is only a custom design implemented for the source application itself. There is no deeper optimization design for application parallelism, data parallelism dimensions, or upper-level scheduling, and no further work on compute compatibility.

13.3.2 Polyhedral Models

13.3.2.1 Concepts

The polyhedral model is the mathematical framework for loop nesting optimization. Loop nesting that satisfies the requirements of the polyhedral model is called static control section (SCoP) [29]. The SCoP is defined as a set of statements with loop boundaries and conditions, affine functions that act as closed loop iterators, and variables that remain unchanged during the execution of the SCoP. Programs in the polyhedral model are typically represented by four parts: entities/states, iteration domains, access relations, and scheduling.

1. *Statement/Instance*: It represents a line of code. And the code in the loop will correspond to an *instance* every time it is executed.
2. *Domain*: The loop corresponding to each instance can be represented as a vector of length N for an N-weighted loop. The set of all possible *vectors* is *Domain*.

3. *Dependency*: There will be data dependencies (read–write dependencies, write–write dependencies, and write–read dependencies) between statements of a program, expressed as an inequality of affine transformations.

4. *Schedule*: Statement S defines a schedule (order) which is represented by a mapping, that is, {S[i, j] → [i, j]}, indicating that statement S[i, j] iterates first in the order of i and then in the order of j.

These concepts are illustrated below using a running example of matrix multiplication (MM). Figure 13.4 shows the sample code. The iteration domain contains loop instances of the statements in the program. The iteration domain of the statement S0 in the example program has the form {S0[i, j, k]: $0 \le i < M \wedge 0 \le j < N \wedge 0 \le k < K$}—the access relation maps statement instances to array indexes. For example, the access relation for read access in statement S0 has the form {S0[i, j, k] → A[i, k]; S0[i, j. k] → [k, j]; S0[i, j, k] → C[i, j]}. Finally, the schedule maps the set of instances to multidimensional times.

The statement instances are executed in the order of the dictionary of multidimensional times. For example, the timetable of statement S0 has the form {S1[i, j,k] → [i, j, k]}. The timeframe of a SCoP program can be represented as a scheduling tree [30]. Figure 13.5 shows the scheduling tree for the example program. The scheduling tree starts with a domain node that defines the iterative domain of the program, followed by a band node that encodes the partial scheduling at each loop dimension. The ISL library manipulates the scheduling tree of the program to perform the loop transformations. An AST is obtained from the scheduling tree to generate the final code and then reduced to the target code (e.g., C).

13.3.2.2 Polyhedron Optimization

Once the program (source code) is converted into a polyhedral model, mathematical analysis can optimize the code. Throughout polyhedral optimization,

```
for (int i = 0; i < M; ++i)
    for (int j = 0; j < N; ++j)
        for (int k = 0; k < K; ++k)
S0:            C[i][j] += A[i][k] * B[k][j];
```

FIGURE 13.4
MM sample code.

$$\textbf{DOMAIN}: \{S0[i,j,k]: 0 \le i < M \wedge 0 \le j < N \wedge 0 \le k < K\}$$
$$\textbf{BAND}: \{S0[i,j,k] \to [i,j,k]\}$$

FIGURE 13.5
Initial scheduling of MM in the form of a scheduling tree.

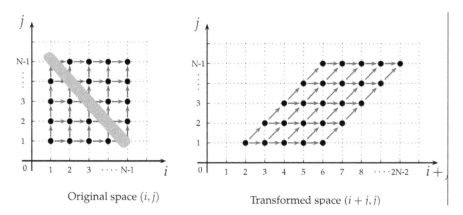

Original space (i, j) Transformed space $(i + j, i)$

FIGURE 13.6
Example program and its corresponding domains and dependencies.

a variety of research has been aimed at using this data to improve code performance.

For example, the code in Figure 13.6 can be easily extracted by visually drawing its Domain and Dependency because it is two-dimensional (two-fold loop).

The domain is one of the black dots on the top of the left diagram, and the arrows between the black dots indicate the dependencies. We can see that the five nodes covered by the green line in the chart have no dependencies on each other and are, therefore, parallel (exactly any node that lies on the same 45° line has no dependencies). If we're using OpenMP, however, we can only parallelize two loops, that is, one row or column of nodes. Diagonal lines cannot be parallelized.

The polyhedral model's representation of programs is all done with sets and mappings. We get the form shown on the left when we represent the dependencies between statement instances in the iteration space with blue arrows. According to the Fundamental Theorem of Dependency, statement instances without dependencies can be executed in parallel with each other, and there are no dependencies between all the points within the green band (on the diagonal) in the figure so that these points can be executed in parallel with each other. But we find that the base of this two-dimensional space is (i, j), that is, it corresponds to two layers of loops i and j. It is impossible to mark circles that can be parallelized because this green band is not parallel to any of the axes. So the polyhedral model transforms the base (i, j) using affine transformations so that the green bar can be similar to one of the axes of the bottom of the space so that the loops corresponding to the axes can be parallel so that we can transform the area shown on the left into the form displayed on the right.

At this point, the scheduling of statement S can be expressed in the form of $\{S[i, j] \rightarrow [i + j, j]\}$. So, the transformation process of the polyhedral model is

Left table

SOURCE CODE	PARTITION	TRANSFORMERS CODE

`for(i=0; i<=N; i++)`
`  Y[N-i] = Z[i];   /*s1*/`
`for(j=0; j<=N; j++)`
`  X[j] = Y[j];   /*s2*/`
	Reversal
	$s_1: p = N - i$
	$(s_2: p = j)$
		`for(p=0; p<=N; p++) {`
		`  Y[p] = Z[N-p];`
		`  X[p] = Y[p];`
		`}`

`for(i=1; i<=N; i++)`
`  for(j=0; j<=M; j++)`
`    Z[i, j] = Z[i-1, j];`
	Permutation
	=
		`for(p=0; p<=M; p++)`
		`  for(q=1; q<=N; q++)`
		`    Z[q, p] = Z[q-1, p];`

`for(i=1; i<=N+M-1; i++)`
`  for(j=max(1, i+N);`
`      j<=min(i, M); j++)`
`    Z[i, j] = Z[i-1, j-1];`
	Skewing
	=
	+
		`for(p=1; p<=N; p++)`
		`  for(q=1; 1<=M; q++)`
		`    Z[p, q-p] = Z[p-1, q-p-1];`

Right table

SOURCE CODE	PARTITION	TRANSFORMERS CODE

`for(i=1; i<=N; i++)`
`  Y[i] = Z[i];   /*s1*/`
`for(j=1; j<=N; j++)`
`  X[j] = Y[j];   /*s2*/`
	Fusion
	$s_1: p = i$
	$s_2: p = j$
		`for(p=1; p<=N; p++){`
		`  Y[p] = Z[p];`
		`  X[p] = Y[p];`
		`}`

`for(p=1; p<=N; p++){`
`  Y[p] = Z[p];`
`  X[p] = Y[p];`
`}`
	Fission
	$s_1: i = p$
	$s_2: j = p$
		`for(i=1; i<=N; i++)`
		`  Y[i] = Z[i];   /*s1*/`
		`for(j=1; j<=N; j++)`
		`  X[j] = Y[j];   /*s2*/`

`for(i=1; i<=N; i++){`
`  Y[i] = Z[i];   /*s1*/`
`  X[i] = Y[i-1];  /*s2*/`
`}`
	Re-indexing
	$s_1: p = i$
	$s_2: p = i - 1$
		`if (N>=1) X[1] = Y[0];`
		`for(p=1; p<=N-1; p++){`
		`  Y[p] = Z[p];`
		`  X[p+1] = Y[p];`
		`}`
		`if (N>=1) Y[N]=Z[N];`

`for(i=1; i<=N; i++){`
`  Y[2*i] = Z[2*i];   /*s1*/`
`for(j=1; j<=2N;j++)`
`  X[j] = Y[j];   /*s2*/`
	Scaling
	$s_1: p = 2 * i$
	$(s_2: p = j)$
		`for(p=1; p<=2*N; p++){`
		`  if (p mod 2 == 0)`
		`    Y[p] = Z[p];`
		`  X[p] = Y[p];`
		`}`

FIGURE 13.7
Optimization of polyhedral models for different scenarios.

also called the process of scheduling transformation, and the process of organizing shift is the process of changing bases and realizing cyclic shifts [31].

Figure 13.7 also demonstrates how the polyhedral model can be optimized for various scenarios, which will not be presented here.

13.3.3 Summary

The main goal of source-to-source optimization for custom hardware accelerators is to reduce the user's burden and provide automated means of optimizing partially tailored scenarios.

The Merlin compiler utilizes the ROSE compiler's basic structure and polyhedral model for AST analysis and transformation. Host and compute kernels can be automatically partitioned and refactored. However, it still requires the user to manually specify critical parameters of the hardware implementation, such as parallelism coefficients.

The polyhedral model itself is more deeply optimized for the cyclic computation part of the code but not significantly optimized for the computational control part and the underlying hardware search.

The result of this source-to-source conversion can only be said to make it easier for the next level of tools to implement the hardware design, and there is undoubtedly a performance advantage over the source program. Still, it is not a better representation of the reconstructed and optimized hardware architecture than the manual analysis.

13.4 Domain Customization Languages and Intermediate Expressions

13.4.1 Domain Customization Languages

Domain-specific languages (DSLs) are mini-languages created for specific application domains. Because they are domain-specific, DSLs typically have simpler syntax than general-purpose languages with many convenient language constructs and are, therefore, easier to learn and use.

13.4.1.1 Halide

Halide [32] is an open-source DSL for fast and portable computation on images and tensors. It is designed to help programmers quickly write high-performance image-processing code on modern machines. One of the most significant advantages of Halide is that it separates the algorithmic description of a program from the scheduling—its execution strategy. When trying to optimize Halide code, the programmer can modify the scheduling part of the code without changing the algorithmic position to alter how the program executes. Figure 13.8 shows a Halide program where the programmer can quickly shift the traversal order using reorder. For equivalent C or C++ code, the programmer would have to change the entire loop of their code. Halide currently targets CPUs and GPUs, software platforms without hardware customization capabilities.

13.4.1.2 HeteroCL

HeteroCL [33] is a Python-based DSL for software-defined reconfigurable accelerators. Like Halide, HeteroCL separates algorithms from scheduling, as shown in Figure 13.9. A critical difference between HeteroCL and Halide is that HeteroCL supports compilation flows for FPGAs with multiple backends, including SODA [34], PolySA [35], and Merlin compiler [36]. As a result, customized schedules can be ported to the hardware design in subsequently generated HLS/RTL code. HeteroCL categorizes hardware customizations into three types: computational, data type, and memory architectures, which allow programmers to explore performance/area/precision trade-offs.

```
1  // Algorithm
2  Var x("x"), y("y");
3  Func B("B");
4  B(x, y) = (A(x, y) + A(x + 1, y) + A(x + 2, y)) / 3;
5
6  // Schedule
7  B.reorder(y, x);
```

FIGURE 13.8
An example of a Halide program.

```
1  # Algorithm
2  A = heterocl.placeholder((height, weight), name='A')
3  B = heterocl.compute(A.shape,
4                       lambda x, y: (A[x, y] + A[x + 1, y] + A[x + 2, y]) / 3,
5                       name='B')
6
7  # Schedule
8  s = heterocl.create_schedule([A, B])
9  s.reorder(B.axis[1], B.axis[0])
```

FIGURE 13.9
An example of a HeteroCL program.

Heterogeneous backends supported by HeteroCL generate HLS code and then synthesize it into RTL code using vendor tools. These backends target different types of programs and achieve decent performance. PolySA [35] for pulsed arrays is an architecture consisting of a set of identical processing elements (PEs). This architecture is suitable for various applications, including convolutional computation and matrix multiplication. In addition, the Merlin compiler [36] is a more general-purpose backend that generates optimized HLS code for Intel and Xilinx platforms, greatly enhancing the versatility of HeteroCL.

13.4.1.3 HeteroFlow

HeteroFlow [37] is a recently proposed programming model for FPGA accelerators that supports data placement specifications separate from algorithm descriptions and other hardware customizations. Data schemes between them are as follows: (1) inter-core data placement, which allows efficient on-chip data flow (via First-In, First-Out (FIFOs) and multi-buffers) to be easily implemented between different compute cores within an accelerator and (2) intra-core data placement, which permits efficient and expressive specification of a wide range of fine-grained data flow patterns commonly used in spatial architectures such as pulsed arrays.

Figure 13.10 illustrates the HeteroFlow workflow and samples; the HeteroFlow compiler backend emits OpenCL or HLS C/C++ code that can be compiled and deployed on mainstream FPGA platforms. This backend generates high-performance code for communication channels with vendor-specific libraries and pragmas and leverages the existing HeteroCL compiler to implement optimized accelerators based on other user-specified hardware customizations. Figure 13.11 shows the HLS code snippet generated by HeteroFlow with different levels of data placement specification, in the computational kernel functions mapped to pulsed arrays. HeteroFlow causes parallel PEs connected by FIFOs for in-kernel data movement (L3–9). In the top-level parts of the FPGA accelerator, HeteroFlow allocates different memory interfaces based on memory access patterns to achieve optimal

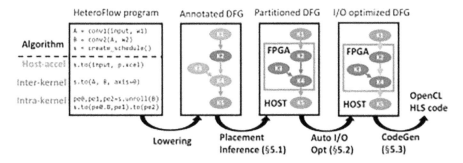

FIGURE 13.10
Compilation flow of HeteroFlow.

```
 1  // intra-kernel data placement with FIFOs
 2  void conv_systolic_array(stream<DTYPE>& fifo_inter0,
        stream<DTYPE>& fifo_inter1) {
 3    #pragma HLS dataflow
 4    stream<DTYPE> fifo_in[M], fifo_out[N];
 5    #pragma HLS stream var=fifo_in[0]
 6    data_loader(fifo_inter0, fifo_in);
 7    PE<0,0>(fifo_in[0], fifo_out[0]);
 8    ...
 9    PE<M,N>(fifo_in[M-1], fifo_out[N-1]);
10    data_drainer(fifo_in[M-1], fifo_inter1);}
11  // top-level function on accelerator
12  void fpga(DTYPE* dma_mm, stream<DTYPE>& dma_fifo, int iter) {
13      #pragma HLS interface m_axi port=dma_mm burst=factor
14      #pragma HLS interface axis port=dma_fifo burst=factor
15      for (i=0; i<K;i++) {
16        DTYPE in1 = dma_fifo.read();
17        DTYPE.in2 = dma_mm[INDEX[i]];
18        compute1(in1.range(31,0), in2.range(63,32), ...);}
19      // inter-kernel FIFOs and double buffer
20      stream<DTYPE> fifo_inter[N];
21      #pragma HLS stream var=fifo_inter[0]
22      DTYPE double_buf[2][SIZE];
23      conv_systolic_array(fifo_inter[0], fifo_inter[1]);
24      compute2(fifo_inter[1], double_buf[iter%2]);
25      compute3(double_buf[1-iter%2]);}
```

FIGURE 13.11
Example of HLS code generated by HeteroFlow.

memory bandwidth with minimal hardware overhead (L13–14). In addition, HeteroFlow automatically applies memory aggregation in the data loading loop to saturate off-chip memory bandwidth (L15–18). On-chip FIFOs and double buffers are automatically generated for inter-core data placement (L20–25).

13.4.1.4 Summary

The DSL domain customization language aims to allow programmers to move away from the hardware part of the implementation and focus on the design of the algorithms and the upper-level scheduling model, with more in-depth optimizations coming from the bottom of the programming model. However, quite a few challenges are still present in the current work. As shown in Table 13.2, it demonstrates the efforts made by most of the DSL-related work.

Halide is geared toward fast and portable computation on images and tensors. Halide was an early mover in separating the algorithmic description of a program from the scheduling—its execution strategy. However, there are no targeted hardware architecture-level optimizations, as its primary computing devices are CPUs and GPUs.

Whereas HeteroCL, inspired by Halide and TVM, separates algorithmic specifications from temporal computation scheduling (e.g., loop reordering and tiling), HeteroCL further separates algorithms from on-chip memory customization and data quantization schemes. However, it provides no programming support for explicit management of data placement.

Heteroflow provides a decoupled and unified programming interface for expressing data placement in different levels of memory hierarchies, resulting in modular and composable design specifications. With FPGAs as the primary supporting device, it supports fully decoupled data placement and co-optimization with other hardware customizations such as tiling and data quantization. However, the underlying hardware implementation still aims at complete mapping of the computational part, which may not be satisfactory for large-scale computational applications such as the various deep learning applications currently available. There are no optimizations for task- and data-level parallelism and the search is also aimed at minimizing latency.

TABLE 13.2

Comparison of HeteroFlow with Other Programming Frameworks

	Design Entry	Decoupled Compute	Decoupled DP*	Unified DP* Interface	Design complexity
HLS	C++	No	No	No	Complete design
Spatial [23]	DSL	No	No	No	Complete design
SODA [9]	DSL	No	No	No	single kernel (stencils)
AutoSA [43]	C++	No	No	No	Single kernel(systolic)
HeteroHalide [27]	DSL	Yes	No	No	Complete design
T2S [40]. Susy [25]	DSL	Yes	Partially	No	Single kernel(systolic)
HeteroCL [24]	DSL	Yes	No	No	Single kernel
HeteroFlow	DSL	Yes	Yes	Yes	Complete design

13.4.2 Intermediate Expressions

The basic principle of Halide IR [1] is the separation of computation and scheduling. Instead of giving a specific solution directly, the optimal solution is found among various scheduling solutions. Handwritten scheduling templates: e.g., Halide and TVM, their idea is to divide the computation of each operator (conv2d) into analysis and scheduling. Math does not need to consider the underlying hardware architecture to write computation rules; scheduling is to optimize the underlying computation, including how to access memory and parallel. Moreover, it can achieve the overlay of data loading and algorithmic analysis to cover the delay caused by data loading. The programmer can specify Halide's scheduling to specify some strategies, the hardware's buffer size, and the relevant settings' buffer line so that it can be based on the characteristics of different computational hardware to achieve high-efficiency computational units of the scheduling. At the same time, the image algorithm of the computation of the implementation of the algorithm does not need to be modified. The disadvantage is that the space for describing the optimization is limited, i.e., the original language that can be applied is determined.

In the Sara project [38], a specialized standard data stream mapping structure has been developed specifically to align with the unique characteristics of CGRA devices. The overall computational part is expanded into a CFG for mapping and optimization as shown in Figure 13.12.

To maximize the throughput of the entire pipeline, it is critical to balance the pipeline stage delay for each level of the coarse-grained channel after Control Flow Graph (CFG) segmentation is performed. SARA captures a separate parallelization factor for each loop nesting in the CFG. When the user parallelizes the innermost loop, SARA vectorizes the computation along Plasticine's SIMD data path. When parallelizing the outer circles, SARA expands the loop's body between distributed computational units to form a larger graph. By combining

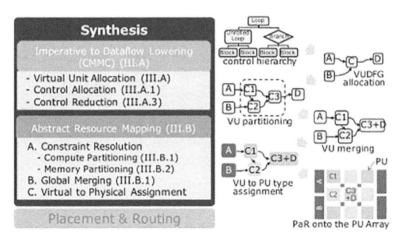

FIGURE 13.12
Compilation flow of SARA.

multiple levels of pipeline parallelism and loop-level parallelism in arbitrarily nested CFGs, SARA can efficiently scale the performance of small computational kernels over many resources. Unlike multiprocessors that utilize thread-level parallelism across distributed units, SARA uses multiple levels of pipeline parallelism across compute and memory units, significantly improving overall computational throughput. However, such a design fails to fully exploit the computation's data reuse and potential parallel features by preserving the source program's computational scheduling.

A data-centric optimization strategy, MAESTRO [39], is designed for the characteristics of Deep Neural Network (DNN) applications. To evaluate how various data streams affect the runtime and power consumption associated with a specific DNN model and its hardware configuration, as shown in Figure 13.13, the computational processes are assigned to different PEs for scheduling through their unique expression afterward.

However, this data-centric representation is imprecise and overly restrictive. It lacks support for complex data flows and skewed data access. This uneven data access requires the introduction of a new dimension by combining the tensor dimensions i and j using affine transformations. Sample irregular data scheduling significantly affects the detection of data reuse

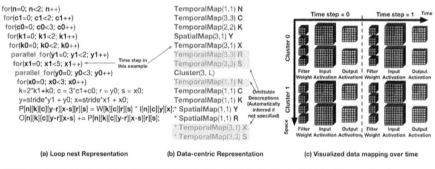

(a) Loop nest Representation   (b) Data-centric Representation   (c) Visualized data mapping over time

(d) Data mapping and reuse of each tensor

FIGURE 13.13

Maestro's data-centric mapping and data reuse strategy. (a) Loop nest Representation. (b) Data-centric Representation. (c) Visualized data mapping over time. (d) Data mapping and reuse of each tensor.

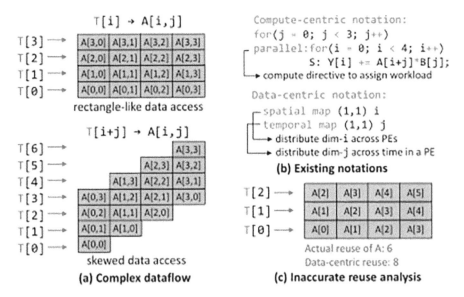

FIGURE 13.14

Limitations of the two representations, computation-centered and data-centered. (a) Complex dataflow. (b) Existing notations. (c) Inaccurate reuse analysis.

(Figure 13.14a), and the actual reuse of tensor A is 6, whereas the result of MAESTRO is 8 (Figure 13.14c).

TENET [40], on the other hand, is designed as a relation-centric notation to model the hardware data flow of tensor computation. The relation-centered representation is more expressive than the computation-centered and data-centered representations. By representing data flow, allocation, and interconnections as relationships in a unified way, the relationship-centric picture forms a complete design space for hardware data flow, providing more opportunities for optimization.

As the sample shown in Figure 13.15, the relation-centered design expresses not only the data flow of computation but also the allocation of PEs and their interconnections in the spatial computing architecture. However, it is limited only to the spatial computing architecture.

13.5 Accelerator Template Mapping

13.5.1 Streaming Architecture Stream Dataflow

Streaming applications are a particular type of task-parallel applications that do not require complex control over inter-task communication and are often exposed to massive data parallelism in addition to task parallelism. There is some previous work dedicated to this type of application.

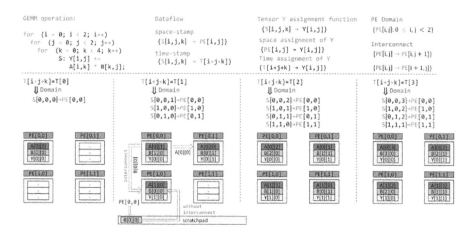

FIGURE 13.15
Analysis of data reuse in the relationship-centered representation proposed by TENET.

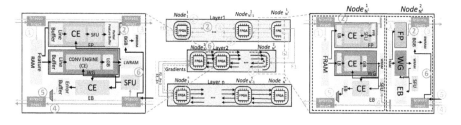

FIGURE 13.16
Mapping strategy for FPDeep.

ST-Accel [41] is a high-level programming platform for streaming applications with an efficient host–kernel communication interface exposed as a virtual file system (VFS). It uses Vivado HLS as its hardware-generated backend, and its software emulation is done through sequential execution.

Fleet [42] is a massively parallel streaming framework for FPGAs with an efficient memory interface for processing large instances of elements in parallel. Programmers write Fleet programs using a Chisel-based [43] domain-specific RTL language to write Fleet programs. These programs can be simulated in Scala (where Chisel is embedded).

In summary, although these frameworks are dedicated to the streaming paradigm, neither provides peek and transaction interfaces in the kernel. Both run software simulations sequentially, which has no correctness issues for streaming applications but can be limiting for general task-parallel programs.

FPDeep is a Stream approach mapping Convolutional Neural Networks (CNN) single-layer and cross-layer pipeline structures [44]. As shown in Figure 13.16, it allocates a separate processing unit for each layer, which can be directly applied and deployed on FPGA clusters. FPDeep uses inter-layer mapping and intra-layer partitioning, as well as weight-load balancing strategies, which can reasonably allocate the tasks of each FPGA to make the algorithm's implementation deeply pipelined, and the computational performance of the method obtains an approximately five-fold improvement compared to the single-FPGA implementation.

Auto CodeGen includes parameterized hardware blocks supporting CONV, POOL, NORM, and FC layers [45]. The CONV block consists of convolutional units that perform dot product operations in a fully expanded manner. The instantiated convolutional units are further contained in an adjustable number of groups, and the input feature mapping is shared among all groups. Each group processes the input feature maps using different weights to compute independent output feature maps. The FC layer is mapped to computational units called FCcores, which can be tuned to exploit input neuron parallelism and can be time reused. Similarly, the POOL block exploits the equivalence of the output feature maps to schedulability. The NORM layer maps to a fixed hardware block that uses a segmented linear approximation scheme for exponential operations and a single-precision floating-point algorithm to minimize the loss of precision. In contrast to the data-driven control mechanisms of the rest of the tool streams of the Generative Streaming Architecture, the Auto CodeGen performs the scheduling and control of each hardware block in a distributed manner in which a dedicated local FSM coordinates the operation of each block.

The streaming architecture is designed with the advantage that each block is individually optimized to take advantage of the parallelism of its layer, and all heterogeneous blocks are linked to form a pipeline. Computation is completed as data is transferred through the stream. Thus, this design approach exploits the parallelism between layers through pipelining techniques, enabling them to execute concurrently. Thus, high computational performance is accomplished. However, the disadvantage is that for large computing applications, both data dependency and control dependency make the pure linear stream mapping approach challenging to implement, and even if it is barely implemented, the resource overheads associated with the overall mapping of an extensive application are not always met by the platform.

13.5.2 Fluctuating Arrays Spatial Dataflow

Kung and Leiserson introduced the term pulsed array in 1978 [46]. The architecture consists of a grid of regular and straightforward processing units (PEs) connected by local interconnections. Systolic derives from the computational pattern in pulsating arrays, where input and output data flow through the PE network rhythmically.

Pulsating arrays have two main architectural advantages: (1) a simple and regular design and (2) a balance between computation and communication. As shown in Figure 13.17, pulsed arrays exploit parallelism through identical

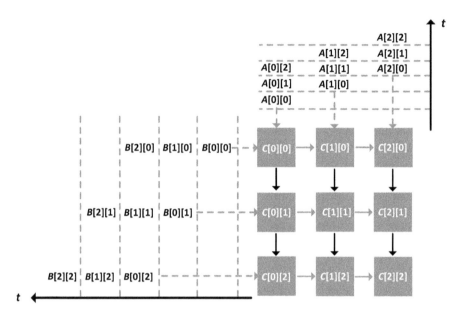

FIGURE 13.17
Sample matrix multiplication for a 2D pulsating array.

PE grids with local interconnections. Such a simple architecture can be easily scaled with minimal additional development costs. In addition, pulsating displays use data locality by reusing data through regional interconnections. This feature helps generate more balanced designs with high performance and energy efficiency potential.

With these benefits, the architecture was intensively studied over the next two decades after the introduction of pulsed arrays. Many pulsed array designs were proposed for different applications, such as pulsed arrays designed for other fields: linear algebra [47], signal processing [48,49], image processing [50], dynamic programming [51], and dynamic programming.

Despite ongoing academic interest, pulsed arrays have yet to enter the real world. One of the critical milestones was the iWarp machine [52], a general-purpose pulsed array processor designed by researchers at Carnegie Mellon University and Intel in the 1990s. However, the work stopped a few years after the machine was first released.

The reasons for this predicament are multiple. First, most pulsed array designs in publications are still "paper designs" that focus only on the design of the computational arrays, ignoring the storage system and integration with the host processor. Pulsed array designs considering storage systems and integration are primarily targeted at Very Large Scale Integration (VLSI) circuits and require significant development costs. The last and most important reason is that the performance gains of such architectures are quickly

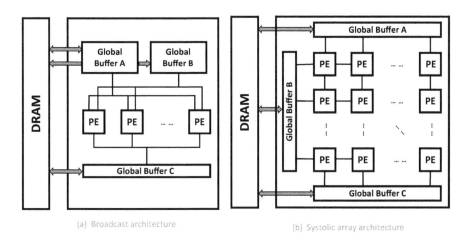

(a) Broadcast architecture

(b) Systolic array architecture

FIGURE 13.18
Comparison of matrix multiplication using (a) broadcast and (b) systolic array architectures.

overshadowed by the exponential performance gains of general-purpose processors that take advantage of Moore's Law.

However, the new challenges facing today's computer architecture community and several technological advances have led to a renewed opportunity for the development of pulsed array architectures:

Demand for More Energy-Efficient Architectures: The powerwall challenge has created a strong need for energy-efficient architectures. Pulsed array has proven to be one of the architectures that meet this requirement. It reduces the power of the control logic through a simple lock-step execution model and minimizes the energy of memory access through local communication. Figure 13.18 compares the broadcast architecture with the pulsed array used for matrix multiplication. In the broadcast design, the data from matrices *A* and *B* are broadcast to the PE through an on-chip cross-switch. The results from matrix *C* are collected into an on-chip global buffer through another cross-switch. In contrast, in a pulsed array, matrices A, B, and C data are sent or collected at the array boundary and transmitted between PEs via a local interconnect.

According to the research, inter-PE communication consumes three times less energy than global buffer access, indicating the potential for achieving higher energy efficiency on pulsed arrays than broadcast designs. Based on this observation, the authors in [53] implemented a systolic array-like architecture called Eyeriss for deep learning applications, which achieves higher energy efficiency compared to other hardware designs. In recent years, shrink arrays have been widely used to accelerate deep learning applications [53–58]. A few representative examples include the tensor processing unit from Google [54], neural network accelerators from Tesla and Xilinx [55], and the Xilinx ML accelerator [57].

Advances in Heterogeneous Platforms: Heterogeneous hardware, such as FPGAs, is increasingly important in modern computing systems. These platforms typically offer several orders of magnitude higher performance and energy efficiency than CPUs and achieve much lower development costs than VLSI circuits. FPGAs are a natural target for implementing pulsed arrays. The island architecture perfectly matches the lattice structure of pulsed arrays. We can start by mapping a PE to the FPGA and then quickly scale to occupy the entire chip by copying the PE. In addition, the local interconnect of the pulsed array facilitates the routing process on the FPGA, resulting in a design with high resource utilization and frequency.

Maturity of compilation tools: The barriers to entry into pulsed arrays are very high because designers must thoroughly understand the application characteristics and the hardware architecture. Automating such a design process has been an important topic since the inception of pulsed arrays. These efforts use temporal transformation [59] to convert algorithms into pulsed arrays and generate RTL code for VLSI circuits or FPGAs. Although previous work is more complete, the manual design process is still the norm. This is because previous work on automated pulsed array synthesis failed to balance the three metrics of generality, performance, and productivity, all of which are critical to the design process. For example, several previous efforts required the use of custom inputs, such as recursive equations [60], which required significant effort on the part of the average programmer to implement, thereby reducing productivity. There are some frameworks [61] that use C programs as input. Still, these efforts are limited in terms of other factors, such as the generality of the frameworks in terms of the types of programs they support or the performance of the generated designs.

However, as the compiler community continues to progress, especially with two notable technological improvements in the last decade, there are new opportunities to embrace the idea of automatic pulsed array synthesis once again:

The first improvement is the **maturity of the polyhedral compilation tool**. The polyhedral compilation framework is a cyclic transformation framework strongly related to pulsed array synthesis. It can be used to perform accurate dependency analyses and apply spatiotemporal transformations to generate contraction arrays. The polyhedral model used to be "blamed" for the limited range of supported programs and immature compilation tools. However, over the years, the polyhedral model has been extended to support a wide range of applications covering most high-performance computing applications and has been integrated with LLVM [29] and has been integrated with modern compilation infrastructures such as LLVM, Multi-Level Intermediate Representation (MLIR), and Halide [62–64].

The second **improvement comes from HLS technology**. HLS tools raise the abstraction level of the hardware programming model from traditional RTL to high-level programming languages such as C/C++. It dramatically reduces development cycles and generates performance comparable to

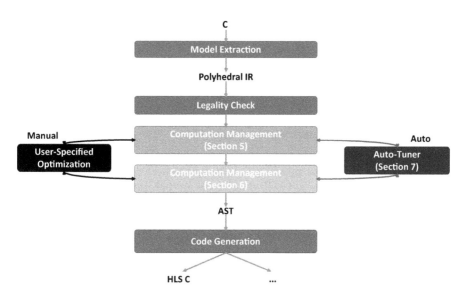

FIGURE 13.19
Compilation flow of AutoSA.

manual designs. Commercial tools such as Xilinx HLS, Intel OpenCL, and LegUp are being adopted by academia and industry at an increasing rate.

Therefore, AutoSA [65] came into being, and Figure 13.19 illustrates the overall compilation flow of AutoSA. First is model extraction; this step extracts the polyhedral model of iteration domains, access relations, scheduling, and data dependencies from the input C program. This is followed by legality checking, which checks whether the input program can be legally mapped to a pulsed array. There are three constraints in total: (1) Transformations should remain semantic. (2) All dependencies should be consistent (constant dependency distance). (3) The dependency distance of spatial loops should not exceed one, so data communication occurs only between neighboring PEs. If the new plan fails to satisfy these constraints, AutoSA will skip the following steps and dump the CPU code from the current project.

The following workflow is compute and communication management. A complete pulsed array architecture comprises a PE array and an on-chip I/O network. AutoSA divides the process of building these two components into two phases: compute and communication management. The compute management phase builds the PE and optimizes its microarchitecture. After that, the communication management phase builds the I/O network for data transfer between the PE and external memory. Then comes the code generation, where AutoSA generates the AST from the optimized program after the previous phases. The AST is then traversed to create the final design of the target hardware.

```
for (int i = 0; i < M; ++i)
    for (int j = 0; j < N; ++j)
        for (int k = 0; k < K; ++k)
S0:             C[i][j] += A[i][k] * B[k][j];
```

FIGURE 13.20
Sample code for matrix multiplication.

Finally, there is the optimizer, as the compute and communication management phase involves several optimization techniques, each of which introduces several tuning options. AutoSA implements adjustable knobs for these techniques, which the user can set manually or tune via the auto-tuner.

Figure 13.20, on the other hand, gives a sample mapping for MM computation, where AutoSA can generate six different pulsation arrays for MM. This is done by choosing cycles ❶*i* ❷*j* and ❸*k* as spatial loops of one-dimensional arrays, cycles ❹(*i*, *j*) ❺(*i*, *k*) and ❻(*j*, *k*) as spatial loops of a two-dimensional array are implemented. We denote these six arrays in turn as Designs 1–6. Of these six designs, Designs 1 and 2 and Designs 5 and 6 are symmetric. Finally, we have chosen to experiment with Designs 1, 4, and 5 for simplicity. Figure 13.21a–c depicts the architecture of these three designs.

As shown in Figure 13.21a, in Design 1, loop *i* is designated as a spatial loop. Therefore, matrix *A* is associated with the internal I/O and is fed directly to each PE. Elements of matrix *B* are reused along the *i* axis. Each PE accumulates the pieces of matrix *C* locally. Therefore, we allocate a local buffer for matrix *C* in the PE to store intermediate results. After the computation is completed, the final result of matrix *C* is drained and sent to the DRAM. Such an architecture can be found in previous works [55,62].

As shown in Figure 13.21b, Design 4 is generated by selecting cycles *i* and *j* as spatial cycles. The elements of matrices *A* and *B* are repeated along the *j* and *i* axes, respectively. The data of matrix *C* is accumulated inside the PE and is discharged when the computation is completed. This architecture can be found in previous works [52].

As shown in Figure 13.21c, Design 5 is generated by choosing cycles *i* and *k* as spatial cycles. The main difference between Design 5 and Design 4 is that the elements of matrix *C* are now accumulated along the *k* axis. Therefore, a local buffer (bufC) is saved. However, data from matrix *A* needs to be sent directly to each PE. Data from matrix *B* is reused along the *i* axis. This architecture can be seen in previous works [54,66].

Design 1 vs. Design 4: 1D pulsating arrays limit the design space to one less spatial dimension to explore. The optimal 1D pulsating array found by AutoSA has 128 PEs with a SIMD factor 8. Placing more PEs will result in routing failures or wasted cycles to compute the filler elements that reduce the effective GFLOP. However, 1D pulsation arrays are more frequent than

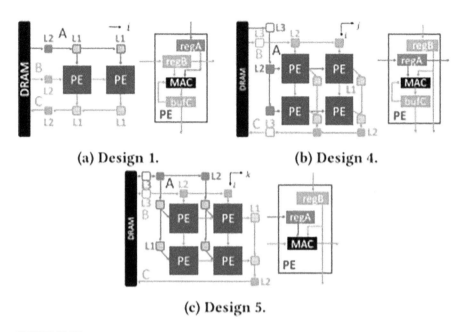

(a) Design 1.

(b) Design 4.

(c) Design 5.

FIGURE 13.21
Matrix multiplication to design the array architecture for (a) 1, (b) 4, and (c) 5.

their 2D counterparts, which is a combination of a more regular architecture and fewer resources.

Design 4 vs. Design 5: AutoSA can place more PEs for Design 4 than Design 5, although this requires more resources. This is due to the simpler I/O network. Figure 13.21b shows that Design 4 uses matrices A and B for data reuse and only generates L2 I/O modules at PE boundaries. However, Design 5 (shown in Figure 13.21c) utilizes only the reuse of matrix B. The data elements of matrix A need to be sent to each PE individually through the L1 I/O modules. This adds complexity to the wiring and limits the design size we can explore.

Design 4 balances resources and cabling complexity to achieve the highest performance in these designs (Table 13.3).

As shown in Table 13.4, it demonstrates the recent years of work on mapping pulsed array structures. However, the pulsating array structure can achieve very high computational performance and DSP efficiency in the case of computational regularity. However, since their design and size are fixed after compilation, peak performance is difficult to reach in practice. At the same time, each PE can only run a very set number of computations, which makes it difficult to solve the branching problem in the computation process. Meanwhile, the latest pulsed array work, AutoSA, still requires the computational program to satisfy three constraints to generate the corresponding structure, which is still a significant limitation.

TABLE 13.3

Performance Comparison of Different Matrix Multiplication Designs

Designs	SA Sizes	MHz	GFLOPs	LUT	FF	BRAM	DSP
1	128×8	346	555	38%	31%	10%	42%
4	13×16×8	300	934	52%	42%	41%	68%
5	13×12×8	300	660	46%	37%	10%	51%

TABLE 13.4

Comparison of Different Frameworks

Feature	AutoSA	MMAlph [17]	[7]	PolySA [10]	SuSy [30]
Generality					
Imperfectly Nested Loops	Yes	No	No	No	No
Multi-Statement	Yes	Yes	No	No	Yes
Performance					
Array Partitioning	Auto	No	Auto	Auto	Semi-Auto
Latency Hiding	Auto	No	No	Auto	Semi-Auto
SIMD Vectorization	Auto	No	No	Limited	Semi-Auto
Double Buffering	Auto	No	No	Auto	Semi-Auto
Data Packing	Auto	No	No	Limited	Semi-Auto
Productivity					
Input	C	DSL	C	C	DSL
Auto-Tuning	Yes	No	No	Yes	No
Space-Time Transformation	Auto	Semi-Auto	Auto	Auto	Semi-Auto

13.6 Chapter Summary

FPGAs are reconfigurable hardware that has received much attention in the post-Moore era. To make FPGAs easier and more efficient, efforts have been made to optimize the FPGA toolchain, especially HLS tools, by transforming high-level languages into HDLs. However, complex optimization primitives remain a burden for users. For this reason, there has been a shift toward compilation optimizations such as the Merlin compiler and polyhedral models. These optimization techniques can make code easier to write and more efficient. In addition, the emergence of domain-tailored programming languages and intermediate languages (e.g., Halide, HeteroCL) has dramatically improved development and optimization efficiency. Optimized middle languages can be mapped to corresponding hardware templates, enabling a fully automated accelerator design flow. This design flow makes FPGA design and programming more straightforward and more efficient, making FPGA applications in more fields possible.

References

1. Dennard R. H., Gaensslen F. H., Yu H. N., et al. Design of ion-implanted MOSFET's with very small physical dimensions. *IEEE Journal of Solid-State Circuits*, 1974, 9(5): 256–268.
2. Wulf W. A., McKee S. A. Hitting the memory wall: Implications of the obvious. *ACM SIGARCH Computer Architecture News*, 1995, 23(1): 20–24.
3. Cong J., Huang M., Wu D., et al. Heterogeneous datacenters: Options and opportunities. *Proceedings of the 53rd Annual Design Automation Conference*. 2016: 1–6.
4. Huang M., Wu D., Yu C. H., et al. Programming and runtime support to blaze FPGA accelerator deployment at datacenter scale. *Proceedings of the Seventh ACM Symposium on Cloud Computing*. 2016: 456–469.
5. Putnam A., Caulfield A. M., Chung E. S., et al. A reconfigurable fabric for accelerating large-scale datacenter services. *ACM SIGARCH Computer Architecture News*, 2014, 42(3): 13–24.
6. Guo L., Chi Y., Wang J., et al. AutoBridge: coupling coarse-grained floorplanning and pipelining for high-frequency HLS design on multi-die FPGAs. *The 2021 ACM/SIGDA International Symposium on Field-Programmable Gate Arrays*. 2021: 81–92.
7. Guo L., Lau J., Chi Y., et al. Analysis and optimization of the implicit broadcasts in FPGA HLS to improve maximum frequency. *2020 57th ACM/IEEE Design Automation Conference (DAC)*. IEEE, 2020: 1–6.
8. Cong J., Liu B., Neuendorffer S., et al. High-level synthesis for FPGAs: From prototyping to deployment. *IEEE Transactions on Computer-Aided Design of Integrated Circuits and Systems*, 2011, 30(4): 473–491.
9. Cong J., Zhang Z. An efficient and versatile scheduling algorithm based on SDC formulation. *Proceedings of the 43rd annual Design Automation Conference*. 2006: 433–438.
10. Cheng J., Fleming S. T., Chen Y. T., et al. EASY: Efficient Arbiter SYnthesis from multi-threaded code. *Proceedings of the 2019 ACM/SIGDA International Symposium on Field-Programmable Gate Arrays*. 2019: 142–151.
11. Cheng J., Josipovic L., Constantinides G. A., et al. Combining dynamic & static scheduling in high-level synthesis. *Proceedings of the 2020 ACM/ SIGDA International Symposium on Field-Programmable Gate Arrays*. 2020: 288–298.
12. Haj-Ali A., Huang Q. J., Xiang J., et al. Autophase: Juggling HLS phase orderings in random forests with deep reinforcement learning. *Proceedings of Machine Learning and Systems*, 2020, 2: 70–81.
13. Hsiao H., Anderson J. Thread weaving: static resource scheduling for multithreaded high-level synthesis. *Proceedings of the 56th Annual Design Automation Conference 2019*. 2019: 1–6.
14. Chen Y. T., Kim J. H., Li K., et al. High-level synthesis techniques to generate deeply pipelined circuits for FPGAs with registered routing. *2019 International Conference on Field-Programmable Technology (ICFPT)*. IEEE, 2019: 375–378.
15. Josipović L., Sheikhha S., Guerrieri A., et al. Buffer placement and sizing for high-performance dataflow circuits. *ACM Transactions on Reconfigurable Technology and Systems (TRETS)*, 2021, 15(1): 1–32.

16. Cong J., Wei P., Yu C. H., et al. Automated accelerator generation and optimisation with composable, parallel and pipeline architecture. *Proceedings of the 55th Annual Design Automation Conference.* 2018: 1–6.

17. Intel. Intel FPGA SDK for OpenCL Pro Edition: Programming Guide (2021)[EB/OL]. (2021-10-04)[2023-08-14]. https://www.intel.com/content/www/us/en/docs/programmable/683846/21-3/programming-multiple-fpga-devices.html.

18. Xilinx. Vivado Design Suite User Guide: High-Level Synthesis (UG902)[EB/OL]. (2021-05-04)[2023-08-14]. https://www.amd.com/content/dam/xilinx/support/documents/sw_manuals/xilinx2020_2/ug902-vivado-high-level-synthesis.pdf.

19. Nane R., Sima V. M., Pilato C., et al. A survey and evaluation of FPGA high-level synthesis tools. *IEEE Transactions on Computer-Aided Design of Integrated Circuits and Systems*, 2015, 35(10): 1591–1604.

20. Najjar W. A., Bohm W., Draper B. A., et al. High-level language abstraction for reconfigurable computing. *Computer*, 2003, 36(8): 63–69.

21. Coussy P., Chavet C., Bomel P., et al. GAUT: A high-level synthesis tool for DSP applications: From C algorithm to RTL architecture. *High-Level Synthesis: From Algorithm to Digital Circuit*, 2008: 147–169. doi: 10.1007/978-1-4020-8588-8_9.

22. Muslim F. B., Ma L., Roozmeh M., et al. Efficient FPGA implementation of OpenCL high-performance computing applications via high-level synthesis. *IEEE Access*, 2017, 5: 2747–2762.

23. Kobayashi R., Oobata Y., Fujita N., et al. OpenCL-ready high speed FPGA network for reconfigurable high performance computing. *Proceedings of the International Conference on High Performance Computing in Asia-Pacific Region.* 2018: 192–201.

24. Falcon Computing. merlin Compiler[EB/OL]. (2020-07-13)[2023-08-14]. https://github.com/falconcomputing/merlin-compiler.

25. Zhang P., Huang M., Xiao B., et al. CMOST: A system-level FPGA compilation framework. *Proceedings of the 52nd Annual Design Automation Conference.* 2015: 1–6.

26. Quinlan D., Liao C. The ROSE source-to-source compiler infrastructure. *Cetus Users and Compiler Infrastructure Workshop, in Conjunction with PACT.* Citeseer, 2011, 2011: 1.

27. Zuo W., Li P., Chen D., et al. Improving polyhedral code generation for high-level synthesis. *2013 International Conference on Hardware/Software Codesign and System Synthesis (CODES+ ISSS).* IEEE, 2013: 1–10.

28. Cong J., Jiang W., Liu B., et al. Automatic memory partitioning and scheduling for throughput and power optimisation. *ACM Transactions on Design Automation of Electronic Systems (TODAES)*, 2011, 16(2): 1–25.

29. Benabderrahmane M. W., Pouchet L. N., Cohen A., et al. The polyhedral model is more widely applicable than you think. *International Conference on Compiler Construction.* Berlin, Heidelberg: Springer, 2010: 283–303.

30. Verdoolaege S., Guelton S., Grosser T., et al. Schedule trees[C]//International Workshop on Polyhedral Compilation Techniques, Date: 2014/01/20-2014/01/20, Location: Vienna, Austria. 2014.

31. CSA IISc. uday-polyhedral-opt [EB/OL]. [2023-08-14]. https://www.csa.iisc.ac.in/~udayb/slides/uday-polyhedral-opt.pdf.

32. Ragan-Kelley J., Adams A., Paris S., et al. Decoupling algorithms from schedules for easy optimization of image processing pipelines. *ACM Transactions on Graphics (TOG)*, 2012, 31(4): 1–12.

33. Lai Y. H., Chi Y., Hu Y., et al. HeteroCL: A multi-paradigm programming infrastructure for software-defined reconfigurable computing. *Proceedings of the 2019 ACM/SIGDA International Symposium on Field-Programmable Gate Arrays.* 2019: 242–251.

34. Chi Y., Cong J., Wei P., et al. SODA: Stencil with optimised dataflow architecture. *2018 IEEE/ACM International Conference on Computer-Aided Design (ICCAD).* IEEE, 2018: 1–8.

35. Cong J., Wang J. PolySA: Polyhedral-based systolic array auto-compilation. *2018 IEEE/ACM International Conference on Computer-Aided Design (ICCAD).* IEEE, 2018: 1–8.

36. Cong J., Huang M., Pan P., et al. Software infrastructure for enabling FPGA-based accelerations in data centres. *Proceedings of the 2016 International Symposium on Low Power Electronics and Design.* 2016: 154–155.

37. Xiang S., Lai Y. H., Zhou Y., et al. HeteroFlow: An accelerator programming model with decoupled data placement for software-defined FPGAs. *Proceedings of the 2022 ACM/SIGDA International Symposium on Field-Programmable Gate Arrays.* 2022: 78–88.

38. Zhang Y., Zhang N., Zhao T., et al. Sara: Scaling a reconfigurable dataflow accelerator. *2021 ACM/IEEE 48th Annual International Symposium on Computer Architecture (ISCA).* IEEE, 2021: 1041–1054.

39. Kwon H., Chatarasi P., Pellauer M., et al. Understanding reuse, performance, and hardware cost of DNN dataflow: A data-centric approach. *Proceedings of the 52nd Annual IEEE/ACM International Symposium on Microarchitecture.* 2019: 754–768.

40. Lu L., Guan N., Wang Y., et al. TENET: A framework for modelling tensor dataflow based on relation-centric notation. *2021 ACM/IEEE 48th Annual International Symposium on Computer Architecture (ISCA).* IEEE, 2021: 720–733.

41. Ruan Z., He T., Li B., et al. ST-Accel: A high-level programming platform for streaming applications on FPGA. *2018 IEEE 26th Annual International Symposium on Field-Programmable Custom Computing Machines (FCCM).* IEEE, 2018: 9–16.

42. Thomas J., Hanrahan P., Zaharia M. Fleet: a framework for massively parallel streaming on FPGAs. *Proceedings of the Twenty-Fifth International Conference on Architectural Support for Programming Languages and Operating Systems.* 2020: 639–651.

43. Bachrach J., Vo H., Richards B., et al. Chisel: Constructing hardware in a scala embedded language. *Proceedings of the 49th Annual Design Automation Conference.* 2012: 1216–1225.

44. Geng T., Wang T., Sanaullah A., et al. A framework for acceleration of CNN training on deeply-pipelined FPGA clusters with work and weight load balancing. *2018 28th International Conference on Field Programmable Logic and Applications (FPL).* IEEE, 2018: 394–3944.

45. Liu Z., Dou Y., Jiang J., et al. Automatic code generation of convolutional neural networks in FPGA implementation. *2016 International Conference on Field-Programmable Technology (FPT).* IEEE, 2016: 61–68.

46. Kung H. T., Leiserson C. E. Systolic arrays (for VLSI). *Sparse Matrix Proceedings 1978.* Philadelphia, PA: Society for Industrial and Applied Mathematics, 1979, 1: 256–282.

47. Gentleman W. M., Kung H. T. Matrix triangularization by systolic arrays. *Real-time signal processing IV. SPIE*, 1982, 298: 19–26.

48. Kung S Y. VLSI array processors. *IEEE ASSP Magazine*, 1985, 2(3): 4–22.
49. Kalson S., Yao K. A systolic array for linearly constrained least squares filtering. *ICASSP'85. IEEE International Conference on Acoustics, Speech, and Signal Processing*. IEEE, 1985, 10: 977–980.
50. Kulkarni, Yen. Systolic processing and an implementation for signal and image processing. *IEEE Transactions on Computers*, 1982, 100(10): 1000–1009.
51. Lipton R. J., Lopresti D. A systolic array for rapid string comparison. *Proceedings of the Chapel Hill Conference on VLSI*. NC: Chapel Hill, 1985: 363–376.
52. Peterson C., Sutton J., Wiley P. iWarp: A 100-MOPS, LIW microprocessor for multicomputers. *IEEE Micro*, 1991, 11(3): 26–29.
53. Chen Y. H., Emer J., Sze V. Eyeriss: A spatial architecture for energy-efficient dataflow for convolutional neural networks. *ACM SIGARCH Computer Architecture News*, 2016, 44(3): 367–379.
54. Jouppi N. P., Young C., Patil N., et al. In-datacenter performance analysis of a tensor processing unit. *Proceedings of the 44th Annual International Symposium on Computer Architecture*. 2017: 1–12.
55. Tesla. fsd Chip - Tesla[EB/OL]. (2021-09-27)[2023-08-14]. https://en.wikichip. org/wiki/tesla_(car_company)/fsd_chip.
56. Kung H. T., McDanel B., Zhang S. Q. Packing sparse convolutional neural networks for efficient systolic array implementations: Column combining under joint optimization. *Proceedings of the Twenty-Fourth International Conference on Architectural Support for Programming Languages and Operating Systems*. 2019: 821–834.
57. Xilinx. vitis AI [EB/OL]. [2023-08-14]. https://www.xilinx.com/products/ design-tools/vitis/vitis-ai.html.
58. Sohrabizadeh A., Wang J., Cong J. End-to-end optimisation of deep learning applications. *Proceedings of the 2020 ACM/SIGDA International Symposium on Field-Programmable Gate Arrays*. 2020: 133–139.
59. Kung S. Y. VLSI array processors. *IEEE ASSP Magazine*, 1985, 2(3): 4–22.
60. Bednara M., Teich J. Automatic synthesis of FPGA processor arrays from loop algorithms. *The Journal of Supercomputing*, 2003, 26: 149–165.
61. Bondhugula U., Ramanujam J., Sadayappan P. Automatic mapping of nested loops to FPGAs. *Proceedings of the 12th ACM SIGPLAN Symposium on Principles and Practice of Parallel Programming*. 2007: 101–111.
62. Grosser T., Zheng H., Aloor R., et al. Polly-Polyhedral optimization in LLVM. *Proceedings of the First International Workshop on Polyhedral Compilation Techniques (IMPACT)*. 2011: 1.
63. Vasilache N., Zinenko O., Theodoridis T., et al. The next 700 accelerated layers: from mathematical expressions of network computation graphs to accelerated gpu kernels, automatically. *ACM Transactions on Architecture and Code Optimization (TACO)*, 2019, 16(4): 1–26.
64. Lattner C., Amini M., Bondhugula U., et al. MLIR: A compiler infrastructure for the end of Moore's law. arXiv preprint arXiv:2002.11054, 2020.
65. Wang J., Guo L., Cong J. AutoSA: A polyhedral compiler for high-performance systolic arrays on FPGA. *The 2021 ACM/SIGDA International Symposium on Field-Programmable Gate Arrays*. 2021: 93–104.
66. Genc H., Haj-Ali A., Iyer V., et al. Gemmini: An agile systolic array generator enabling systematic evaluations of deep-learning architectures. arXiv preprint arXiv:1911.09925, 2019, 3: 25.

Index

Note: **Bold** page numbers refer to tables and *italic* page numbers refer to figures.